T0271666

ROUTLEDGE LIBRARY EDITIONS:
ACCOUNTING

Volume 62

THE AUSTRALIAN ACCOUNTING
STANDARDS REVIEW BOARD

THE AUSTRALIAN ACCOUNTING STANDARDS REVIEW BOARD

The Establishment of its Participative Review Process

ASHEQ RAZAUR RAHMAN

Routledge
Taylor & Francis Group

LONDON AND NEW YORK

First published in 1992

This edition first published in 2014
by Routledge
2 Park Square, Milton Park, Abingdon, Oxon, OX14 4RN

and by Routledge
711 Third Avenue, New York, NY 10017

Routledge is an imprint of the Taylor & Francis Group, an informa business

© 1992 Asheq Razaur Rahman

British Library Cataloguing in Publication Data
A catalogue record for this book is available from the British Library

ISBN: 978-0-415-53081-1 (Set)
eISBN: 978-1-315-88628-2 (Set)
ISBN: 978-0-415-72014-4 (Volume 62)
eISBN: 978-1-315-86712-0 (Volume 62)

Publisher's Note
The publisher has gone to great lengths to ensure the quality of this book but points out that some imperfections in the original copies may be apparent.

Disclaimer
The publisher has made every effort to trace copyright holders and would welcome correspondence from those they have been unable to trace.

THE AUSTRALIAN ACCOUNTING STANDARDS REVIEW BOARD

The Establishment of its Participative Review Process

Asheq Razaur Rahman

Garland Publishing, Inc.
New York and London 1992

Library of Congress Cataloging-in-Publication Data

Rahman, Asheq Razaur.
The Australian Accounting Standards Review Board : the establishment of its
participative review process / Asheq Razaur Rahman.
p. cm.—(New works in accounting history)
Originally presented as the author's thesis (Ph.D.—University of Sydney)
Includes bibliographical references.
ISBN 0-8153-0802-7
1. Australian Accounting Standards Review Board. 2. Accounting—Standards—
Australia. I. Title. II. Series.
HF5616.A8R34 1991   91-41423
657'.021894—dc20

All volumes printed on acid-free, 250-year-life paper.
Manufactured in the United States of America.

Design by Marisel Tavarez

To my mother
Razia Rahman
and my wife
Naseem Jahan Rahman
for their
encouragement and
understanding

ACKNOWLEDGEMENTS

I wish to thank my supervisor, Professor Murray C. Wells, for his guidance, patience and encouragement. I am indebted to Professor Muzaffer Ahmed, Institute of Business Administration, University of Dhaka, for arranging financial assistance and encouraging me to pursue higher studies. I acknowledge with gratitude the financial assistance provided by the Australian International Development Assistance Bureau.

I would also like to acknowledge the assistance and cooperation of my teachers, in particular, Professor Allen T. Craswell, Mr. Graeme W. Dean, Professor Michael J.O. Gaffikin and Professor Greg P. Whittred. Professor Frank L. Clarke, Mr. T.S. Ramanathan, and Professor Peter W. Wolnizer guided me at the initial stages of this research, for which I am very grateful to them.

Amongst others, without whose encouragement and support this study would be difficult to complete, were the members of my and my wife's families, and my friends Fawzi Laswad and Bosco Kim. They assisted me in various ways in the duration of this study. I am also indebted to John and Sue Bergwerth, Mrs. Pamela Wells and Roger and Christabel Wescombe for arranging, the often unmentioned, extra-curricular activities that reduce the stress that accompanies intensive research. The liveliness and agility of my little son, Asif, provided me strength and lightened my load.

Finally, I thank Mrs. Justine Harding, for her secretarial services, and Massey University, for providing the facilities, for preparing the final manuscript of this book.

TABLE OF CONTENTS

LIST OF TABLES

LIST OF FIGURES

ABBREVIATIONS

A.A.A.N.Z.   Accounting Association of Australia and New Zealand

A.A.R.F.   Australian Accounting Research Foundation

A.A.S.E.   Australian Associated Stock Exchanges

A.C.A.R.S.F.   Australian Chartered Accountants Research Service Foundation

A.C.T.U.   Australian Conference of Trade Unions

A.F.R.   Australian Financial Review

A.I.A.   American Institute of Accountants

A.I.C.P.A.   American Institute of Certified Public Accountants

A.I.D.A.   Australian Industry Development Association

A.I.M.   Australian Institute of Management

A.L.P.   Australian Labour Party

A.L.S.C.A.L.   Alternating Least-square Scaling

A.P.A.I.S.   Australian Public Affairs Information Service

A.P.C.   Accounting Principles Committee

A.P.S.   Accounting Practice Statement

A.R.C.   Accounting Research Committee

A.R.F.	Accounting Research Foundation (former name of A.A.R.F.)
A.S.A.	Australian Society of Accountants
A.S.C.	Australian Securities Commission
A.S.R.B.	Accounting Standards Review Board
Ac.S.B.	Accounting Standards Board
B.H.P.	Broken Hill Proprietary Company
B.R.W.	Business Review Weekly
C.A.C.	Corporate Affairs Commission
C.A.P.	Committee on Accounting Principles
C.A.P.A.P.	Committee on Accounting Principles and Audit Practice
C.A.S.B.	Cost Accounting Standards Board
C.A.T.	Committee on Accounting Terminology
C.C.A.	Current Cost Accounting
C.I.A.	Commonwealth Institute of Accountants
C.L.R.C.	Company Law Review Committee
C.P.A.	Certified Public Accountant
D.A.	Discriminant Analysis
E.M.H.	Efficient Market Hypothesis

F.A.S.B.	Financial Accounting Standards Board
G.A.A.P.	Generally Accepted Accounting Principles
I.C.A.A.	Institute of Chartered Accountants of Australia
I.C.A.C.	Interstate Corporate Affairs Commission
I.C.A.E.W.	Institute of Chartered Accountants of England and Wales
M.D.S.	Multi-dimensional Scaling
N.A.	Not Available
N.C.S.C.	National Companies and Securities Commission
N.L.	Non-Labour parties
N.S.W.	New South Wales
P.A.O.	Principal Accounting Officer
P.S.A.S.B.	Public Sector Accounting Standards Board
S.E.C.	Securities and Exchange Commission
S.P.P. Model	Stigler-Posner-Peltzman Model
U.K.	United Kingdom
U.S.	United States
U.S.A.	United States of America
W.A.	Western Australia

ABSTRACT

This research is aimed at providing an explanation for the creation of the Accounting Standards Review Board (A.S.R.B.) in Australia and the establishment of its functions. The Board is capable of approving standards recognized by the legislature. The interest in this subject has been inspired primarily due to the dearth of research on it and by the methodology adopted by R. Walker (1987). R. Walker (1987) used the "capture" argument to explain that the accounting profession, being the regulated party, influenced the regulatory process preceding the creation of the Board and in the two years after its creation, in order to have a board which would be in its control.

Contrary to R. Walker's (1987) observations it is observed here that the Board was dependent on several interest groups and that there was scope for those groups to influence the activities of the Board. Based on the findings regarding the significance of the roles acquired by the interested parties in the A.S.R.B. mechanism, it is hypothesized, that in order to achieve an influential role in the functioning of the A.S.R.B. all identifiable interest groups participated actively in the Board's establishment.

The model for this research is based primarily on the "Theories of Economic Regulation" developed by the Chicago School [Stigler (1971), Posner (1974) and Peltzman (1976)] and also draws from the arguments of other schools of thought in the area of regulation and public choice. The model illustrates that regulatory policies are initiated by perceived crises. Crises stimulate the demand for such policies. The regulators respond by supplying the policies. Both the demanders and suppliers are motivated by self-interest rather than public-interest. The resulting policy is the equilibrium outcome of the demand and supply functions. In a dynamic regulatory process, such policies are subject to change with changing demand and supply patterns.

From the analysis of the Board's creation and the establishment of its functions it is established that the A.S.R.B. and the mandatory accounting issue originated and existed well before it entered the political debate. The politicians turned the underlying problems, on which the idea for an A.S.R.B. was based, into a crisis. It was further fueled by the news media, and the A.S.R.B. issue eventually entered the political arena. There were several effective participants or participating groups/bodies which acted as demanders of policy measures in the formation of the Board. The bureaucrats, the accounting profession and the companies were the main participants on the demand side. The suppliers of the Board and its functions were the politicians who made-up the Ministerial Council for Companies and Securities. The Council responded to the demands of a majority of the effectively participating interest groups and interested individuals.

The arguments for and against an A.S.R.B., placed by the demanders and the suppliers, were mainly aimed at satisfying their respective self-interests. Significant cases were that of the bureaucrats lobbying with an intention to alleviate the problems of rule enforcement; the accounting profession acted to strengthen its position as a profession and as a standard-setter; the companies joined the debate to secure themselves from over-regulation; and the regulators, the Ministerial Council, accepted the notion of the Board and supplied it to achieve their own political ambitions. This is consistent with the premise of this thesis, that the suppliers and demanders of regulation act rationally on the basis of self-interest.

The major contribution of this research is that, it provides an elaborate and neutral explanation about the activities which precede the formulation of accounting regulatory policies. The knowledge gained from it can be applied to understand the formulation of regulatory policies in other areas and to predict or explain the behaviour of interest groups in the preparation of accounting standards and regulations. The notions of self-interest, supply and demand and the dynamic nature of the regulatory environment are easy to comprehend. The merger of the A.S.R.B. with the Ac.S.B., its proposed merger with the P.S.A.S.B., the imminent creation of the Australian Securities Commission and the forthcoming national companies and securities legislation in Australia are all explainable from the perspective adopted in this thesis. Such developments have also enhanced the need for similar research of this nature.

Chapter 1

INTRODUCTION

The Problem and the Hypothesis:

There has been renewed interest in accounting research regarding the creation and demise of accounting regulatory bodies. The creation of the Accounting Standards Review Board in 1984 in Australia prompted a major study into its creation and the establishment of its functions by R. Walker[1] (1987).[2] In the U.S.A. Davis and Menon (1987) investigated the creation and demise of the Cost Accounting Standards Board using Bernstein's theory of "life-cycle of regulatory commissions".

The subject of this study is the creation of the A.S.R.B. and the establishment of its functions. The interest in this subject has been instigated mainly due to the dearth of research on it and by the methodology adopted by R. Walker (1987). R. Walker used the notion of "regulatory capture" in his description of the Board and in investigating the process of its creation. He showed that the accounting profession, being the regulated party, influenced that process in order to ensure that the Board would be under its control.

The inadequacies and anomalies in R. Walker's study are discussed under various headings in Chapters 2, 3, 4 and 11. In essence, it is asserted that R. Walker's approach was biased towards showing that the accounting profession was the only influential participant in the Board's creation and the determination of its functions. This is evident

---

1   Since Professor R.G. Walker's and Mr. Frank Walker's (former Attorney-General of N.S.W.) names are mentioned frequently in this book, they are distinguished by their first initials and are called R. Walker and F. Walker, respectively.

2   There have been several reviews of the A.S.R.B. in the context of the company law and company accounting in Australia. One elaborate review was that by Parker, Peirson and Ramsay (1987).

Board's creation and the determination of its functions. This is evident from his choice of the "capture" notion without any reference to other theories of regulation. Without a review of those other theories it is not possible to judge the efficacy of the "capture" approach.

Again, R. Walker's description of the Board being captured by the accounting profession is limited to a study of certain aspects of the Board's operations. A systematic review of the Board's organization and functions (before its merger with the Ac.S.B. of the A.A.R.F.), within the regulatory framework of the Co-operative Scheme for Companies and Securities, in Chapters 2 and 3 indicates that the Board was dependent on and susceptible to influence from several interest groups. The influence of the profession on the preparation and review of standards is noted as R. Walker did, but it is found here that other parties had also secured important roles through which they could constantly scrutinize and influence the Board's activities. To identify a few, the Board, being dependent on its creator the Ministerial Council for its basic authority, had to operate with the notion that all its approved accounting standards were subject to political approval. This implied that the political consequences of its standards had to be minimal.

Within the time-frame of this study, the Board was also found to be dependent on the N.C.S.C. for the enforcement of the approved standards. The presence or absence of any standard which was an impediment to the efficient administration of company law was liable to receive the attention of the N.C.S.C. and its delegates, the State C.A.C.s. Furthermore, R. Walker (1987) failed to mention the conspicuous presence of a number of company executives on the Board. Companies or more specifically their directors were, in fact, the primary object of accounting regulations, such as the approved accounting standards. Auditors or the accounting profession as a whole, as R. Walker assumed, were affected because they were actively involved in the preparation and authentication of company financial statements. As a result the companies, along with the accounting profession, were also one of the regulated parties because their activities and interests could be affected by the approved accounting standards. The considerable representation of company executives on the Board was devised, presumably, to help secure the interests of that group of regulated parties.

Accounting regulatory recommendations have ranged from free financial information market proposals to suggestions for central government bureaucratic control, with regulated markets as an intermediary option.[3] In Australia the regulated market option is favoured by the policy makers and has been in use for a long time.[4] According to Peirson and Ramsay (1983) three different means of regulation have been in use in Australia. These are Government legislation, professional accounting standards and the official listing requirements of the Australian Associated Stock Exchanges (A.A.S.E.). The choice of the Accounting Standards Review Board (A.S.R.B.) and its approved accounting standards showed a preference for a mixed form of regulation. Under that form, accounting standards were reviewed through a "due process" mechanism by the interest groups and on approval received legislative support.

Such a board seems to be the outcome of various proposals for and against its establishment. For example, F.J.O. Ryan, the N.S.W. Companies Registrar and later the Commissioner of Corporate Affairs, demanded a statutory commission with the power to prepare standards (Ryan, 1967, p. 106). Frank Walker, the N.S.W. Attorney-General in 1977, called for an accounting standards tribunal for reviewing accounting standards (F. Walker, 1981b, p. 23). The Accounting

---

3   For example see Bromwich (1985) chapters 3, 4 and 6 and Solomons (1986) mainly chapters 9 and 10. In Australia indications of probable bureaucratic control were made by F. Walker (1981) as an alternative to a semi-autonomous Accounting Tribunal.

4   See Peirson and Ramsay (1983). Similarly, Fels (1982, pp 29-30) remarked that, in general, government intervention has increased in recent years in Australia. Morgan (1976, p 2-4) identified 40 different kinds of economic regulations in U.S.A. Such regulations not only include regulation of commodities markets through price fixation, barrier to entry, etc., but also regulation of securities and financial information market.

Standards Review Committee of N.S.W. Report (1978, p. 145) recommended the establishment of an accounting standards review board capable of setting priorities and authoritative enough to direct the professional accounting standard-setting process. As a part of its responsibilities as a company law enforcer, the N.C.S.C. demanded the right to set disclosure requirements for company accounts (Durie and Kelly, 1982, p. 38 and Australian Financial System, Final Report of the Committee of Inquiry, 1981, p. 372). Coming to terms with the surge in the call for Government intervention in standard-setting, the accounting profession accepted intervention to the extent of review by an independent or profession sponsored board ("Australian Accounting Profession", Submissions of March and August 1982 to the N.C.S.C.).[5] All those proposals had one common feature - legislative backing for accounting standards. Others, such as Winsen (1980) and the Australian Industries Development Association (1982), argued to the contrary and suggested the continuation of the process of self-regulation or no government intervention.

The variety of proposals made for an accounting standards review board and the involvement of several interest groups in the final outcome implies a pluralistic formation process. The basic impetus for a board, as we shall see later, was provided by failures in the securities market, but the outcome - the Board, seems to be the product of pressures from different parties trying to safe-guard or enhance their own interests. The regulators (the Ministerial Council), in the process of establishing a standard-setting body under the Co-operative Scheme for Companies and Securities, apparently were influenced by the interest groups.[6] Therefore, the major problem addressed in this study is that:

---

5   Suggestions for legislative backing for professional accounting standards were
       made as early as 1978 by the professional accounting bodies (R. Walker 1986,
       p. 6).

6   A closer scrutiny of the Board's organization and functions conducted in
       Chapters 2 and 3 reveal this. Also see R. Walker (1986).

Despite various forms of existing regulations and various recommended forms of regulation, why was the A.S.R.B. set up in a form that left it dependent on and subject to the influence of several interest groups?

The scope of influence of several interest groups and the Board's dependence on them for efficient functioning casts doubts on R. Walker's (1987) "capture" argument. It leads us to hypothesize that:

In order to ensure that they played an influential role in the functioning of the A.S.R.B. all identifiable interest groups actively participated in the Board's establishment.

Importance of the Research:

The A.S.R.B., due to its unique mechanism of securing the support of the major interest groups and legislative backing for accounting standards, was a noteworthy innovation in the field of accounting regulation in Australia. This research is directed towards understanding why and how a board with its unique attributes was installed.

Until now only R. Walker (1987) has attempted to provide an explanation of the nature of the Board and its process of establishment. Because of the economic consequences that emanate from the accounting standards (See Chapter 5), R. Walker's argument that the Board was captured by the accounting profession could have far reaching implications for those who depend on company financial statements with the understanding that they were prepared on the basis of standards which are the outcome of "due process". Acceptance of the capture argument may also provoke changes for the Board leading to its demise. For example, if the Board is seen as a profession dominated body its standards may lose support of important allies such as the politicians in power, the law enforcing agencies, and the preparers of financial statements, as was the case of professional accounting standards (See Chapter 8). That could, in turn, reduce the support received by the Board from those allies. The loss of support could be to the extent that it could terminate the existence of the Board (The A.P.B. in the United

States had a similar fate (Moonitz, 1974, pp. 74-75)).[7] This necessitates further investigation of the Board's organizational and functional features. If our observations are different from R. Walker's we need to provide an alternate explanation for the creation of the Board. This study, therefore, is an investigation of the Board's organizational and functional features (before its merger with the Ac.S.B.) and provides a description of how they were determined.

Methodologically, R. Walker (1987) used a narrow approach in the sense that he looked only at the behaviour of the accounting profession in the Board's creation. The behaviour of other parties, especially that of the members of the Ministerial Council (the creators of the A.S.R.B.), had not been studied by him. His "capture" approach covered a time frame too short to illustrate adequately the Board's establishment. The time frame, he adopted, was sufficient to highlight the activities of the accounting profession and not those of other parties. He mainly examined the phase after the creation of the Board, and he highlighted the participation of the accounting profession. He almost completely ignored the involvement of other parties. The omission of a description of the "gestation" phase which preceded the creation of the Board and in which the idea of a review Board evolved, also contributed to the lack of examination of the involvement of other parties in the creation of the Board. This study will try to fill this void.

The A.S.R.B. since its creation was a public body financed by the Australian Treasury. The Board's contributions towards the improvement of securities market efficiency, reduction of frauds in the securities market or any other "measurable" objective to assist users of financial information, are not clear. Since the Board's budget and expenditure had increased rapidly from the initially proposed budget of $ 18,000 in 1981 (See N.C.S.C. Release 401, 1981 p. 4) to $ 210,000 in 1985-86 (See A.S.R.B. Annual Report 1985-86, pp. 18-19) and as it had

---

7   Although the C.A.S.B. in the United States was also closed because of loss of support, but "capture" was not the main reason for it (See Davis and Menon, 1987).

no clear or readily discernible benefits for its beneficiaries - users of accounting information - it is important to understand why and how the A.S.R.B. was created.

In this respect, we also need to understand why the regulators, in their decision to create an A.S.R.B., overlooked the main purpose of having accounting standards as instruments of maintaining the quality of financial information in securities markets. As it is understood, initially the regulators saw the need for an A.S.R.B. in the context of the Co-operative Scheme for Companies and Securities for the improvement of the capital markets (See Australian Financial System, Final Report of the Committee of Inquiry, 1981, Chapter 21). They seemed to have overlooked their objective in the process of reconciling their views with those of others, specially with those having a significant stake in the Board's creation.

In this research the A.S.R.B. is regarded as a part of an on-going regulatory process rather than a new regulatory set-up. R. Walker (1987) assumed the latter in explaining that the accounting profession, as a regulated party, managed to capture the newly formed A.S.R.B. through its influence. The "capture" notion is certainly applicable under such an assumption, and it only helps to explain and predict the situation from a narrow single party perspective. In this study an attempt is made to look at the creation of the A.S.R.B. as a "two-way" "process", that is to study the behaviour of the suppliers and the demanders of the Board in an on-going regulatory process for company disclosure that probably co-existed with the company form of business organization since its inception. Such an approach can help us study and predict the behaviour of all interacting parties. Accordingly, it can also assist in suggesting future changes in the regulatory capacity of the Board taking into account the interests of all the parties in the regulatory process. It can also provide a frame of reference to understand or predict the behaviour of interest groups in the accounting standard-setting process.

The potential importance of this study has enhanced because of the recent changes in the accounting regulatory policy in Australia. The merger of the Board with the Ac.S.B. of the A.A.R.F. and its reconstitution testifies to an important feature of the regulatory process, that is stressed in this thesis - that the developed from this research can help us understand why such a change took place.

Scope of the Study:

This research deals with the reasons for and the process of the creation of the A.S.R.B. in Australia. It is not a detailed study of the Board's standard-setting process. Inquiry into the demand for and the supply of standards has been conducted only to reveal the reasons for the demand and supply of the Board.

The study is descriptive in nature. It uses a descriptive model which is considered superior to others because of its greater capacity to explain interest group behaviour. The model provides a neutral perspective of assessing the behaviour of all the identifiable interest groups (See Chapter 5). The nature of participation of interest groups and the corresponding changes in the organization and functions of the Board, which can affect the process of establishing financial disclosure standards, is investigated. It is not intended to use any other view point, for example, investigate why the A.S.R.B. was created as a part-time board and not as some other form of regulatory body (such as a full-time board or a commission). There are two reasons for avoiding such an approach. First, according to the problem and the hypothesis specified in the first section, the regulatory capacity of the Board is of primary importance and not its organizational form. Second, till now no organizational theory has been developed which can provide an adequate explanation for the preference for various forms of public bodies (Hood, 1978).[8]

---

8   Among the arguments for the creation of public bodies reviewed by Hood (1978), the "managerial theories" seem to partially explain why the A.S.R.B. was created as a part-time board. Such theories view organizations as being built up from basic operational tasks and imply that the top structure which emerges will be closely related to the dictates of the basic tasks. From this view point, it can be

The intention in this study is to investigate the initial establishment of the organization and the functions of the Board and <u>not</u> its entire life-cycle. According to the discussion in Chapter 5, the embryonic development of regulatory bodies normally takes place in two stages: "gestation" and "youth". For the purpose of determining the time span of this study those stages have been considered (See Chapter 5 for further details). Notwithstanding the difficulty in identifying an accurate starting point of the "gestation" period,[9] this study commences with a review of the forms of company disclosure regulation which preceded accounting standards. It covers the evolution of the concept of mandatory accounting standards and the events leading to the creation of the Board. The time period of the study extends up to December 31, 1986, in order to study the determination of the Board's functions and organizational changes that took place after its creation. The time period stops short of the recent merger of the Board with the Ac.S.B., but sufficiently covers R. Walker's (1987) adopted time frame. Although it is beyond the scope of this thesis to review in detail all procedural controversies confronted by the Board after its creation, the significant ones, such as those discussed by R. Walker (1987) and those that were responsible for the reconstitution of the Board, are examined.

As for the explanatory capacity, this research may have wider implications - for example, in explaining the creation of other regulatory bodies. In this respect there are three points about which the reader should be <u>cautioned</u>. First, the A.S.R.B., unlike many other regulatory bodies, had (and still has) very limited regulatory capacity (explained in Chapters 2 and 3). Secondly, it dealt (and still deals) with accounting

---

inferred that the A.S.R.B. emerged as a part-time board because initially its primary objective was only to review standards created by others. But, such a theory does not explain why the Board had been empowered to review standards only and in whose interest was it to ensure that the Board did not have any other powers. This and other weakness (see Hood, 1978) of this strand of theories make them only partially capable of explaining the creation of regulatory bodies.

9   According to Bernstein (1955) the "gestation" period is normally over twenty years, but it may not be so in all cases.

standards which, due to their nature, could be different from many other forms of regulations. Finally, the context of the A.S.R.B. is Australian and in Australia the overall mechanism for securities regulations is different from other countries. That is, the structure and administration of the Co-operative Scheme for Companies and Securities is unique and no other country has a similar system.[10]

Outline of Chapters:

This book is composed of eleven chapters. These chapters are briefly described in this section.

Chapter 1 introduces the thesis by describing the problem and specifying the hypothesis. The importance of the research, scope of the study and the outline of its chapters are also described in this chapter.

Chapter 2 deals with the organization and function of the A.S.R.B. before its merger with the Ac.S.B. First, the institutional framework in which the Board existed is described. Then its organization and regulatory capacity is analyzed. Finally, the parties on which it was made to depend by its creators have been identified.

Chapter 3 further investigates the role of the Board, specially in terms of its independence. The scope of influence by interest groups on its activities is examined.

In Chapter 4 the competing theories of regulation, that have been applied in accounting, are evaluated. From this evaluation the most descriptive theoretical framework that is applicable to this research is identified.

---

10   It has been shown later that this Co-operative Scheme has been instrumental in the creation of the A.S.R.B.

From that theoretical framework a model - having the concept of a market for regulatory policies - is developed in Chapter 5. The regulatory theories, in general, are briefly examined to identify the nature of regulatory policies and substantiate the explanatory status of the preferred model amongst those theories. The method of applying the model with the support of some other related theories is outlined. The advantages and limitations of the model are also noted.

In Chapter 6 major forms of company accounting regulations in Australia are identified. The events and crises leading to accounting regulations and the nature of demand for and supply of various forms of accounting regulation prior to the inception of the idea of government backed mandatory accounting standards is studied. It is shown that changing accounting regulatory forms in Australia are evidences of a dynamic regulatory process. The emergence of financial accounting standards as a regulatory form is seen as a product of this process.

In Chapter 7 it is established that the accounting standards which evolved as a mode of professional development, in the light of subsequent company failures, received attention and recognition from outside the profession and eventually turned into a means of company financial disclosure regulation.

In Chapter 8 the trend towards mandatory accounting standards in a changing regulatory environment of the 1970's is analyzed.

Chapter 9 focuses on the stage of the regulatory process through which the A.S.R.B. was created and its functions determined. The various arguments forwarded for a Board or a similar organization and the way the final outcome was determined is reviewed. The review is based on publicly available literature and submissions to government authorities.

In Chapter 10 we analyze the behaviour of the demanders and suppliers of the A.S.R.B. The analysis reveals that the Board was indeed an outcome of the participation of several groups.

Chapter 11 comprises a summary of this dissertation and lays down the major conclusions and implications. The procedural changes that were criticized by R. Walker (1987) are discussed in this chapter, in the light of the conclusions. A postscript is also appended to this chapter to briefly reenact, on the basis of the model adopted in this thesis, the recent changes made to the Board.

Chapter 2

THE A.S.R.B. - ITS ORGANIZATION AND FUNCTIONS

Introduction:

R. Walker (1987) revealed the dependence of the Board on the Australian accounting profession and its standard-setting mechanism. In this chapter we review the organization and functions of the Board before December 31, 1986, within the framework of the Co-operative Scheme for Companies and Securities in Australia. The review is aimed at determining whether the Board was dependent on the accounting profession alone or also on other parties.

Note that the A.S.R.B. has recently been merged with the Ac.S.B. and may soon be merged with the P.S.A.S.B. of the A.A.R.F. The change of the Co-operative Scheme for Companies and Securities into a national Commonwealth based scheme is also imminent. The organization and functions of the Board under the changed/changing regulatory conditions are not the subject of study here. This review is in the context of the conditions prior to those changes.[11]

In Section 2 of this chapter the institutional framework of which the Board is a part is described. In Section 3 the organization of the Board is examined. In Section 4 its regulatory capacity is investigated. And, Section 5 summarizes the nature of the Board's organization and functions and identifies the other parties on which the Board is dependent on.

---

11   The changed regulatory conditions are briefly discussed in Chapter 11.

The Institutional Framework:

The establishment of the A.S.R.B., unlike its counterparts in North America or U.K.-Ireland, cannot just be seen as an outcome of the criticisms faced by the accounting profession.[12] It is also an off-shoot of the reform of companies and securities legislation in Australia.[13] In this respect R. Walker (1985) very rightly stated:

> one cannot sensibly examine the role of the A.S.R.B. without some understanding of the role of the Ministerial Council and the operations of the Co-operative Scheme for Companies and Securities (p. 3).[14]

The key features of the Co-operative Scheme for Companies and Securities[15] are highlighted in Figure 2.1 and briefly described as follows:

(i)   The Formal Agreement:

It is an agreement reached between the six States and the Commonwealth and it was executed in December, 1978. It is the charter for the Co-operative Scheme for Companies and Securities. The objectives of the Co-operative Scheme are, that there should be uniformity in the laws relating to companies, the regulation of the securities industry and in the administration in the States and territories of Australia in order to promote commercial certainty to bring about a reduction in business costs and greater efficiency of the capital markets, and that the confidence of the investors in the securities market should be maintained through suitable provisions for investor protection. It sets out the role of the

---

12   For example see Bromwich (1985, p. 14 and p. 22).

13   For example see Parker (1986, p. 5)

14   For an elaborate discussion about it see R. Walker (1985, pp. 3-5).

15   The Co-operative Scheme as a scheme for the supply of an A.S.R.B. is discussed in detail in Chapter 8.

Ministerial Council, the N.C.S.C. and the States' and territories' administrations. It forms a schedule to the various Acts and codes and directs the N.C.S.C. and the C.A.C.s to observe the formal agreement (the Schedule to the National Securities and Conpanies Commission Act 1979 and Business Review Weekly, June 27, 1981, p. 30). In the 'formal agreement' the States agreed to cede powers to the Commonwealth whereby the States agreed not to enact separate companies or securities legislation but automatically adopted Commonwealth legislation (R. Walker, 1985, p. 3).

(ii)   **The Acts and Codes:**

The States still maintain their own codes but the text of those are that of the Commonwealth Acts as translated and adopted by the State's Companies (Applications of Laws) Act. There are four codes in each jurisdiction:

1.   The Companies (Acquisition of Shares) Code;
2.   The Securities Industry Code;
3.   The Companies and Securities (Interpretation and Miscellaneous Provisions) Code, and
4.   The Companies Code.

The legislative requirements relating to the establishment of the A.S.R.B. were incorporated in the Companies and Securities Legislation (Miscellaneous Amendments) Act 1983. These provisions are now consolidated in the Companies Act and Code at sections 266B-F (A.S.R.B. Release 200, 1985, p. 3 - see Appendix B.1.).

Figure 2.1.: A.S.R.B. and Its Environment. (Over page)

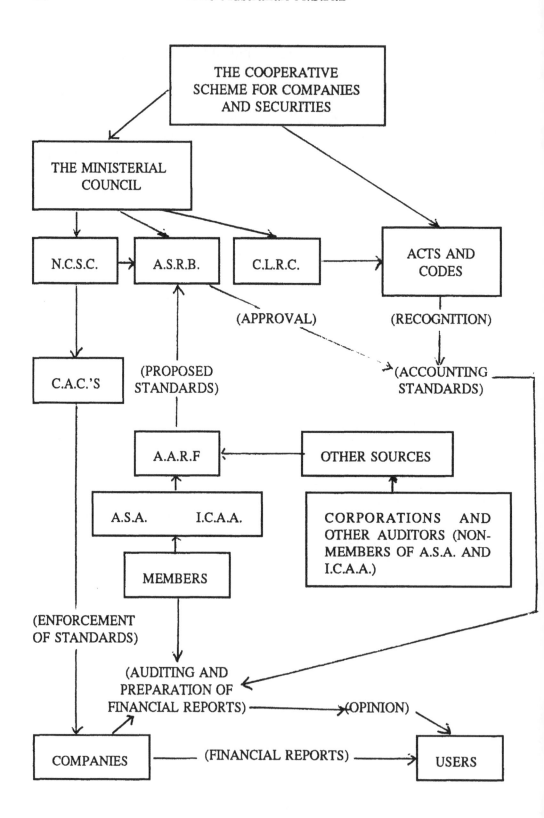

(iii)   **The Ministerial Council:**

The Ministerial Council is the collegiate body which has ministerial responsibility for the policy and administration of the co-operative scheme. It consists of the six States' and the Commonwealth Attorneys-General and it has the ministerial responsibility to the exclusion of individual ministers. Decisions of the Council are by majority vote. Each minister has one vote (the Schedule to the National Securities and Conpanies Commission Act 1979 and Business Review Weekly, June 27, 1981, p. 30). It is the principal body of the Co-operative Scheme.

In practice the Council is a body composed of the politicians who hold a certain government office, namely that of the Attorney-General. Their membership is subject to their transfer from that office or their party's stay in power. Therefore, as R. Walker (1987, p. 281 and p. 285) noted, the members of the Ministerial Council can change and so can the general attitude of the Council towards company regulation.

(iv)   **The N.C.S.C.:**

The N.C.S.C. is the central administrative and coordinating body in the Co-operative Scheme. It is a Commonwealth statutory authority and it receives its powers under the N.C.S.C. Act of the Commonwealth and the N.C.S.C. (State Provisions) Acts of the States, as well as under the various substantive laws. It is also authorized to determine policy measures and adjudicate on matters arising from those legislations, on a national basis (R. Walker, 1985, pp. 3-4). It consists of three full-time members. It is empowered to delegate its powers and functions to the State C.A.C.s, and to give directions to those Commissions with respect to those powers and functions. The N.C.S.C. is obliged by law to obey the directions of the Ministerial Council (Business Review Weekly, June 27, 1981, p. 30). In general the Commission is responsible for ensuring that:

- information which is made available to investors in securities markets is sufficiently accurate, timely and objective to enable investors to make rational investment decisions;
- an open and informed market exists so that all shareholders have equal access to information bearing on investment decisions;
- the efficiency of securities markets will be encouraged by regulating the conduct of securities business to promote desirable market practices;
- high standards of corporate behaviour are maintained, and there are adequate remedies and penalties for breaches of company law (Australian Financial System, Final Report of the Committee of Inquiry, September, 1981, pp. 364-365).

These responsibilities show that the maintenance of an informed securities market is a priority for the N.C.S.C. For that reason the Commission had shown great interest in the creation of the A.S.R.B. and was in fact entrusted with the operational aspects in respect of the creation of the Board (For example, see N.C.S.C. Media Release 401 and 405). When the A.S.R.B. commenced its activities in January, 1984, the N.C.S.C. in conjunction with the N.S.W. C.A.C., was entrusted by the Ministerial Council to make interim arrangements for its operations.

(v)   The C.A.C.s:

The C.A.C.s are autonomous state commissions. They administer the day-to-day aspects of the companies and securities legislation. In particular, all documents (including financial statements) that are required to be lodged under the various acts of the scheme and all applications for the exercise of the N.C.S.C.'s powers are to be lodged with the C.A.C.s (Business Review Weekly, June 27, 1981, p. 30). They are subject to the direction of the N.C.S.C. They were responsible for the enforcement of the approved accounting standards of the A.S.R.B.

(vi)   The Companies and Securities Law Reform Commission:

Responsibility for formulating certain law reform proposals lies with the Companies and Securities Law Reform Commission, established in 1983. It undertakes assignments on reference from the Ministerial Council (R. Walker, 1985, pp. 3-4).

(vii)   **The A.S.R.B.:**

The A.S.R.B. was established by the Ministerial Council. It has no separate legal identity. It is described in the Code as "the body known as the Accounting Standards Review Board established by the Ministerial Council" (A.S.R.B. Annual Report 1984-85, p. 2). The A.S.R.B. commenced its activities in January 1984 with the assistance of the N.C.S.C. In July 1984 it received a separate budget allocation. Action was taken concurrently to establish a full-time staff. Its first director was appointed on November 12, 1984 (A.S.R.B. Release 200, 1985, p. 3). The main function of the Board as an organ within the Co-operative Scheme was to establish and monitor financial disclosure standards recognizable under the Companies Act 1981. Its features are discussed in greater detail in this and the next chapter.

(viii)   **The A.A.R.F.:**

It is a research and standard formulating body established jointly by the two professional accounting bodies in Australia, the A.S.A. and the I.C.A.A. The standards formulated by it, upon receiving approval from the National Councils of the two professional bodies, take the shape of professional accounting standards. It was recognized by the A.S.R.B. as the main source of proposed accounting standards (A.S.R.B. Release 200, p.10).

(ix)   **The Companies:**

Subject to the provisions of Section 266B to 266F inclusive of the Companies Act and Codes, approved standards must be used in preparing the financial statements of companies incorporated in all States of Australia, the Northern Territory and the Australian Capital Territory. Therefore approved accounting standards were enforceable on all companies incorporated in Australia and those companies were the object of A.S.R.B. regulations.

(x)   **The Auditors:**

The auditor of a company registered under the Companies Act 1981 has specific obligations in respect of whether accounts or group accounts conform with approved accounting standards and in particular to furnish a copy of the audit report to the Board where he or she is not satisfied that the accounts or group accounts comply with the approved accounting standards. In this respect the obligations of the company auditor have been laid down in sub-paragraph 285 (3)(a)(ii), paragraph 285(3)(aa) and sub-section 285(11) of the Companies Act and Codes.

Since approved accounting standards were rules stating the procedure or procedures which must be followed in the preparation of accounting reports (A.S.R.B. Release 200, p. 2) and the company auditor was obliged to refer to them in forming an opinion about company and group accounts, the auditor's activities could be seen as being regulated by the standards. Therefore, we may regard the auditor as one of the regulated within the purview of approved accounting standards.

The auditor of a company under the Act and Codes need not be a member of the A.S.A. or the I.C.A.A. The qualifications for registering as an auditor with the relevant C.A.C. has been specified in sub-section 18(2) and Regulations 20-22 of the Act.

(xi)   **The Professional Accounting Bodies:**

The A.S.A. and the I.C.A.A. are normally considered as the Australian professional accounting bodies. They fund and manage the A.A.R.F. but, as mentioned earlier, they do not represent the whole of the accounting and auditing profession in Australia.[16] The A.S.R.B. recognized that the

---

16   See Section 18(2) and Regulations 20-22 of the Companies Act 1981 for the eligibility requirements for becoming a company auditor. These requirements show that non-members of A.S.A. and I.C.A.A. can also become registered company auditors.

primary responsibility for the development of accounting standards should remain with those bodies (<u>A.S.R.B. Annual Report 1985-86</u>, p. 7).

(xii)   The Users of Financial Information:

The prime users of financial reports are the shareholders (or potential shareholders) and the creditors (or potential creditors), but the A.S.R.B. also recognized other users, like governments or government agencies, consumer groups, employees or unions (<u>A.S.R.B. Release 100</u>, p. 6 - see Appendix A.1.).

The Organization of the A.S.R.B.:

Composition:

The A.S.R.B., before its reorganization through the merger with the Ac.S.B., was a part-time board[17] (It still is so). It was composed of seven part-time members (<u>A.S.R.B. Release 200</u>, p.3). Its members were appointed by the Ministerial Council in the following manner:

- the Chairman
- a member selected from a panel of names submitted by the Australian Society of Accountants.
- a member selected from a panel of names submitted by the Institute of Chartered Accountants in Australia.
- four members selected from panels of names submitted by the following organizations and bodies:
  the National Companies and Securities Commission;
  the Australian Associated Stock Exchanges;
  the Institute of Directors in Australia;
  the Australian Council of Trade Unions;
  the Business Council of Australia;
  the Australian Merchant Bankers Association;

---

17   Also see R. Walker (1985, p. 9)

the Institute of Chartered Secretaries and Administrators;
the Accounting Association of Australia and New Zealand;
the Australian Accounting Research Foundation; and
the Australian Shareholders' Association.

While members were selected from panels of names submitted by those organizations, they are appointed in their own right and not as delegates or representatives of the organizations and bodies which advance their names (A.S.R.B. Release 200, 1985, pp. 3-4).

A list of A.S.R.B. members appointed since its inception is in Table 2.1.

Table 2.1. List of A.S.R.B. members since its creation and up to 1987.

NAME	YEARS SERVED (as at 31/12/86 and including those appointed for 1987)[18]	PAST AND/OR PRESENT AFFILIATIONS
J.N. Bishop	3	I.C.A.A.+ - auditor
G.W. Bottrill	3 (as Chairman)	A.S.A.+ - A.A.R.F. - company executive
P.L. Calder	*	A.S.A. - company executive
R.L. Coppel	1 *	I.C.A.A. - A.A.S.E. - auditor
R.J. Cotton	3	A.S.A.+ - company executive
S.J. Droder	3 **	I.C.A.A. - A.A.R.F.+ - company executive
B.H. Edwards	*	I.C.A.A. - auditor
W.A. Gibson	*	A.S.A. - company executive
A. Holland	2	I.C.A.A. - company executive
C.A. Martin	1 *	A.S.A. - academic
P.A. Pearce	1 *	I.C.A.A. - A.S.A.+
D. Sly	2	A.S.A. - company executive
R.G. Walker	2	I.C.A.A. - academic

18   Although those members selected for the year 1987 fall outside the period of this study, they are included to provide a better idea of membership background.

*	Appointment commenced on January 1, 1987.
**	Appointed Chairman from January 1, 1987.
+	Past president or former chairman.

Source: <u>A.S.R.B. Annual Reports</u> (1984, 1985 and 1986) and <u>A.S.R.B. Media Release 86/9</u>, December 1, 1986.

The data in Table 2.1. is further analyzed according to career background and professional membership of each member.

Table 2.2. Career Background and Professional Membership Affiliations of A.S.R.B. Members.

Membership Affilitation	Company Executive	Auditor	Academic	Others
A.S.A. or I.C.A.A	7	3	2	1
Held/Holds Senior Position in A.S.A. or I.C.A.A. or A.A.R.F.	3	1	0	1
Non-members of A.S.A. or I.C.A.A. or A.A.R.F.	0	0	0	0

From Table 2.1. and 2.2. we find the following:

1. All members of the Board were members of the A.S.A. or the I.C.A.A.
2. A number of members (five out of thirteen) had been affiliated to the A.S.A., the I.C.A.A. and the A.A.R.F. at senior levels. Others may have been involved with those bodies at lower levels (for example see R. Walker, 1986, p. 37).
3. The two chairmen appointed so far had held senior positions in the A.A.R.F. - the standard-setting organ of the A.S.A. and the I.C.A.A.

4.   A large number of the members (seven out of thirteen) were affiliated with companies.

Since the above information only provides a broad idea of the affiliations of the members, it cannot help us to find whether any particular group dominated the Board's membership numerically at a point in time. To do so another table has been constructed to breakdown the membership of the Board on a yearly basis. This helps us in identifying any particular years in which any party could have significantly dominated the Board numerically.

Table 2.3. Background of the A.S.R.B. Members on an Annual Basis.

Background	1984	1985	1986	1987
Company Executives	5	5	3	3
Auditors	1	1	2	2
Academics	1	1	1	1
Stock Exchanges	1	0	1	1
Total	7	7	7	7
Past-presidents and Ex-chairmen of A.S.A., I.C.A.A. and A.A.R.F.	4	4	5	2
Members directly involved with the Accounting and Auditing Profession	6	6	6	6

Table 2.3. reveals that:

1.   The company executives (all of them senior accountants) held a majority in the first two years after the Board's creation and their representation remained high.
2.   The practicing auditors at no point had a majority.

3. Members who had been affiliated with the A.S.A., I.C.A.A. and the A.A.R.F. at senior levels held a majority in the first three years after the Board's creation.

4. Members who had direct involvement in the accounting and auditing profession, combined together, always held a large majority in the Board.

5. There had been some representation from the academics and the stock exchanges.

The official composition of the Board provided for only two representatives from the A.S.A. and I.C.A.A. (one from each body). At no point in time could they, along with other independent members of the accounting and auditing profession, have dominated the Board numerically. To achieve a majority they inevitably would have to seek support from the larger group - the representatives of the companies.[19] In other words, the representatives of the companies could play a powerful role in the activities of the Board, provided they acted as a bloc.[20] There was the possibility of those representatives acting in the general interest of the A.S.A. and the I.C.A.A. because all of them were members of one or both of those bodies and most of them had been

---

19   The number of academics was too small to form a viable coalition with the profession, and academics like Professor R. Walker, who seemed to dissent with the moves of professional bodies (For example, see R. Walker, 1985, 1986 and 1987), were unsuitable for a coalition with those bodies.

20   Like the F.A.S.B., it is not necessary that the A.S.R.B. members affiliated to particular groups would vote as a bloc. For example see Meyer (1974), Rockness and Nikolai (1977), Hussein and Ketz (1980) and Brown (1981). Those studies mainly dealt with specific issues of standard-setting and did not reject the possibility that the members of the professional bodies, the most dominant group, could work together to safeguard the general interests of the accounting profession as a whole. Again, professional body members, specially employed as company accountants or academics, may not directly work in the interest of the professional bodies. They may be work in their own or some other group's interest. An example of this is the behaviour of Professor R. Walker (See R. Walker, 1985 and 1986). He is a member of the I.C.A.A., but he has been critical of the domination of both the A.S.A. and the I.C.A.A. in A.S.R.B. matters.

senior office bearers in the executive councils of both the bodies - provided their actions were not detrimental to the interests of the companies and industries that employed them.

As for A.S.R.B.'s staff, the Board was initially provided secretarial assistance by the N.C.S.C. Later, it had a Director (a member of the A.S.A. and an ex-Assistant Commissioner of the N.S.W. C.A.C.) and an executive secretary. It also had a panel of consultants (A.S.R.B. Annual Report 1985-86, p. 7).

Appointment, Tenure and Removal:

As mentioned earlier the Board's members were appointed by the Ministerial Council from various panels of nominees which in turn determined the composition of the Board. There was no specific set of criteria for appointment, but the nature of appointments made indicated that opportunity for participation by interest groups (specially the companies and the professional accounting bodies, the A.S.A. and the I.C.A.A.), employment of expertise and prominence in the field of accounting and auditing were emphasized.[21]

Members were appointed for a term of two years on a staggered term basis with the possibility of reappointment.[22] To ensure the staggered term concept the first set of Board members included three members (the Chairman and those members nominated by the A.S.A. and I.C.A.A.) having three year terms. Subsequently chairmen and members had terms of three years and two years, respectively (A.S.R.B. Annual Report 1986-87, p. 6). Therefore, every year three or four members including the chairman could be replaced, if any of them were not reappointed.

---

21   See the background of the Board members in the A.S.R.B. Annual Reports of 1984-85 (pp 4-5) and 1985-86 (pp.5-7) and Tables 2.1., 2.2. and 2.3.

22   Mr. Stan Droder was reappointed (A.S.R.B. Annual Report 1985-86, p. 6)

There were no definite rules for the removal of A.S.R.B. members, except that they could be denied reappointment by the Ministerial Council or denied renomination by the body which nominated the member in the first instance. Since the Board was not an independent statutory body and was established through a resolution of the Ministerial Council, the Council, as its creator, could dissolve it, as and when necessary. In this respect R. Walker (1985, p. 3) observed that the Board, presumably, could exist for as long and in such a form as was the wish of the Council.

Finance:

The budget estimates for the A.S.R.B. had risen continuously since it was mentioned in the N.C.S.C. Media Release of December 3, 1982. The initial estimate by the N.C.S.C. for the A.S.R.B. was $18,000 per annum, which it later increased to $35,000 (N.C.S.C. Media Release, December 3, 1982). Compared to that, the expenditure for the first six months of the Boards activities (January 1 to June 30, 1984) was $34,244 (A.S.R.B. Annual Report 1984) which was paid out of the N.C.S.C. budget. The allocation for 1984-85 was increased almost six times to $200,000 and the expenditure for the same year stood at $199,916 (A.S.R.B. Annual Report 1984-85). The allocation for 1985-86 was $210,000 and the expenditure stood at $209,939 (A.S.R.B. Annual Report 1985-86).

The A.S.R.B., in respect of financial accountability, did not have a distinct status. Initially the N.C.S.C. provided all the necessary finance and facilities for the Board's operation. Later, even though the Board received a separate budget allocation, its accounts were kept as a part of the N.C.S.C. accounts. The N.C.S.C.'s accounts were audited by the Commonwealth Auditor General and a separate audit certificate was not issued in respect of A.S.R.B. accounts (A.S.R.B. Annual Report 1984-85, p. 11). The A.S.R.B. prepared annual reports each year which were addressed to the Ministerial Council for Companies and Securities. The Commonwealth Attorney-General presented the reports, on behalf of the Council, to both the houses of the Commonwealth Parliament (See A.S.R.B. Annual Reports 1984, 1984-85 and 1985-86).

A.S.R.B.'s Regulatory Capacity:

The A.S.R.B. was established by the Ministerial Council in an attempt to have a set of approved accounting standards recognizable under the provisions of the Companies Acts and Codes and to impose obligations upon the directors and auditors of companies in respect of those standards.[23] It is also noted in Chapter 5 that mandatory accounting standards are regulations. For such reasons the A.S.R.B. may be considered as having regulatory functions.

Basic Authority:

Legislative support can be provided in two ways. The first method involves the creation of a regulatory body through a statute - a statutory regulatory authority. The second case is that of a regulatory body being created by another body which has been authorized to do so by the legislature or that the legislature recognizes its creation, and then supports the regulations formulated by such a regulatory body and also provides it with the means of enforcement (Wettenhall, 1977). The A.S.R.B. falls in the second category. It was not a statutory body and did not have a separate legal identity (A.S.R.B. Annual Report 1984-85, p. 2). Section 266 of the Companies Act 1981 as amended in 1983 stated:

> "Board" means the body, known as the Accounting Standards Review Board, established by the Ministerial Council.

The aim of the 1983 amendments to the Companies Act 1981 was to establish a system for bringing into existence "approved accounting standards" and to impose obligations upon the directors and auditors of companies in respect of those standards (A.S.R.B. Annual Report 1984-85, p. 2). The broad guidelines regarding the duties of the Board were set down in Sections 266B-F of the Act. The obligations of

---

23   See A.S.R.B. Release 200, 1985, p. 4; A.S.R.B. Annual Report 1984-85 pp.2; and R. Walker, 1985, pp. 4-7; Companies Code, 1981, sections 266 and 269.

the directors and the auditors regarding compliance with the accounting standards approved by the A.S.R.B. were laid down in Sections 269 and 285, respectively, of the Act (Also see A.S.R.B. Release 201, 1985 - see Appendix B.2.).

The Act mainly provided the basis for a mechanism for the enforcement of the approved accounting standards. It said little about the process of formulating and approving those standards. The procedures for the evaluation of standards were outlined in the A.S.R.B. Release 100 (1985) and that for the approval of standards were set out in the A.S.R.B. Release 200 (1985) (See also Figure 3.1.). Although those releases, contained statutory provisions of the Act and the directives of the Ministerial Council, they were A.S.R.B. documents. Even the envisaged conceptual framework was expected to be such a document (A.S.R.B. Annual Report 1984-85, p. 3). It meant that they did not carry statutory support like that received by approved accounting standards, and they were in effect only guidelines for the review and approval of standards. The powers and duties granted to the Board by the Ministerial Council were specified in A.S.R.B. Release 200 (1985) and in the A.S.R.B. Annual Report 1984-85. Those documents indicated that the A.S.R.B. functions were closely guided by the Council and its major policy decisions had to be ratified by the Council. That implied that the A.S.R.B. drew its basic authority to operate for the purpose of reviewing standards from the Ministerial Council and the enforcement rules for the standards were provided by the legislature. Neither the Council nor the statute defined its standard-setting procedures precisely. It was up to the Board to develop its procedures under the scrutiny and approval of the Council and within the guidelines of the statute.

Functions:

Fesler (1946, pp. 213-221) described the nature and conduct of independent regulatory agencies and noted that the legislature provided a broad discretionary authority to such agencies. He classified their functions as legislative, judicial and executive. The A.S.R.B. functions are discussed in this perspective as follows:

(i)   **Legislative Function:**

Legislative function is basically rule making. If the emphasis is placed on a legislative technique, the agency will set about doing what the legislature failed to do - define with some exactness the types of acts that will be treated as lawful. It will do this by issuing rules and regulations (Fesler, 1946, pp. 213-228). Spann (1979) emphasized this in the Australian context as follows:

> ... parliaments have neither the time, the expertise, nor adequate processes to undertake the detailed formulation of every necessary law. Usually they must content themselves with declaring the policy or outline of legislation and empowering some administrative authority to prescribe most of the machinery by which, and the circumstances in which, that policy is to be implemented. This is done by conferring power in the Act or minister or other authority to make regulations, orders, rules or by-laws, which when made are 'delegated regulations', sometimes also called 'sub-ordinate legislation' (p. 153).

In Australia such delegation is normally made to the Governor-General in Council or a Ministerial Council or to a special authority (Spann, 1979, p. 153).

The A.S.R.B. had the legislative characteristics of a regulatory agency. Its powers outlined in <u>A.S.R.B. Release 200</u> (February, 1985, p. 4) and the <u>A.S.R.B. Annual Report 1984-85</u> (November, 1985, p. 3) were indicative of it:

> The Ministerial Council has empowered ('advised' as per the <u>Annual Report 1984-85</u>) the Accounting Standards Review Board to:
>
> - determine priorities in consideration of proposed accounting standards referred to it;
> - specify a conceptual framework, not having the force of an approved accounting standard, against which it will evaluate standards submitted for approval; *
> - review standards referred to it;
> - review appropriate standards, or portions thereof, of national accounting standards of other countries or of International Standards; *

- sponsor the development of standards; *
- seek expert advice as it deems necessary;
- conduct a public inquiry into whether a proposed accounting standard should be approved;
- invite public submissions into any aspect of its public functions;
- change the form and content of accounting standards submitted to it for approval without it being necessary for the submitter to agree to the changes;*
- approve or revoke accounting standards.**

---

*   These powers did not exist when the A.S.R.B. Release 200 was published in February, 1985. They were later added in the A.S.R.B. Annual Report 1984-85 published in November, 1985. Also see R. Walker (1985) for a detailed discussion on those amendments.

**   The power to revoke was added in the A.S.R.B. Annual Report 1985-86 (p. 4). This was already present in the Companies Act sub-section 266B(4).

The principal functions of the A.S.R.B. as revealed from its objectives (See A.S.R.B. Annual Report 1985-86, pp. 2-3) were to review accounting standards proposed by the A.A.R.F. or those proposed by other bodies (with the prior consideration of the A.A.R.F.).[24] As per its operating philosophy, the A.S.R.B. recognized that the primary responsibility for the development of accounting standards should remain with the accounting profession (A.S.R.B. Annual Report 1985-86, p.7). This was further confirmed by the "Fast Track" procedures adopted by the Board from December 1985 whereby:

1.   the Board's "Procedures for Approval of Accounting Standards" (See A.S.R.B. Release 200) were temporarily relaxed and

2.   the Board could seek comments directly on the professional standards without first redrafting them.[25]

---

24   A.S.R.B. Annual Report 1985-86, p. 7 and A.S.R.B. Release 200, p. 3.

25   A.S.R.B. Annual Report 1985-86, pp. 9-10.

The A.S.R.B. could be classified as a legislative regulatory body because it was delegated by the Ministerial Council the powers to identify, review and approve the financial disclosure rules (standards) for companies. An approved accounting standard was defined in the Companies Code as being an accounting standard approved by the A.S.R.B. by "notice in writing published in the (Commonwealth of Australia) Gazette" (Companies Act 1981, Section 266B). A standard to be approved required the affirmative vote of at least five members of the Board (A.S.R.B. Release 200, p. 10). Only the Ministerial Council had the power to disallow an approved accounting standard, within 60 days of its publication in the Gazette (Companies Act 1981, Section 266B(3)). In the absence of such rejection by the Ministerial Council or revocation or amendment by the A.S.R.B. the approved standard became a disclosure rule. In short, approved accounting standards were rules stating a procedure or procedures which had to be followed in the preparation of company accounting reports. It could deal with the form or content of company financial statements, or it could concern how information was to be presented in those statements or in accompanying notes. It could deal with how money magnitudes in financial statements were to be calculated or define the constituent terms (A.S.R.B. Release 100, 1985, pp. 3-4).

The A.S.R.B. basically had powers for establishing and monitoring[26] standards. The power to establish standards is divisible into two parts: (1) reactive power and (2) proactive power (see Cranston 1982, p. 15; R. Walker, 1985, p. 5). Reactive power means the power to react to proposals or cases presented by outsiders. Proactive power is the power to sponsor, investigate and determine standards. The A.S.R.B. was initially expected to approve only standards that were submitted to it (see R. Walker 1985, p. 5 and N.C.S.C. Media Release, 1982). This function was expanded to include sponsoring and development of standards (A.S.R.B. Release 200, p. 4), which was further enhanced to include the specification of a conceptual framework, reviewing standards

---

26   Monitoring function has been discussed under the heading "Executive Functions".

of other countries or International Standards and changing standards proposed to it without the approval of the proposing body (A.S.R.B. Annual Report 1984-85, p. 3). Although the A.S.R.B. had both reactive and proactive powers, it intended to remain mainly reactive. Proactive powers were expected to be used only if there was no other viable alternative to set a required standard within a reasonable time (A.S.R.B. Annual Report 1984-85, p. 4). The addition of proactive powers was important because it reduced the dependence of the A.S.R.B. on outsiders, if such a need arose. That, along with the power to change standards, could act as a deterrent to those who intended to influence the A.S.R.B. by proposing unacceptable standards in areas where suitable standards were needed.

(ii)   Judicial Functions:

It involves rule setting as cases arise and are presented for decision by the agency (Fesler, 1946, p. 213). Fesler (1946) felt it to be more useful in the settlement of disputes rather than standard-setting. According to him this mode of standard-setting ignored interests which were not represented in the agency.

The powers of the A.S.R.B. did not signify any judicial functions.[27] The Board's role was not that of an adjudicator. In case of controversies or objections regarding its standards the affected party could make representations to the Ministerial Council (see R. Walker (1985, p. 10)). R. Walker (1985, p. 2) noted that the N.C.S.C., as the central administrative agency of the Co-operative Scheme, was obliged to enforce the compliance of A.S.R.B. standards through courts rather than administrative edict.[28] Ford (1988, p. 11) added that an appeal

---

27   In 1977 Frank Walker, the N.S.W. Attorney General, referred to the establishment of an accounting tribunal (Business Review Weekly, November 28, 1981, p. 46).

28   See R. Walker 1985, pp. 2-3 for a detailed description of the current regulatory system.

from a decision of the N.C.S.C. lay with the Supreme Court of the appropriate State or Territory. In this respect it may be pointed out that the courts can define the scope of the legislative power granted to prepare delegated legislation, such as those of the A.S.R.B. Spann (1979) stated that:

> Delegated legislation is ultra vires and invalid when it exceeds the power granted by the Act of Parliament to the subordinate authority (p. 154).

In the case of the Co-operative Scheme the power to regulate the behaviour of companies and securities was delegated to the Ministerial Council, which in turn had delegated the authority to formulate financial disclosure regulations to the A.S.R.B.. It is evident from this arrangement that the Courts, as in the case of other legislations and regulations, could also define the scope of financial disclosure regulations.

To sum up, it can be said that the judicial powers to decide in case of controversies arising from approved accounting standards was fractionally with the Ministerial Council and the N.C.S.C., and mainly with the Courts. The A.S.R.B. had no such powers.

(iii)   Executive Functions:

The regulatory agency may be entrusted to administer the regulations set by itself or the legislature or some other body and ensure that the regulations are followed by the regulated firms (Fesler 1946, p. 214). The functions and duties of A.S.R.B. in this respect were minimal. The A.S.R.B. itself was not empowered to enforce any approved accounting standard on the companies. The Companies Code provided the statutory requirements for the enforcement of those standards. Sections 266, 269 and 285 of the Companies Code imposed responsibilities on company directors and auditors in connection with compliance with 'approved accounting standards' in the preparation of accounts and group accounts.

The approved accounting standards applied to the first year of a company that commenced after the day on which the accounting standard was approved and in relation to subsequent financial years of the company (Companies Act 1981, Section 266C (1)(a)). The A.S.R.B. was also empowered to vary the date from which a standard was applicable subject to the possibility of disallowance by the Ministerial Council (Companies Act 1981, Section 266C(1)(b) and 266D(1)). The A.S.R.B. could replace, revise or revoke its approved standards, subject to review by the Ministerial Council (Companies Act 1981, Sections 266B and 266C). The Council could also disallow approval, replacement, revision or revocation of any approved accounting standard within 60 days of the A.S.R.B.'s decision being published in the Gazette (Companies Act 1981, Sections 266B, 266C and 266D).

Under Section 285(11) of the Companies Act 1981, an auditor of a company or holding company was required to send to the A.S.R.B. a copy of his/her report on the accounts or group accounts within seven days of submitting that report to the directors where he/she was not satisfied or was of the opinion that the accounts or group accounts had not been drawn up in accordance with a particular approved accounting standard. Section 266F of the Act empowered the A.S.R.B. to require the company by notice in writing, to furnish it within seven days of the notice, a copy of the accounts or group accounts to which the auditors' report pursuant to Sub-section 285(11) related. The A.S.R.B. monitored non-compliance with the approved accounting standards and maintained a register of such accounts which was available to the N.C.S.C. and the C.A.C.s (R. Walker, 1985, p. 8 and A.S.R.B. Release 200, p. 9).

The rules enacted by the legislature in Australia are administered, currently, through a Commonwealth-cum-States mechanism. Prior to the establishment of such a system the States administered the companies legislation independently. The enactment of the Uniform Companies Act was followed by the gradual upgrading of the State Company Registrars from filing authorities to Commissioners of Corporate Affairs empowering them with the additional task of enforcing financial disclosure provisions of the Companies Act.

Following the signing of the Co-operative Scheme for Companies and Securities Agreement in 1978, the State administrations were supplemented by the the creation of the N.C.S.C. in 1980. The N.C.S.C. as a Commonwealth body, was entrusted with the administration of the Commonwealth Companies Legislation adopted by each State under the Co-operative Scheme. The N.C.S.C. was empowered to conduct its activities through its delegates the Corporate Affairs Commissions of the respective States and Territories (See N.C.S.C. Third Annual Report and Financial Statements 1982, Appendix A and Appendix C Release 109). Amongst the responsibilities of the Commission some of the following related to company financial disclosure:

> ... the Commissions' objectives will be to ensure:
>
> ...
>
> ...
>
> (iii)   that high standards of corporate governance and accountability are recognized, encouraged and maintained by directors and officers of companies;
>
> ...
>
> (v)   that auditors and liquidators of companies observe high standards of professional competence and personal integrity in performing their duties;
>
> ...
>
> (vii)   that information concerning companies which is maintained in public registries is up-to-date, complete and accurate; ... (See N.C.S.C. Third Annual Report and Financial Statements 1982, p. 60).

The power to administer the standards, through the imposition of sanctions outlined in the Companies Code, were assigned to the N.C.S.C. and, on appeal, to the judicial system.[29] R. Walker (1985) briefly stated the pivotal role of the N.C.S.C. as follows:

---

29   See R. Walker 1985, pp. 2,3 and 8 for detailed discussion and also Peirson and Ramsay, 1983, p. 300.

The N.C.S.C. has responsibility for administering the Commonwealth
legislation and the state legislation applying the provisions of the
Commonwealth legislation and regulations. The N.C.S.C. was also
given authority to exercise responsibility for policy making and
adjudication arising from that legislation, on a national basis (p. 3).

The N.C.S.C.'s could also exempt and modify the application of
legislation (Ford, 1988, p. 10). It could issue Class Orders granting relief
to companies and or their auditors from the accounts and audit provisions
of the Companies Act and Codes. In this respect the Notes on the
Inclusion of N.C.S.C. Materials in the A.S.R.B. Manual (1986) stated:

Section 273 of the Companies Act and Codes vests in the National
Companies and Securities Commission the power to grant orders
relieving the company or relieving the auditor of a company from any
specified requirements of the Companies Acts or Codes relating to, or
to the audit of, accounts or group accounts or the Directors' report
required by sub-section 270(1) or (2). The orders can be made in
respect of an individual company or for classes of companies.

Including those Class Orders, till now, the N.C.S.C. has issued the
following types of pronouncements clarifying its position in respect of
company financial disclosure :

(1)   N.C.S.C. Release 600 N.C.S.C. Pronouncements
       (regarding accounting regulations of the Companies Acts
       and Codes).
(2)   N.C.S.C. Release 625 Relief from Accounts and Audit
       Provisions (of the Act): Section 273 orders.
(3)   N.C.S.C. Release 650 Schedule 7 (revised).

The powers of the N.C.S.C. indicated that the Commission could
exempt or defer the application of approved accounting standards. Under
its Release Series 600 the Commission has issued seven Class Orders
affecting the application of approved standards issued by the A.S.R.B.
It has also issued pronouncements under its Release Series 600A
providing directions for the application of certain accounting standards.
Such powers clearly indicate the role played by the N.C.S.C. and its

delegates, the C.A.C.s, in the enforcement of approved accounting standards.

In short, the enforcers of companies legislation, the N.C.S.C. and the C.A.C.s, were authorized to issue directives in the course of conducting their duties with a view to facilitating the implementation of standards issued by the Board. R. Walker (1985, p. 4) also mentioned that arrangement for standard-setting and comprehensive feedback concerning compliance had also broken new ground. The feedback regarding standards was designed to assist the N.C.S.C. to impose sanctions on the non-complier and serve the A.S.R.B., through the reports of the company directors and auditors, in knowing the weaknesses of approved standards.

Inference:

The functions of the A.S.R.B., as observed here, were predominantly legislative and slightly administrative (executive) and not at all judicial. Under its powers, it could mainly play a standards reviewer's role, with the additional power for monitoring compliance with approved accounting standards. A major portion of executive functions were given to the N.C.S.C. and the judicial functions were shared by the N.C.S.C. and the Courts. In the case of legislative functions, the over all authority was with the Ministerial Council which itself was the creation of the legislatures of the States and the Commonwealth.

The Board's role was primarily in the field of delegated legislation which made it to rely on the three branches of government - the legislature, the judiciary and the executive, for the effective enforcement of its standards. A.S.R.B.'s standards were enforceable only through the provisions of the Companies Code; the judiciary could define the scope of its functions and its standards, and the executive (the Ministers) appointed its members and provided it with its powers.

Although the A.S.R.B. did not have complete control over the mechanism for standard enforcement (that is the powers to institute sanctions for non-compliance), it was equipped to provide an essential ingredient for rule administration - the monitoring of compliance. The A.S.R.B. also recognized that for rule development to be effective, it should proceed in tandem with rule administration (R. Walker, 1985, p. 21). In fact, one of the reasons for which the A.S.R.B. was established was to ensure that the accounting rules which were to be imposed on the corporate sector should have some legitimacy in the eyes of preparers of financial statements, auditors, shareholders and other users of accounting reports - and that those rules were enforceable (R. Walker, 1985, p. 21). In that respect, in order to enhance the legal enforceability of the approved accounting standards, the A.S.R.B. had to change the drafting style used by the A.A.R.F. on advice from the Commonwealth Attorney-General's Department (A.S.R.B. Annual Report 1984-85, p. 6; and R. Walker, 1986, p. 17). Therefore, the legislative functions of the A.S.R.B. were closely linked to the administrative functions of the N.C.S.C. and the judicial functions of the N.C.S.C. and the Courts, and were aimed at better enforceability of the standards.

Summary:

The Board was a legislative regulatory organ of a greater regulatory system - the Co-operative Scheme for Companies and Securities. The role of that scheme is to regulate corporate and securities market activities in Australia, within which the financial accounting standards play a significant role. In that scheme of regulations, the A.S.R.B. was delegated, by the Ministerial Council, the function of establishing those standards and monitoring the compliance with them by the companies.

As a part of the Co-operative Scheme, the Board was dependent on other government organs within and outside the scheme. For basic authority and existence, it was dependent on the Ministerial Council, an entity composed of politicians. All standards approved by the Board were also subject to the approval of the Council. Therefore, the Board had to function to the satisfaction of the Ministerial Council.

The implementation of the approved accounting standards of the Board was the responsibility of the N.C.S.C. and its delegates - the bureaucratic organs of the Government. In this respect, we have noted that the Commission could modify the nature and timing for the enforcement of the standards. Accordingly, the Board was dependent on the Commission and the State C.A.C.'s for the purpose of implementing the standards. And as for matters that needed resolution, the ultimate authority lay with the courts.

In the case of the involvement of the regulated parties in the organization of the Board, as a bloc, numerically the members affiliated to the companies and those closely associated with the accounting bodies (the A.S.A and the I.C.A.A.) had held a majority in the membership since the creation of the Board. Although bloc voting could not be guaranteed because there could be disagreements within the bloc, the possibility of dominance of the regulated groups for the preservation and enhancement of their interests was there.

Under normal circumstances, the Board had to rely on the accounting profession for the preparation of standards. The organization of the Board was indicative of greater participation of a wider circle of interest groups in the accounting standard-setting process, but that participation was mainly limited to the review and approval of standards. The creation of the Board did not significantly change the nature of participation in the standard formulation stage. In that stage the parties other than the professional accounting bodies could only contribute through submissions to the A.A.R.F. Even though there was scope for participation in the A.A.R.F. process, the power to propose standards was mainly with the national councils of the A.S.A. and the I.C.A.A.

Although the Board, as an organization, was given an independent appearance, it was dependent on others for almost all the activities which were essential for its efficient functioning. Such dependence provided the scope of influence on its activities by several interest groups. This observation necessitates a further analysis of the influences. That analysis is contained in the next chapter.[30]

---

30   See Curran (1983, p. 531) for further details of the A.A.R.F. standard-setting process. Although Coombes and Stokes (1985) tried to show the plurality of of the process, Curran mentioned that some of the past issues were selected by the A.A.R.F. due to pressures to do so and that a minor fraction of those assumed to be interested in accounting standards, responded to the exposure drafts of the Foundation.

Chapter 3

THE A.S.R.B. - ITS INDEPENDENCE

Introduction:

The A.S.R.B., as we have seen in the previous chapter, was created separately from other company financial disclosure rule setters, such as the N.C.S.C., the A.A.R.F., the A.A.S.E., and all the other legislative, judicial and executive departments. The criteria of appointment for the members of the Board also confirmed that feature as follows:

> ... they are appointed in their own right and not as delegates or representatives of the organizations and bodies which advanced their names. (A.S.R.B. Release 200, 1985, p. 4).

Explaining that criterion, Masel (1983) regarded A.S.R.B. as an independent body representative of (not representatives of) the interest groups (p. 541). The N.C.S.C. Release 401 (1981, p. 4) and N.C.S.C. Release 405 (1982, p. 12) and the Joint Report of the N.C.S.C. and the N.S.W. C.A.C. (1983) in recommending a separate standards review board emphasized the independence criterion. In short, A.S.R.B. was intended to be an independent regulatory agency.

It must be noted here that the A.S.R.B. was not the only regulatory agency in Australia which was granted an independent status. Wettenhall (1977, p. 329) in a survey of 103 statutory authorities reported that 42 of the authorities were created primarily to provide them impartial and independent status. Seven out of the ten regulatory authorities studied in the same survey were created for the same reasons. From those observations, it is fair to claim that "independence" is regarded as an important feature of most regulatory agencies in Australia.

Contrary to the "independence" notion, we noted in the previous chapter that the Board was dependent on several institutions and groups, which gave rise to the scope of influence from various interests on its activities. Therefore, in this chapter the Board's presumed independence from or dependence on outside influences is analyzed in the light of notable literature on independent regulatory agencies.

In section 2 of the Chapter the reasons for which an independent board was created are identified. In section 3 the independence of the Board is tested. The influence and dominance of interest groups is analyzed in section 4. In section 5 the manner in which the Board was established is hypothesized.

Identification of the Reasons for an Independent A.S.R.B.:

The reasons for the creation of independent regulatory agencies have been reviewed by Fesler (1946, pp. 223-224), Bernstein (1955, pp. 24, 54, 56, 71 & 72), Wettenhall (1975, p. 74 and 1977, p. 349) and Cranston (1982, pp. 7-9). Those reasons are reviewed here and an attempt is made to identify the reasons which had been instrumental in the formation of the A.S.R.B. as an independent regulatory agency.[31]

The Reasons:

1.   Public interest (Bernstein, 1955, p. 24; Cranston, 1982) through interest group participation (Wettenhall, 1977) is one reason for having an independent regulatory agency. The public interest argument, in the case of the A.S.R.B., was placed or discussed, for example by F. Walker (1979), the Australian Development Association (1982, p. 13), Bottrill (1982, p. 12), Hines (1983, p. 27), Peirson & Ramsay (1983, p. 300), Craig (1985, p. 83), and R. Walker (1985, p. 6). The constitution and powers of the

---

31   Those reasons do not include the reasons that relate to aspects of the Board other than independence.

A.S.R.B. and the procedures set by the Board signified an attempt to incorporate the public interest argument. The Ministerial Council, by selecting the members of the A.S.R.B. from several panels (A.S.R.B. Release 200, pp. 3-4), intended to give a public image to the Board. The powers of the A.S.R.B. included responsibilities to enhance public participation:

> - conduct public hearings into whether a proposed accounting standard should be approved;
> - invite public submissions into any aspect of its public functions; (A.S.R.B. Release 200, 1985; A.S.R.B. Annual Report 1984-85).

Provisions for participation were also made within the procedures for the approval of standards. The A.S.R.B. was expected to consult regularly with the users and preparers of accounting information and the public in general through submissions, meetings, public hearings and talks (A.S.R.B. Release 200, pp. 6-8; A.S.R.B. Annual Report 1984-85, pp. 7-8). In this manner the A.S.R.B. was not only organized as a public body, but also as an organ which could serve private interests. Wettenhall (1977, Table 4, p. 350) observed such a purpose of regulatory bodies in Australia. His survey revealed the participation of private businesses in regulatory bodies (Table 27, p. 360), which showed that the A.S.R.B. was not the first organization of its kind to possess such features.

2.   The second reason for which independent regulatory agencies are supposedly established, is to reduce the cost of extensive litigation (Bernstein, 1955, p. 24; Cranston, 1982). This is not applicable in the case of the A.S.R.B. The A.S.R.B. was neither a tribunal nor a judicial body. It could only approve or set standards and monitor compliance. The capacity to enforce such standards was assigned to the N.C.S.C. In case of controversies the ultimate authority to decide was with the courts (see R. Walker 1985, pp. 1-2, also see A.S.R.B. Release 200, 1985 p. 4

and A.S.R.B. Annual Report 1984-85, p. 3). Under that
arrangement the N.C.S.C. was responsible for persuading a court
that the company concerned failed to meet its statutory
obligations of "true and fair" disclosure. The A.S.R.B. could
play an advisory role for both the N.C.S.C. and the Courts.
According to Bernstein (1955, p. 24), such advisory services
have been provided by regulatory authorities in the U.S.A. With
no such case arising in the case of approved accounting
standards, it is difficult to say whether the A.S.R.B. could help
in reducing litigations and litigation costs.

3.   Independent regulatory agencies are expected to limit the
involvement of courts in the administration of social policy
(Bernstein, 1955, p. 72; Cranston, 1982). This notion could apply
in the case of A.S.R.B. approved standards. The courts
previously had to depend mainly on the guidelines of the
Companies Code and its schedule 7 and the standards of the
professional accounting bodies. Mannix and Mannix (1982)
described the situation without approved accounting standards as
follows:

> When questions of accounting procedure and
> method have arisen, courts have shown a marked
> reluctance to offer guidelines upon what
> accounting principles ought to be applied possibly
> because of the fact that the accounting profession
> itself has not laid down any extensive guidelines.
> Instead the courts have restricted themselves as
> they must do in any case before them and have
> tended to accept evidence of any established
> practice of sound commercial accounting, as long
> as it is applied consistently. Generally evidence
> from other accountants and representatives of
> accounting bodies as to what constitutes sound
> accounting practice is accepted and applied (p.
> 31).

The standards approved by the A.S.R.B. could provide guidelines to a greater specificity and they could be given greater importance by the Courts in deciding cases because of their statutory backing and the amount of public exposure they had already undergone during the formulation process. Since accounting standards have economic consequences[32] which lead to social impacts, certain expertise would be needed to formulate policies and standards which were not possessed by the courts. In the past, reformers had feared legalistic approaches, applied by judges without a real appreciation of the context in which regulation occurred (Cranston, 1982, p. 7-8). In the case of accounting, the courts could follow the essence of approved accounting standards in deciding the cases regarding financial disclosure because of the seal of community acceptance given to those standards by the A.S.R.B. This implied that the courts did not need to be too involved in deciding which information was "true and fair" and which was not.

4.   The fourth reason for the establishment of independent regulatory agencies is, that it employs expertise which is not present with the legislature, the judiciary and the executive branches (Fesler, 1946; Bernstein, 1955, p. 24; Wettenhall, 1977, Table 28, p.360 and Cranston, 1982). Cranston (1982) quoted Landis's classical statement to elaborate this reason and stated:

> the case for the independent regulatory agency
> was to concentrate and nurture expertise and to
> free administration from political and judicial
> pressures (J.M. Landis, The Administrative
> Process, 1974)

---

32   See Chapter 3, also see Hines, 1983; Craig, 1985, p. 83; Zeff, June 1978 & December 1978, pp. 58-62; Rappaport, 1977, pp. 89-98; F.A.S.B., 1978; Wyatt, 1977, pp. 92-94; Sweiringa, 1977, pp. 25-39; Prakash & Rappaport, 1977, pp. 29-38.

It applies well in the manner the A.S.R.B. was formed and put into operation. Emphasis on expertise was placed by the N.C.S.C. Media Release (1982), Masel (1983, p. 542), F. Walker (1981b, p. 23) and Kelley (1982). In fact both the N.C.S.C. Release 401 (1981, p. 3) and N.C.S.C. Release 405 (1982, p. 13), while recommending the membership of the A.S.R.B., gave high priority to expertise as a qualification for the selection of the Board's members. The manner in which A.S.R.B. operated showed an active involvement by the people who participated in or were associated at the policy making levels with the accounting standard-setting process of the A.A.R.F. and the professional accounting bodies. Table 2.3. provides evidence that there was a tendency for former senior officials of the A.S.A., I.C.A.A. and A.A.R.F. to be appointed to the Board. Although the Board as a whole represented a wide cross-section of the business, academic and professional community, the individual members all possessed professional accounting qualifications and most of them had had close association with the accounting bodies.

Another example of the dependence of the Board on professional accounting expertise was, that the Ministerial Council, during the Board's establishment endorsed the expectation that:

(i)   accounting standards to be considered by the Board for approval would normally emanate from the A.A.R.F.; and

(ii)   the Board would not approve accounting standards emanating from other sources without first giving the A.A.R.F. the opportunity to comment. (A.S.R.B. Release 200, 1985, p. 5 and see Figure 3.1.).

The "fast track" procedure, described in Chapter 2, can also be seen as an evidence of the dependence of the Board on the professional accounting bodies.

Figure 3.1

SUMMARY CHART – REVIEW OF PROPOSED STANDARDS

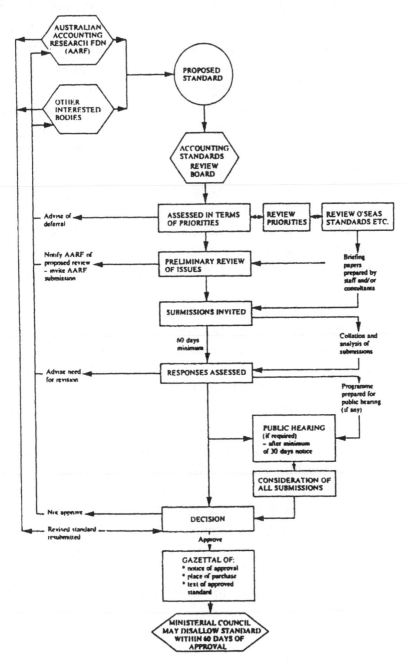

Source: A.S.R.B. Release 200, p.10

5.   Another reason for having an independent regulatory agency is
            that it could have organizational and functional flexibility
            (Bernstein, 1955, p. 24; Cranston, 1982; Wettenhall, 1975 &
            1977). This was not a significant issue for the establishment of
            the A.S.R.B. Since the A.S.R.B. was established by the
            Ministerial Council and worked under the supervision of the
            Council (A.S.R.B. Annual Report 1985-86, p. 3), it had to
            maintain its allegiance to the Council. It had no separate legal
            identity from that of the Council (A.S.R.B. Annual Report
            1984-85, p. 2). Its powers were drawn from the powers of the
            Ministerial Council (See previous chapter). The extent to which
            the Ministerial Council could interfere in the operations of the
            A.S.R.B. was defined in the Companies Code Section 266B-F.
            For example, it could disallow any standard prepared, or any
            standard revised or any standard revoked by the A.S.R.B. within
            a period of 60 days (Sections 266B(3) & (5), 266C(3)).

            The A.S.R.B. could also come under the influence of
            other advisory and administrative bodies which advised the
            Ministerial Council from time to time. Leading amongst them
            has been the N.C.S.C. As noted earlier, it played a
            policy-making and administrative role in the Co-operative
            Scheme. It was instrumental in the formation of the A.S.R.B.[33]
            and continued to play a major advisory role. In addition to the
            N.C.S.C. the A.S.R.B. may also have been influenced by the
            Commonwealth Attorney-General's Department, and the
            Corporate Affairs Commissions (R. Walker, 1985, p. 3-4). For
            instance, the A.S.R.B. abandoned the idea of approving the
            Australian Accounting Standards of the Professional Accounting
            Bodies because the Commonwealth Attorney-General's
            Department suggested the need for extensive redrafting of those
            standards if they were to be legally enforceable (R. Walker,

---

33   For example see N.C.S.C. Release 401 (1981) and N.C.S.C Release 405 (1982).

1985, p. 11; A.S.R.B. Annual Report 1984-85, p. 6).[34] The A.S.R.B. could also be influenced by the Courts in the sense that the Courts had the ultimate power to define the scope of approved accounting standards (R. Walker, 1985, pp. 1-3).

Apart from the perceived influences of the legislature, the executive and the judicial branches, the A.S.R.B. review and approval process was left open for the intervention of the public, in general, and the interest groups, in particular. The active intervention and close interest shown by the interest groups was noticeable when the joint accounting bodies expressed concern about having to relinquish copyright in standards submitted to the A.S.R.B. After the affirmation by the A.S.R.B. in February 1985 that the parties submitting standards to the Board would be required to assign copyrights to the Board (A.S.R.B. Release 200), on 27th June 1985 the joint accounting bodies formally communicated their unwillingness to comply with this requirement and expressed their intention to make representations on the matter to the Ministerial Council (R. Walker, 1985, p. 10). This clearly indicates that the A.S.R.B. decisions could be subjected to review by its creating authority the Ministerial Council due to effective interest group pressures.

6.   Independent regulatory agencies are also demanded because the courts and the executive may apply legalistic and administrative approaches respectively, overlooking the context in which the regulation occurred (Cranston, 1982). In this respect the A.S.R.B. could reduce some problems. Mannix and Mannix (1982) showed concern in the way the courts depended on the accounting profession in judging "the truth and fairness" of information audited by professional accountants. They felt that it led to an unhelpful circularity of reasoning:

---

34   This procedure was relaxed under the "fast track" method adopted in December, 1985 (A.S.R.B. Media Release No. 85/63, December 1985).

> The reasonable auditor would accept accounts
> which present a true and fair view and a true and
> fair view is given by accounts which a reasonable
> auditor would accept (p. 31).

Under such circumstances the Courts could overlook the very essence of developing accounting principles. The method used by the Courts was fragmentary - that is case by case, and did not conceive of the problem of financial disclosure as a whole.

As for the administrative approach of the executive branch, it is difficult to comment because there was no significant proposition from any quarter for the setting of accounting standards by a particular ministerial department.[35] Again, it may be recalled that the A.S.R.B. had no powers, except for monitoring, to administer the approved accounting standards. Therefore, there was a remote possibility that it would use an administrative approach similar to that of the executive branch.

7. Detachment from political control is another reason for having independent regulatory agencies (Bernstein, 1955, p. 71; Wettenhall, 1975 & 1977). In this context, political control means control by the major political parties or a direct influence of their party policies. The A.S.R.B. was an instrument of the Ministerial Council. The Council was composed of the Attorney-Generals of the States and the Commonwealth (R. Walker, 1985, p. 3). The Ministerial Council itself could be dominated by a particular political party only if the majority of the Governments in Australia and their Attorney-Generals were

---

35 Bromwich (1985, p. 107) considered Companies Acts as regulations designed by the bureaucracy. In U.K., under the Companies Act of 1981, such involvement of the bureaucracy had increased. In Australia the Schedule 7 of the Companies Code states the form and content of accounting disclosure by the companies, but did not specify measurement rules.

from a single party. For example, in 1986 four out of the six State and the Commonwealth Governments were Labour Governments. Although there was no defined arrangement for political party involvement in the accounting standard-setting process, there was ample scope for political influence by the parties through their lobbying to the Ministerial Council.

8. Impartiality and procedural due process is another suggested object of independent regulatory agencies (Bernstein, 1955, p. 54; and Wettenhall 1975 & 1977). This was an important reason for the creation of the A.S.R.B. as an independent agency. Arguments in this respect were placed or noted by F. Walker (1979), Australian Industries Development Association (1982, p. 13), Hines (1983, p.24), Bottrill (1984, p. 12) and Craig (1985, p. 83).[36] Most of their criticisms were aimed at the moral right of the professional accounting bodies to issue accounting standards. They argued that the need for accounting standards arose out of Government Legislation or had economic consequences and community implications. Public interest was involved and a system of developing and enforcing accounting standards completely in the hands of the professional accounting bodies was not acceptable by them. These arguments led to the belief that there was a need for broader community participation in the accounting standard-setting process and that the process should be independent of any particular interest group. This notion was characterized in the appointment of the members of the A.S.R.B., as mentioned in the previous chapter (Also see A.S.R.B. Release 200, p. 4).

---

36   Also see Peirson and Ramsay (1983, p. 296) and R. Walker (1985, p. 6).

The process of standards approval laid down in <u>A.S.R.B.</u> <u>Release 200</u> (pp. 3-5) also emphasized community participation[37] and due process through:

a. Submission of standards by any interested party (subject to review by the A.A.R.F).
b. Consultation with preparers and users.
c. Public exposure of draft standards.
d. Submissions on drafts by interested parties.
e. Public hearings.

9. Necessity of confidentiality (Wettenhall, 1977) is another reason for establishing an independent agency. It was never demanded by any one as a reason for the creation of the A.S.R.B. As explained above, the Board was established to encourage and enhance public participation rather than curtail it. According to the <u>A.S.R.B. Annual Report 1984-85</u>:

> The A.S.R.B. has taken the view that an essential element in the review process is the collection of the views of the participants in the accounting process (p. 7).

The only evidence of maintaining confidentiality in the A.S.R.B. publications was, that the Board stated that it would treat submissions to it as public documents unless the submission specifically requested confidentiality (<u>A.S.R.B. Release 200</u>, 1985, p. 14 and <u>A.S.R.B. Annual Report 1984-85</u>, p. 7).

10. Independent regulatory agencies may also be established to cover Federal and State responsibilities (Wettenhall, 1977). This was a reason not only for the creation of the A.S.R.B., but also for the Co-operative Scheme for Companies and Securities as a

---

37   Also see Australian Financial Systems, Final Report of the Committee (1981, p. 372) and <u>N.C.S.C. Release 405</u> (1982, p. 14).

whole (R. Walker, 1985, p.3). The Ministerial Council, at the apex of the Scheme, had representatives from all the State Governments and the Commonwealth Government. The A.S.R.B., as the Council's instrument, covered both Federal and State responsibilities for the formulation of approved accounting standards.[38]

11.   Experimental or investigational purpose can be another reason for an independent agency (Fesler, 1946). This reason was not very prominent in the establishment of the A.S.R.B.

As mentioned in the previous chapter, the activities of the Board could be both "proactive" and "reactive", that is it could sponsor standards itself in addition to those proposed by others. Its following "proactive" powers would require experimentation and investigation by the A.S.R.B. itself:

- review appropriate standards, or portions thereof, of the national accounting standards of other countries or of International Standards.
- sponsor the development of standards.
- change the form and content of accounting standards submitted to it for approval without it being necessary for the submitter to agree to the changes. (A.S.R.B. Annual Report 1984-85, p. 3, see also R. Walker, 1985, p. 5, for a detailed discussion).

The A.S.R.B. intended to be proactive only if there was no viable alternative available for bringing into existence a required accounting standard within a reasonable time.

---

38   This is also in line with the N.S.W. Accounting Standards Review Committee Report (1978, p. 145).

Therefore, the A.S.R.B. regarded the powers to amend submitted standards and to commission the preparation of standards as reserve powers (A.S.R.B. Annual Report 1984-85, p. 4).

12.   Another reason for independence is that the functions cover legislative, judicial and executive responsibilities and no branch is competent to do it alone (Fesler, 1946). This reasoning seems quite obvious in case of accounting standards, but was not expressed as such by any group for the establishment of the A.S.R.B. The expression by certain quarters[39] that the professional accounting bodies were more capable than others to formulate accounting standards, could be considered as an argument in this direction.

13.   The argument that the legislature does not want to enhance the power of the executive and or that the legislature differs in philosophy from that of the executive has also been placed as a reason for having an independent regulatory agency (Bernstein, 1955, p. 56; Fesler, 1946; Wettenhall, 1977). This issue was not used in the creation of the A.S.R.B. The creation of the A.S.R.B. was not a product of a struggle between the legislature and the executive to usurp the power to control corporate financial disclosure. In fact, its establishment promoted a balance between the legislative function of rule making and the executive function of rule enforcement. The A.S.R.B. was an outcome of a quest for enforceable rules (See R. Walker, 1985, p. 21; and also Chapter 8), that was to make the financial disclosure requirements of the legislature under the Companies Act and Codes executable. Accordingly, the A.S.R.B. closed the gap between the aims of the legislature and the executive in respect of financial disclosure regulation.

---

39   For example N.C.S.C. Media Release (1982), Masel (1983, p. 542), F. Walker, (1981, p. 23) and Kelley (1982).

14.   Independent regulatory agencies can also serve as a tribunal to safeguard the interests of the producer (the regulated) (Bernstein, 1955, p. 24). It was to some extent true in case of the A.S.R.B. The primary regulated group as pointed out in Chapter 2 was composed of the Companies. In addition the auditors had to fulfill certain requirements under the Companies Code and could be affected by the A.S.R.B. standards.[40] The debate regarding the creation of the A.S.R.B. was actively participated by the companies or their representatives and the auditors. For example, the N.C.S.C. Media Release of 6th December 1982 revealed that out of a total of 22 responses to the A.S.R.B. issue, 10 submissions were from preparers of financial statements (that is companies) and 6 were from the auditors (see Attachment A of that Release). This provides a fair idea of the extent of lobbying by those who would be directly affected by the A.S.R.B. approved accounting standards. Again, the current composition and the composition of the first set of members of the A.S.R.B. clearly indicated that the Board was dominated by senior company financial executives and members of the professional accounting bodies in Australia. From such evidence it is implied that the "safeguarding the interest of the regulated" notion was strongly built into the A.S.R.B. review process. As for the A.S.R.B. being a tribunal, the Board did not have any judicial or quasi-judicial powers. Therefore, it was not a tribunal.[41] This implies that the A.S.R.B. could safeguard the interests of the regulated only through the standard-setting process.

---

40   See A.S.R.B. Release 201, 1985 for details of the Companies Code requirements of the company directors and auditors.

41   Only Frank Walker the Attorney-General of N.S.W. in 1977 wanted a tribunal for accounting standards (Durie and Kelly, 1982, pp. 1 and 38).

Inference:

The above discussion reveals the major reasons for granting an independent status to the A.S.R.B. Those which were prominently expressed and were later incorporated in the A.S.R.B. set-up, were:

(i)   Public interest and also serving competing (private) interests.
(ii)   Employment of expertise.
(iii)   Impartiality and procedural due process.
(iv)   Safeguarding the interests of the regulated.

Other reasons, with lesser importance, that were perhaps inadvertently incorporated into the organizational features of the A.S.R.B., were:

(i)   Limiting the involvement of courts in standard-setting.
(ii)   Reducing legalistic and administrative approaches.
(iii)   Detachment of control from the political parties.
(iv)   Covering Federal and State responsibilities.
(v)   Experimental and investigational purpose.
(vi)   Incapability of the legislature, the judiciary and the executive branches of the Commonwealth and the States to prepare accounting standards.

Having noted that the Board was expected to be an "independent" body we further test and analyze the Board's features that were reviewed in the previous chapter, in the following sections.

Test for Independence:

Fesler (1946, p. 298) discussed the difficulty of determining when an agency could be called independent. He felt that we could only deal with the degree of independence - greater or lesser - and not complete independence or complete dependence. He laid a framework under which independence of regulatory bodies could be tested. Such testing involved assessment of:

(i)   Institutional safeguards of independence.
(ii)   Appointment, tenure and removal of members and that of the staff.
(iii)   Financial support.
(iv)   Basic authority.
(v)   Political factors.

In the light of this framework we can judge the nature of organizational and functional independence of the A.S.R.B. as follows:

1.   Institutional safeguards:

Fesler (1946) pointed out that boards and commissions were most common devices of preserving organizational independence. The A.S.R.B. was also provided with a board form of organizational structure. As mentioned earlier, it had seven members including a chairman, all of whom worked on part-time basis (A.S.R.B. Release 200, p. 3). R. Walker (1985, p. 9) therefore, called it a part-time board.

Fesler (1946) had doubts about the independence of commissions and boards because their members could be party loyalists or allied to political parties. Although the members of the A.S.R.B. may have been free from political affiliations, there were other forms of affiliations such as membership of professional accounting bodies and in some cases as ex-executives of those bodies or the A.A.R.F. A significant number of them were also senior company executives. They had undoubtedly brought with them their prior expertise and ideologies which could influence the proceedings of the A.S.R.B. Therefore, there were ample reasons to believe that the A.S.R.B. decisions could be influenced directly by the interest groups whose behaviour was in fact the object of A.S.R.B. regulation.

Outside influence could also be exerted through other channels. Recalling the earlier discussion on the reasons for an independent A.S.R.B., we find that there was scope for the political parties to influence the Board through their dominance in the Ministerial Council.

If the political interests were an extension of the interests of the regulated parties, the regulated could exert pressure through the Council. In addition to that the scope of the approved accounting standards could also be challenged in the Court. Again, the Board relied on the N.C.S.C. and the C.A.C.s for the enforcement of its standards. On those grounds it is evident that the A.S.R.B. was not provided sufficient institutional safeguards to operate independently. Apart from that, as discussed earlier, the A.S.R.B. was not a statutory body and was an instrument of the Ministerial Council. Not only its activities but also its existence could be decided upon by the Council.

Contrary to those disadvantages, Spann (1979) noted that part-time boards, being the commonest form of board in Australia (p. 131), had the following advantages:

(i)   Easier public accountability.
(ii)   Easier to change when necessary.
(iii)   Represent wider interests.

He pointed out that some statutes provided for the representation of various interests on the board (Spann, 1979, p.132, also see Wettenhall, 1977, p. 343) which had the following objectives:

(i)   Interest groups select a person with certain personal qualities.
(ii)   Promotes the confidence of the group in the board.
(iii)   Means of liaison between the group and the board.
(iv)   Views of the interest groups are presented.

The problems which he noted with such boards were, that qualifications of members were rarely specified and that there was a fear that political appointments could deprive the board of its independence (p. 132; also see Cranston, 1982, p. 19). In the case of the A.S.R.B. the only qualification mentioned was expertise in the area of accounting (N.C.S.C. Release 405, 1982, p. 13). This did not ensure a board's independence from political or interest group interference. In fact, "expertise" seems to have been interpreted as membership of professional accounting bodies or prior standard-setting knowledge. This led to a numerical dominance by members having close affiliations with the professional accounting bodies on the Board.

2. Appointment, Tenure and Removal:

Fesler (1946) suggested some other solutions to overcome the problems of institutional safeguards. Those were sufficiently lengthy and secure terms of office, appointments on overlapping basis ensuring that the appointing authority should not be allowed to appoint a majority of the members at one time (p. 209). He also emphasized the length of the term of office as an instrument for maintaining independence and added:

> One of the principal justifications for the independent commissions is the argument that, because of their staggered-term arrangement and relative freedom from executive domination, they have greater continuity of policy than executive departments (p. 223).

Spann (1979, p. 130) mentioned that for Boards in Australia, the appointments were normally made by the Governor-General at the advice of the Executive Council - the Cabinet. Compared to such appointments the A.S.R.B. members were appointed by a less authoritative body - the Ministerial Council for Companies and Securities. The mode of staggered-term arrangement allowed the Ministerial Council to appoint four members including the chairman every alternate year. The other three members could also be changed in a similar manner. That provided the Ministerial Council the power to change the membership of the Board rapidly and significantly, if it desired.

The two year terms for members and three year term for the chairman was somewhat shorter than that noted by Spann (1979) in the case of other Australian boards and Bernstein (1955) found in the case of U.S. regulatory commissions. Spann (1979, p. 130) revealed that the term of board members in Australia normally ranged from three to five years and that for chairmen it could extend to seven years or to retiring age. Bernstein (1955, p. 9), in the case of U.S. regulatory commissions, found the terms of members ranging from five to seven years. Spann (1979) emphasized the importance of the length of the term as follows:

> These provisions regarding tenure are important as they can influence the importance of the board. Where appointments are made for short periods or may be terminated at the will of the minister, the influence of the latter can be considerable (p. 131).

Unlike other agencies, the appointment and removal of members of the A.S.R.B. was made by the Ministerial Council and not by a minister or any other individual. Since the Council met periodically and needed to vote on all issues, the removal of members could be more difficult than if it was made by a Minister. Still, as the members were appointed for short periods, and as the Board was part-time, there was ample scope for lack of continuity and indifference towards taking bold steps. Under such circumstances the staggered term basis would not serve its purpose. Moreover, the nominees of the professional accounting bodies had a term of three years initially as compared to two years for those from other bodies, and the chairman of the Board and a number of members in the first set of members were company executives. This increased the likelihood of accounting bodies' ideologies and methods and company interests prevailing over that of others within the Board during the Board's infancy.

There were no definite rules for the removal of A.S.R.B. members, except that they could be denied reappointment at the end of their terms by the Ministerial Council or they could be denied renomination to the selection panels by the nominating bodies.

Wettenhall (1977) emphasized that the agency should have control over its staff to attain a greater degree of independence from the centralized government apparatus (p. 314 & 343). The A.S.R.B. was initially provided with secretarial assistance by the N.C.S.C. Later, it appointed a full-time Director and secretary. The Director had the status and privileges equivalent to that of an Assistant Commissioner - Special Grade in the N.S.W. Public Service. This appointment was made by the A.S.R.B. with the assistance of the N.C.S.C. (A.S.R.B. Annual Report

1984, p. 1). The total control of the Board over its staff, including their appointments, was consistent with what Wettenhall (1977, p. 343) recommended for the statutory authorities and the regulatory authorities in Australia. Since the size of the staff was small and their involvement in the standard-setting process minimal, they were an insignificant issue in the determination of the independence of the Board.

3.   Financial Control:

Spann (1979) emphasized that for boards "Financial Control was the most important of all forms of control" (p. 136). He found that the degree of financial autonomy could vary (p. 136). Fesler (1946, p. 211) also pointed out that the freedom from reliance upon the executive and the legislature for financial support was an important criterion of independence. He argued that agencies that could finance themselves were free from this form of executive and legislative control. Cranston (1982, p. 19) also noted the use of political influence on regulatory bodies through budgeting pressures. He felt that budget constraints could lead to lack of aggressiveness (p. 16).

Wettenhall (1977) pointed out that close financial control through the budgetary system could be used as a basis of control by the central government system (p. 314). He found significant legislative and ministerial controls, regarding budget and finance, on Australian statutory authorities including regulatory agencies (p. 324; also see Table 20A p. 357). He suggested minimal ministerial intervention and accountability through annual reports to the parliament (p. 342). He also proposed accountability through accounts maintaining the distinctive character of the body (p. 342).

Financially, the A.S.R.B. was dependent on the Ministerial Council. It had no resource of its own to finance its activities nor could it receive financial assistance from private sources. Since the N.C.S.C. played a crucial role in organizing the creation of the A.S.R.B. (R. Walker, 1985, p. 4; also see Chapter 9) and as the A.S.R.B. was treated as a segment of the N.C.S.C., financially and resource-wise, the

N.C.S.C.'s advice to the Ministerial Council regarding A.S.R.B. affairs could carry significant weight. This was similar to the following conclusion drawn by Coombes (1983) before the Board started functioning:

> The N.C.S.C. will be the conduit for decisions of the Ministerial Council in appropriating money to, and providing staff for the Board (p. 4).

4.   Basic Authority:

Citing the U.S. example Fesler (1946) stated that regulatory authority of independent establishments were created by the legislature. They depended on the legislative body for growth of regulatory authority. Similar instances of regulatory bodies depending on the statute for its authority were mentioned in Wettenhall (1977). His survey of statutory authorities identified a number of regulatory bodies in Australia which had been created by the statute. He showed (Wettenhall, 1977, Table 11, p. 352) that those regulatory authorities were closer to the legislature than to the responsible ministers.

From our discussion in Chapter 2 and this chapter, there is reason to believe that the A.S.R.B. drew its powers from those of the Ministerial Council. The Council could also scrutinize the standards, if necessary. The legislature only provided statutory support for the enforcement of approved accounting standards. On the other hand the judiciary could define and limit the scope of its standards if the standards were challenged by any one in the courts - but no such instance had occurred. Again, the Board was dependent on the N.C.S.C. and the C.A.C.s for the enforcement of its standards and on the accounting profession for the preparation of proposed standards.

5. Political Factors:

Too much political control by the executive and the legislature on the regulatory body could be against the notion of autonomy. In the case of the A.S.R.B. the Ministerial Council left the door open for political pressures of the political parties represented in the Council. Fesler (1946, pp. 111-112) suggested two ways of warding-off such influences by the agency. First, it could get sufficient backing of the interest groups who had sufficient economic and political power to restrain the executive and the legislature from influencing it. Secondly, it could receive some relief from executive power if its members themselves belonged to major political parties or factions which could prevent the executive from interfering.

In the case of the A.S.R.B., the scope for the second mode of receiving independence was minimal as there was no special provision in the A.S.R.B. for political party representation, as was the case of some of the U.S. regulatory agencies (see Bernstein, 1955, p. 9). The first mode of maintaining independence from the political parties in the executive and the legislature was possible due to the representation of major companies, auditing firms and professional accounting bodies in the A.S.R.B. Those interest groups could effectively counter interference by the Ministerial Council, specially when it affected them directly. Therefore, it is felt that adverse Ministerial Council dominance would not be accepted by the Board without being thoroughly debated within and outside the Board.

Since, "regulation is essentially political, that is concerned with the formulation of public policies" (Fesler, 1946, p. 212), the A.S.R.B. would need on the one hand the support of the Ministerial Council to remain free of any excessive interest group influence, and on the other hand need support of the interest groups to develop an identity of its own which could be seen to be independent and be independent from the Ministerial Council.

Scope for Participating Interests' Influence:

The A.S.R.B. occupied a strategic place in the network of organizations that were set up under the Commonwealth-States Co-operative Scheme for Companies and Securities. It was established by the Ministerial Council for Companies and Securities as one of the organs of the Co-operative Scheme to ensure the formulation and maintenance of approved accounting standards (financial accounting rules for the companies).

The A.S.R.B. had very few features of an independent body. From the discussion in this and the previous chapter it is evident that there were four major sources of influence on the organization and functions and the framework within which the A.S.R.B. could operate. The scope of the influence of those sources are summarized here.

Politicians:

The politicians secured their control over the operations of the Board through the framework of the Co-operative Scheme. Institutionally the Board had to rely mainly on its creating authority the Ministerial Council which was composed of politicians in State and Commonwealth Governments. With respect to appointment, tenure and removal, it was dependent on the Ministerial Council. The part-time nature of the board and the short terms of office of the members posed as a threat to the continuity of policies and a deterrent towards taking bold steps. Financially, it was completely dependent on the Ministerial Council and the parliamentary appropriations procedure. Its basic source of authority was the Ministerial Council and the legislature only provided support for its approved standards. Hence, the Board was susceptible to the influences of political interests through the Ministerial Council.

It is felt, that the Board was a solution provided by the politicians to solve the problem of information asymmetry in the securities markets. The A.S.R.B.'s approved accounting standards were a form of delegated legislation as they were meant to specify the form and content of the 'true and fair' financial statements that were required under the Companies Act 1981. Neither the Statute nor the Board defined the 'true and fair' concept (nor is it definable). Again, from the Board's set-up there is hardly any reason to believe that it could improve the accounting standard-setting or its standards qualitatively. The only expected improvement could be in the enforcement of standards.

The politicians, in their quest to solve the securities market information asymmetry problem, found a solution which served dual purposes. First, the Board, at least in form, seemed to be independent and serving community/public interest. Second, it provided a balancing mechanism for safeguarding the interests of all politically effective private interest groups. Both ways the politicians in Government gained - that is, they gained public support as well as private interests' support.

Bureaucrats:

The Board also had to rely on government bureaucracies, such as the N.C.S.C. and the C.A.C.s. Those organizations were the company law enforcers and it was their responsibility to enforce the financial disclosure provisions of the Companies Act and Codes of which the enforcement of the "true and fair view" requirement was one important aspect. The preparation and application of the approved accounting standards was seen as one manner of fulfilling this requirement.

Approved accounting standards were legislatively backed and their enforcement could be seen by the law enforcing bodies, to some extent, as the fulfillment of the duty of the "true and fair" requirement of the Act and the Codes. That indicates that the supply of such standards and the establishment of a Board capable of providing those standards may be perceived as being in the interest of the bureaucrats responsible for the efficient functioning of the activities of the N.C.S.C. and the State C.A.C.s.

Apart from that, the N.C.S.C. and C.A.C.s, having been delegated by the legislature the sole authority to enforce and apply standards, could modify the timing and class of industry for the application of standards, if necessary.

The N.C.S.C., because of its pivotal role as a policy formulator within the Co-operative Scheme for Companies and Securities, could influence the decisions of the Ministerial Council pertaining to the Board. Such interference could be expected in cases where a standard under the review of the Board faced problems of enforcement, for example due to excessive corporate opposition. Vice versa the Commission and its delegates could see a need for a new standard and could place pressure on the Board directly or through the Ministerial Council for it. In this respect Gavens and Carnegie (1987, p. 20) noted that the N.C.S.C. proposed the standard on foreign currency translation disclosure (A.S.R.B. 1003). Dissatisfied with the failure of the professional accounting bodies to issue a standard in this respect the N.C.S.C. issued a class order requiring disclosure of foreign currency accounting policy. It sought and succeeded to have this class order approved as an approved accounting standards. That situation clearly signifies that the Commission could, without any direct representation on the Board, steer the activities of the Board (Also see Parker et al, 1987, p. 237).

The Accounting Profession:

The A.S.R.B.'s organizational and functional features revealed the influencing capacity of the professional accounting bodies. The A.S.R.B. was like a market place for financial disclosure regulations. It had the power to supply mandatory (approved) accounting standards on the basis of effective demand. To secure evidence regarding effective demand we can observe the sources of proposed standards and the number of standards proposed by them. The supply to meet such demands can be measured by looking at the number of standards that were approved out of the proposed standards. Such evidence is provided in Table 3.1.

Table 3.1   Number of Standards Proposed and Approved (as at 30/6/86).[42]

Sources	Standards Proposed	Standards Approved	Standards Rejected	Standards Pending
A.A.R.F.	15	6	0	9
Australian Shareholders Association	1	0	0	1
N.C.S.C.	1	1	0	0

Table 3.1. reveals that the accounting profession was the only source that had succeeded considerably in getting its standards approved by the Board. The profession was also the most frequent source of proposed standards. Furthermore, the influencing capacity of the professional bodies was institutionalized into the review process of the Board due to the Board's acceptance that under normal circumstances the A.A.R.F. would be the sole supplier of proposed standards; that it would keep the A.A.R.F. informed of its activities of assessing priorities amongst proposed standards; and allow the Foundation to conduct a preliminary review of standards coming from other sources.

The fact that the Board was a Government sponsored body and capable of being influenced by the professional accounting bodies, it provided the following benefits to those bodies and their members:

1.   The Board through its approved accounting standards made the enforcement of professional accounting standards possible on both members and non-members of professional accounting bodies.

---

42   A.S.R.B. Annual Report 1986-87, p. 14, showed that, apart from the parties mentioned in this Table, the Australian Merchant Bankers Association have also proposed standards.

2.   The Board's cost of reviewing and approving the standards were borne by the Government. That is, the process of getting public recognition for professional standards was being subsidized by the tax payers.

3.   As the mechanism for enforcing the standards on non-members of the accounting bodies, such as company directors, was provided by the Government, the cost of enforcement was also subsidized by the tax payers.

4.   The professional bodies, through their influence on the Board, could ensure that the standards that were approved were not contrary to the interests of their members. Such members included both company accountants and auditors.

Companies:

Company executives had considerable representation in the Board, which indicates that they could act as the mouth-piece of their respective organizations and industries. In that manner they could, on specific occasions and also generally, safeguard the interests of the regulated parties - the companies. In addition, as the A.S.R.B. was under the overall jurisdiction of a political entity - the Ministerial Council, the companies could exert influence on its activities through the Council.

Gavens and Carnegie (1987, p. 20 and p. 24) argued that the cost of non-compliance was higher in the case of approved accounting standards than that for the professional accounting standards. That, they believed, gave the companies a greater incentive to participate in the standard-setting activities of the Board and also that of the A.A.R.F.

Others:

In addition to those major sources of influence there were other parties which also had the scope of communicating their views to the Board. Through their representation in the Board the academics and the stock exchanges could voice their views. But, as their representation was minor they would have to use other avenues to effectively affect the decisions of the Board.

The Board would also have to rely on the courts in matters of judicial nature to determine the scope of its functions and standards.

Inferences:

Fesler (1946) described two major issues regarding independent regulatory establishments:

> The first is the end sought - the formation and administration of public policies without undue pressure from political and economic interests. The second is the supposed means to the end - the organizational status of "independence" or isolation from political and economic centres of power (p. 208).

Sufficient proof has been provided here to substantiate that both the "end" - the approved standards, and the "means to the end" - the Board's organization and functions, could be influenced by several interest groups.

The reasons for such dependence were related to the reasons for which an independent status was sought for the A.S.R.B. Public interest and serving competing private interests, employment of expertise, impartiality and procedural due process, and safeguarding the interests of the regulated seems to be the major reasons for which the Board had acquired its organizational form and functional features. Its creation and the attempted non-representative form of appointment by the Ministerial Council supports the traditional 'public interest' argument. The provision to select members from different interest groups or bodies is indicative of the 'serving of competing private interest' notion. The possession of professional qualifications and affiliations of most of the members of the Board and the A.A.R.F. background of some of them provides evidence for the 'employment of expertise' argument. The part-time board form of A.S.R.B., being represented by a variety of interests and the provision of public exposure for standards before approval, supports the 'impartiality and procedural due process' argument. The overwhelming presence of company financial executives, who also happened to be members or senior members of professional accounting bodies, in the Board is indicative of the 'safeguarding the interests of the regulated' argument.

Two more points, the historical development of the A.S.R.B. and the background and attitudes of its members, are of interest. These could undoubtedly arouse the "capture" notion in the minds of some critics. Cranston (1982) pointed out that the historical development of a regulatory agency could influence its behaviour. He specified that if an agency began as a small and poorly endowed organization it could adopt a restrictive view of its powers and that view could continue to shape its consciousness. He also ascertained that the background of the regulators was a central feature of the "capture theory". Regulators who had served in the regulated industry would be indoctrinated with its views (p. 17). He quoted an empirical study in the U.S. which found that the appointment of former employees of a regulated industry to a regulatory agency increased the likelihood of decisions favourable to the regulated industry (p. 17). The regulators could become too concerned about their own security and would be reluctant to create conflict with the regulated (p. 18).

Those arguments seem to be applicable to the A.S.R.B. Historically, the inventory of submissions in respect of its establishment was dominated by the professional accountants and the companies.[43] Its outcome was a board dominated by members of the accounting profession and company executives. With respect to its resources and its regulatory capacity, the Board was poorly resourced than most of the bodies it was expected to regulate. For the beneficiaries who were poorly represented on the Board the following statement by Olson (1965) amplifies the situation:

---

43   For example see Attachment A of the N.C.S.C. Release 405, 1982). Also see
        Chapter 9 of this thesis.

Potential beneficiaries of regulation are generally not organized ... have diffused interests and little individual incentives to combine, although their stakes might be high in aggregate" (Cranston, 1982, p. 21).

Although the Board as a regulatory organization could look "captured" to some, it was wide open to pluralistic[44] influences, that is it could also be effectively influenced from sources other than the accounting profession and/or the companies. The accounting profession mainly had the capacity to influence the operational aspects of the Board, that of standard-setting and review of standards - that also to the extent that it was not contrary to the interests of the other groups. The evidence from Chapter 2 and this chapter do support R. Walker's (1987) arguments to the extent that the accounting profession had considerable influence, from both within and outside the Board, on the activities of the Board, but the "capture" notion, adopted by R.Walker (1987, pp. 281-282; also see Chapter 4), was certainly not applicable in describing the features of the Board. He argued, as if the accounting profession was the only regulated party and that it had succeeded in acquiring control over the activities of the Board. He overlooked the fact that the primary regulated parties were the companies and that they also had the capacity to influence the activities of the Board.

As the creating authority, the Ministerial Council and its political interests were important determinants of the manner in which the Board existed. The control of any group over the Board and its activities could only be to the extent that it was not detrimental to the political interests of a majority of the members of the Council. We also noted the strong influencing capacity of the company law administrators/bureaucrats and the judiciary. Vice versa we may deduce from those observations that none of those parties had the power to independently control the activities of the Board.

The manner in which the Board was left under the influence of the interest groups, seemed to indicate that the Board was established

---

44   See Cranston, 1982, p. 4 for a description of the "pluralist" model.

under a power sharing "political" formula so that it could <u>not</u> be completely controlled or be under the de facto control of any of the groups. For its survival and effectiveness it needed the support of all the groups.

That sort of mechanism could be unacceptable to those who consider politics from a derogatory sense, but it seemed essential for a task of the kind the A.S.R.B. was undertaking. The competing interests would always exist and the A.S.R.B., to survive in an environment where politically effective groups decided the fate of public bodies, had to bring about a balance amongst the different interests it served. That seems logical in the light of what Fesler (1946) contemplated regarding achieving a balance between competing elements of a regulatory process:

> The problem of regulatory procedures will never cease to be perplexing, for it consists essentially of the delicate task of achieving a balance between public policy and private rights, between form and substance, and between men and procedures. The problem is complicated by the fact that this balance is not the same for each regulatory function (p. 221).

The dependence of the Board on other parties and the scope of influence of those parties on the Board's activities casts doubts on R. Walker's (1987) demonstration that the process of the creation of the A.S.R.B. was dominated by the accounting profession. This, as specified in Chapter 1, leads to the hypothesis that

> In order to ensure that they played an influential role in the functioning of the A.S.R.B. all identifiable interest groups actively participated in the Board's establishment.

In order to substantiate this hypothesis, the remainder of this dissertation analyzes the process through which the Board was established.

Chapter 4

EVALUATION OF COMPETING THEORIES OF REGULATION WITH APPLICATIONS IN ACCOUNTING

Introduction:

Various explanations have been forwarded to explain why or how company financial disclosure regulation is established or why it should or should not be introduced. In this chapter such explanations are reviewed. This is followed by the identification of a theoretical framework capable of describing the Accounting Standards Review Board's process of creation, under the institutional and behavioural conditions that prevailed during that process.

Watts and Zimmerman (1979) argued that accounting theories were used to substantiate excuses in a regulatory process. Such theories consist of both normative and positive arguments. Normative theories may have specific prescriptions whereas positive theories may have implications which are or could be used for prescriptions.[45] Studies in accounting regulation based on those theories[46] have implicitly or explicitly used different market models. To understand their regulatory implications, such studies can be looked at from three view points: (1) the type of prescription or description, (2) the market model used and (3) the assumed or expressed market condition.

---

45   For example see Watts and Zimmerman (1986) regarding the normative aspects of E.M.H. studies (p. 5 and pp. 20-21) and Gallagher (1986) regarding regulatory implications of agency model. Watts and Zimmerman (1986, p. 14) also argued that positive accounting theory was important because it could help those who had to take decisions on accounting policy.

46   For example see Lev and Ohlson (1982), Bromwich (1985, Chapters 3 and 4), Solomon (1986, Chapter 10) and Foster (1986, Chapters 1, 2, 9 and 11) Watts and Zimmerman (1986) for a review of such studies.

The types of prescription (implicit or explicit) or description normally communicated by these studies can be classified as:

1.   For Regulation.
2.   Against regulation.
3.   Describing regulation as it is.

In this chapter five types of implicit or explicit market models[47] used in explaining accounting policy measures have been identified.[48] These are:

1.   Market for securities.
2.   Market for financial information.
3.   Market for auditing services.
4.   Market for managerial services.
5.   Market for accounting regulations.

The implied or expressed market conditions in those studies were:

1.   Perfect competition.
2.   Monopoly or oligopoly.
3.   Externalities or public goods argument.
4.   Information asymmetry.
5.   Social priorities other than efficiency of production.

The explanatory capabilities of the three broad categories of prescriptive and descriptive studies in accounting policy have been reviewed below in the light of market models and conditions.

---

47   Later in this chapter it has been shown that all these markets are related to financial information disclosure.

48   Sunder and Haribhakti (1984) mentioned the operation of three markets, capital, managerial skills and auditing services markets, which could affect accounting policy.

Arguments Favouring Accounting Regulation:

Cooper and Keim (1983) summarized the rationale behind the regulation of corporate financial disclosure as: "The fundamental economic rationale for the regulation of corporate financial disclosure is that the information markets will not function efficiently and fairly in the absence of government regulation" (p. 190).

Leftwich (1980) reviewed the market failure argument in financial disclosure. He explained that market failure was said to occur when either the quality or quantity of a good produced in an unregulated market differed from what was purported to be the social optimum. Social optimum is that output which maximizes aggregate social welfare and is attained only if the prices of inputs and outputs are equal to their social marginal costs. Market failure for accounting information leads to (1) under production of information, (2) over production of information or (3) the free rider problem. Government intervention is suggested as a way of moving the actual output of the private market closer to the supposed social optimum.

Such arguments favouring accounting regulation are also known as public interest theories because they are normally based on the "public interest" concern for correcting perceived market failures (inefficiencies and inequities in the market).[49] Five categories of arguments, using implicit or explicit market models, have been used to prescribe accounting regulations. These categories are:

1.   Imperfect competition in the market for securities due to financial information asymmetry, adverse selection and moral hazard, functional fixation and diversity of procedures.

---

49   Also see Watts and Zimmerman (1986, Chapters 7 and 14), Posner (1974) and Phillips and Zecher (1981, Chapter 2).

2.   Imperfect competition in the market for financial information due
        to monopoly, over production of information (speculation
        problem) and insider trading.
3.   Externalities and public goods argument in the market for
        financial information.
4.   Imperfect competition in the market for auditing services due to
        oligopoly.
5.   Social priorities other than market efficiency - enhancing stock
        market confidence and the legal approach.

Studies within these categories are elaborated below:

1.   Imperfect Competition in the Market for Securities:

Perfect markets are based on the assumption of perfect information for
both buyers and sellers. This condition is unlikely to be met in the real
world. Therefore buyers or sellers are highly unlikely to make an optimal
decision under such circumstances and, accordingly, they do not
maximize their or the society's welfare (Strickland, 1980, p 14-15). In a
securities market the products being traded are shares and bonds. Under
perfect competition assumption the price of securities is set by the
demand and supply functions of perfectly informed buyers and sellers.
Financial information, which is a component of the total information set,
is one of the determinants of securities' prices.

In securities markets the market failure possibility may involve
a presumed "asymmetry" (unevenness) in the distribution of financial
information among capital market agents, specially buyers and sellers of
securities and producers and users of financial information (Cooper and
Keim, 1983, p 190). There may be more informed or less informed
investors. In this setting the more informed investors may either be
holders or non-holders of the security and may be either potential sellers

or buyers. In such a situation the more informed buyer or seller has incentives to trade to reap expected abnormal returns.[50]

Some investors are thought to be naive and unable to interpret accounting information, and thus are disadvantaged in the securities market. Investors also suffer from functional fixation because they attach the same meaning to accounting numbers independently of the set of accounting rules used to calculate those numbers (Leftwich 1980, p 200-8).

A related aspect of asymmetrical information among investors is the self-selection that may occur on the part of those offering securities for sale, a phenomenon termed as moral hazard and adverse selection. An example of moral hazard is when company managers, after floating shares, involve themselves in transactions to increase their wealth. This can be done by, say, artificial inflation of share prices by misinforming the market and selling shares owned by the managers themselves or their agents. Later when the market is informed about the true value of the shares the prices will fall.. The wealth transfer that takes place after the sale is for the benefit of the seller at the expense of the buyer. In the case of adverse selection the more informed seller or buyer transacts shares with the prior knowledge that share price may go down or up once the inside information becomes publicly available. The difference between moral hazard and adverse selection is that in the first situation the probability of risk of the lesser informed party is less than one whereas in the latter the risk is unity.[51] This is because in the case of moral hazard the managers or insiders may or may not transact by misinforming the market and the purchaser may or may not be at a risk of losing, but in the case of adverse selection the seller or buyer transacts with prior inside information which is eventually released and affects the other party.

---

50   See Beaver (1981 Chapter 2) for a detailed review.

51   See Beaver (1981 Chapter 2) and Cooper and Keim (1983, pp. 197-200) for a detailed review.

Accounting numbers are some times considered to be distorted or meaningless. Diversity of procedures due to several rules available for accounting may produce non-comparable information. This could be caused by bias on the part of the producer due to the absence of objective criteria for choosing among the set of available accounting techniques (Leftwich 1980, p 200-8).

Another approach is the legal approach. According to Peirson and Ramsay (1983):

> The legal approach does not debate whether regulation is needed per se, rather it considers extensions and revisions to the law. The existence of disputes, public calls for action ... are all indicators that problems exist which may be overcome by legal means.

This approach is normally demanded in the public interest in the wake of company failures (ie., security market failures). It recommends legislative solutions for those market failures (Peirson and Ramsay, 1983, pp. 292-294).

Beaver (1981 p. 47) stated that financial information in a securities market played the role of altering the beliefs of investors and affected the trading and contracting opportunities available to investors.[52] Such consequences included security price effects, which in turn could lead to other consequences (p. 52). Information asymmetry may lead to market failure because some buyers or sellers may release their private information after they have transacted and affect the security prices to their advantage. Such a market will not have a Pareto optimum outcome and the market outcome will be below the purported social outcome. In the extreme case, such market failures may lead to a lack of credibility in the market and to a total breakdown of the system. Under such circumstances regulation of financial reporting is prescribed to ensure even distribution of information to the capital market agents.

---

52   Beaver (1981) provided a list of economic consequences of financial reporting (p. 16 and pp. 50-52).

2.   Imperfect Competition in the Market for Financial Information:

A major criterion for perfect competition is many sellers (in addition to buyers) who as individuals are incapable of affecting the supply of products in the market. In the case of financial information markets the product being traded is financial information. The buyers of information are presumed to be security holders or potential security holders. In the case of sellers of information under imperfect competition, they are hypothetically the company management (but there can be other sellers like analysts, advisors, etc.). The price of accounting information in a securities transaction is assumed to be embodied in the in price of the security. For example, the seller of securities who may have bought the securities at a lower price can sell it at a higher price after some good news is revealed about the relevant firm or its environment. The difference between the old and the new price of the security is the price paid by the purchaser for the good news regarding the security. The same is received by the seller for holding the security until the good news was revealed.[53] Other means of pricing financial information through private contracts has been discussed later under the incentive signalling theory and the agency theory discussions.

One of the claimed defects of the market for financial information is the monopoly control over information by managers because alternative sources of information do not exist or are not used by the investors (Leftwich 1980, p 200-2). In the case of monopoly the "laissez faire" assumption of many sellers is violated. There is a single or dominant supplier of a good. A monopolist can restrict production artificially and increase the market price. By exploiting its unique position, the monopolist maximizes its profits, but not society's welfare.[54]

---

53   See Bromwich (1985, pp. 53-54) for further discussion on pricing of financial information.

54   Strickland, 1980, p. 14 and also see Morgan 1976, pp. 18-20.

Since the assumption under such conditions is that published accounting reports provide exclusive access to information about corporations, the investors cannot corroborate published accounting numbers against any alternative source. Managers may deceive investors by giving erroneous figures and such errors may result in faulty investment decisions. Critics of monopoly control recommend increased government regulation to improve the quality and quantity of accounting information.[55]

Another criticism of the financial information market is found in the insider trading version of the market failure theory. Ross (1979) reviewed this version and explained that it was based on exploitation of inside information by insiders meaning that the insiders could profit at the expense of the outsiders if the outsiders were uninformed of inside information and the actions by the insiders and their effects. Disclosure regulation under such circumstances could enhance the quantity of freely communicated information and lower the cost to investors of observing insider transactions, promoting efficiency and enhancing equity between insiders and outsiders. This presumably facilitated resource allocation (efficiency) and provided fairness to all parties (equity). Another possibility exists, that of insiders selling their information to outsiders up to the point where their marginal costs equal their marginal revenue. But, there is the problem of moral hazard, and some means of verification is necessary. Disclosure regulation can induce insiders to be truthful because monopoly power encourages them to be untruthful or secretive in the short term.

3.   **Externalities and Public Goods Argument in the Market for Financial Information:**

Externalities arise when the benefits or costs of a transaction do not fall completely on the parties of that transaction. That is the individuals actions may impose costs or bestow benefits on others not directly

---

55   For example see Chambers (1973) and Chambers, et al. (1978).

related to the transaction (Also see Bell, p. 5, 1988). Foster (1980) recognized the use of externalities in financial reporting studies and noted,

> References to the existence of externalities in financial reporting are being made increasingly in the literature. For instance, a committee of the American Accounting Association (1977) observed that "financial accounting information shares much in common with the more traditional examples of externalities" and without intervention too little information will be produced. This is one of the standard arguments for ... disclosure policies". (p. 521)

Such externalities can arise from either the timing of information releases or the content of the releases (p. 522).

One major reason for such externalities is explained by the public goods argument of accounting information. The public goods argument relates to the "public goods" nature of financial information, and the argument that the problems of joint consumption and exclusion that characterize such goods may induce market failure (Cooper and Keim 1983, p. 190).

Leftwich (1980, p. 198) explained that the social optimum quantity (Samuelson 1954, p. 55) of a public good was produced when the marginal cost of the goods was equal to the sum of the individual consumers' marginal valuations of the good. The essence of a public good is that its provision to a single individual makes it equally and costlessly available to other individuals. The consumption of such goods by any individual does not diminish the quantity available for others. The price system can not function properly if it is not possible to exclude non-purchasers from consuming the goods in question (Cooper and Keim, 1983, p 190). Due to the non-exclusion or the free rider problem the private producers are unable to charge perfectly discriminating prices (Leftwich, 1980).

Leftwich (1980) pointed out that the accounting literature emphasized the under production of accounting information resulting from the problem of excluding non-purchasers of a public good (p. 198). He noted that the public goods argument was used by advocates of increased regulation (p. 200)

4.   Imperfect Competition in the Market for Auditing Services:

Market failure is also suspected in the market for auditing services. In such markets the products being traded are auditing services. The suppliers are auditing firms. Such services are demanded by shareholders directly and indirectly by other investors through a demand for audited financial statements (Chow 1982).

In U.S.A. the Metcalf and the Moss Reports initiated regulatory pressure under the "structure theory" of anti-trust in reaching the conclusion that the accounting profession is oligopolistic; that is the market is dominated by a few large firms, lacks competition, there are barriers to entry, market concentration, and excessive profits. The structural theory implies a chain of causality flowing from an industry's structure, through its conduct, to its performance (Buckley and O'Sullivan, 1980, p. 4).

With respect to the accounting profession it can be applied to both auditing and accounting standards. According to this theory, the concentrated nature of the accounting profession leads to the prediction of excessive fees and profits, barriers to entry, and domination by a small segment of firms that do not fulfill the high responsibilities of the accounting profession because of lack of competitive pressure. The regulatory prescriptions in this area encompass among other things the accounting disclosure requirements and their formulation (Weston, 1980, pp. 200-203).[56]

---

56   See Buckley and Weston (1980) for further details.

5.   Social Priorities and Other Market Efficiency Arguments:

Merino and Neimark (1982) argued that the Securities Acts were not Acts of political enlightenment, but a mode of resolving a structural contradiction in the American Society between increased economic concentration and public philosophy. They wrote that the Acts were designed to maintain an ideological, social and economic "status quo" and were indirect contributors to the virtual absence of any serious attempt to ensure corporate accountability. (Chua and Clarke, 1984, p. 1)

Morgan (1976) stated that one reason for regulation was the protection of the public where it was uneconomic for citizens to protect themselves (p. 20). Bell (1988) also looked at accounting regulation from a broader socio-economic perspective. Having noted the Pareto Optimality objective of regulation he explained:

> Given a Pareto Optimality objective, everyone in society is a "stakeholder". Everyone has a stake in greater efficiency which yields more goods in a society for a given amount of effort (p. 16). [His italics]

Supporting the need for accounting regulation in this context he proposed that:

> If information is already being collected, and disclosure does not harm anyone, then a strong Pareto case can be made for mandating disclosure of that information. ...

> If disclosure costs are negligible (because the information is already collected) but disclosure improves efficiency in the economy overall, then a case can be made for mandating disclosure even where the entity making the disclosure is hurt, competitively, in the process (p. 17).

In contrast to Bell's (1988) macro economic efficiency considerations, Lev (1988) took an "equity" perspective in an attempt to explain why disclosure of accounting information should be mandated. Lev's concept of equity was ex ante as opposed to the more familiar ex post notions used in literature. He proposed a public interest criterion of equity in capital markets for the purpose of policy making. This criterion he explained meant equality of opportunity, which is obtained

> ... when all investors are equally endowed with information, since in this case risk-adjusted expected returns would be identical across investors (p. 5).

He noted that:

> Inequity in capital markets, in the form of systematic and significant information asymmetries, leads to adverse private and social consequences: high transaction costs, thin markets, lower liquidity of securities, and in general - lower gains from trade (p. 19).

To remove such inequity he suggested that:

> ... the equity orientation provides justification for the regulation of information disclosure; it offers policy makers an operational "public interest" criterion for disclosure choices - the systematic decrease of information asymmetries ... (p. 19).

Conclusion:

Those arguments have one notion in common - that there are imperfections (market failures) in the market under consideration, which may hamper optimal disclosure of financial information. They are frequently used to justify regulation to ensure optimal production of accounting information in the public interest or to enhance social welfare.[57] This is consistent with what Bell (1988, p. 5) noted, that the

---

57   For example see Leftwich, 1980. In economics normative theories are normally proposed in the interest of the public. As per Posner (1974), under the "public interest" theory, it is held that economic regulation is in response to the demand of the public for a correction of perceived inefficiencies and inequities in the market. Phillips and Zecher (1981, Chapter 2) regarded the market failure theory as providing an economic rationale for what regulation ought to do - improve

sought-after benefits of regulation are usually couched in terms of achieving Pareto Optimality - a state where no one individual or firm can be made better off by reallocating resources in an economy without making some other individual or firm worse off.

Generally, those theories are deficient in finding a solution to the major problem of this study. They are incapable of describing the creation of accounting regulatory bodies within the prevailing institutional and behavioural setting. The assumptions under which the public interest theories operate are: (1) economic markets are fragile and apt to operate very inefficiently (or inequitably) if left alone; (2) government regulation is costless; and (3) politicians perceive that the benefits of regulation offset any harmful effects (Posner, 1974, p. 336 and 340). Posner (1974) challenged those arguments because he found that such regulations were not positively correlated with the presence of external economies and diseconomies or with monopolistic market structures. Again, government is not a costless and dependably effective

---

economic efficiency by correcting market failures. Therefore, the market failure explanation of economic regulation is a normative explanation for suggesting why there should be regulation of markets.

Morgan (1976) and Strickland (1980) stated that there were reasons to believe that the market process did not always guarantee an optimum allocation of society's resources. Market failures could occur, causing over or under production of goods. According to this view, market failures required government intervention in order to improve market performance and society's welfare. Strickland (1980) explained that if a market failure did not occur, a "laissez faire" economy prevailed and the responsibility of the government lay in (1) preserving law and order; (2) enforcing contracts; and (3) defining property rights. He termed this as the government's minimum role in a market economy. However, he pointed out that there could be situations in which a laissez faire economic philosophy did not maximize society's welfare. Since market forces failed to bring about an optimal allocation of society's resources, he called those situations market failures. In such cases individual's self-interest conflicted with the interests of the society, and government intervention became necessary. Morgan (1976) stated that economic regulation of business was one set of ways by which choices among alternative production possibilities could be influenced on a public level or assisted at an individual level (p. 5).

instrument (pp. 336-337). And, there is contrary evidence in the accounting literature suggesting that the benefits of regulation do not exceed its costs (Phillips and Zecher, 1981).

Market failure prescriptions in accounting failed to provide an achievable objective function, that is an information set which could lead to an optimum allocation of societies resources.[58] Some writers have suggested that such a social welfare optimum is impossible to achieve.[59] Normally the purported objective of market failure theories is "public interest" - a vague term. It is often used to camouflage the pursuit of self-interest (Peirson and Ramsay, 1983, p. 293). No one has specifically defined "public interest" nor is it definable.

Mitnick (1980) dismissed the potential of public interest approaches on the grounds that there was no single public interest conception (see p. 91 and Chapter 4). He concurred with the view taken here that public interest theories could be viewed as vague and indeterminate because views of public interest were often vague and could be conflicting. They neither described the mechanism of achieving public interest nor did they clarify the role of the regulators and the public interest groups. He also exposed the variety and complexity of public interest concepts adopted by various theorists which supported the view that public interest arguments were not specific (p. 108, 243, 262, 268, and pp. 278-279).

Phillips and Zecher (1981) felt that the market failure theory failed to capture adequately the way in which regulation actually worked in the real world. They pointed out that nearly all regulatory programs have fallen short of dealing successfully with a real market failure in a cost effective manner (p. 19). Commenting on SEC's corporate disclosure program, they stated that it had no clear goal, thus there was no clear

---

58   For example see Leftwich (1980) and Phillips and Zecher (1981, p. 21).

59   Arrow (1963), Demski (1973), Gonedes and Dopuch (1974) and Watts and Zimmerman (1986, p. 157).

way to assess its effectiveness or desirability of changes in the program (p. 21). While it is possible to conceive of better regulatory laws and better administration of regulatory programs that deal with real market failures in a cost effective manner, the wide spread absence of such laws and programs leaves a nagging suspicion that something more fundamental is amiss. Market failure theory failed to capture adequately the way in which regulation actually worked (p. 21).

Lev and Ohlson (1982) in criticizing its methodological approaches stated that normative theorists in accounting have been trying to answer the following questions:

> Can the usefulness of accounting be fostered by public intervention and regulation (the case of "market failure")? If so what is the optimal structure of accounting institutions (e.g., set in public or private sector), and how should accounting choices be made by policy makers and the consequences of such choices be evaluated?

> Methodological approaches to these issues followed by researchers included deductive (a priori) reasoning, laboratory experiments, and questionnaire studies. The result was at best a very limited advancement in the understanding of the basic issues and a negligible impact on practitioners and public decision makers. Missing was a widely accepted, conceptually well-structured, and empirically testable link between accounting (firm-based) information and the specific uses of this information (p. 251).

Arguments that try to explain the deviations of regulations from public interest ends expose the failure of public interest theories to explain regulation in terms of the operation of the political process. Wilson (1974) in this respect stated:

> When government regulation fails to compel businesses to serve socially desirable objectives, it is not usually because of the incompetence or venality of the regulators but because of the constraints placed on them by the need to operate within the political system. (p. 147)

Thus, in regulatory controversy, needs are dramatized and failures emphasized; advocacy and the need to build support can mean that the provisions of regulation will reflect what has been effective in the political controversy, rather than what is likely to work in regulation (Mitnick, 1980, p. 96)

Market failure theories, like most earlier political theories, have suffered because they have not taken into account some economic realities.[60] Researchers have analyzed government action on the assumption that governments were run by perfect altruists whose only motive was to maximize social welfare. An alternative view, acknowledging that governments are composed of people who, like others, act primarily out of self-interest, is a more likely premise. Government policies are mainly a product of self-interest of the politicians (or bureaucrats - that is to gain office (and its benefits) through satisfying constituents' demands (Downs, 1957a, pp. 137-150). Therefore, market failure theories overlook how the public institutions function and how the regulators and other participants behave in the regulatory process.

Finally, it may be added that it is not possible to explain the formation of the A.S.R.B. and its standard-setting process on the basis of any market failure theory. Since the Board was not explicitly based on any market failure theory, the determination of what kinds of market failure the Board was trying to correct was not clear. The expected optimum quality or quantity of information the Board was trying to achieve was also not mentioned. Therefore, it could approve an infinite number of disclosure requirements. The notion of meeting "community expectations" (see A.S.R.B. Release 100) was as vague as the public interest notion. Such a notion was introduced by interest groups.[61]

---

60   For example see Downs (1957a), pp. 149-150.

61   For example see the Joint Submission of the Australian Accounting Profession, March and August, 1982, suggesting an A.S.R.B. in the public interest or Peirson and Ramsay, 1983, pp. 293-294.

Explanations Against Regulation in Accounting:

There exists another class of theories suggesting or implying that markets are efficient and that there is no apparent need for corporate financial disclosure regulations. Using explicit or implicit market models, there have been four categories of explanations put forward to explain the efficiency of unregulated markets. These categories are:

1.   Efficient securities market - the explanation provided by the Efficient Market Hypothesis (E.M.H.) studies.
2.   Efficient financial information market - the explanation provided by signalling theory and agency theory studies.
3.   Efficient auditing services market.
4.   Competitive market for managerial services.

Studies within these categories are elaborated below:

1.   Perfect Competition in Securities Market - Efficient Market Hypothesis:

This set of research is based on the efficient market hypothesis (E.M.H.). Foster (1978)[62] summarized the findings of those studies as follows:

> The evidence on the relationship between capital asset returns and financial information is compelling on the following issues:
>
> (1)   There is a positive contemporaneous association between the sign and size of the accounting earnings change and the size of the securities price change.
> (2)   Much of the market's reaction to accounting earnings is anticipatory; more timely information sources than the earnings announcements are used in the securities price revaluation process.

---

62   Also see Foster (1986) pp. 402-403, Watts and Zimmerman (1986) p. 5 and 17.

(3)   Notwithstanding (2), there is a significant security price and trading volume reaction to the information contained in interim and annual earnings announcements.

(4)   There is not a mechanistic relationship between reported accounting numbers and stock returns; the market uses a broad based information set in interpreting the information content of reported accounting numbers (p. 361-362).

Accordingly Henderson & Peirson (1977) summarized the outcome of E.M.H. researches in the following manner:

(1)   Investors react to new information in a way which causes the prices of shares traded on a stock exchange to change almost instantaneously and without bias.

(2)   The prices of shares traded on a stock exchange fully reflect all publicly available information.

(3)   Abnormal rates of return on share trading cannot be earned by investors (p. 125-126).

The E.M.H. studies assume a set of arguments. First the market under investigation is a market for securities with shares and bonds as the product being traded in the market. The seller of the securities is the supplier and the purchaser is the one who demands the securities. Those studies tend to show that the perfect market criterion, that the buyers and sellers assume that their own buying and selling decisions have no effect on market prices, is present in the securities markets and the equilibrium prices of the securities are determined due to the demand and supply functions of the market.[63]

The E.M.H. arguments tend to negate the market failure argument that the securities market is inefficient with respect to financial information (Watts and Zimmerman, 1986, pp. 19-21). It suggests that there is an association between the accounting earnings change and securities price change. It also tries to show that there are other sources

---

63   Beaver (1981, p. 47) mentioned that under perfect competition it is assumed that all sellers and buyers are equally informed and that no one can individually affect prices. This implies that there is no possibility for abnormal returns.

of information in addition to earnings announcements (Watts and Zimmerman, 1986, p. 69). These sources can be more timely than the later source. In short, the securities market has a broad based information set which supplements (or includes) the reported accounting information and all publicly available information is incorporated into the price of the securities.

The E.M.H. arguments also refute the market failure argument that investors are naive and face difficulties in understanding complex accounting reports leading to erroneous decisions to buy and sell shares. This sophisticated investor hypothesis which implies that the investors are able to distinguish between accounting changes of economic significance and cosmetic changes, and the conclusion that there are other, more timely sources of information, deemphasizes the need for mandatory disclosure of accounting information. Although the E.M.H. arguments do not explicitly reject regulation, it is implied from it that, as accounting reports are of lesser economic significance than they are thought to be, the securities market does not totally depend on them for efficient functioning. Therefore, it implies that mandatory financial disclosure requirements are not essential, and to an extreme it implicitly questions the role of accrual accounting.[64]

An alternate description of efficient disclosure of financial information by firms was given by Sunder and Haribhakti (1984). They explained in terms of firms obtaining capital resources from the capital market (securities market) and described the disclosure mechanism as follows:

---

64   For a detailed discussion on the implications of E.M.H. research see Beaver (1981) pp. 163-167, Bromwich (1985) Chapter 3 and Solomon (1986) Chapter 10.

In arriving at the supply function of capital to a firm, or class of firms,
such suppliers will assess the perceived risks and rewards of the
proposed investment in the light of information available to them
currently and promised to them in the future. Promise of prompt,
accurate and reliable information about the firm in the future forms an
important consideration for investors. Other things being equal, firms
which operate a more satisfactory accounting system, and this depends
to a great extent on the firms' accounting and auditing policy, will be
able to raise capital at a lower cost. the firm will thus, enjoy a
competitive advantage over other firms unless the cost of such an
accounting system outweighs the savings in the cost of raising capital.
(p. 168)

In short, they confirmed that the security market itself provided a
mechanism for the determination of optimum information, which was
based on the cost benefit functions of generating such information.[65]

2.   Perfect Competition in the Market for Financial Information:

There are two sets of studies in this area. These are the signalling theory
studies and the agency theory studies. Both sets assume that there is a
market for financial information in which the product being traded is
financial information. Those who demand are the buyers or holders of
securities and the suppliers are the companies' managers. The price paid
by the buyer of financial information is the cost borne (for example
monitoring costs) or benefits forgone (for example lower dividends or
lower interests for more secure securities). The price received by the
managers are in terms of incentives given to or penalties imposed on the
managers with respect to disclosure of performance.

---

65   A similar explanation is provided by Benston (1973) pp. 133-134.

Both, the signalling theory (discussed in detail by Ross (1979))[66] and the agency theory (introduced by Jensen and Meckling (1976)) are discussed briefly below:

(a)   Incentive Signalling Approach:

The assumptions behind Ross's (1979) argument were, that the managers had a long horizon tied to the firm, the manager's performance was geared to the firm's performance and if no financial information was disclosed (no news) by a firm it meant that some information was being suppressed, therefore it had bad news. It also assumed that the securities market was competitive and no regulations existed.

Ross (1979) argued that the manager's compensation was tied to the firm's performance and the shareholders would not allow the trading of the firm's stock for his personal gain. As the potential gains from such trading described above are generally in excess of the managerial compensation schedules, and since the cost of monitoring these activities to limit the manager's total compensation is quite high, the least cost form of compensation will simply rule out the bulk of insider trading by managers. The stockholders are aware of insider trading incentives and they enter into contracts with managers which penalize such activities. In such a situation where the manager's fortunes are directly linked to that of the firm and where they are precluded from insider trading, they will have a strong self-interest to disclose relevant information to the outside market. Good news if disclosed by the manager's will enhance the value of the firm which will in turn enhance their compensation. Bad news if not disclosed will be interpreted as bad, lowering the firm's value and the manager's compensation. Other no news firms will explicitly disclose that they have no news to disclose to differentiate themselves from the earlier mentioned no news firms. To protect themselves from untruthful information management compensation

---

66   Moris (1986) reviewed other studies in this category of research. He showed that this theory was consistent to the agency theory.

contracts can have bonding provision which if violated by the managers would lower their compensation (p. 182-183). In this manner the good news, bad news and no news firms' managers will have incentives to disclose to the securities market. In this respect the only purpose of the disclosure law would be to see that the contracts to disclose are honoured (p. 183-185). He further stated:

> There is no need for laws legislating that information must be disclosed, since managers have incentives to reveal information. There is need to enforce the private contracts which stockholders and managers would arguably arrive at; these serve to construct management incentive schedules (p. 188).

The incentive signalling theory of Ross held that the private sector would supply the monitoring and penalties necessary to assure the disclosure of inside information either directly or through the use of other procedures supplied by the public sector (p. 192). He demonstrated that the market forces provided strong incentives to managers to disclose information. Any failure in the capital market was due to the presence of non-competitive managerial market (p. 192).

Ross's incentive signalling analysis used a financial information market where financial information as a product is traded between the shareholders as buyers and the managers as suppliers. The price to be paid to the managers is expected to be settled through private contracts. He felt that the incentive signaling approach reinforces the traditional marginal analysis, that information would be disclosed till the marginal benefit from the disclosure equals its marginal cost. This approach purported to provide a mechanism which ensured that information would be disclosed in the absence of disclosure regulation. He felt that using such an approach, the different costs associated with regulatory disclosure could be avoided.

(b)   Agency Perspective:

Advocating a similar theme as the incentive signalling approach, the "agency theory" school (mainly the Rochester School led by Jensen & Meckling (1976)) reacted to the increasing involvement of government agencies with accounting standards. Briefly looking at it, this school defined the agency relationship as 'a contract under which one or more persons (the principal(s)) engage another person (the agent) to perform some service on their behalf which involves delegating some decision making authority to the agent' (Jensen & Meckling, 1976, p 308). Stemming from these relationships are the agency costs consisting of

1.   monitoring expenditure by the principal (the shareholders) for example financial reports and audit fees,

2.   bonding costs by the agent for example contractual arrangements limiting alternative opportunities, the kinds of activities engaged in and stock options; and

3.   a residual loss being the extent of discount in the share price occasioned by shareholders recognizing that the managers may be working more in their own interests than in the interest of the share holders (Jensen & Meckling, 1976, p 308).

The agency theory school regards accounting information as the product of the market for accounting information. It is said to be demanded by the shareholders and creditors who pay a price for such information through the monitoring costs. The managers who are assumed to be the suppliers of the information receive the price through reduced bonding cost imposed on them. Their assumed market is composed of private contracts between the principals (shareholders and creditors) and the agent (the managers) and may be regarded as a private market for accounting information.[67] Since the managers and shareholders have an incentive to reduce agency costs the publication of accounting reports

---

67   Leftwich (1980 and 1983) elaborated the term "private market for accounting information".

will occur as a result of the inherent market forces (Watts & Zimmerman, 1978).

It has also been argued, as Ross (1979) did, that there is a market for managers such that poorly performing firms will be taken over, or poorly performing mangers will be passed over or thrust aside by more ambitious colleagues (Scott, 1978; Fama, 1980). In either event it is concluded, that managers have some incentives to act in a way which benefits shareholders and to issue accounting reports with a view to reducing the residual loss component of agency costs. This constitutes a market solution to the issue of accounting reports, and as a corollary the need for government regulation is denied (Scott, 1978).

Holthausen and Leftwich (1983) cited a number of studies based on the agency cost theory (or those illustrating the economic consequences of accounting choice due to costly contracting and monitoring). They identified that the economic consequences of accounting choice analyzed by various authors, resulted from the following causal links between firms' cash flows and reported accounting numbers:

(1)   management compensation plans,
(2)   government regulations,
(3)   lending agreements, and
(4)   political viability (p. 83-89)

Those studies, instead of proposing what "ought" to be the form of accounting, purport to explain what "is" the case. The reason for this change in direction is the belief that accounting is dependent on (a) the environment in which such information is used, and (b) the differing criteria invoked by competing interests in the financial reporting process.[68] Although these studies can be classified as having a positive

---

68   This positive approach to finding a solution for normative issues is yet to make a significant contribution (Holthausen and Leftwich 1983, p 306).

approach since they examine why firms choose particular accounting techniques, they are implicitly normative (for example see Gallagher, 1986). The agency theory suggests a market solution to the issue of accounting reports instead of government regulation (Wells 1978, p 8). Others (for example Chow, 1982) suggest that firms do have sufficient incentives to hire external auditors indicating that the existence of such private incentives may imply a reduced need for mandatory auditing (Chow, 1982, p 287).

The perfect competition argument in the financial information market shows that there are three bases for the perfect market assumption. These are,[69]

1.   The existence of management compensation contracts and the assumed existence of a complete market for managers are sufficient reasons for public disclosure of financial information by managers.
2.   The incentive contracts between managers and security holders creates a private market for financial information.
3.   From the above two modes of disclosure comes the derived demand for independent auditors to authenticate the information supplied by the managers. This demand in the light of a market for auditing services is discussed next.

3.   Perfect Competition in the Market for Auditing Services:

A perfect market for auditing services can exist when auditing services are being traded between many buyers (security holders) and many sellers (auditors). Earlier under the heading "Imperfect Competition in the Market for Auditing Services" the criticisms of such a market as an oligopoly was discussed. Such criticisms have been refuted by Dopuch and Sumunic (1980). Their findings indicate that there is no market wide

---

69   Also see Beaver (1981) p. 49.

concentration by the large audit firms, there are no real barriers to entry and pricing of services is competitive.

Chow (1982) showed that a private market for auditing services did exist and there was a reduced need for auditing regulations (p. 287). He used the agency theory for his analysis and stated that firms hired external auditors to help control the conflict of interest among firm mangers, shareholders, and bondholders. He added that the demand for auditing depended on certain characteristics of the firm, like leverage, firm size, accounting-based debt covenants and managers' ownership share (p. 287).

In another manner Sunder and Haribhakti (1984) cautioned against the use of accounting and auditing policy in the market for auditing services. They explained that, if a change in an accounting/auditing policy or standard placed a burden of higher risks without compensating rewards on the auditors, they would shift their supply function until their economic interest was optimized in the altered environment. They stressed that the market for auditing services ensured an equilibrium between the demand and supply of auditing services through adjustment of accounting/auditing policy on the one hand and the number of people willing to work on the other (p. 168). That explanation implies that excessive auditing regulation would reduce the number of suppliers of auditing services and hence make the market less competitive, thereby affecting the supply of audited information in the market for financial information.

4.   **Perfect Competition in the Market for Managerial Services:**

Ross introduced the notion of related markets in analyzing the incentive signalling approach of financial disclosure. He pointed out that there was a market for managerial services the efficiency of which could lead to the efficiency of financial information markets. He stated:

In sum, the central message of the incentive signalling analysis is that the source of a failure by insiders to supply relevant and truthful information to outsiders is the existence of noncompetitive forces in related markets - in particular the market for managerial services. (p. 192)

As mentioned earlier, under agency theory, Scott (1978) and Fama (1980) argued that in the market for managerial services, the managers of poorly performing firms would be passed over or thrust aside by more efficient colleagues or such firms would be taken over by other more efficiently performing firms. Fama (1980) attempted to explain that the firm as a whole and the managers in particular were disciplined due to the existence of an efficient managerial labour market. He viewed the firm as a team whose members act from self-interest but realized that their destinies depended to some extent on the survival of the team (the firm) in its competition with other teams (other firms) (p. 289). He explained how the separation of security ownership and control, typical of large corporations, could be an efficient form of organization within a "set of contracts" perspective. His analysis showed that a firm could be disciplined by competition from other firms, which evolved devices for monitoring the firm and the contracting members. Individual participants in the firm, in particular the managers, faced both the discipline and opportunities provided by the markets for their services, both within and outside the firm.

In other words, Fama (1980) emphasized that the set of contracts present in various firms could be combined to form a market for managerial services. Managerial services, he explained, were supplied by the managers and demanded by other parties to the contracts. The price of the services set out in those contracts, he pointed out, were determined on the basis of managerial efficiency. This in conjunction with Ross's (1979, pp. 183-185) arguments implies that the managers of good news firms will try to disclose information in order to distinguish themselves from bad news firms or no news firms.

Sunder and Haribhakti (1984) also recognized the existence of a market for managerial services and described the relationship between this market and accounting policy They suggested that accounting policy, on the margin, must strike a balance between the demands of managers and that of the users of financial information (p. 168).

Arguments Against Social Priorities of Regulation:

Winsen (1980, p. 234) challenged the prevention of frauds and other similar kinds of market manipulation as an argument for instituting regulations. He basically agreed with the competitive solution for enhancing company financial disclosure. Within that competitive solution, he argued, that neither the presence of agreements for auditing and disclosing financial information nor the existence of disclosure regulation automatically prevented frauds. What was needed, he explained, was more direct remedies, such as the application of laws relating to fraud and breach of contract (p. 254-253).

Conclusion:

The above models and arguments have numerous deficiencies.[70] Only a few of the major deficiencies are discussed here.

The normative theories (for and against regulation) using the financial information market model have one common assumption, the assumption of manager's monopoly over financial information production and disclosure. Those favouring regulation used it as a major reason for regulated disclosure, whereas others have argued that the market could take care of it. It must be pointed out that the market for financial information is not similar to a perfect economic market with respect to supplier characteristics (See Bromwich 1985, p. 61). There may be many buyers, as the demand for financial information may be a function of the demand for securities, but the primary source of corporate financial information is the company management. Disclosure may be through

---

70   For example see Wells (1978, pp. 10-12), Kirpke (1979), Watts and Zimmerman (1986) and Bell (1988).

annual reports, interim reports, or other means and may be further elaborated by the investment houses or the news media, but the primary supplier who has the first hand knowledge of the performance of the company is the manager. The incentive signaling approach and the agency theory do not deny this fact and try to explain that there are incentives for these monopolist managers to supply information. The efficient market hypothesis research does not reject this totally, because it does not prove that the financial information is equally timely for the outsiders as for the insiders.

The market for financial information differs from a perfect economic market in another way. The product traded in it is unique to the company to which it relates. The product in the financial information market is not homogeneous (Also see Bell, 1988, p. 13) and each product, as mentioned earlier, can be supplied from only one source, that is the company and its management. There can be other secondary sources of corporate financial information, for example the price of the security itself, but it can be reflected in the price only after the company has disclosed certain information or it has been transmitted due to insider trading.

In this respect Kirpke (1979) criticized Ross's (1979) incentive signaling arguments which is also applicable to the agency and the efficient market hypothesis arguments to some extent.

(1)   The assumption that the insider and his actions can be identified in the market is naive. In real life the insider may be acting through his agents who may be difficult to identify in the securities market.

(2)   Insider's agents can execute the purchases or sales of shares instantly before the outsiders can realize what has happened. The insider can act before the outsiders realize the impact of his actions. Therefore, the outsider may act only after the insider has reaped the abnormal profit.

(3)   Profits from insider trading may be looked as an appropriate means of rewarding the managers and insiders may not sell or disclose information to outsiders.

(4)   Due to technological specialization it may not be possible to have an unrestricted managerial market. The prospective newcomer may have to acquire the necessary expertise to cross the barrier to entry. We might add that there might be other problems like that of interlocking directorates which makes the market for directors closely knit and makes it difficult for outsiders to enter the market.

(5)   Insiders may be penalized for their actions, but it can be done only after they have acted inappropriately. Such penalties may not be good enough to induce information signaling prior to insider trading.

Other flaws in Ross's (1979) argument were the assumptions of management having a long horizon tied to the firm and that the economic fortunes of the manager depended on that of the corporation. This does not provide for those managers who are nearing retirement. They may not disclose as Ross predicts because they may be interested in short term gains through insider trading rather than long term career benefits. Again if the market for managers is efficient, as he suggested, then the economic fortunes of a manager may not be tied to the fortunes of a single company. He may only disclose information to the extent that it enhances his value in the managerial market and not the value of the firm in the securities market.

Ross (1979) also argued that the reason for the failure in the capital market was the presence of non-competitive managerial markets (p. 192). In a way he suggested a perfect market for managers. One of the basic assumptions of a perfect market is the availability of information regarding the product to both the supplier and the person demanding the product. From Ross's arguments it is evident that the financial information of the firm acts as the information necessary for evaluating a manager. It can be argued, that the managerial market cannot be perfect without a perfect market for financial information and the existence of one without the other is not possible. The implication of this argument is that it is not possible to correct the managerial market (as suggested by him) without the correction of the financial information market.

As for the evidence revealed by the agency theory research, Wells (1978, p 10-11) refuted them because, he argued, that they were selective and contrary to a multitude of other (selected) cases documented by Chambers (1973) and Briloff (1972). He argued that in many cases the agency theory view that managers voluntarily disclosed information, failed to work. Managers, he explained, could be interested in issuing reports which would lead to higher share prices than to issue reports which were true but unfavourable (p 12). Evidence of such instances have been documented by Chambers (1973) and Briloff (1972). Wells' argument could be extended to suggest that the normative theories suggesting de-regulation try to argue in terms of efficiency of financial disclosure markets. They overlook the equity aspect of financial disclosure.

Bell (1988, p. 7) noted that the market failure arguments considered Pareto Optimality conditions as the objective criterion. He rejected the notion that such optimality was achievable through the free play of markets. In this respect he observed: "Uncertainty, of course, does exist in any actual real world market economy, thus bursting our "perfect information" Pareto Optimality balloon" (p. 7).

Apart from uncertainty, Bell (1988) pointed out certain problems with the perfect market arguments, of which some have already been discussed above. He noted that unequal consumer power could lead to price and output discrimination, with powerful consumers being able to exact certain kinds of information not available to small consumers. He also referred to the fact that private markets over the years have not developed certain kinds of information which have importance in decision making (pp. 12-14).

Studies in the "against regulation" category have two common aspects. They provide explanations or evidence that the various implied or stated markets are efficient and that market forces can ensure optimal financial disclosure and disclosure of other associated information. They provide reasons why there is no need for disclosure regulations or show how a free competitive market can take care of any market imperfections.

From the view point of this thesis, all anti-regulation arguments have one major drawback - they are not meant to explain why and by whom regulation is sought. The regulatory implications of those theories should be treated with caution because they have not taken into consideration the motives of the suppliers and seekers of accounting regulations and the process through which regulation is sought. Even though evidence from E.M.H. studies tends to negate the market failure argument, those studies overlook the fact that regulation is demanded and supplied in spite of the efficient securities market explanations. The same can be said about other efficient market arguments. All those explanations have ignored the presence of another related market - the market for accounting regulations, and the behavioural aspects of its participants. Therefore, their regulatory implications are weak predictors and suspect in the eyes of positivists.

Descriptive Explanations For Accounting Regulation:

Accounting policy making and the standard-setting process have been frequently described as social choice/political processes.[71] Chambers (1977) noted that the contemporary accounting standards were produced through a bargaining process and the standard-setting programme was opportunistic and piecemeal. Social choice based arguments confirm, that in reality the accounting standard-setting processes do not follow any

---

71   For example see, Gerboth (1973), Horngren (1973), Moonitz (1974), Aranya
        (1974), May and Sundem (1976), Buckley (1976), Watts (1977, pp. 64-65),
        Solomons (1978), Watts and Zimmerman (1979), Dopuch and Sunder (1980, p.
        18), Beaver (1981, p. 18), Sunder and Haribhakti (1984, p. 166, pp. 167-168) and
        Zeff (1972, 1978 and 1986).

specific market failure/public interest theories or market efficiency theories.

Descriptive theories of economic regulation which have been used in accounting standards research,[72] provide economic explanations of the social choice/political process view. Those theories regard regulation as an economic good and implicitly or explicitly use a market for regulation model. Their application in explaining accounting standard-setting is discussed under the following taxonomy:

1.   Capture Theory:

Capture theory provides a positive explanation by describing why and how interest groups capture the regulatory process in their own interest. There are basically two versions of this theory - the Marxist and the political scientists' versions. In general they provide incomplete explanations of the regulatory process as shown below:

a.   Marxist Approach:

Posner (1974) explained that the Marxist version of "capture" asserted that big business - the capitalists - controlled the institutions of our society and therefore controlled the regulations. Under this theory the market for accounting standards is considered to be a monopoly because the supply side, in general, is seen to be captured by the large accounting firms and their large clients as a single bloc. For example, in the U.S.A., the Metcalf Report alleged that large auditing firms (mainly the "big eight" firms monopolized the auditing of large corporations and controlled the standard-setting process. Through their control of the A.I.C.P.A., it was suspected, that the "big eight" controlled the Financial Accounting Foundation and hence the F.A.S.B. The report further argued, that as the S.E.C. recognized the F.A.S.B. established standards, the corporate accounting standards were being prepared in the interest of the

---

72   For example see Watts and Zimmerman 1986, Chapter 10.

"big eight" accounting firms and their large corporate clients. (See Hussein and Ketz 1980, p. 354, Newman 1981, p. 247 and Belkaoui (1985), pp. 45-47).

This view has been refuted by Rockness and Nikolai (1977), Haring (1979) and Hussein and Ketz (1980) because the regulators' preferences do not always correspond to those of a single group nor do the regulators vote in a single bloc.

In economics Posner (1974, p. 341) rejected the Marxist capture theory explanation for regulation as being baseless because many regulations also served the small businesses and individuals of different professions.

b.   Political Scientists' Approach - R. Walker's (1987) Methodology:

The political scientists explain that over time regulatory agencies come to be dominated by the industries that are regulated. They see the interest groups - the regulated firms - as prevailing in the struggle to influence legislation, and predict the regular sequence, in which the original purposes of a regulatory programme are later thwarted through the efforts of the interest group (Posner 1974, pp. 341-43).

R. Walker (1987) used this version of capture argument to explain the conversion of the A.S.R.B. from a broad based participative organization to a body which was captured by the professional accounting bodies in Australia. He analyzed the Board since its creation and found that the accounting bodies and their joint standard-setting body, the A.A.R.F., through a series of successful moves in the first few years of its life, achieved considerable control over its functions. From this perspective, he tried to explain that the A.S.R.B. was initially created as an organization which would be responsive to the demands of all interested parties, but it was eventually captured by a single interest group, the accounting bodies, in a manner that it would respond only to the demands of those bodies.

R. Walker's (1987) capture argument was based on the following definition of capture:

> "Capture is said to occur if the regulated interest *controls* the regulation and the regulatory agency; or if the regulated parties succeed in *coordinating* the regulatory body's activities with their activities so that their private interest is satisfied; or if the regulated party somehow manages to neutralize or insure *nonperformance* (or mediocre performance) by the regulating body; or if a subtle process of interaction with the regulators the regulated party succeeds (perhaps not even deliberately) in *coopting* the regulators into seeing things from their own perspective and thus giving them the regulation they want; or if, quite independently of the formal or conscious desires of either the regulators or the regulated parties the basic structure of the *reward system* leads neither venal nor incompetent regulators inevitably to a community of interests with the regulated party." (Quoted by R. Walker, 1987, pp. 281-282 from Mitnick, 1980, p. 95)

Walker's explanation of the Board and its process of establishment has certain methodological deficiencies. Most of those deficiencies seem to emanate from his use of the "regulatory capture" model. Those issues are discussed in the following paragraphs.

R. Walker (1987) provided no reason for the choice of the "capture" theory. He concentrated more on a segment of the A.S.R.B.'s life when there was greater participation by the professional accounting bodies in the activities of the Board. Perhaps, because of the intensity of such participation he overlooked the participation of others, and studied only the demands of the profession and their impact on the functions and activities of the Board. This introduced a bias which emphasized the influence of the profession on the Board's operations. This scenario appears to have led Walker to the choice of the capture model - a model which is capable of describing the behaviour of a single party/interest group in the choice of regulatory methods (See Walker, 1987, pp. 281-282).

Bernstein's (1955) arguments regarding the life cycle of regulatory commissions highlights the limited explanatory capacity of the "capture" model in terms of the segment of the regulatory body's life it is capable of describing. He noted that a situation like "capture" may occur only during a regulatory body's "youth" phase, that is the phase that immediately follows the creation of the body (See Mitnick, 1980, p. 46). He examined the creation of a body capable of producing a new form of regulation which would affect the regulated parties, such as the case of Cost Accounting Standards Board (C.A.S.B.) in the U.S.A. (See Davis and Menon, 1987). There, that board was empowered to produce a new form of regulation (cost accounting standards) to regulate defence cost contracts. In the case of the A.S.R.B. the form of regulation was accounting standards. Accounting standards came into existence well before the creation of the Board (See Chapter 6). As we shall see later in this dissertation, the A.S.R.B. was the outcome of a demand for mandatory/legislatively backed accounting standards and not for a completely new regulatory device. The demand for such standards arose from the problems that existed in the accounting profession's standard-setting and enforcement process. Similarly, professional standard-setting received regulatory status due to the deficiencies that existed in earlier forms of company disclosure requirements. From this sequence of adjustments in accounting regulation we can infer that the A.S.R.B. and its form of approved accounting standards were yet another step in the on-going regulatory process. Therefore, it would be misleading to assume that the Board and its standards created a new regulatory environment with a new set of regulated parties. The regulated parties such as the companies and the professional accountants already existed. Besides that profession's mechanism for the preparation of accounting standards and other professional pronouncements had been in existence well before the idea that accounting standards be used as company disclosure requirements. The profession had installed such a mechanism for the maintenance of professional identity and status (discussed in Chapter 7). Therefore any development in that area would receive substantial attention from the professional bodies.

In this respect, R. Walker's approach of assuming that the A.S.R.B. and its standards were a new regulatory scheme and studying a small segment of its life cycle overlooked the relationship of this development with that of earlier and existing forms of company disclosure regulation. A study in such isolation does not help us understand the place of the A.S.R.B. in its environment. R. Walker portrayed the accounting profession as the regulated party, but ignored the fact that the professional accounting bodies were and still are the major source of accounting standards. For the creators of the A.S.R.B. to avoid the profession and to create a completely new form of regulation would be to invent a new device to tackle certain anomalies which were mainly noticed in the area of enforcement of standards. To gain acceptance from the companies for a new device would also be an unprecedented task. Therefore, the acceptance of accounting standards as the regulatory form and the role granted to the accounting bodies in the preparation and review of standards was perhaps inevitable from the view that approved accounting standards were an adjusted form of an existing form of regulation.

Again to look at the Board in isolation from its regulatory environment was problematic because the Board *per se* was responsible mainly for only one aspect of the accounting regulatory function. We have noted in Chapter 2 that the Board was dependent on the accounting profession for only the preparation and review of accounting standards. It was completely dependent on a political entity, the Ministerial Council, for its basic authority. Its standards could be reviewed by the Council. It relied on the N.C.S.C. and its delegates, the State C.A.C.'s, for the enforcement of its standards. The companies, the prime target of approved accounting standards, had significant representation on the Board. Such reliance made the notion of independence a fallacy. On the other hand we have seen in Chapter 3 that the Board bore the mark of influence from more than one interest group and had to function to the satisfaction of all effective participants of its regulatory process.

To overlook the behaviour of other major participants in the regulatory process keeps us ignorant of how they have acted in the past, which on the other hand makes it difficult to predict their future behaviour. For example, R. Walker's arguments presented a case of accountants as the regulated party trying to achieve regulatory capture.

He did not note that in that case the companies were the prime target of regulation, whereby he failed to examine the participation of this group of regulated entities. The absence of any discussion of companies' interests does not mean that the accounting profession could establish standards at will ignoring the interests of the companies and their directors.

R. Walker (1987, p. 285) did predict that in the future "a new set of key players" might emerge. He did not identify those players. In the absence of any description about the behaviour of other major parties in the creation of the Board it is impossible to identify such players from his study.

R. Walker's description also lacked an analysis of the supply aspect of the A.S.R.B. and its functions. In other words, he did not sufficiently explain why the Ministerial Council which once wanted to introduce a stringent accounting policy contrary to the demands of the accounting profession changed its tough attitude towards regulation of the profession. R. Walker (1987) did try to clarify by partially explaining why the profession's demands were satisfied by the regulators - the Ministerial Council. He used the concept of "neo-corporatism"[73] and explained that in the case of the A.S.R.B., the government, through the Ministerial Council and its A.S.R.B. had transferred its responsibility for the regulation of financial reporting to a private interest-group: the accounting profession (R. Walker, 1987, p. 283). His explanation was partial in the sense that he did not explain why its more recent members had a less stronger attitude towards regulation of the profession as opposed to the earlier members who had established the Board. He also did not explain why the N.C.S.C. approved the "fast-track" method of reviewing standards. Apparently the N.C.S.C.'s acceptance of such a

---

73   Neo-corporatism represents a model of political behaviour whereby efforts to
          secure consensus are achieved through government recognition of interest-groups
          and the granting to those groups of privileged access to the policy-making
          process (R. Walker, 1987, p. 283).

method was to speed up the production of standards, which would in turn help it in administering company law disclosure requirements.

The choice of the time period for his study also helped R. Walker (1987) to substantiate his capture argument. He chose a period when the profession had some success in getting its demands met. By concentrating his study mainly on the two years immediately following the creation of the Board he overlooked the acquisition by other parties of important roles in the A.S.R.B. standard-setting process. As is shown in Chapters 9 and 10, those other parties acquired their roles during the process of the creation of the Board and the establishment of its functions. The possibility of distortion of results due to the misspecification of the time period was pointed out by Merino et al (1987, p. 755).

Generally, we can observe from this discussion that the political scientists' approach of explaining accounting regulation in the form of regulatory capture is of limited use because it has insufficient explanatory and predictive power. No reason is suggested as to why the regulated industry should be the only interest group able to influence a regulatory agency. In a situation where the A.S.R.B. as a regulatory agency regulated more that one industry with varying interests, the model fails to explain why one industry, such as the accounting profession should participate more actively than the others. Lastly, it ignores a good deal of evidence that the interests promoted by regulatory agencies can also be in accord with those of other groups rather than that of the regulated firms alone (Also see Posner 1974, pp. 341-343).[74]

---

74   This is also noted in the case of the A.S.R.B. in Chapter 11. The procedural changes that were criticized by R. Walker (1987) as being those that were demanded by the profession, were also congruent to the earlier demands of other parties.

2.   The Public Choice Theories:

Public choice theories seek to demonstrate that economic regulations are an outcome of a competitive market for regulations with a long-term view of the regulatory process.

Public Choice has been defined by Mueller (1976) as "the economic study of non-market decision making or simply the application of economics to political science" (p. 395).

Public choice theories are an outcome of the response to issues arising in political economics and use the basic behavioural postulate of economics, that man is an egoistic, rational, utility maximizer (Mueller 1976, p. 395).

Studies in accounting which have used the public choice argument are reviewed below:

a.   Stigler-Posner-Peltzman (S.P.P.) Model:

Wells (1978) was one of the first who recognized the explanatory capability of this model in explaining the nature of accounting standard-setting. His objective was to show why it was so difficult to achieve agreement on accounting standards compared to that in the case of auditing standards and why the need for government regulation arose when efforts to achieve consensus failed. He explained that accounting regulation was sought primarily by the accounting profession and others on cost-benefit terms. That is the standards were demanded as long as those interests perceived that they would gain if such standards were established. But, when the interests conflicted and when it was not possible to absorb outsiders into the accounting profession to reap the interests of its cartel conditions it became necessary for the profession to demand government regulation or government support for the professional standards. He further elaborated this view with his C.C.A. example. Here he explained the demand-supply concept of the determination of standards. He explicated that standards would be supplied by the policy makers as long as the demand for it effectively exceeded the opposition for it. In the case of C.C.A. the opposition by managers, based on their cost-benefit perception, has surpassed the demands of the profession, and the C.C.A. standard is yet to be fully installed.

In other words Wells (1978) in explaining the establishment of accounting standards adopted Posner's (1974) view of "regulation as a service supplied to effective political groups, at a cost" (Bell, 1988, p. 5).

Phillips and Zecher (1981, Chapter 2) noted that the public choice theory provided an economic rationale for understanding why regulatory agencies and programs did not deal effectively with the economic problem of inefficient allocation of resources.[75] They challenged the presumption that the S.E.C.'s corporate disclosure program served the public interest (p. vii). They analyzed the effect of that program on the allocation of resources and how the groups affected by those reallocations determined the evolution and enforcement of new rules (p. 2). They sought to prove that the S.E.C.'s primary role seemed to be to referee or nurture an interest group of experts in securities regulations (p. 4). For this, they chose the public choice theory (Chicago School) to understand why regulators who were mandated to correct allocational inefficiencies, appeared to serve many masters - not just the consumers or the public.

Phillips and Zecher (1981) were critical about the central principles of the S.E.C., that is, (1) full disclosure and (2) anti-fraud provisions and self-regulation (p. 15). Those principles were based on the market failure notion of regulation - improving efficiency by correcting market failure (p. 17). They mentioned that nearly all regulatory programs had fallen far short of dealing successfully with a real market

---

75   Strickland (1980) and Morgan (1976), mentioned that economic regulations could be instituted not for the benefit of the society, but for the benefit of the regulated firms. Firms traded the uncertainty and competitiveness of the free market for the financial security of the regulated environment (p. 303).

failure in a cost effective manner (p. 20). In their analysis they abandon the notion that correcting market failure was a serious goal of regulatory agencies and instead viewed those agencies as an integral part of the political - economic system, that had a major function of reallocation of wealth among competing groups. In that respect they found that the S.E.C. corporate disclosure program had no clear goal, thus there was no clear way of assessing its effectiveness or the desirability of changes in its programs (p. 21). They argued that while it was possible to conceive of better regulatory laws and better administration of regulatory programs that dealt with real market failures in a cost effective manner, the wide spread absence of such laws and programs left a nagging suspicion that something else was amiss (p. 21). In that respect, market failure theory fails to explain, adequately, the way in which regulation actually works.

They conducted a cost-benefit analysis of S.E.C. disclosure regulation, that is the mandatory filing of corporate information with the S.E.C. From the benefits view point they concluded that such requirements did not significantly improve the pricing of securities in the secondary or new securities markets. Most financial analysts viewed the reports filed with the S.E.C. as vital for their work, whereas the investors found them to be of much less use. From the costs side, the disclosure costs were high, and higher for smaller companies. On the one hand it taxed a large number of investors through the cost of preparing mandatory reports and on the other hand it benefited the securities analysts, security lawyers and accountants in terms of securing jobs for them. The investors per capita tax was very small and hence they did not have the incentive to lobby against the S.E.C. program. The per capita benefit of the beneficiaries was high, therefore they had the incentive to lobby to maintain or enhance the disclosure rules.

Their arguments revealed that the disclosure regulations were not effectively sought to meet the cost benefit criteria of the investors or the assumed "public", but they were sought by the interest groups in their own interest. They confirmed Stigler's (1971) and Peltzman's (1976) arguments that individual's response to regulatory proposals depended on how it would affect their wealth. Their conclusions conformed to the Chicago School's predictions in the following manner:

1. On the demand side:
   (a) The securities analysts, security lawyers and accountants had a large stake in the S.E.C.'s regulations which led them to organize themselves effectively and bid for and against the proposed regulations.
   (b) The larger groups, like that of investors, had a low per capita perceived gain to lobby for or against proposed regulations, but had a high per capita cost to organize and lobby. Therefore, they were passive participants in the regulatory scene.
   (c) Groups, in which the per capita stake was higher than per capita cost, approached the law maker or regulator in the political-economic market place and indicated the strength of their support or opposition to the regulator.

2. On the supply side, the success of S.E.C.'s disclosure program hinged not on its capability to correct market inefficiencies, but on the balancing of interests of effectively organized groups.

Johnson and Messier (1982) also applied this version of public choice theory to study the determination of accounting standards by the F.A.S.B.. In their regulatory market model they suggested that a firm or coalition would demand a standard only if it had the need (perceived benefit) and that its efforts could influence the supply of the standard. On the supply side, supply for an alternative would be granted when demand for it was high, it was the most acceptable compromise to opposing parties and it did not threaten the existence of the standard-setting organization. In short, they provided an insight into the existing standard-setting process and provided some explanation for the demand for and the supply of accounting standards.

b.　　Downsian Analysis:

Sutton (1984), in explaining the lobbying of accounting standard-setting bodies, used the Downsian voting model and noted that "a rational individual will only allocate resources to lobbying if the expected benefits to him from doing so exceed the costs" (p. 93).

Sutton's analysis mainly covered the demand side of the regulatory market. He ascertained that lobbying was considered worth while by large producers of financial statements and undiversified producers rather than consumers of financial statements. Standards with economic consequences arouse more interest with the producers than disclosure standards, whereas consumers favoured disclosure standards. The higher the cost of non-compliance, the higher was the level of producer lobbying. Lobbying was most productive when the regulators preferences were undecided. Despite free riders, a lobbyist would lobby as long as the perceived benefits from lobbying exceeded its costs.

3.　　Crisis Theory/"Bush Fire" Approach:

Wells (1978, pp. 15-18) adopted another theory to explain the difficulties faced in obtaining agreement with accounting standards. He used the crises theory explicated in Wells (1976), to provide an alternate view of the process of creation of standards. His view was that regulations were the result of crises which arose, or were manufactured, from time to time.

He explained that practitioners appeared to suffer a loss of confidence due to crises such as corporate failures. Such crises substantiated the shortcomings in their practices. Their deficiencies were publicized by various quarters, which eventually loosened the traditional views of the profession. In that situation it became politically inexpedient to oppose proposals for overcoming the deficiencies, and a politically acceptable alternative was adopted. Providing an answer to his question of why it was difficult to obtain agreement on accounting standards, he added: "We have not had enough crises".

This argument of Wells (1978) based on the crisis theory has its origins in the theory of scientific revolutions provided by Kuhn (1970). In this respect, Wells (1978, p. 16) recognized that the consensus which emerged from accounting crises was different from that of scientific revolutions. The latter was based on intellectual argument and evidence; whereas consensus over accounting policy matters was political in kind where power and influence played a significant role. His arguments, did not go far enough in describing the behaviour of the parties involved in the consensus process. Furthermore, he did not describe the mechanism of the consensus process. But, his assertions do elucidate that demand for standards are associated with or follow a crisis and that the intensity of the demand for and the subsequent supply of standards may be related to the intensity of the crisis.[76]

Watts (1977) pointed out the intentional use of "crises" to create regulation. He argued that "crises" were either the creation of the media in order to entertain the layman or could be created by politicians. Whichever the case, the political entrepreneurs used it to suggest simplistic solutions understandable by the layman or his constituents he represented. Those solutions he argued were not necessarily of any use to solve the perceived crisis. On the other hand bureaucrats responsible for law enforcement also suggested the establishment of regulations in order to avoid blame. Both the politicians and the bureaucrats through the institution of regulations tried to strengthen their position as lawmakers and law enforcers, respectively. So crises are used to establish regulations with a view to enhance self-interest.

Although Watts' (1977) did show that his "crises" theory could explain the creation of the S.E.C. with its power to establish corporate disclosure rules, he did not explain why the power to prepare financial accounting standards was delegated to a private body, the F.A.S.B., and

---

76   This argument has been adopted in the preferred model, explained in the next
        chapter, to identify event which lead to demand for and supply for mandatory
        accounting standards.

what role did the accounting profession, the companies and others play in that delegation of power.

4.   Other Studies:

There have been some other studies exploring various aspects of the behaviour of the lobbyists and the standard setters. Those studies have implicitly examined the demand or the supply function of accounting standards. For example, Watts and Zimmerman (1978), Kelley (1982 and 1985) and Puro (1984) used the agency model to explain the behaviour of demanders (for and against) of accounting standards; Hussein (1981) used Zaltman *et al*'s "innovation model" to explain the reasons for and the process of lobbying in standard-setting; and Meyer (1974), Rockness and Nikolai (1977), Jarrel (1979), Haring (1979), Hussein and Ketz (1980), Brown (1981), Newman (1981a and 1981b) and Coombes and Stokes (1985) studied different aspects of the supply of standards to de-fuse or verify the Ruling Elite/Capture theory in accounting.

If seen from the public choice perspective, those studies provided a useful insight into the nature of the standard-setting process, but none of them provided an explanation capable of linking the two main aspects of standard-setting, the demand and the supply functions, to show how the equilibrium point (the policy) is determined. The main reason for their inability to do so was the absence of the use of a theoretical framework which covered the two aspects adequately. But, those studies, combined together, indicate the existence of a market for accounting standards with a demand and a supply side. In that manner they supported the S-P-P argument that accounting standards were determined in a market for regulations environment.

Another descriptive study which, as shown in the next section, lent support to the public choice framework was that of Davis and Menon (1987). Their study discussed the circumstances leading first to the creation and later to the termination of the Cost Accounting Standards Board (C.A.S.B.) in the U.S.A. To explicate the formation of that board they used the arguments of Wilson (1974 and 1980) and showed that it was a case of diffused benefits and concentrated costs. Policy crusaders' perception of immediate benefits for government departments dealing with defence procurement, in particular, and for the public, in general, along with the negative image of the defence industry in the American Congress led to its creation. Davis and Menon saw the subsequent life of the Board in the pattern of decay of regulatory organizations as portrayed by Bernstein (1955). They showed that the continued opposition that the Board faced from the defence industry throughout its life followed by the subsequent loss of support from its advocates, which seemed to happen at a time of rising trend towards deregulation, made the Congress to terminate its life.

Inference:

The use of the prescriptive theories of accounting regulation is minimal for the purpose of this thesis. Apparently they are also not that effective in extending support for what they themselves intend to propose. In this respect Bell (1988) stated:

> anything approaching the "perfect information" needed for Pareto Optimality, which might be theoretically feasible in an uncertain world, is unlikely to be produced by either private markets or by public regulation. The claim that it is more likely, or at least as likely to be achieved through private market forces incorporating agency and signalling relationships as with government regulation is at best unproven (p. 14).

Amongst the descriptive arguments, the Public Choice version of explaining economic regulation is preferred here because it can provide a more complete and conclusive framework for positive research in financial disclosure regulations. It explains the determination of regulatory policies in a pluralistic political environment using basic economic and behavioural concepts.

Posner (1974, pp. 341-344) asserted the greater explanatory capacity of this model over the "capture" or "public interest" theories because it (1) discarded the unexplained, and frequently untrue, assumption of pristine legislative purpose; (2) replaced the capture metaphor by the more neutral terminology of supply and demand for regulations provided it satisfied the cost-benefit conditions of those who sought it and that of the regulator who supplied it; (3) contained a more acceptable assumption that people seek to advance their self-interest rationally (as opposed to government acting on the basis of market failure or market efficiency theories) and (4) suggested regulations could be sought by any politically effective group acting in their private interest. It also provided an answer to why cartels (for example accounting bodies), which could regulate its members, sought the coercive powers of the State to regulate outsiders. Thus, this model has the capacity to explain "why" and "how" regulations are demanded and supplied.[77]

The essence of public choice in accounting was emphasized by Gerboth (1973) in the following manner:

> In a society committed to democratic legitimization of authority, only politically responsive institutions have a right to command others to obey their rules. (p. 478)

Moonitz (1974) and Wells (1978) also pointed out the importance of political and constituent support for the survival of standard-setting agencies and their established standards. Aranya (1974) and Hein (1978) provided evidence regarding pressure group influence in the determination of the British Companies Acts disclosure requirements.

---

77   Such a view is supported by Johnson and Messier (1982, p. 197). In explaining the reason for the demand for financial reporting regulation Phillips and Zecher (1981) stated:

> "... some groups in society clearly benefit from this (the SEC's) regulatory programme: for example those who enjoy increased demand for their services to produce the disclosures such as securities lawyers, financial accountants, auditors" (p. 44).

Those and other studies (see footnote 27) indicate that the public choice criteria of the supply of and demand for regulatory policies, on the basis of self-interest, are also present in the accounting standard-setting process. Therefore, the Public Choice framework has the capacity of describing the determination of accounting regulations in terms of participants' behaviour in the political process.[78]

In assessing the survival of professional accounting standards Wells (1978) predicted that: "Accounting standards as we know them, however, would survive only as long as the professional accounting bodies maintained their alliance with other influential groups" (p 1).

The A.S.R.B. was in a similar situation in its initial years. It functioned on the basis of majority rule rather than unanimity rule.[79] Achieving unanimity (or consensus) on a conceptual framework has been of little success in U.S.A. and U.K.[80] The A.S.R.B. Release 100 also fell short of being a conceptual framework as it refrained from specifying important aspects, such as measurement rules. The reason for it was that there was no goal congruence amongst the various groups participating in the standard-setting process.[81] In the approach used by the standard setters, the interest groups seem to play a game of wealth transfers.[82] The goal of each party is to have a standard which helps in enhancing or at least maintaining the wealth of its constituents. This may have an equal and opposite likelihood of reducing the wealth of the members of another group. This indicates that it is difficult to achieve goal

---

78   Also see Peirson and Ramsay (1983, p. 294-295) and Watts and Zimmerman (1986, p. 173).

79   See Mueller (1976) for discussion on unanimity and majority rules.

80   See Belkaoui, (1985), pp. 206-208 and Ashton, 1983, pp. 223-226.

81   Bromwich (1985, p 76) noted that different groups may have different economic consequences due to the mandatory accounting rules.

82   Watts and Zimmerman (1979, p. 275).

congruence amongst opposing parties. Again as those groups have varied interests,[83] there is low cohesiveness amongst them. This can be illustrated as follows:

Goal Congruence	Cohesiveness	
	High	Low
High	(1) High Consensus	(2) Medium Consensus
Low	(3) Low Consensus	(4) No Consensus

As mentioned above the likelihood for (1) or (2) is low and that for (3) or (4) is high. Therefore consensus through unanimity will be rare. The obvious method is the public choice method of majority rule. The majority in this case as expressed in the S-P-P model is that of the effectively participating groups. Without such majority support for its standards the survival of the A.S.R.B. would be at stake. This in turn implies that for the formation of the Board a similar support of the effectively participating groups was necessary and such support would have to be maintained for its survival.

The case of the C.A.S.B. in the U.S.A. testifies to the fact that an accounting standard-setting body needs the support of influential parties on both the supply and the demand sides. The study by Davis and Menon (1987) indicated that the C.A.S.B. was capable of surviving and functioning so long as the concerned executive branches of government on the demand side and the American Congress on the supply side supported the need for a cost accounting standards board. In the presence of continued opposition from the defence industries, when the executive

---

83   Like companies may try to satisfy the shareholders through showing higher profits, whereas the auditors may try to provide true and fair information to the shareholders. In doing so there may be disagreement in selecting an acceptable accounting method.

branches lost interest in the Board and the trend in the Congress shifted towards deregulation, the C.A.S.B. met its inevitable end.

Therefore, amongst all the models discussed in this chapter, the Public Choice model has the greatest explanatory power as a regulatory theory. It is used in this thesis to explain why the regulators (the Ministerial Council) chose the A.S.R.B. based method of standard-setting.

Chapter 5

THE THEORETICAL MODEL

Introduction:

The review and analysis in Chapters 2 and 3 led to the hypothesis that the A.S.R.B. was the outcome of a multi-party process. Schaffer (1977) described such a process as follows:

> The public policy process is then a multi-person drama going on in several arenas, some of them likely to be complex large-scale organizational situations. Decisions are the outcome of the drama, not a voluntary, willed, individual initial action. "Drama is continuous. Decisions are convenient labels given post hoc to the mythical precedents of the apparent outcomes of uncertain conflicts" (p. 148).

Hawker et al (1979) explained this further by stating that

> Public policy consists of continuing patterns of political and administrative activity that are shaped both by deliberate decisions and by the interplay of political and environmental forces. The sources of policy include strategic individuals in powerful organizations who attempt to shape policy to their own design, past patterns of policy, the political processes and structures through which policy proposals pass, and the political and social environment in which relevant activity takes place. Public policy is not simply an aggregation of decisions and programmes; it is wider than the results of discrete decisions and it does not necessarily have the coherence and definition of a programme. It includes non-purposive as well as purposive elements and unintended as well as intended consequences (pp. 22-23).

Fainsod and Gordon (1941) emphasized that an understanding of the nature and methods of the major parties-in-interest and the environment in which they operate, as well as the political instruments of regulation, was critical to an understanding of regulation. Mitnick's (1980, p. 83) observations also clearly portrayed the complexity of a regulatory process. Despite the complexity, he recognized the need for a theory which adequately dealt with all or most of the aspects of that process.

Recognizing that complexity, in this chapter a model, based on the public choice framework of the previous chapter, has been developed for a methodical study of the regulatory process which created the A.S.R.B. First, the regulatory theories, in general, are briefly examined to substantiate the nature of regulatory policies and identify the explanatory status of the preferred model amongst those theories; second, it is established that accounting standards are economic regulations and can be studied in a market context; third, it is shown why a regulatory policy, allowing the creation of such standards, can also be studied in a market context; fourth, the public choice model - a market for regulatory policies in which the demand and the supply functions are capable of determining the type of accounting regulatory agency and its regulations - is elaborated and explained; fifth the expected behaviour of identifiable interest groups on the demand side is discussed; sixth the method of applying the model with the support of some other theories is outlined; and finally, the advantages and limitations of the model are noted.

The Nature of Regulatory Theories and the Status of the Model:

Mitnick (1980) reviewed the theories of regulation. He observed that in a broad sense regulation can be defined as "the intentional restriction of a subject's choice of activity, by an entity not directly party to or involved in that activity" (p. 20).

He noted that regulation in practice was a dynamic process rather than a static outcome (pp. 7-10, p. 20 and p. 101). According to his typology of regulation (see Figure 5.1.) the kind of regulation that is the subject of this thesis is the traditional regulation.

Regulator	Regulate	
	Public	Private
Public	Government Self-Regulation	Traditional Regulation
Private	"Capture"	Private Self-Regulation

Figure 5.1. Typology of regulation.

Source: Mitnick (1980) p. 14.

Mitnick (1980, Chapter 2) examined the dynamic elements in the regulatory system, including the evolutionary/life cycle patterns of two major elements in the regulatory system - the regulatory agency and the regulated industry. His evaluation of the life cycle theories revealed that they had numerous weaknesses (pp. 73-75), and he concluded that their status as satisfactory descriptive or explanatory mechanisms was questionable (p. 76). In this respect it is important to point out, that it is not possible to apply the life cycle theories alone to study the A.S.R.B., because it has not yet undergone one full cycle as depicted by those theories. Also, recalling the scope of this dissertation, it is not the intention here to study the whole life cycle of the Board, but only to study those stages which cover the establishment of the Board's organization and functions.

The theories of regulatory origin reviewed by Mitnick (1980, Chapter 3) are more appropriate for describing the establishment of the Board. He noted that the creation of regulatory organizations, and the creation, implementation, and administration of regulation, may be understood as special cases of the general policy-making process. He pointed out that the theories of regulatory origin analyzed by him are partial theories because they looked at certain specific aspects and not at all the facets of the regulatory process (p. 79). Development of a complete theory, he said, was not possible because, unlike disciplines such as economics, no powerful tool existed to do so (p. 79).

For a better understanding of the theories of regulatory origin Mitnick (1980) reviewed various descriptions of the policy-making process. He identified five major stages: (1) access (issue creation, issue expansion and agenda entrance); (2) decision; (3) implementation; (4) administration and (5) impacts. He emphasized that a full theory of regulation must explain all these stages; whereas a full theory of regulatory origin must at minimum extend from the access stage into the administration stage (pp. 80-81). He also found that to a large extent, theories of regulation have always been theories of "interest" (public or private). Regulation, as he viewed evolved or changed over time due to the change in interests served. Explanation of this phenomenon, he saw, was an important issue for the regulatory theories (p. 84).

Mitnick (1980) also accepted that the life cycle theories and the origin theories were complementary to each other and not substitutes. This notion, he recognized, was essential for developing a more robust model (p. 126). Again, reviewing the private interest theories of regulation, he observed that legislators also behaved like interest groups and tried to design regulations to serve their own self-interest rather than some "public interest" (p. 119 and 122).[84] This indicated that to have a broader theory of regulatory origin assistance may also be sought from theories that explain Government/politicians' behaviour. He concluded that there are obvious areas of complementarity among the various approaches towards describing regulatory origin. He suggested an integrating approach to develop a theory. His model centred on the regulatory organization and the incentive system faced by organizational members. His was a step towards explaining the whole process of regulation under an existing regulatory system rather than a theory of regulatory origin capable of describing the creation of a new regulatory

---

84   This is also explained by Downs (1957a and 1957b) and Abrams and Settle (1978) as reviewed later.

system. In the case of the task delineated for this thesis we need a theory of the latter type.

To avoid duplicating Mitnick's (1980) review of theories of regulatory origin and to keep the discussion short, it can be summed up from his findings that in order to develop an adequately explanatory theory of regulatory origin, arguments may have to be drawn from, for example organizational life cycle theories, public interest theories, group behaviour theories, economic theories, theories of Government and public administration, agency theory, behavioural theories and capture or partial capture theories. This leads to Mitnick's (1980) observation that developing such a theory is an insurmountable task and is certainly not an object of this dissertation. Such a theory, for the sake of identification, can be called a public choice theory[85] because it would explain the choice between regulatory policy alternatives. Mitnick (1980) described this as follows:

> Regulation can be seen as the outcome of rational choices by public officials maximizing their utility (p. 120).

In this chapter a simplified model within the Public Choice Theory domain has been developed. According to the scope of this study laid down in Chapter 1, the model that has been described later is primarily based on the premise that man (individuals including politicians in government) is an egoistic, rational, utility maximizer (See Mueller, 1976 p. 395 and Downs 1957a and 1957b). The overall framework of demand and supply, adopted in the model, is drawn from the theory of economic regulation of Stigler (1971), Posner (1974) and Peltzman (1976). Mitnick (1980) distinguished their economic theory of regulation in the following manner:

---

85   See Mueller (1976) to assess the wide range of theories that can be classified as public choice theories. Phillips and Zecher (1981) classified theories of economic regulation, on which our model is based, as a public choice theory.

One can perhaps distinguish an *economic theory of regulation*, with the supply-demand framework and the assumptions about individual actors, from an *economic approach to modelling regulation*, which relies mainly on the assumptions and techniques of economics but not necessarily on the structure of, parallelism with, or appropriation of, existing models of economics. (p. 119) [His italics]

Mitnick (p. 119) felt that the structure of the economic theory of regulation needed further explication based on the basic supply-demand, rational choice framework. To determine the nature of demand for accounting regulatory policies, arguments are drawn from Posner's (1974) description of cartels seeking regulations; the studies on accounting professional bodies' behaviour by Buckley (1980) and Willmott (1986). Downs' (1957a and 1957b) and Abrams and Settle's (1978) explanations of Government and politicians' behaviour are used to outline the nature of supply for such policies.

To apply the model for this thesis, the life cycle theory of Bernstein (1955) and the stages of regulatory policy making identified by Mitnick (1980, pp. 80-84) are used to determine the length of the period of origin of the regulatory policy comprising the A.S.R.B. The crisis theory, as adopted by Wells (1976 and 1978) to describe the development and demise of accounting theories and standards, is used to identify major events which have led to intermittent occurrences of demand and supply for accounting regulatory policies within the period selected for this study. In the case of regulations, Mitnick (1980) called this aspect regulatory entry and referred to Cobb and Elders (1972) agenda-building model. That model methodically explained (1) issue creation, (2) issue expansion and (3) agenda entrance in the process of regulatory entry.

Reverting to the scope of regulatory theories, Mitnick (1980) identified theories which dealt with explaining the creation of new regulations or developments in existing regulations or the origin of regulatory policies or the creation and conduct of regulatory bodies or the behaviour of the regulators. The model developed for this study is intended to describe the origin of the regulatory policy and the subsequent creation of the A.S.R.B. - its organization and functions.

Table 5.1. The Theoretical Bases of the Preferred Model.

Theories	Authors	Aspect for which used	Remarks
Public Choice and Democracy	Mueller (1976) Downs (1975a and 1975b)	Premise	To assume the basic behavioural properties of individuals in the regulatory process.
Economic regulation	Stigler (1971) Posner (1974) Peltzman (1976)	Demand and supply	To establish the core theoretical base of the model
Cartel/group behaviour	Posner (1974) Buckley (1980) Willmott (1986)	Demand	To substantiate the behaviour of accounting bodies
Government/ politicians' behaviour	Downs (1957a and 1957b) Abrams and Settle (1978)	Supply	To describe the behaviour of government as supplier of regulatory policies
Life cycle	Bernstein (1955) Mitnick (1980)	Demand and supply	To identify the stages of the life cycle in regulatory origin
Crisis and Agenda-Building	Wells (1976 and 1978) and Cobb and Elder (1972)	Demand and supply	To identify the events leading to demand for and supply of policies

Accounting Standards as Economic Regulations:

Wells (1978, p. 4, p. 19) explained that the accounting profession and the managers sought or rejected regulations on the basis of their cost-benefit relationship. His arguments suggested that financial disclosure standards like other economic regulations[86] are economic goods and are sought only when their benefits to the demander exceed the costs of acquisition. Others, such as Watts and Zimmerman (1978), Phillips and Zecher (1981) and Johnson and Messier (1982) also held a similar view of the S.E.C. and F.A.S.B. disclosure requirements.[87]

To confirm that financial disclosure standards are economic regulations, we first need to establish whether such standards are regulations. Secondly, we need to check whether financial disclosure, which can be altered by disclosure standards, has any economic consequences. Thirdly, the consequences of such disclosure standards have to be noted to verify that these standards are capable of allocating scarce resources (presumably wealth) among competing demands. Finally, we need to demonstrate that those standards are established through a demand and supply mechanism.

Financial Accounting Standards are Regulations:

Financial accounting standards are regulations because they may (1) restrict the choice of accounting methods available to management and (2) force companies to report in a form which those companies may not have chosen voluntarily (Sutton, 1984, p. 81).

---

86   Economic regulations have similar characteristics as economic goods according to Stigler (1971) and Peltzman (1976).

87   Also see the previous chapter.

A.S.R.B.'s definition of accounting standards fits this scenario. A.S.R.B. Release 100 (1984) defined accounting standards as:

> In broad terms "accounting standards" are rules stating a procedure or procedures which must be followed in the preparation of accounting reports. An accounting standard may deal with the form and content of financial statements ... or it may concern how information is to be presented in financial statements or accompanying notes. A statement may deal with the manner in which money magnitudes reflected in those financial statements are to be calculated. A given standard may incorporate 'definitions' of constituent terms. (pp.3-4)

Professional accounting standards in Australia are primarily enforceable on the members of professional accounting bodies.[88] A.S.R.B.'s approval of such standards could strengthen those standards and make them enforceable on all companies incorporated in Australia and their auditors (A.S.R.B. Release 100, p. 2). The Australian Accounting Standards with the approval of the Board could become government backed regulations with a wider sphere of enforcement.[89] That conforms with Mitnick's (1980) view (See previous section), of regulations, because A.S.R.B. standards could restrict the choice and form of company financial disclosure and accounting methods for the companies. Likewise, it could restrict the scope of audit opinion of the company auditors. The entities which were involved in setting up such restrictions and enforcing them, such as the Board itself, the N.C.S.C. and the C.A.C.'s, were not directly involved in the activity of preparing or using financial reports for economic gains. Therefore, approved accounting standards of the Board were, in fact, government regulations because they regulated the activities of companies or company directors and the auditors.

---

88   Even though they do not have legal force the C.A.C.s use them as prima facie evidence of true and fair view (Miller, 1978, p. 92 and Australian Financial Systems, Final Report of the Committee of Enquiry, 1981, p. 370fn).

89   Companies Code 1981 Section 266.

Economic Consequences of Financial Information:

Accounting information is an economic good because it has consequences that are economic in nature. Zeff (1978) defined economic consequences of financial information as "the impact of accounting reports on the decision making behaviour of business, government, unions, investors and creditors" (p. 56).

Almost all accounting changes can have real effects (Lev and Ohlson, 1982, p. 250). Holthausen and Leftwich (1983) reviewed the economic consequences of voluntary and mandatory choices of accounting techniques and standards. They specified that accounting choices are likely to have economic consequences if changes in rules used to calculate accounting numbers alter the distribution of firm's cash flow, or the wealth of parties who use those numbers for contracting or decision making.[90]

The economic consequences studies indicate that releasing accounting information has consequences which are economic in nature. Accounting information is a means of wealth transfer[91] and can affect wealth distribution in the securities market. This reinforces the argument that financial accounting disclosure can affect resource allocation amongst competing demands.

---

[90]   May and Sundem (1976), Prakash and Rapport (1977), Solomons (1978) and Bromwich (1985, chapter 5) also pointed out the importance of economic consequences of accounting numbers.

[91]   See Zeff (1978, p. 62), Watts and Zimmerman (1979, p. 275) and Holthausen and Leftwich (1983, p.77).

Economic Consequences of Accounting Standards:

To elaborate the argument further it is shown that financial accounting standards, as regulations, are economic goods or economic regulation because of their economic consequences. Watts and Zimmerman (1979) explained that government regulation of accounting procedures created incentives for individuals and interest groups to propose alternate procedures backed by suitable theories. In this respect they analyzed theories as economic goods. Accordingly, regulations which eventually adopted such theories could also be regarded as economic goods. To this Watts and Zimmerman (1979, p. 275) added, that accounting standards had wealth transfer capabilities. Such wealth transfers could be seen as the allocation of scarce resources amongst competing demands, which implied that accounting standards could be demanded because it is in a way demand for wealth.[92] As mentioned earlier, Wells (1978) also regarded accounting standards as economic regulations. His analysis of C.C.A. standards substantiated this notion, because he showed that on the one side the accounting profession demanded such a standard to avoid criticisms of its existing practice which could eventually affect the demand for their services and on the other side the managers opposed it when they became aware of the fact that no extra benefits were forthcoming to cover the extra costs imposed on them by such standards. C.C.A., as it seems, is still in an unacceptable state because the opposition for it effectively out ranks its demand.

Considerable descriptive and empirical research has been conducted describing financial accounting standard-setting. Such studies can be classified into: (1) studies describing the economic consequences of accounting standards and (2) the studies which describe the behaviour of the participants in the standard-setting process.

---

92   Morgan (1976) stated that regulation could serve the purpose of allocating power and wealth without exclusive reliance on market mechanisms.

The "economic consequences studies" highlight the fact that financial accounting standards may not only facilitate disclosure of economic consequences of firms' operations but also impart consequences of their own. Seven empirical studies have been reviewed here. These studies can be classified into two categories:

1.   those that studied the economic impact of standards requiring increased disclosure: For example see Dhaliwal (1978) and Abdel-khalik, et al (1978), and

2.   those that studied the economic impact of standards requiring changes to alternate disclosure methods: For example see Makin (1977), Winn (1978), Benston and Krasney (1978), Harison (1978) and Collins, et al (1981).

These studies revealed favourable and unfavourable economic impact of standards on different parties, under varying circumstances. Such impacts varied across firms due to the presence of various catalysts which Collins, et al (1981) demonstrated by revealing the relationship between economic consequences and variables such as presence of loan agreements and firm size. Holthausen and Leftwich (1983), from their review of research into the economic consequences of mandatory choices and voluntary choices of accounting technique reiterated this by concluding that accounting choices have economic consequences if changes in the rules used to calculate accounting numbers alter the distribution of firms' cash flows, or the wealth of parties who use those numbers for contracting or decision making (p. 77).

A more detailed review of the empirical studies of the economic impacts of accounting regulations by Chow (1983) revealed a similar finding "accounting regulations do seem to have economic effects." (p 85)

From the conclusions of those studies it is not possible to generalize the nature and direction of the economic consequences, but it can be inferred that certain standards do have economic consequences which can be favourable or unfavourable to the interacting parties. The consequences may, in some cases, be substantial enough to arouse interest amongst certain groups to participate in the standard-setting process. The studies relating to the behaviour of interest groups are reviewed next.

The Nature of Supply of and Demand for Accounting Standards:

Economic consequences of regulations can lead to demand for regulations and, based on the effectiveness of demand, there can be a supply of regulations by the regulatory agencies. Such a situation may imply that there exists a market for regulations. In accounting the use of such a market model can give a more elaborate and objective description of the "so called" social choice process[93] of accounting standard-setting in economic terms.

The studies describing the behaviour of participants in the standard-setting process exposed that the process has two major aspects - the supply of and the demand for standards. This provides preliminary evidence that there exists a market for accounting standards. Twenty recently conducted studies have been reviewed and classified as follows according to their theoretical underpinnings:

I.   Economic Regulation Theory: Johnson and Messier (1982) and Puro (1984)

II.   Economic Theory of Democracy: Sutton (1984)

---

93   For example see, Gerboth (1973), Horngren (1973), Moonitz (1974), Aranya (1974), May and Sundem (1976), Buckley (1976), Watts (1977, pp. 64-65), Solomons (1978), Watts and Zimmerman (1979), Dopuch and Sunder (1980, p. 18), Beaver (1981, p. 18), Sunder and Haribhakti (1984, p. 166, pp. 167-168) and Zeff (1972, 1978 and 1986).

III.   Agency/Contracting Cost Perspective: Watts and Zimmerman (1978), Kelley (1982 and 1985), Leftwich (1983) and Puro (1984)

IV.   Evolutionary Notion:
        (a)   Inductive Process: Hussein (1981)
        (b)   Ideological/Social, Political and Economic Influence: Merino and Neimark (1982) and Cooper and Keim (1983)

V.   Ruling Elite/Capture Theory: Meyer (1974), Rockness and Nikolai (1977), Jarrell (1979), Haring (1979), Hussein and Ketz (1980), Brown (1981), Newman (1981a and 1981b), and Coombes and Stokes (1986).

In respect of the "demand for" and "supply of" standards the following inferences can be drawn from the above studies:

I.   The demand for standards:

        1.   Standards may not only facilitate the reporting of economic consequences of a firm's operations, but may also impart consequences of their own on the managers, creditors, shareholders, auditors, etc. Those who perceive that they are affected by such consequences may participate in the standard-setting process and try to influence the outcome in their own favour. (For example the Economic Consequences studies and also see Johnson and Messier (1982) and Sutton (1984)).

        2.   There are other variables also which may act as catalysts. Their presence may create variations in the intensity of economic consequences of standards. (For example see Collins, et al (1981) and Holthausen and

Leftwich (1983)) Under such circumstances certain groups or individuals may participate more than others in the standard-setting process.

3. Lobbyists lobby in their own interest which may be directly derived or derived through the fulfilment of the interest of others, like auditors lobbying for or with their clients, the producers of financial statements. (For example see Watts and Zimmerman (1978), Kelley (1978 and 1985), Hussein (1981), Johnson and Messier (1982), Sutton (1984) and Puro (1984)).

4. Inter-personal channels of lobbying play an important role at the earlier stages (attitude formation stage) of standard-setting. (For example see Hussein (1981) and Sutton (1984)).

5. The amount of lobbying may vary with the radicalness of a proposed alternative. (For example see Hussein (1981)).

6. Number of submissions are higher for standards which materially affect the contents of financial statements than those that affect only the form. (For example see Hussein (1981) and Sutton (1984)).

II. The supply of standards:

1. Regulators having similar employment affiliations do not necessarily vote alike every time - there are no significant coalitions. (For example see Meyer (1974), Rockness and Nikolai (1977), Haring (1979) and Hussein and Ketz (1980)).

2. Even with the bloc voting assumption, on the basis of employment affiliations, no single coalition dominates or

has the capability of dominating the standard-setting body. (For example see Hussein and Ketz (1980), Newman (1981a), Brown (1981) and Coombes and Stokes (1985)).

3.   But the possibility of domination by producers of accounting reports and large accounting firms through indirect or informal means cannot be over ruled. (For example see Hussein and Ketz (1980)).

4.   The regulators respond to the constituents' demands in the case of direct lobbying, like written submissions. (For example see Brown (1981), Coombes and Stokes (1985)).

5.   Regulators preferences do not consistently correspond to that of a single group, which supports the pluralistic supply argument. (For example see Hussein and Ketz (1980), Brown (1981) and Coombes and Stokes (1985))

6.   Government agencies, like the S.E.C., that provide statutory backing to accounting standards and enforce them on the producers, have veto powers - therefore possessing immense influencing capacity. (For example see Newman (1981b)).

7.   The supply of standards is the out-come of a socio-political process where economic variables play an important role. (Merino and Neimark (1982) and Cooper and Keim (1983)).

Accounting Regulations and Accounting Regulatory Policies:

We have noted that accounting standards are economic regulations and they are determined in a process which is similar to an economic market. Regulations may be prepared and imposed in various forms as shown in

Figure 5.1. In the case of accounting, U.K. follows the private self-regulation pattern. In the U.S.A. it is a mix between private self-regulation of the F.A.S.B. and the government (traditional) regulation of the S.E.C. In Australia the current situation reflects a transition from self-regulation of the profession to government (traditional) regulation. Generally speaking, the Governments of the respective countries have adopted specific regulatory policies. In case of self-regulation, the government adopts a policy of allowing the profession to regulate its members; whereas in the case of government regulation it adopts a policy of assuming the regulatory responsibility itself.

The nature of regulations differ in the two cases. For example, in terms of creating standards under self-regulation the professional bodies and their members can be the only direct participants, whereas government regulation necessitates the direct participation of other groups like managers, investors, etc. Similarly, enforcement of professional standards is possible only on the members of the profession, whereas government backed standards can be more widely enforced. Therefore, the nature of regulations differ depending on the regulatory policy adopted.

Mitnick (1980, p. 79), in this respect, pointed out that regulatory organizations, and the creation, implementation, and administration of regulation, may be understood as elements of the policy making process. Accordingly, if regulations are capable of imparting economic consequences, the overall regulatory policy, under which a body capable of preparing such regulations exists, can also be said to have economic consequences. Therefore, such a regulatory policy can be seen as an economic commodity in the same manner as economic regulations are treated. The creation, change and demise of such policies can also be studied from an economic market view point, as in the case of economic regulations. Consequently, if accounting standards can have the traits of economic regulations, so can the regulatory policy creating and enforcing them. The next section provides a model, in that framework, for the study of the creation of the regulatory policy under which the A.S.R.B. was established and empowered with its function of standard-setting.

The Preferred Model - A Market for Regulatory Policies:

The Public Choice model provides a scheme to explain the creation of an agency capable of establishing mandatory accounting standards in terms of a market.[94] The product in that market being the regulatory policy creating the agency (in this case the A.S.R.B.). The nature of the policy (specification of the organization and functions of the agency) is determined by the demand and supply functions of that market. Stigler (1971) asserted that public resources and powers to improve the economic status of economic groups provided a scheme of the demand for regulation[95] and the political process provided elements of a theory of supply of regulation. The demand and supply and other aspects of this market are discussed below.

The Premise:

Downs (1957a and 1957b) provided an economic theory of democracy and explained how democratic governments acted rationally to maximize political support. As a forerunner to Stigler's (1971), Posner's (1974) and Peltzman's (1976) arguments, his arguments were based on rational action and economic behaviour of individuals and the government. He

---

94   Watts and Zimmerman (1986) p. 21.

95   Stigler (1971) believed that regulation is actively sought by an industry, acquired by that industry and operated primarily for its benefits. But why would an industry solicit the coercive powers of a state? The reasons he provided were: (1) direct subsidy of money, (2) control over new entries, (3) power to restrict substitute products and services (4) price fixing. These political bonuses were not obtained by the industry in a pure profit-maximizing form. The political process erected certain limitations upon the exercise of cartel policies by an industry. These limitations were: (1) change in the distribution of control of the industry among firms. Small firms were sometimes numerous in number having greater political strength. This could change the market structure through the imposition of quotas, by the government, which would reduce the market share of large firms. (2) The procedural safeguards required of public process are considered to be costly. (3) The political process would automatically admit powerful outsiders to the industry's councils.

provided a rationale that laid down the premise for a market model of regulatory process - that individuals in government and society supplied and demanded regulation, respectively, primarily to fulfill their self-interest in a rational manner.[96] Emphasizing that premise Stigler (1971) stated: "We assume that political systems are rationally employed, which is to say that they are appropriate instruments for the fulfilment of desires of members of the society." (p. 4)

The Supply Side - Politicians:

Downs (1957a) argued that political parties in a democracy formulated policies and served interest groups strictly as a means of gaining votes in order to gain office. They sold policies for votes instead of products for money. Their social function - which was to formulate and carry out policies when in power as the government - was accomplished as a by-product of their private motive - which was to attain the income, power, and prestige of being in office (p. 137). In other words, Downs suggested that regulators supplied policies in their own interest[97] and in doing so served the interests of the groups or individuals who could affect their stay in office or in getting elected into an office.

Stigler's (1971) theory extended Downs's (1957a and 1957b) notion of government policy making into the economic regulation arena. Peltzman (1976) elaborated Stigler's theory and explained, that the choice of amount and type of regulation was the result of a political auction where the regulator served as the auctioneer and the successful bidder won the right to tax the wealth of others. The regulator sought to maximize the support of his programmes and balanced off the support received by the beneficiaries of regulation against the opposition to those

---

96   Also see Stigler (1971), Phillips and Zecher (1979) and Peirson and Ramsay (1983, pp. 294-295).

97   Also see Abrams and Settle (1970, pp. 247-248), Hawker *et al* (1979, p. 6 and pp. 22-23) and Mitnick (1980, p. 119 and 129).

programmes. The regulator maximized a majority M generated by[98]

$$M = n . f - (N - n) . h \quad \text{...... Equation 5.1.}$$

where

M = majority of support
n = number of potential voters in the beneficiary group
f = probability that a beneficiary will grant support
N = total number of potential voters
h = probability that he who is taxed (every non-n) will oppose the regulatory policy/regulation/ legislation

The variable f is a function of per capita net benefit that a potential voter (lobbyer) in the beneficiary group will derive if the regulation is granted in his favour. Whereas, h is a function of the per capita net loss of a potential voter (lobbyer) in the opposition group.

On the supply side, the study of the nature of the politicians as regulators is essential for this thesis, because the A.S.R.B. was basically created by the legislators of the Commonwealth and State Governments in Australia through their ministers in the Ministerial Council. The politician-regulators behaviour was further substantiated by Mitnick's (1980) review of studies in this area.[99] He noted that in a situation where politicians were the regulators, the central role on the supply side was played by the politicians (pp. 121-122).

Weller (1980) also highlighted the importance of political forces in the determination of public policy. He stated:

---

98   See Peltzman (1976), pp. 214-216 for further details.

99   Like Downs (1957a and 1957a), Mitnick (1980) revealed that politicians sought survival, that is reelection, by choosing regulatory policies to serve groups who may offer him support; and survival led to benefits such as salary, status and future security.

> The study of public policy must be concerned with political activity,
> with the development and content of policies, with the processes that
> shape them and the institutions which mold them. These factors simply
> cannot be readily separated. Whether individual studies concentrate on
> policy or processes or institutions, the drawing together of those
> threads is at the centre of our concern (p. 499).

Therefore, for this study, the behaviour of the members of the Ministerial
Council for Companies and Securities and other politicians before the
creation of the Council is a subject for further investigation.

The Demand Side:

Fainsod and Gordon (1941) felt that:

> The regulatory machinery ... does not operate in a vacuum. Important
> parties-in-interest have a vital stake in the formulation, execution, and
> - on occasion - frustration of public policy. They seek to make their
> influence felt. A realistic examination of the regulatory process must
> take them into account, consider their claims, their demands and the
> intensity of the pressure which they are able to bring to bear on the
> contest to determine policy. (p. 238)

Explaining the demand for policies, Downs (See Sutton, 1984) asserted
that a rational citizen will only allocate resources to influence
government policies directly if the expected benefits to him/her from
doing so exceeded the costs. That is when

$$P \ (U_A - U_B) - C > 0 \quad ...... \text{ Equation 5.2.}$$

Where,
$U_A =$ Utility of the preferred outcome,
$U_B =$ Utility of the alternate outcome,
$P =$ Probability/Certainty of getting the preferred outcome, and
$C =$ Cost of achieving the preferred outcome, that is cost of
organizing, lobbying, mitigating opposing, etc.

In other words the determinants of demand (for or against the regulation) are the expected benefits to be received from a policy measure or loss forgone by having or not having a particular regulation; and the cost of participating effectively in the regulatory process. An individual will lobby for a policy measure only if the expected net benefit from doing so is positive; and he/she will lobby against it if the net expected loss is positive.[100]

The Equilibrium:

Hirshleifer (1976 p. 243-244) specified that regulatory equilibrium was one where a balance was struck among the marginal costs and benefits of different interest groups affected and one which included the interests of the regulator. Watts and Zimmerman (1986) explained this as follows:

> Under the economic theories, the existing set of laws and regulations are the equilibrium result of two opposing forces - those who receive benefits and those who provided benefits. In equilibrium, those receiving the benefits are incurring costs at the margin just equal to their expected marginal benefits and those providing the wealth transfer are incurring costs at the margin just equal to the expected marginal reduction in the wealth transfer (p. 224).

Becker (1976) added that Peltzman's (1976) economic approach was a vote maximizing model in which the major assumption was that voters perceived the gains and losses from all policies. His and Peltzman's arguments implied that the regulations which survived the keen competition for votes tended to be relatively efficient ways to redistribute resources.

Recalling that regulation is a process, Mitnick (1980, pp. 138-139) noted that parties in the environment could disturb the equilibrium in their efforts to achieve their interests. Depending on the effectiveness of the parties' lobbying, the rational utility maximizing

---

100   The Downsian analysis used by Sutton (1984) also reiterated this.

regulators in their pursuit of gaining the greatest possible support for their programmes may change the existing regulatory policies. Therefore, unlike R. Walker's (1987) static view of a "captured" A.S.R.B., this model considers the state of the Board at a point in time as temporary, and that it will keep on changing in the future depending on the nature of the demand for and the supply of such changes.

Determinants of Pressure Group Size:

As they organize, gainers and losers face transactions and information costs. The size of these costs must be weighed against the net benefits of opposing or supporting the regulation. This relative balance will determine the probability of support or opposition given to the regulatory programme. The per capita net benefit or the net loss which are the determinants of the probability of demand for regulations [support (f) or opposition (h) in Equation 5.1.] in turn are also the determinants of the size of the beneficiary and opposing groups. In general the winning group would tend to be small,[101] with large relative per capita wealth arising from the establishment of the regulation. The large taxed group tends to include ineffective lobbyers, because of the high information and organization costs associated with successful lobbying and the problems of free riders in large groups. Although there may be some economies of scale in lobbying, diminishing returns to group size and the dilution of the per capita gains or losses often render small groups more effective in the political process. The regulators are also likely to maximize their political support by concentrating benefits on a few and taxing a large group. The large taxed group normally bears a small per capita tax and its members have little incentive to organize against the tax (that is the policy imposing the tax).[102]

---

101   Compared to the number of all participating and non-participating constituents.

102   See Peltzman (1976) pp. 212-213, and Phillips and Zecher (1981) pp. 61-62.

Demand by Interest Groups (Cartels):

Mitnick (1980) surveyed the "group" private interest theories of regulation. He concluded that regulation was seen as a process; seeking government control and the use of its powers was the prize variable in group conflicts; and supply of regulation, including its form and effects, could be responsive to group demands. Wells (1978) explored this issue in accounting standard-setting. Recognizing the economic regulation nature of accounting standards and using Posner's (1974) cartel view, he argued that standards, like most commodities, were apparently sought through private cartels (for example the professional accounting bodies) or through government regulation.

Posner's (1974) extension to Stigler's theory elaborated the reasons for interest groups (cartels) seeking regulations. His arguments were based on the economic theory of cartels. He sought to explain that regulation was demanded when cartels failed to serve its members or when cartelization was not possible. The value of cartelization was greater in cases of a less elastic demand for the industry's product and the more costly or slower, was new entry into the industry. Costs of cartelization were the seller's cost of arriving at a price and the cost of enforcing the agreement on outsiders or free riders. The benefits of having cartels were raising price above competitive levels, price fixation, barriers to entry and exemptions from anti-trust laws. The per capita benefits of cartelization were higher and costs of maintaining cartels were less if the size of members was small and if the members had homogeneous interests. A large number of parties with low group cohesiveness and asymmetry of interests, that is, lack of goal congruence, led to a lack of participation among members in an industry or society which made the cost of cartelization excessive, discouraging large cartels and encouraging interest groups or smaller homogeneous cartels to seek regulatory solutions.

Therefore, like cartelization, in a political process regulation can protect industries by bringing about shared rules of behaviour - rules which ensure higher than competitive rates, protection from potential competitors and so on (Mitnick, 1980, p. 117).

Interest Groups in the Demand for a Government Sponsored Accounting Standard-Setting Body:

In this thesis the behaviour of the accounting professional bodies as an interest group in the regulatory process is an object of study, but interpretation of its activities cannot be made in isolation, without considering the activities of other groups. Specially, when we have noted the scope of influence of other parties in the A.S.R.B.'s regulatory framework. Such a study was also emphasized by Mitnick (1980, p. 109). Accordingly, we discuss here the expected behaviour of all the interest groups identified in Chapters 2 and 3. We have already discussed the behaviour of politicians on the supply side in the previous section. We have also identified the broad reasons of demand for regulations in that section. Here we discuss the behaviour of those on the demand side.

Bureaucrats:

We noted in Chapter 2 and 3 that the bureaucrats in the N.C.S.C. and the C.A.C.s were one of the beneficiaries of the establishment of the A.S.R.B. Their capacity to enforce the "true and fair view" requirement of the Companies Act and Codes was expected to be enhanced due to the mandatory nature of the approved accounting standards and the perceived gap that they filled in the absence of a legislative definition of the "true and fair view". The N.C.S.C. and its delegates had also been delegated the power to enforce such standards, which could alleviate the problems faced before in the area of standards enforcement.

The improvement in their capacity as law enforcers leads us to believe that they were one of the major participants in the A.S.R.B.'s creation process. Hawker, et al (1979) described the behaviour of bureaucrats in a policy-making process as follows:

> Behaviour of individual bureaucrats are directed both by organizational constraints and the need to participate in the game of bureaucratic policies. ... Bureaus tend to maximize their budgets, expand their programmes, reward their staffs, and defend their own turf. Bureaucratic advise is not disinterested; bureaucratic battles are a vital contribution to the mix of factors giving shape to policy (p. 14).

They added:

> Public servants are often not pliable or neutral. They are often involved in initiating policy, aggregating demands, and settling means, ... (p. 30).

In respect of disclosure regulation, Watts (1977) described bureaucratic behaviour in terms of crisis avoidance. He stated:

> I assume bureaucrats appointed to administer corporate disclosure laws maximize their own expected utilities. The bureaucrats' careers and hence their expected utilities are affected by the likelihood of being blamed for future "crises". Thus, I expect bureaucrats to consider the effects of alternative regulations on the likelihood of blame when they draft and interpret regulations on corporate financial statements (p. 67).

He elaborated further that:

> The S.E.C. was established as a "solution" to the crisis "caused" by inadequate corporate disclosure. One of the "inadequacies" of the disclosure was the diversity of accounting procedures used by corporate management. The bureaucrats at the S.E.C. were motivated to reduce the diversity to avoid the blame for future crises (p. 70).

This can also be backed by Winsen's (1980) argument:

> Since regulatory agencies ... prefer to minimize risk and criticism should the future turn out to be worse than expected, they tend to require conservative, uniform procedures ... (p. 250)

Although bureaucratic crisis management is used by the bureaucrats to their own advantages but it has its limitations. Watts (1977) explained it as follows:

> The bureaucrats involved in reducing the diversity of accounting procedures have conflicting incentives. They have an incentives to appear to reduce diversity in order to avoid blame. They also have an incentive to avoid imposing costs on corporate managers and other individuals. Those managers could lobby with members of Congress to offset the bureaucrats' decisions, to reduce the S.E.C.'s budget etc. The bureaucrats will choose the course which maximizes their own expected utilities (p. 70)

From the arguments placed here we can expect that the bureaucrats, to strengthen their position as company regulators, played a substantial role in the creation of the Board.

Accounting Profession:

Professional accounting bodies satisfy the criteria of cartels.[103] Wells (1978) emphasized this as follows:

> ... professional organizations, such as the Australian Society of Accountants, the various Institutes of Chartered Accountants and the American Institute of Certified Public Accountants have the characteristics of economic cartels. They function for the benefit of their members and restrict entry to the market. They are also costly to maintain, and as Posner points out in relation to most large cartels (p. 344), there is a substantial 'free rider' effect. (p. 3)

Accounting standards assist in achieving certain benefits, and standards which are imposed on the clientele of its members adds certainty to these benefits. Such benefits are achieved at a cost and will only be sought by the cartel if the expected per capita benefits of its members exceed their expected per capita costs. These benefits and costs are explained as follows:

---

103   Buckley (1980) and Willmott (1986) explained the nature and objectives of accounting bodies, which is in conformity with Posner's (1974) view of cartels.

Buckley (1980) and Willmott (1986), using the group behaviour theory, explained why these bodies demand financial disclosure standards to serve their interests. They basically argued that, like any other professional body, the accounting bodies' primary interest was to achieve higher prices for its products. They could do this in two ways: (1) restricting supply and (2) increasing demand for its services. They argued that accounting standards could help both ways.

Supply is controlled, in part, by limiting the number of sellers in the market. This can be done by generating increasingly complex standards which on the one hand raises the "absolute cost" of entry and on the other hand improves the qualitative outlook of the profession. In either case members can justify higher prices.

Demand is generated by issuing new compulsory accounting rules, preferably mandatory ones which can be enforced on those who are current and potential customers of its members' services. In this manner the cartel can not only improve and ensure the demand of its current clientele but also expand its clientele. This raises the demand curve and also makes it less elastic which in turn helps increase prices of services.[104] See Figure 5.2.

---

104   Watts and Zimmerman (1986, pp. 321-324) reviewed the various ways of increasing demand for auditors services through regulation and threatened regulations in U.S.A. Those were (1) the 1933 securities act's requirement of auditing by "independent or certified auditors. This and subsequent S.E.C. and S.E.C. supported F.A.S.B. requirements have broadened the nature of audit and increased the demand for auditing. (2) Accounting standards have added a new service to the list of auditors services. There is now demand for lobbying which the auditors can provide - but at a cost. (3) Increasingly complicated standards also increase the demand for auditing services and the demand for auditors.

Figure 5.2.: The impact of accounting standards on the pricing of accountants' services

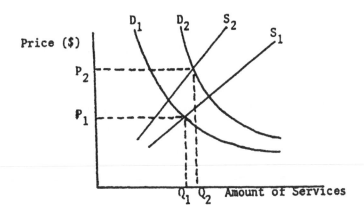

P_1 = Price of services with no new standards.
P_2 = Price of services after imposition of new standards.
Q_1 = Quantity of Services with no new standards.
Q_2 = Quantity of Services after imposition of new standards.
S_1 = Supply curve with no new standards.
S_2 = Supply curve after imposition of new standards.
D_1 = Demand curve with no new standards.
D_2 = Demand curve after imposition of new standards.

The demand for a government created standard-setting body is derived from the demand for mandatory standards. Such a body, under the *de facto* control of the accounting profession, serves essentially three purposes. First, its standards are mandatory and enforceable on members and non-members. Secondly, as a public body most of its costs and the cost of enforcing standards is borne by the Government. Thirdly, the profession can ensure that the standards approved by it are not contrary to the interests of its members.

From those remarks Posner's cartel argument can also be noted in the case of the A.S.R.B. For example, Stamp (1979, p. 5) pointed out that unenforceable standards (of the profession) were non-standards and R. Walker (1985) alleged that the A.S.R.B. was essentially the product of a political compromise to gain both government and constituency support for enforcing professional accounting standards (p. 21). The A.S.R.B.'s approval of professional standards not only guaranteed enforcement but also widened the sphere of enforcement to include company managers and auditors who were non-members of the Australian professional accounting bodies. This was a far less costly means of expanding the dominance of the professional accounting bodies than trying to recruit those outsiders into the profession's cartel. Such a dominance is expected to secure the position of professional body members as accountants and the professional accounting standards as approved standards.

The approved accounting standards could reduce the risk involved in authenticating accounts. Such standard could fill the void in the financial reporting requirements of the Companies Code regarding uniform accounting rules, subject to the over riding requirement of "true and fair view". In that respect Winsen (1980, p. 250) noted that accountants preferred conservative and uniform reporting procedures to minimize risk and criticism.

The cost of achieving those benefits are incurred through the cost of organizing and the cost of enforcing the standards on outsiders.

The per capita cost to members of organizing reduces with the increase in size of the organization, but increases with the heterogeneity of the organization. On the other hand per capita benefits reduce with the increase in the size of the organization. These factors help determine and limit group size to a level where the marginal cost from organizing is equal to its marginal benefits (Watts and Zimmerman, 1986, pp. 225-226).

The per capita cost to members of enforcing the standards on non-members, like company directors, through government support, depends on the cost of being informed about government action; the cost of lobbying; and also the cost of organizing for that purpose, say the cost of running the A.A.R.F. (Watts and Zimmerman, 1986, p. 222).

Normally those costs are borne by the members in the form of membership fees and other related expenses. The members will vote for additional accounting standards to a point where their marginal cost for acquiring such standards are equal to their marginal benefits.

In terms of cost and benefits of accounting regulations the behaviour of the accounting profession in the regulatory process has been described by Wells (1978) in the following manner.

Traditionally, regulation of the accounting profession has come from within. This is characteristic of all professions. Codes of ethics, self-discipline and the exercise of judgment together with some recognized proficiency provide the justification for the privilege position enjoyed by the members of the profession. This reinforces the suggestion that regulation may be viewed as an economic good. The maintenance of the professional structure involves significant costs to its members (in the form of high educational standards for entrance, annual dues, time and effort devoted to professional activities) and to the public (in the form of registration requirements, charges for professional services, and other monopoly provisions). The continuing high level of demand from people wanting to enter the profession, and the continued acceptance by the public of the privileges accorded to members of the profession are evidence of the benefits perceived by those groups from belonging to and tolerating the profession, respectively. Clearly the benefits are seen to exceed the costs at both the individual and public levels. (p. 4-5)

Wells (1978, pp. 5-7) also supported Posner's (1974) argument that accounting cartels would seek government regulation or government support for its regulations if the scope of such regulations extended beyond the profession itself. For example, he explained that it was easier to gain agreement for auditing standards because they were internal regulations and compliance with them was a part of the cost of belonging to the cartel. As long as benefits exceeded costs those regulations would be accepted. As for accounting standards, they extend beyond the cartels and compliance with them is expected from company managers in addition to that of the members of the accounting bodies. The managers also weigh their options on cost-benefit terms and would not accept standards which impose a net cost, even if it is accepted by the members of the accounting bodies. To reap the benefits of such standards, the accounting bodies have two options open to them - to include the managers in their cartel or to seek government support for their regulation. Since it is difficult to imagine what benefit would flow to the managers by joining the accounting cartel, the second option of government regulation is quite obvious. This option also promises benefits to investors or other members of the public, presumably in the form of avoided losses or minimized risks, with no direct costs, and thus generate public support for such regulations. This, Wells (1978) noted, has been the pattern of developments in the U.S.A., U.K. and Australia.

The Companies:

We have noted earlier that companies or company directors are the prime targets of accounting standards within enhanced enforceability such as the approved accounting standards. They certainly were not one of the beneficiaries of a board which catered to greater regulation of companies. Companies, perhaps, could even consider the creation of the Board as a part of the increasing trend towards regulation that followed the company collapses of the 1960s and 1970s. The Uniform Companies Acts, the Corporate Affairs Commissions in the States, the Interstate Corporate Affairs Commission and finally the formation of the Co-operative Scheme for Companies and Securities with a national commission, the N.C.S.C., are enough proof of a growth and tightening of company regulations in Australia since the 1960s. In this respect Winsen (1980) had this to say:

> Perhaps Australia has never before witnessed such pressures as appear to exist now for the government to become directly involved in the regulation of financial reporting standards used by limited liability companies . The formation of the National Companies and Securities Commission (N.C.S.C.) and the deliberations of the Committee of Inquiry into the Australia Financial System (CIAFS) may assist such pressures to "bear fruit" (p. 232).

Therefore we can expect considerable concern by company directors and managers towards any form of new regulatory measures.

We have noted in the third section of this chapter that the companies, managers or preparers of accounting information do participate and lobby in the preparation of accounting standards. The lobbying activities of preparers or companies have been noted and/or described, for example, by Watts (1977), Wells (1978), Watts and Zimmerman (1978), Hussein (1981), Johnson and Messier (1982), Sutton (1984) and Kelly (1985). We have noted that companies with different traits will lobby differently. For example those which are more interested in lobbying can be expected to be large (Watts, 1977, pp. 68-69, Sutton 1984, p. 93 and Kelly, 1985, p. 629); directly affected by the standard through earning changes, political costs, cost of information production and higher cost of non-compliance (Watts and Zimmerman, 1978, pp. 115-116, Hussein, 1981, p. 28, Sutton, 1984, p. 81, p. 86 and p. 93 and Kelly, 1985, p. 629); undiversified producers (Sutton, 1984, p. 93); effect on management compensation plans (Watts and Zimmerman, 1978, pp. 116); and other specific company characteristics such as management ownership and leverage (Kelly, 1985, p. 621 and p. 629). In this respect Watts and Zimmerman (1978) emphasized two important aspects of accounting standard-setting. First is that the management plays a central role in the determination of standards and second is that the management lobbies on accounting standards on the basis of self-interest to maximize their own utility through maintenance or enhancement of their compensation.

Since we noted that standards have economic consequences and the management lobby mainly in the light of those consequences, we expect the managers to lobby in the case of a standard-setting body, provided it perceives such consequences being imparted from them. We have already noted in the fourth section of this chapter that a regulatory body, such as the A.S.R.B., being part of a regulatory policy, could be seen to have the capacity to impose economic consequences. Accordingly, it is expected in this study to find that the companies and their representative organizations did participate in the creation of the Board. The effect of such participation is already evident in the extent of the representation of companies on the Board.

Others:

Apart from the major interest groups identified above, we have noticed members of the Board who were academics or from the stock exchange. Johnson and Messier also noted the participation of the financial/security analysts in the standard-setting process of the F.A.S.B. Again, Jensen (1977) pointed out the role of the press in the regulatory process.

It is not within the scope of this research nor is it possible to briefly deal with the role of the academia in accounting research and provision of guidance. Their contribution has been mainly pedantic and persuasive in value. This was also pointed out by Mr. F. Walker the N.S.W. Attorney-General when he warned the profession

> ... never to underestimate the influence of academics on Government. Great change is initiated from their writings and they exert a tremendous influence on public opinion and our bureaucracy (Quoted by Winsen, 1980, p. 247)

Before the concept of accounting pronouncements and regulation developed, they provided leadership in respect of accounting methods. One example of the latter in Australia is the role played by Sir Alexander Fitzgerald in guiding the infant profession with regards to practical problems of accounting practice (For example see Zeff 1973 and Chapter 6). Having borne the responsibility of guiding the profession in technical matters it is quite normal to expect the academics to participate in the setting of accounting standards and the creation of standard-setting organizations.

Stock exchanges, as we shall see in Chapter 6, have adopted the practice of establishing their own disclosure rules in addition to those provided by company law. Their rule setting efforts are directed towards the establishment of order in the securities market which in turn serves the interests of its members through the stability and growth in such markets (Discussed in more detail in Chapter 6). Although it is in the interest of the stock exchanges to have proper measurement standards for the disclosure of financial information in the securities markets, traditionally they have left that responsibility to the accounting profession. Notwithstanding such a convention, the members of the stock exchanges are expected to observe the accounting standard-setting process closely, and if possible, through the Board's review procedures.

The security analysts do benefit under a regulatory process which mandates disclosure of information preferably "true and fair" because it reduces their cost of information procurement and validation. Phillips and Zecher (1981, p. 44) have noted the interest of the analysts towards securities laws which enhanced compulsory disclosure. Since the approved accounting standards mandated the use of certain methods of disclosure and could also require disclosure of certain information not disclosed in the earlier regime, it is in the interest of the securities analysts to have a Board which is capable of producing such standards.

As for the press Watts (1977, p. 65) argued that if individual voters had little incentive to demand information on the effects of their representative's actions and related political phenomena, then the media had little incentive to supply such information. As a consequence he predicted that news programs and coverage would provide simple explanations of the political process: explanations which entertained rather than informed. He argued that crises (impressions of impending disaster caused by natural phenomena or by individuals) are entertainment and thus the news media had incentives to create crisis. As crises are responsible for initiating demand for accounting standards (For example see Wells, 1978) and as the press plays a role in creating such crises, we may notice that the press is also partly responsible for the creation of the Board.

The motive of the media in producing news was identified by Cohen and Young (1973, p. 97). They noticed that the media manufactured news using a manipulative model to suit the needs of its ownership. In an attempt to make news more entertaining, the media has often been critisized for mis-reporting. For example, the editor of The Chartered Accountant in Australia once criticised the financial press of trying to emphasize particular items through the choice of headings, not reporting important facts related to the reported news or quoting information out of the context of the news it was related to (The Chartered Accountant in Australia, August, 1971, p. 2).

As for the beneficiary of the A.S.R.B.'s approved accounting standards the investor, both small and institutional, Winsen (1980, p. 247) noted that in recent investigations, such as the Committee of Inquiry into the Australia Financial System, no such party complained about the alleged deficiencies in corporate financial reports. He also found from recent studies in the U.S.A. that there was no desire on the part of investors for greater accounting regulation. The only reason suggested by such studies was that the investors felt that adequate financial data was available.

Another reason for the lack of demand from the investors for more regulations in accounting may be because such investors are numerically large in number and the benefits or costs of such regulation to them may be insignificant and un-identifiable. According to Wilson's (1974, 1980) argument (See Davis and Menon, 1987, pp. 191-192), we may say that the benefits and costs to the beneficiaries of greater accounting regulation are diffused as compared to that of other parties. Hence, they do not find it expedient to lobby either for or against such regulations.

Application of the Model:

The above regulatory model is based on the notion that regulatory policies are adopted on the basis of regulation as a process and the instances of demand and supply for the policies occur within that process. Since the whole process can be cyclical and a never ending one and as the objective of this study is only to investigate the establishment of the A.S.R.B. and its functions, we need to explain only a part of the regulatory process. The identification of this segment and the method of applying the demand-supply model, within this segment, is explained in this section.

Determining the Time Period of the Study:

The life cycle theories of regulation reviewed by Mitnick (1980) indicate that regulation is not created as a static instrument and its creation itself takes time which can be, according to Bernstein (1955, pp. 74-79), as long as twenty or more years. The A.S.R.B. as a regulatory organization is the subject of discussion here. As Mitnick (1980) has identified Bernstein's (1955) life cycle theory as a suitable framework to describe the general pattern of evolution of regulatory agencies including their functions, that theory is used to identify the time frame necessary for this study. An out-line of Bernstein's model is given in Figure 5.3. Intuitively, the first two stages of that model seems to cover significant aspects of the origin of the regulatory policy creating the organization and functions of the Board.

The *Gestation* phase encompasses a period of rising distress leading to the formation and activation of groups who demand legislative remedy to protect their interests. After a struggle, a statute covering "vague language" and reflecting "unsettled national economic policy" is passed. It is a compromise, which largely succeeds in passage only because of crisis or near-crisis conditions. (Bernstein, 1955, pp. 74-79)

Figure 5.3: Bernstein's (1955) Life Cycle of Regulatory Commissions

Gestation:
- twenty years or more
- sparked by crisis
- marked by group struggle
- regulation is compromise
- regulatory statute out of date when enacted
- regulation emphasizes short-term over long-term considerations

Youth:
- crusading, aggressive in conflictual environment
- agency lacks experience
- agency has vague objectives
- untested legal powers are tested, but legal process is incomprehensible to public
- experienced, well-organized opposition from industry
- loss of public support and political leadership as groups who pushed for regulation retire; regulated industry successful in rewarding regulators and affecting attitudes

Maturity:
- passivity/apathy; adjusts to conflict it faces
- agency lacks Congressional and public support
- acts as manager rather than policeman
- relies on precedent and routine
- maintains good relations with industry
- most of time spent in litigation
- parochial professionalism
- backlog of cases develops
- Congress and Budget Office refuse appropriation increases
- "becomes a captive of the regulated groups"

Old Age:
- debility
- procedures sanctified
- "working agreement" with industry to maintain status quo
- "recognized protector of agency"
- Congress and Budget Office refuse funds
- staff declines in quality; poor management
- agency fails to keep up with societal change

But scandal/emergency/crisis can trigger new drive for regulation: cycle repeats

Source: Mitnick (1980), p.46

During the *Youth* phase, the agency with its unspecified frame of reference has to operate in a conflictual environment. Lacking administrative experience, possessing vague objectives and untested legal powers, the agency faces well-organized experienced interference from the regulated and other interested groups. This leads to a struggle to determine the scope of its powers including an effort by those groups to determine appointments to the agency. (Bernstein, 1955, pp. 79-86).

As mentioned in the second section Mitnick (1980, pp. 81-83) identified five stages of the process of regulatory origin: (1) access; (2) decision; (3) implementation; (4) administration and (5) impacts. The access stage resembles Bernstein's gestation phase. This phase ends with the decision of whether to regulate or not. If the decision is to go ahead and regulate then the access phase is followed by implementation and administration. The implementation and early steps towards administration approximately covers Bernstein's youth phase. A study of the initial impact of those stages can give evidence of the nature of the outcome of the demand-supply process within those phases.

Administration or the operational set-up of the Board has already been reviewed in Chapters 2 and 3. Access, decision and implementation stages are the object of study in the later chapters. Although important, a detailed study of the impact of having a board is beyond the scope of this study. It is also not possible to determine the impact adequately till the Board has produced a substantial number of standards.

In the case of the A.S.R.B., as in other cases (Mitnick, 1980, p. 49) it will be difficult to clearly identify the points where those phases (Bernstein's life cycle's) exactly commence and end. Therefore, the best possible way of determining the time period of gestation and youth is to include all major events which led to the creation of accounting standards in Australia which subsequently led to a search for regulatory solutions. The adoption of disclosure standards can be traced as far back as the enactment of Companies Acts and Codes in the Colonies in Australia. The gestation period for a regulator policy leading to mandatory standards in Australia can be considered to have commenced with events leading to the demand for and supply of disclosure rules under those Acts and Codes. Therefore, the history of those rules is briefly studied first (in Chapter 6) followed by a detailed review of the evolution of accounting pronouncements and standards (in Chapter 7). For that reason, although this study commences from the second half of the nineteenth century, it is more elaborate from the time the profession started releasing its pronouncements.

On the other hand, the gestation period can be said to have ended with the establishment of the A.S.R.B. on January 1, 1984. The establishing process of the Board did not end with its creation because most of its functions were specified after its establishment. The Board's formation conforms to Bernstein's description. It was born with a vague and heavily contested set of powers. And, in fact, the legislation (The 1983 amendments to the Companies Act 1981) recognizing the Board did not specify any function for the Board. The functions were eventually set by the Board (see <u>A.S.R.B. Release 100, 200 and 201</u>) with the approval of the Ministerial Council. Since the establishment phase of the Board continued up to the installation of its functions in 1985 and its initial settling down activities (For example, see R. Walker, 1987), this study continues up to the end of 1986 to cover those aspects.

Identifying Events Initiating Demand:

Although regulation can be recognized as a process, the actual instances of demand and supply for regulatory solutions, like the creation of agencies and empowering those agencies with certain functions, are responses to certain events [or, as Bernstein (1955, in both gestation and youth phases), Wells (1978, p. 17 and 18) and Mitnick (1980, pp. 168-169 and 204-205) have termed them as *crises*]. For accounting standards Wells (1978, pp. 15-18) elaborated this issue in terms of his crisis theory (see Wells, 1976). He explained that certain upheavals, like company failures exposed certain shortcomings of accounting practitioners. Such crises created a loss of confidence amongst the practitioners. The community became aware of professional deficiencies and their criticisms loosened the traditional and conservative views of the accountants. This made it politically inexpedient to oppose proposals for overcoming the deficiencies, and a politically acceptable alternative was adopted.

Wells' (1978) C.C.A. example was a good representation of the combined application of the crisis theory and the demand-supply model explained above. It clearly supported the view that the crisis theory can assist in the application of that model. In that example, he explained that exceptionally high inflation led to crises within professional accounting and managerial circles. Professional accountants faced lack of confidence in their existing accounting practices; whereas managers sought tax relief in the wake of high inflation. Demands were made by both professional accountants and managers, on economic grounds, for the adoption of C.C.A. standards. Government committees in different countries reviewed the situation but failed to provide sufficient tax relief. Managers realized that the forthcoming benefits were insufficient to meet C.C.A. costs and reversed their demand for C.C.A. standards into an opposition to it. Eventually, the policy makers refrained from supplying a C.C.A. standard because the opposition for it surpassed its demand.

Watts (1977, pp. 65-67) also explicated the role of crises in the creation of regulation. He argued that politicians (in addition to the press, see above) created crises and then came to the rescue with simple legislative solutions. He noted that crises had a long history in justifying legislative actions which affected corporations. He accepted that events, such as stock market crash were of significant economic consequence, but he found that the simplistic explanations forwarded by legislators to justify legislation to remedy the crisis were of doubtful validity. For example he challenged the blaming of the crash on the lack of disclosure and perceived the regulation of disclosure as a convenient "solution" provided by the political entrepreneurs.

To be systematic this pattern of crises leading to a demand for and supply of regulatory solutions, is studied in this thesis in the light of the elements and factors of regulatory entry described by the Cobb and Elder (1972). Their agenda building model, shown in Figure 5.4.

provided a detailed insight into the process of issues, generated by crises, which entered the regulatory agenda.

Other Issues:

As specified in the model the major aspects of this study are investigations of the supply side and the demand side and the process which led to the equilibrium/outcome of an A.S.R.B. Although this study involves a long time frame, it mainly concentrates on the issue of demand for and supply of mandatory standards. Importance is given to the debate on mandatory standards, especially in the light of the Co-operative Scheme for Companies and Securities. That scheme was drawn-up to provide a basis for uniform companies law throughout Australia and still the government regulation of companies in Australia is normally conducted within its framework.

Applying the model to the creation of the A.S.R.B., it is explained that the Co-operative Scheme for Companies and Securities provided a mechanism for the supply of the A.S.R.B. Such a mechanism developed, over time, to correct the perceived failure in the market for securities due to suspected information asymmetry - specially the asymmetry in the quality of financial information made available to investors by listed companies. Although initially the intentions of the regulators in supplying the A.S.R.B. could have been to correct information asymmetry, the supply of the Board, applying our hypothesis, has been based on the demands for it by effectively participating interest groups. The demand for the Board is shown to be derived from the demand for mandatory accounting standards.

"Pros and Cons" of the Model:

The model is aimed at explaining that the A.S.R.B. is the outcome of a pluralistic political process where policies are set on the strength of the demands of effectively participating interest groups and to fulfill the needs of the suppliers - regulators. It has the following advantages and limitations.

Figure 5.4: Cobb and Elder's Agenda - Building Model

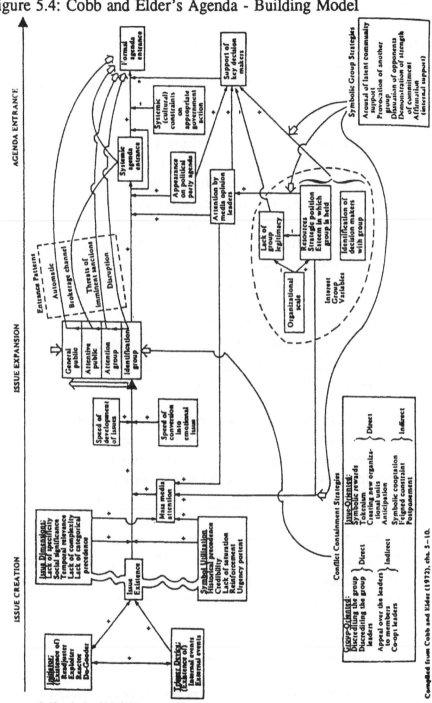

Source: Mitnick (1980), p.170

Advantages:

The model described above is a comprehensive one with a powerful explanatory capacity. Other than using the simple and neutral notions of economics,[105] that is demand and supply, it has some other important features.

First, this model has been reinforced by other theories which have already been used and tested in explaining various elements of the regulatory process (for example see Mitnick, 1980). The model has been developed keeping in view the drawbacks of other models. It has been constructed in a manner that it draws its essence from Stigler (1971), Posner (1974) and Peltzman's (1976) economic theory of regulation and it is also strengthened by other theories. In this manner the weaknesses that existed in the economic theory have been minimized.

Second, the concept of regulation as a dynamic process has been adopted. This concept is essential for an adequate study of any kind of regulation because of the active environment (for example see Fainsod (1940), Bernstein (1955), and Mitnick (1980)).[106]

Third, within the process notion, the model includes most of the necessary steps and elements needed for this study. This has been possible because it looks at the creation of a regulatory body and its functions as elements of a dynamic regulatory process and not as static issues.

Fourth, the demand-supply view adopted in the model is applicable to all stages and for all elements of the regulatory policy. For example, it can describe the creation, change or demise of the regulatory agency or its functions, or the whole policy framework.

---

105   Some other features have already been explicated in Chapter 4.

106   For a review of theories using the concept of regulation as a process see Mitnick (1980, Chapters 2 and 3).

Fifth, its premise, rational choice on the basis of self-interest, is a basic human trait and as shown by Mueller (1976) and Mitnick (1980, Chapter 3) it has been adopted in many theories of regulation and public policy. As opposed to "public interest" theories, in which regulations which are not serving the "public interest" are considered anomalous, this model explicates that such outcomes are logical products of the actions of self-interested regulators and demanders of regulations. Therefore, regulatory policies are treated as outputs of economic actions of interest groups and individuals.

Sixth, it helps in identifying the interest groups and in explaining their behavioural pattern. (The selection of a sufficiently long time period, as in this study and unlike R. Walker's (1987) study, can be helpful in identifying all major interest groups who were active before and after the establishment of a regulatory policy).

Seventh, it is applicable to any regulatory method, that is regulation by legislature, by regulatory agencies, etc.

Finally, as Mitnick (1980, p. 111) claimed, a model of this nature exposes the mechanism that functions within the regulatory "black box". This mechanism has normally been described vaguely by accounting policy experts as the social choice/political/socio-economic/ evolutionary/revolutionary process or they have narrowly concluded that it is a "captured" mechanism under the complete control of the accounting profession. It has been recognized earlier that the regulatory process is complex. This model can help in conducting a more objective study of the various aspects of the regulatory process, than the ones that can be conducted under other models.

Limitations:

As mentioned in sections 1 and 2, the complexity of regulatory processes makes it difficult to construct a complete regulatory model (Also see Hawker et al, 1979, pp. 22-23). Although, this model has been made as comprehensive as possible it may still have many weaknesses. Apart from that, the comprehensiveness of the model can also lead to an enormous task which may have to be covered in more than one study. Adding to this limitation, it is quite challenging to provide sufficient empirical evidence for all the intricate details of the regulatory process, as described by this model, in a single study (for example see Posner (1974)).

Finally, the demand and supply framework incorporated in the model in no way implies that the model represents a perfect economic market. Stigler (1971) held that in market decisions, individuals decided on their own and their decisions, unlike political decisions, affected the market to the extent of the market share they controlled. Political decisions were considered different from market decisions because they were made simultaneously by a large number of persons and their representatives and included both interested and uninterested voters. This did not allow participation in proportion to the extent of their interest. Such political decisions imposed costs, like the cost of affecting minorities, political party costs, campaign contributions of industries and free riders.

Summary:

Following are the salient features of the model described above:

1.   Regulatory policies are initiated by perceived crises.

2.   Regulatory policies are demanded.

3.   Regulatory policies are supplied.

4.   "Self-interest" is the motive behind the demand and supply of regulatory policies.

5.   Resulting features of regulatory policies are the equilibrium outcomes of the demand and supply functions.

6.   Regulatory policies represent a certain state, at a point in time, in a dynamic regulatory process. It is subject to change and is related to the preceding and future states.

7.   The regulatory process has at least two participants, one demander and one supplier.

8.   A reasonably long time interval should be used to identify all major participants in the regulatory process.

9.   All major participants should be identified, their roles in the policy outcome understood and their behaviour in the process preceding the outcome analyzed before any conclusions are drawn about a regulatory policy.

Despite all its limitations and weaknesses, comparatively this model is more powerful than the other regulatory theories that have been applied in accounting, as shown in the previous chapter. Hence, it will be used as a framework for describing the establishment of the A.S.R.B. and its regulatory functions.

Chapter 6

THE HISTORY OF ACCOUNTING REGULATORY POLICIES
IN AUSTRALIA UP TO 1970

Introduction:

Chapters 2 and 3 outlined the nature of the regulatory policy for accounting (the organization and functions of the A.S.R.B. and its regulatory framework) adopted in Australia since the creation of the A.S.R.B. As explained in Chapter 5, a regulatory policy is the outcome of a regulatory process. Various types of company financial disclosure regulatory policies were adopted in Australia prior to the adoption of the concept of mandatory accounting standards and the creation of the A.S.R.B. A review of those policies is conducted here to gain an idea of how they had been adopted, what were the sources of regulations, what forms of regulations were supplied and why they were supplied. The discussion mainly covers the period before the 1970s, that is up to the time when professional accounting standards started gaining prominence as financial disclosure regulations.[107]

Section 2 of the Chapter identifies various major forms of company accounting regulations in Australia. In Section 3, the events and crises leading to accounting regulations and the nature of demand for and supply of various forms of accounting regulation prior to the inception of the idea of government backed mandatory accounting standards is studied. In Section 4 the discussion is summarized and the state of accounting regulation around 1970 is specified.

---

107   It is difficult to provide distinct starting and ending dates for each regulatory cycle because regulatory processes are continuous and new regulatory policies may only supplement the existing ones, as we shall see has happened in the case of financial disclosure.

It should be noted at the outset that it is neither the purpose of this chapter nor is it within the scope of this thesis to provide a detailed history of accounting regulations in Australia. Although the Appendix 1 to 5 of this thesis venture into such history, the information accumulated in them are used only as reference for gaining a better insight into the changing pattern of financial disclosure regulatory policies adopted over the years in Australia.

Forms and Sources of Accounting Regulation in Australia:

Mitnick (1980, Chapters 6, 7 and 8) classified the types of regulatory designs into two classes: (1) Regulation through directives and (2) Regulation through incentives. Within the first type Peirson and Ramsay (1983) identified three main sources of accounting rules in Australia: (1) Government legislation and the rules of the N.C.S.C. under such legislation; (2) professional accounting standards jointly set by the A.S.A. and I.C.A.A., and (3) the Official Listing Requirements of the A.A.S.E. In addition to those sources, Graham, Jager and Taylor (1984, pp. 4-8) pointed out three other sources of rules: companies' memorandum and articles of association; trust deeds; case law or court sanctions.

As for the second type of regulation - regulation by incentive - only one such regulation of reasonable importance exists in Australia. That is the A.I.M. Annual Report Award.[108] It rewards companies by recognizing the degree of excellence achieved by them in reporting with a view to enhancing the quality of company disclosure, thereby regulating company disclosure through incentives.

Amongst those forms of rules the following five are considered here as forms of externally imposed accounting regulation. They have been listed below along with their sources.

---

108   See Mitnick (1980) Chapters 6, 7 and 8 for a discussion on regulation by incentive.

Table 6.1.: Forms of Accounting Regulation in Australia and their Sources.

Form of Regulation		Main Sources
(1)	Case law	Courts.
(2)	Government legislation and rules.	The Legislature and its delegates, like the N.C.S.C.
(3)	The Official Listing Requirements for companies listed in stock exchanges.	The A.A.S.E.
(4)	The professional accounting standards.	Jointly set by the A.S.A. and the I.C.A.A. through the A.A.R.F.
(5)	The A.I.M. Annual Report Award.	The A.I.M.

All of the above fit the definition of "regulation" specified in Chapter 5. They come from sources which are separate from the regulated entities, the companies, and they can restrict or enhance the choice of the form and substance of company disclosure. Although companies can influence the outcome of such regulatory sources, they cannot individually control those sources. The remaining two sources, the memorandum and articles of association and the trust deeds, are framed by or through the involvement of the promoters (who can later become directors) and the directors of the companies concerned. Due to the involvement of company directors or their appointed officers, those forms of rules do not fit the definition of (externally imposed) regulation adopted in this thesis.

In addition to the sources of financial disclosure regulation, there are other sources of influence which are frequently overlooked. Those sources of influence are the academic and professional literature, the financial press, foreign regulatory bodies, security analysts, the Financial Executives Institute and the Institute of Directors in Australia.

The academic and professional literature is a major source of influence guiding company financial reporting and their regulations. The arguments and evidence amassed by the academics and the professional authorities have persuasive value. An example of the immense wealth and influence of such literature in the area of "true and fair" reporting is provided by Wolnizer (1985, pp. 155-159), from where it is noted that such literature preceded the courts and the legislature in providing an elaborate explanation for the term "true and fair" view. Likewise he commented that:

> The idea that accounts should represent the actual affairs of companies in a true or factual manner was established in the literature before the first public Act to make reference to a "full and fair" balance sheet was enacted in the U.K. in 1844 (p. 155; emphasis added).

Such literature affects all accountants and auditors through the educational and professional development process. In addition, it has also had an impact on regulators in forming their judgments. One such example is the use of academic literature by Ryan (1967, pp. 102-3) in the discussion, again, on "true and fair" view. Although, the academic and professional literature can play a persuasive role in financial disclosure by companies, it lacks the coercive authority to direct the disclosure activities of companies, nor does it possess the capacity to provide incentives in that respect. In short, it does not provide regulations under the definition adopted in this thesis.

The financial press also plays a major role in influencing company accounting practice and the regulation of such practices. Zeff (1973) briefly reviewed its role, and commented that, the press had been a potent factor in accelerating the efforts of the accounting profession to review its standards (p. 54). Birkett and Walker (1971) while studying the response of the profession to the crises of the sixties also noted the criticisms by the press of published financial information and the role of accountants.

Decisions of foreign regulatory bodies may also have persuasive authority in Australia. Instances of such influence are noted in the next section. The reason for such persuasive authority in the case of statutes and the case law is mainly the similarity between the Australian and foreign statutes and the general similarity between the Australian and foreign legislative and judicial mechanisms (for example, see Evans, 1974, p. 62; and also see Ford, 1982, p. 120, for his argument on the persuasive authority of the U.K., New Zealand and South African legislations in Australia).

Apart from the statutes and case law, Zeff (1973) noted that the Australian professional accounting standard-setting process was considerably influenced in the past by the activities of foreign accounting bodies. For example, the I.C.A.A. from its outset followed the lead of the I.C.A.E.W. Its first set of Recommendations were based on the I.C.A.E.W. Recommendations (p. 5). Initially the influential members of the Institute were persistent advocates of the English pronouncements (p. 9) and some were even opposed to the idea of I.C.A.A. developing its own recommendations (pp. 2-3). In addition to the specifics of the I.C.A.A. pronouncements, the general nature of its standard-setting process was based on the English pattern. For example, Zeff (1973) found that the naming of Australian pronouncements as "recommendations", "principles", and "statements of accounting practice" coincided with the use of such names by the I.C.A.E.W. (p. 20). Moreover, the decision by the I.C.A.E.W. in late 1969 to regenerate and fortify its own programme of developing accounting pronouncements served to reinforce the view of leaders of the Australian Institute that they were heading in the right direction (p. 25). Apart from the English influence he noticed some U.S. and Canadian influence, from the later half of the sixties, on the initiation and drafting of some I.C.A.A. standards (p. 16 and pp. 25-26). Similarly in the case of enforcement of standards on the members, both the I.C.A.A. and the A.S.A., followed the enforcement policies adopted by the American, Canadian, English, Scottish and Irish Institutes (p. 22).[109]

The other sources of influence on financial disclosure and their regulation, like the security analysts, the Financial Executives Institute and the Institute of Directors in Australia were reviewed by Zeff (1973, Chapter 5). From his study we can infer that those sources do not play a very active role in the regulation of financial disclosure, but they are aware of the regulating activities and are important and potent interest groups in this area.

Since none of the above mentioned sources of influence are sources of financial disclosure regulation, they will not be afforded any further attention in this chapter.

Accounting Regulatory Policies Before the 1970s:

In this section a review of the history of company accounting regulatory policies, adopted in Australia up to 1970, is conducted. The review is based on various sources, as cited in Appendixes 1 to 5.

The investigation covers the events and crises and the resultant demand for and supply of various modes of regulation, rather than that of individual standards and rules. First, the events/crises leading to the demand and supply are identified for each category of regulation. This is followed by an examination of the trend in demand and supply. Finally, the outcome of each period of demand and supply is summed up.

The events and crises that prompted the demand for and supply of accounting regulations in Australia are listed in Appendix 1. In that

---

109   Also see Faggotter, 1978, p.175 for a discussion on the influence of U.K., U.S., Canadian and New Zealand institutes and multinational accounting firms and corporations.

Appendix the terms event and crisis are used with similar meanings. The only difference is in the extent of impact they had on company accounting disclosure. For example, events include occurrences, incidents and other related matters regarding individual or various companies; whereas the term crisis encompasses a series of events and emergencies creating a dilemma capable of bringing about turning points in the trend of company financial disclosure regulatory policies.

The process of demand for regulations, due to its intricacies and complexities is difficult to list clearly. The major instances of demand are listed in Appendix 1, because of their inseparability from related events and crises. Moreover demand itself, if intensively pursued, can be one of the reasons which turns events into crises. Demand, in the form of direct lobbying, is difficult to trace. And even if it is possible, it would be an arduous task to list all instances of demand in favour of or against various forms of regulations over the time span covered in Appendixes 1 to 5; and the list itself would be of enormous length and hence incomprehensible.[110]

The supply and formation of different regulatory policies and promulgation of regulations, over time, in Australia, are listed in Appendixes 2 to 5. Those Appendixes also look at the organization and reorganization of the regulatory set-ups of the various sources of accounting regulation.

The following discussion in this section, unless otherwise indicated, is based on the facts listed in Appendixes 1 to 5.

---

110   Research attempting to explain or predict the demand for accounting rules itself
       is an emerging branch of accounting research. A brief review of various studies
       in this branch has been conducted in Chapter 5 in the sub-section "The Nature
       of Supply of and Demand for Accounting Standards". Griffin (1983) reviewed
       those studies in this area which dealt with explaining and predicting management
       preferences for accounting rules. Apparently it is not possible to study all
       instances of demand in the lengthy time period of accounting regulations under
       review in this chapter.

The Courts:

Australian States adopted prevailing English laws up to a date extending between 1828 to 1836 (different states adopted different dates), and established cut-off dates after which they enacted their own laws (Gibson, 1971, pp. 24-25). Despite such arrangements, case laws developed in England and elsewhere, originally in the British Empire and more recently in the Commonwealth, continued to have a persuasive value and effect on accounting disclosure practices in Australia. From Appendix 2 it is easy to draw the inference that such cases and the judgment and dicta of judges have been quoted/cited widely by company law authorities and in the company accounting literature in Australia.

It can be noted from Appendixes 2 to 5 that before the Victorian Companies Act of 1896 the courts prescribed enforceable disclosure requirements to be followed by companies. The early cases on company accounting dealt with both issues of disclosure and measurement. Disclosure requirements seem to have been initiated in the form of defining the rights of members and directors to inspect books of accounts and to prescribe the format of disclosure to members. On the other hand measurement rules evolved due to the problems arising from dividend distribution through the maintenance of capital. In solving those problems efforts were made by the courts to determine methods of calculation and/or define terms like profit, capital, floating and fixed capital, dividend, depreciation, expense, liabilities, assets, etc. In the *Re Ebbw Vale* case, searching for methods of calculation for profit, led to the idea of making out a balance sheet for profit calculation. A quest for the establishment of a capital maintenance rule led to the still unresolvable problem of asset valuation (French, 1977, pp. 310; also see Reiter, 1926, Chapter 8). The courts in establishing case law depended on the professional accounting methods and practices, and in some cases they even expressed satisfaction for such methods and practices (as for example, see *Leeds Estate Building* case in Appendix 2). But, the courts in some contentious cases did pass judgment contrary to the practices of the profession (As for example in *the Lee v. Neuchatel* case in Appendix

2).[111] Baxt (1970, pp. 543-48) and Wolnizer (1985, pp. 146-54) have documented, in detail, the cases regarding "true and fair" reporting where the judgments and the dicta of the courts either depended on the prevailing accounting practices or on the independent view of the judges.

Appendix 2 contains evidence to suggest that the case law and dicta of judges, developed over the years, are the outcome of various single company related events. Such events occurred because of conflict of interest between parties (for example the shareholders, directors and creditors) often due to the absence, or non-specification, of important issues in the articles of association or in the relevant statutes (see Reiter 1926, Chapter 5 and French 1977 for further details of such cases listed in Appendix 2). The interest was normally self-interest of individuals or groups which is consistent with the premise of this thesis, that the actors in the regulatory process act on the basis of self-interest.

In the early dividend cases the courts tried to protect the interests of creditors from the actions of the directors or shareholders. In this respect French (1977) concluded that, the courts provided an effective approach to creditor protection together with a great deal of freedom for directors to allocate scarce resources to their best use (p. 326). Other early cases tried to determine the rights of directors and shareholders to inspect books of accounts in order to protect their interests or in other words to determine how far the company should be forced to disclose to those two interested parties (For example see *Baldwin v. Lawrence, Moller v. Spencer* and *Burn v. London and New South Wales Coal Co.* in Appendix 2).

In addition to the self-interest motive, we also find the element of demand for and supply of disclosure requirements in case laws. The judicial system in Australia like its English counterpart, is capable of providing legally binding remedies to specific instances of conflict. Its

---

111   The dependence of courts on accounting principles and practice is discussed further in the next chapter.

due process mechanism is also tuned towards dealing with specific cases. This allows the parties seeking resolution of contentious issues, to demand solutions to their conflicts from the judicial system or more specifically from its courts. The courts to the extent of their capacity to deal with the matters presented to them and in the light of precedents, legislation and the nature of the specific issue, supply relief, if necessary, to the affected party/parties in the form of judgments and orders. Such judgments and orders and their supplementary dicta have provided specific accounting requirements for companies (see Appendix 2).

The rulings of the courts have the force of law for the litigants of the case in issue. They can also be applied to other cases of similar nature as a precedent. Such rulings and the dicta of the judges, apart from having direct legal implications, have in the past attracted considerable attention from the legislature, the accounting profession and companies. Thus they have acted as catalysts in shaping the company disclosure requirements over the years. Evidence of such impacts have been provided by, for example, Gibson (1971, Chapters 9, 14 and 19), Edwards (1976) and Morris (1986b). The capacity of the courts, as providers of laws which can directly regulate the activities of the litigants of specific cases brought before it and their influence on others, provides regulatory capacity to the courts. The requirements imposed upon the litigants can be called regulations according to the definition put forward in Chapter 5 of this dissertation, because such requirements are imposed upon the companies by an external authority - the courts - and because they restrict or direct the activities of the affected companies.

The impact of such case laws were not limited by national boundaries because accounting and business practices were often similar in different countries. Although English laws were adopted directly in Australia up to certain cut-off dates in the early half of the nineteenth century (See Appendix 2), a substantial amount of case law in England regarding joint-stock companies was developed after those dates. Such case law may not provide precedent for Australian cases, but it does carry persuasive value. English case law has influenced Australian company accounting practices and regulations because of similarities in business practices and the close business relations between Australia and England. (For example see Gibson, 1971, Chapters 9, 14, and 19). A relevant example is that of the Australian case, *Phillips v. Melbourne and Castlemaine Soap and Candle Co.* where the decision in *Lee v. Neuchatel Asphalt Co.*, an English case was followed (Morris, 1986, p. 76). More recently, in the twentieth century, case laws developed in U.S.A. have attracted the attention of the Australian accounting profession and the legal authorities. Major examples include the *McKesson and Robbins* case (see Gibson, 1971, p. 150), and the *Continental Vending* Case (see Chambers, 1973, p. 152).

Summing up, we find that the courts were the earliest suppliers of company accounting regulations in Australia. Their supply was initiated due to the conflict of self-interest between parties who were financially involved in different companies. Such conflicts gave rise to demand for judicial remedies and the judiciary in its capacity as a law maker provided remedies for the specific situations. Although the ruling of a court as a law may be applied to other cases through the system of precedence, such application is possible only if similar cases are brought before the courts. Despite such limitations, cases frequently drew the attention of the legislature, the accounting profession, the companies and the investors, and have worked as important catalysts for the development of company accounting practices and rules of those other sources of regulation.

The Legislature:

The courts were followed by the legislature as a supplier of company accounting regulations. The courts remained active in areas where the legislature did not provide for any requirements and in those cases where interpretation of the Acts was necessary.

Formative Years:

From the evidence gathered in Appendix 3 it is possible to infer that the legislatures of Australian States, till about 1896, were quite satisfied with the English Statutory provisions and the case law developed in both England and Australia. The only reason for such satisfaction that can be suggested is that the State legislatures, in particular, and the economy, in general, did not face any major crisis which could have been derived or seen to be derived from the fragmentary and optional financial disclosure requirements of the Companies Acts. But, it must not be overlooked that the provisions for disclosure and other provisions of the Acts of that period, which had been derived from those of the English Acts, were themselves the outcome of major crises faced in England (For example see Ford, 1982, Chapter 1) and the demand placed by various interests in the face of such crises (Evans, 1974, p.27 and Hein, 1978, Chapter 5 and 6). The early history of English joint stock companies shows that the development of the company form of organization and requirements through various legislations were due to the situations of booms followed by busts. Booms boosted the need for the company form of business organization, whereas busts revealed its weaknesses. As will be shown in the following paragraphs, the development of accounting provisions in the Companies Acts in Australia over those inherited from the English ones, were also due to such crises in Australia generally or in specific states.

The difference between the events and crises which led to court rulings and those of the legislature is that, in the case of the latter the events and crises were not limited to individual companies or affected only a few individuals, but had more widespread implications. Accordingly, when the legislature reacted, it imposed regulations on all companies through additional legislation. This is unlike court rulings where it effects only the company in question and, others only if they are brought before the courts. In both cases (courts and legislature) there may have been only one case (event or crisis) - but its ramifications were greater if legislations followed.

Before the Victorian Companies Act of 1896 accounting by joint stock companies was substantially unregulated by parliament (Gibson, 1971, Chapter 6 and Morris, 1984). Because company legislation was in an early stage of development with only fragmentary and optional disclosure requirements, Gibson (1971) called these early years "formative years". During this period some preliminary excursions were made into the realm of compulsory disclosure. Disclosure requirements were introduced to specific sectors such as companies involved in banking, mining, life assurance, and to no-liability companies and companies incorporated by charter and by private acts of parliament (Gibson, 1971, Chapter 6 and Morris, 1984).

Campaigns by activists like William Clay in England in the middle of the nineteenth century, for "limited liability: paid-up capital: perfect publicity", did have some effect initially on the Companies Act. The 1844 Joint Stock Companies Registration and Regulation Act in England did require certain definite rules for audit and publicity through the publication of a balance sheet (Gibson, 1971, p. 6 and Evans, 1974, pp. 4-7). Though the Act of 1844 introduced the concept of formation of companies through registration[112] it did not provide limited liability. Limited liability was introduced in the Limited Liability Act of 1855 (Ford, 1982, p. 10). The subsequent English Companies Acts were more comprehensive and encompassed most matters relating to companies. But, these Acts until the Act of 1908 (Evans, 1974, p. 24 and Hein, 1978, p. 192), relegated the 1844 Act's compulsory disclosure requirements to an optional status. Those requirements were laid down in Table A of the Articles of the Act, the adoption of which by companies was voluntary (Gibson, 1971, p. 6).

In the period between 1856 to 1862 the colonies in Australia except South Australia adopted English companies legislation. After this period they started passing their own legislation, nevertheless they maintained the English principle of optional disclosure by retaining a Table A similar to that of the English Companies Act (Morris 1984, p. 56).

---

112   Complete incorporation still needed a deed of settlement (Ford, 1982, p. 9).

Turning Point:

Companies legislation of this kind seemed quite adequate for most of the second half of the nineteenth century and even in the early decades of the twentieth century in all states except Victoria. The 1880's mining boom in Australia, generally, and the real estate speculation in Victoria, in particular, were the two major phenomena which highlighted the deficiencies of the company form of business organization, specially the weaknesses in disclosure requirements. The situation reached its climax when the "boom" slid into a "bust" in Victoria. Bankruptcies and company insolvencies reached their peak between 1890 and 1892. Many saw inadequate information dissemination by companies to investors as an important contributing factor. This led to a public outcry and demand for disclosure requirements for companies (Gibson, 1971, p. 39).

Politicians pledged reform and in 1894 the Liberal-Protectionist Party, with similar pledges, swept to victory in the Victorian Parliamentary elections (Gibson, 1971, p. 39). Cannon (cited in Gibson, 1971, p. 41) had this to say about that victory:

> The government had been elected with an overwhelming popular mandate to pass laws dealing with the glaring abuses of finance and investment system,....

Sir Isaac Isaac's, who was portrayed by Gibson (1971, Chapters 7 and 8) as a person obsessed with the objective of reforming company law, was appointed the Attorney General of Victoria. He then became the most ardent proponent of statutory provisions for minimum disclosure by companies (Gibson 1971, Chapters 7 and 8). These events support the proposition that politicians, in order to achieve their objective of gaining office, provide policies compatible to the electorates' desires or, more specifically, to the more vocal interest groups' demands.[113]

---

113   See Chapter 5 of this dissertation.

Gibson's (1971, Chapters 7 and 8) account of the passing of the Companies Act of 1896 in Victoria revealed that the Act was not so easily passed. The initial crisis created by the "land bust" in Victoria was acutely felt by the people of that state (Gibson, 1971, p. 39). It was followed by a surge of demand for reform by the public and the media. This demand was transmitted to the Parliament by the newly elected government, which in fact had gained victory by proposing a policy of reform to the people of Victoria. But the endeavours of those who moved for reforms were challenged by the representatives of those who benefited from the earlier boom - the land owners and speculators. The process which the Act of 1896 had to endure was summarized by Gibson (1979) as follows:

> Isaacs took up the idea (of minimum disclosure) through the Victorian Parliament in 1896 requiring every company in which there were publicly held shares to present to the annual meeting and to send to each shareholder an annual report including a balance sheet which disclosed a minimum range of information. The bill was opposed bitterly by the land owners and businessmen who dominated the leglative Council, the upper house of Victorian Parliament. After the bill had see-sawed between the houses, been referred to a Select Committee and had been endlessly amended, Isaacs accepted the amended bill ... (p. 25).

The Select Committee, mentioned above, was created by the leglative Council at the request of and intense lobbying by the professional accounting bodies and the business community. The witnesses who were examined by the Committee represented company directors, members of companies holding managerial positions, managers and secretaries of banks and companies and accountants. The findings of the committee coincided with the interests of the business community, thereby providing the answers the leglative Council was seeking as an excuse to send the bill back to the Assembly (Gibson, 1971, p. 42).

The Victorian Companies Act 1896 marked the end of the era of freedom of action with respect to company reporting, and signified the recognition by the legislature of the necessity to regulate company reporting to ensure the protection of shareholders and creditors through the establishment of minimum disclosure requirements (Gibson, 1971, p. 47).[114] Although this was a victory for those who demanded minimum disclosure requirements, it was achieved at a cost - by satisfying some of the demands of those who opposed such requirements. One major compromise was the establishment of proprietary companies with no disclosure requirements (Gibson, 1971, p. 44).

Uniformity with English Legislation:

The adoption of the Act of 1896 drifted Victoria away from the other States of Australia and England. Early in the twentieth century some Victorians realized that such a drift could threaten investment from English investors, because such investors were shy of investing under an alien legal environment. They saw a need to reduce or eliminate the gap between the Victorian and English legislations. The agitation for such a change was also supported by the British Government and legal and accounting authorities in Victoria. Such demands finally prompted a bill in the Victorian Parliament in 1910 (Gibson, 1971, pp. 48-49).

The bill of 1910 saw tactics similar to those of 1896 by the Upper House of the Parliament to delay and reduce the provisions demanded by the bill. On the other hand there was considerable lobbying by the professional accounting bodies to preserve the requirement of a compulsory balance sheet and to add the requirement of presenting a detailed profit and loss account. Although the accounting bodies partially achieved this objective, they failed to acquire a requirement for a detailed profit and loss account. The profit and loss account required under the Act of 1910 was to be in the form of an annexure to the balance sheet without any specified details (Gibson, 1971, Chapter 8).

---

114   Legislature of other States adopted compulsory disclosure requirements at later stages. For example N.S.W. started adopting such requirements in 1936 (Evans, 1974, p. 62).

The Act of 1910 in Victoria brought very little change to the disclosure provisions of the Act of 1896. The reason for this lay in the nature of the problem that prompted its initiation. The Act was initiated to reduce the differences between the Victorian Act of 1896 and the existing English provisions. The differences in the financial disclosure provisions, like the provision for the presentation of a balance sheet, had already been adopted by the English legislation under the Companies Act of 1908 (Evans, 1974, p. 24 and Hein, 1978, p. 192). Consequently there was very little to be changed in the case of the disclosure provisions. In the light of the model adopted in this thesis, we can infer that the insignificant nature of the changes was mainly due to the weak form of demand because of the moderate nature of the crisis. But what ever changes were made, like the presentation of profit and loss accounts, there was an apparent demand for them.

Trend Towards Greater Disclosure Requirements:

The next stage of changes in the leglative policies towards company disclosure were the result of a conjunction of events in and outside Australia due to business volatility and the increasing abuse of the company form of organization. The crash of 1929 was also felt in Australia due to its trade links with U.S.A. and other depressed economies at that time (Gibson, 1979, p. 26). Again, the mining and land speculation between 1931 and 1933 in Australia and the increasing need for uniform legislation between states led to strong demands for legislative measures (Gibson, 1971, p. 57).

Specific deficiencies in the disclosure requirements were highlighted by cases like the Royal Mail case in U.K. in 1931 (Gibson, 1979, p. 26). The Royal Mail case pointed out the uninformative nature of acceptable financial statements. It identified the need for a clear statement of current operating profits and the isolation of other extraordinary items. The fact that the chairman and the auditor, in approving the accounts that allowed transfers from secret reserves to profits, did not violate the acceptable accounting practice at that time, indicated that it was not only them but also the accounting principles that were on trial. This case attracted the attention of the legislators both directly and through the reaction and subsequent lobbying by the accounting profession (For example, see Edwards, 1976, pp. 302-3, Jager, Taylor and Craig, 1979, pp. 204-205, Gibson, 1979, p. 26 and Ashton, 1986).

Since the company is a creation of a statute of the legislature, state legislatures in Australia again acted to mitigate the effects of those crises. Initially between 1920 and 1943, all other states introduced compulsory disclosure requirements similar to those of Victoria. Secondly, Victorian legislators, spurred by the active lobbying of the accounting profession extended the disclosure provisions in 1938 to require adequate profit or income statements and the presentation of consolidated statements for groups. Such provisions were later adopted by other states (Gibson, 1979, p. 26).

Uniformity Between States:

Proposals for uniform laws in Australia had been considered by the State Premiers almost since the Federation. As for company reporting, the professional accounting bodies had shown the desire for uniform legislation since 1924. The stock exchanges joined the accountants in the demand for uniformity in 1929. But, the prospect of uniformity diminished when Victoria moved ahead with its Companies Act of 1938 (Gibson, 1971, p. 268).

Because of inconvenient differences between companies legislation of the various States and Territories moves were again made in the late 1950s to obtain uniform companies legislation. Professional accounting bodies were once again involved in such moves (Gibson, 1971, pp. 270-74). Finally, a bill was drawn up by the representatives and officers of the states and the Commonwealth. Between 1961 and 1962 all states passed a Companies Act based on the bill and the Commonwealth made Companies Ordinances for the territories (Ford, 1982, p. 15). The important aspects of the financial disclosure requirements were, the presentation of balance sheet and profit and loss accounts, consolidated financial statements or separate statement for each subsidiary, data on fixed assets and directors' declaration regarding the realizable value of current assets (Gibson, 1971, p. 273). Again, the power of the Companies Registrars was enhanced, for example in N.S.W. where their powers were to include investigative powers along with the filing authority (Morley, 1979, p.26).

The "True and Fair View":

One of the most important and widely affecting innovations of the company disclosure regulations introduced by the leglisators was the requirement for a company's profit and loss account and balance sheet to give a "true and fair view" about the companies operations and affairs. The term "true and fair view" was first used in the U.K. Companies Act 1947 and was introduced in Australia in the Victorian Companies Act 1955 (N.C.S.C. Release 405, 1982). Although, this term modified the previous requirement of the Victorian Act 1938 that "true and complete" accounts be kept, the notion of fairness was introduced much earlier. Johnston and Jager (1963, p. 312) traced back and noted that Companies Statutes 1864 (Victoria) and Companies Act (Victoria) 1890 required the directors to cause "true" accounts to be kept; that every item of expenditure "fairly" chargeable against the years income be brought into account so that a just balance of profit and loss could be laid before the general meeting; and that the auditors to form an opinion whether the balance sheet was a "full and fair" balance sheet.

Johnston and Jager (1963, p. 312) found the term "true and fair" as broad and indefinite and identified three ways of interpreting it:

    (a)   literally, and in their ordinary meaning, that is without regard to possible technical interpretations;

    (b)   technically, and meaning in accordance with accounting principles either recommended by leading accountancy bodies or followed in best practice; or

(c) technically, and meaning in accordance with accepted accounting or business practice which may in the extreme mean merely that "somebody has tried it".

The term was first introduced into U.K. Companies Act 1947 on the approval by the Cohen Committee on Company Law of a recommendation made by the I.C.A.E.W. The I.C.A.E.W.'s recommendations were in support of the then extant principles of accounting, such as historical cost accounting and the going concern principle (Johnston and Jager 1963, p. 313). In 1958 the Institute clearly stated that the term implied "the consistent application of generally accepted [accounting] principles" (Houghton, 1987, p. 143).

Ever since its introduction its meaning has been debated and it has been used on a variety of occasions to justify various accounting methods and theories (Johnston and Jager, 1963; pp. 312-315; Ryan, 1967; Baxt, 1970; Wolnizer, 1985, Chapter 5; and Houghton, 1987, p. 143) and its effectiveness has been contested in comparison to the requirements, such as that in the U.S.A. (Ryan, 1967 p. 106 and 1974 p. 8 and 16).

Ryan, formerly the N.S.W. Registrar of Companies and then the Commissioner of Corporate Affairs, showed his distaste for the "true and fair" requirement in the following manner:

> The prospect of becoming involved in a controversy in which the various protagonist had already taken up forceful and conflicting views had only a limited appeal. And yet the words 'true and fair' do appear in the Act of Parliament in relation to which I have some responsibility (Ryan, 1967, p.95).

As an officer entrusted to enforce the Company Law in N.S.W. he tried to form a view regarding the term in an A.S.A. convention in 1967. Due to the ambiguity of the term he came to the following conclusion:

> I would like to see the words abandoned in favour of the American formula under which auditors report their opinion that the accounts present fairly the financial position of the company and the result of

its operations in conformity with generally accepted accounting principles applied on a basis consistent with that of the preceding period (Ryan, 1967, p. 106).

Disillusioned with the meaning of "true and fair" he expressed that as a regulator he would take other avenues for the enforcement of the company laws. In this respect he stated that:

> At the lodgment stage my officers are concerned only to see that the accounts comply with the Ninth Schedule. Obviously it is impracticable for them to form any judgment as to their truth or fairness, which at that stage must be matters for the directors and auditors alone. On happening of some subsequent event which raises doubts as to the validity of the accounts, I would not for one moment contemplate a prosecution based on so slippery a concept as truth and fairness. In those circumstances it is my practice to consider the applicability of s 375 of the Act or s 175 of the Crimes Act (Ryan, 1967, p. 107).

Although ambiguous, the term "true and fair view" was the only legislative requirement in respect of the quality of accounts. The Uniform Companies Acts of the various States (and later the national Companies Act of 1981) provided various disclosure rules including adherence to approved accounting standards, but the overriding requirement for the quality of disclosure has been the provision of opinion regarding the "true and fair view" of the financial statements by the directors and the auditors (See For example, Sections 162 and 167 of the N.S.W. Companies Act 1961 and Sections 269 and 285 of the Companies Act 1981).[115]

---

115   In recent years it has again become the object of controversy and debate, specially with the publication of the N.C.S.C. document "A True and Fair View" and the Reporting Obligations of Directors and Auditors (Houghton, 1987, p. 143). Despite its lack of clarity, the provision of the "true and fair view" still remains as the basis for company financial reporting and auditing (N.C.S.C. Release 405, 1982; also see Sections 269 and 285 of the Companies Act 1981).

Towards Greater Investor Protection:

The 1960s was a very hectic period for the legislature in Australia. It was a period of company collapses to some extent similar to those which occurred in U.S.A. in 1929. The series of crashes was initiated by the credit squeeze which began in November 1960 - a squeeze for which many companies were ill prepared (Dean, 1985). Although the crashes occurred throughout the decade, the legislature and the accounting profession, as will be shown later, drew more and more criticism as Inspectors' reports were tabled in parliament.

The initial reaction to the crashes was the enactment of the Companies (Public Borrowings) Act in 1963 by all the States (Evans, 1974, p. 65). The purpose of the Act was to protect the investors in respect of borrowing and guarantor corporations and it required greater disclosure by companies to trustees for debenture holders and the investors, including half yearly balance sheet and profit and loss accounts (Miller, 1978, p. 35). These requirements were enhanced in 1965 to include, specification of duties and responsibilities of the trustees, provision of quarterly reports to the trustees, and publication of mid-year and annual reports.

The supply of the provisions of the Companies (Public Borrowings) Act was in response to demands and allegations made regarding improper borrowing and lending practices of companies[116] in particular finance companies such as Latec, Sydney Guarantee and wholly owned finance subsidiary companies of companies such as Reid

---

The prevailing conditions regarding the "true and fair view" was appropriately described by F. Walker as follows: "The Acts do not attempt to define the expression "true and fair"; nor has there been any useful judicial decision on the point" (F. Walker, 1980, p. 11).

116   Also see Baxt (1970, p. 541).

Murray and Stanhill Development Corporation. Gibson (1979, p. 28) stated that it was found during the companies investigations that certain holding companies raised secured loans and passed them on as unsecured loans to their subsidiaries and associate companies. Meanwhile, one company which had made a mid-year loss, kept on raising funds without disclosing the loss. Such instances led to the enactment of the aforementioned disclosure requirements aiming at protecting the debenture holders and other creditors and investors.

During the 1960s the legislature, though concerned about the problems of accounting measurement (for example see Birkett and Walker, 1971, p. 112 and p. 116), did not face too much direct criticism in that respect. Criticisms in that area were mainly directed towards the accounting profession and its practices (Craswell, 1983, p. 180).
Among other steps taken by the legislature, an important step was the establishment of Company Law Advisory Committee (Eggleston Committee) in 1967. The first interim report of this committee proposed an Australian Companies Commission, which among other duties, would be empowered to alter statutory requirements for companies' accounts, group accounts and directors reports (Gibson, 1971, p. 302). In the meantime, along with other activities, the state governments, improved the capacity of their Companies Registrars to enforce company legislation. For example, the Corporate Finance and Accounting Division was established in the office of the N.S.W. Registrar of Companies and was entrusted with the task of administering and developing the protection afforded by the disclosure provisions of the Companies Act. Later the N.S.W. Securities Industry Act was passed creating the N.S.W. C.A.C. (Morley, 1979, p. 35). In other states also the Registrars of Companies were empowered with the authority to check certain features of accounts and prospectuses (Evans, 1974, p. 67).

The State Company Registrars were gradually upgraded from filing authorities to Commissioners of Corporate Affairs empowering them with the additional task of enforcing financial disclosure provisions of the Companies Act. This change brought a new source of influence in the accounting regulations arena - that of a bigger and stronger bureaucracy to enforce company regulations.

The Commissioners' offices held regular consultations with those affected by the legislation and its administration. One area of consultation was regarding conflicts between directors and auditors as to the appropriate accounting principles to be applied in the preparation of accounts. Consequently, the N.S.W. Commission commenced issuing information bulletins in 1972 to assist practitioners, directors and the general public (Morley, 1979, p. 35). Apart from such activities Corporate Affairs Commissions instituted quality checks for financial information that were disseminated through annual reports of companies.[117]

Stock Exchanges:

Since 1904 the stock exchanges have supplemented the Companies Acts in terms of regulating company financial disclosure in Australia (Gibson, 1979, p. 26-27, Ford, 1982, p. 614 and Morris, 1984, p. 62). Their jurisdiction has been limited to those companies which have been listed in the exchanges having such rules. From Morris's (1984) description of early stock exchange disclosure rules in Australia, it can be inferred that the inception of stock exchanges was based on the self-interest of its founders and subsequent members (pp. 60-63). This is consistent with histories of formation of other exchanges elsewhere, such as the London Stock Exchange. Regarding the London Stock Exchange King (1947) had this to say:

> The Stock Exchange community governs itself by an elaborate set of rules - and does so more speedily, stringently and yet more flexibly than any legal control could do. ...

---

117   See Morley (1979) for a detailed review of such checks instituted by the N.S.W. Corporate Affairs Commission.

Yet in the eyes of the law the Stock Exchange is a most informal body. It shoulders great public responsibilities, but is not a public corporation. It has no Charter, nor is it even a registered company. A lawyer, ... would call it an "unincorporated body of persons operating under a trust deed". ... It came into being simply to promote the common interests of its members (p. 7).

Stock exchanges developed in N.S.W. from the individual independently conducted practices of a small number of brokers. In the middle of the nineteenth century those brokers provided lists in the newspapers of companies in which they traded. The mining boom of the 1870's boosted the demand for the shares of mining companies, which led to the creation of a number of stock exchanges. The slump in share trading and the depression of the 1890s brought the demise of most of the exchanges.[118]

The surviving stock exchanges are essentially similar to their early predecessors. Ford (1982) described stock exchanges in Australia as companies incorporated by guarantee, the members being brokers engaged in the business of share broking (p. 611). The members of those exchanges run and maintain the exchanges in their own self-interest, by providing an organized market to the investors for the transaction of shares in listed companies. The exchanges are not open markets in the sense that investors cannot deal in the exchange themselves. They have to use the services provided by the members of the exchange at a certain cost. This leads one to believe that it is in the interest of the members of the exchanges to keep their respective exchanges in order and require the companies to disclose in such a manner that the investors can rely on the exchanges as a market for transacting in shares and bonds.

The evidence gathered in Appendixes 1 and 4 suggests that most actions have been taken by the management of the respective exchanges

---

118   For a detailed account of the development of the stock exchanges in Australia see The Role and Functions of the Australian Stock Exchanges (A.A.S.E., 1981, Appendix B).

and later by the A.A.S.E. to keep their house in order. Most early requirements by the Stock exchange of N.S.W. required companies to disclose specific information about their paid-up capital, reserves (for banks), dividends, mining output, etc. From Appendix 4 it is apparent that initially the companies agreed to supply, or the exchanges recommended the supply of financial statements by companies. With the introduction of formal listing requirements those disclosure requirements were made compulsory. The extent of information to be disclosed has been enhanced over the years and has considerably exceeded the requirements of the Companies Acts. Some requirements, for example the disclosure of group accounts, have preceded the adoption of similar requirements in the Companies Acts (Also see Gibson, 1979, p. 27 and Whittred, 1986, p. 107). Requirements have been imposed not only to furnish the shareholders with reports, but to publish the information publicly in order to inform prospective as well as present shareholders. Publishing of information in that manner may encourage new participants into the market. Clearly, that is in the interest of the stock brokers of the exchange. Again, the exchanges have been concerned with the frequency and timing of the reports. The requirements to publish interim reports in the form of six monthly reports, which dates back to 1939 for newly listed companies, has not only been made compulsory for other companies but has also been expanded in respect of the nature and amount of information.

The stock exchanges in Australia also preceded the legislature in another important area. This was in respect of uniformity in listing requirements. Although steps towards uniformity were taken by the Sydney and Melbourne exchanges as early as 1925,[119] (Gibson, 1971, p. 75) formal unification of all exchanges was completed in 1937 with

---

119   The first interstate conference of representatives of the stock exchanges in the
       States was held in Melbourne in 1903 (The Role and Functions of the Australian
       Stock Exchanges, A.A.S.E., 1981, Appendix B).

the establishment of the A.A.S.E.[120] At first this unification was simply a formal arrangement and each exchange continued issuing its own listing requirements. The first "common" A.A.S.E. listing requirements were published seventeen years later in 1954 - six years before the Uniform Companies Acts.

The most important aspect of listing requirements has been its regulatory capacity. First, those requirements are regulations for listed companies, because they have been imposed on the listed companies by the managements of the stock exchanges. The only way in which a company can avoid a compulsory requirement is by delisting, and that limits the companies' ability to, and increases its cost of, raising funds due to loss of the facilities provided by an organized capital market.[121] Secondly, Gibson (1979) observed that the exchanges have been remarkably effective in securing compliance relying primarily on the threat of delisting from what has become the sole organized market for securities in Australia (p. 27). Seal of approval to the A.A.S.E. and its predecessors, the individual exchanges, has been provided by the legislatures. One recent development has been the passing of the Securities Industry Act 1980 and State Codes by the Commonwealth and State Parliaments which has made compliance with the A.A.S.E. listing requirements mandatory. Section 42 of the Securities Industry Act 1980 stipulates the powers of the Court to order observance or enforcement of business rules or listing rules of stock exchange. In this respect the obligation of the companies has been specified in the Act as follows:

---

120   Sydney and Melbourne Exchanges started issuing identical listing requirements since 1936 (Gibson, 1971, p. 27).

121   Ford (1982) elaborated this as follows: "Companies usually have an interest in securing and maintaining listing of their securities since the provision of a ready market for their shareholders encourages raising of capital" (pp. 613-14).

A body corporate shall, for the purposes of sub-section (1), be deemed
to be under an obligation to comply with, observe and give effect to
the listing rules of an exchange if that body corporate has been
admitted to the official list of that stock exchange and has not been
removed from that official list (Sub-section 42(2)).

That legislation also allows the government and its agencies to control
the creation of new exchanges and the functioning of existing ones
(Sections 37 to 41; also see Ford, 1982, pp. 614-15). The N.C.S.C., with
the approval of the Ministerial Council for Companies and Securities, has
been given certain powers under that Act to prohibit trading in particular
securities on any exchange (Section 40; Ford, 1982, p. 636).

In 1946 companies applying to list in Sydney and Melbourne
Stock Exchanges were required to enter into a "form of agreement" to
abide by the Stock Exchanges' Official List Requirements. This "form
of agreement" was amended in 1954 to include a dragnet clause aimed
at making future amendments to the listing requirements retrospective
(Gibson, 1971, p. 81 and Whittred, 1986, p. 106). This was reinforced
by the dicta of courts which suggested that while listed, a company was
contractually bound to observe the listing requirements (Ford, 1982, p.
614).

This indicates that stock exchange requirements are regulations
for listed companies or companies utilizing the facilities of organized
securities markets according to the definition of regulations adopted in
Chapter 5 of this thesis.

The Professional Accounting Bodies:

**Inception of a New Form of
Disclosure Regulation:**

Before the 1940s technical development was the responsibility of
individual members of the accountancy profession. Very little systematic
attention was devoted to research and technical matters by the Australian
accountancy bodies (Graham, 1978, p. 56). For example the General

Council of the I.C.A.A. believed that its role should be confined to the administration of the Institute. A majority of the councillors were reluctant to advise the members on the conduct of their professional engagements (Zeff, 1973, p. 4).

Within the accounting profession only a few could foresee the need for technical development. In 1936 Sir A. Fitzgerald in the Australasian Congress on Accounting, suggested a joint standing committee of major accountancy bodies to consider the question of accounting terminology. Following a motion by him the General Council of the Commonwealth Institute of Accountants (C.I.A.), in 1937, decided that the Institute would issue opinions on general principles regarding professional practice of universal application. A committee appointed to look into the Institute's developmental matters later recommended the creation of committees on accounting principles and terminology (Zeff, 1973, p. 29).

The Commonwealth Institute of Accountants (C.I.A.) appointed a Committee on Accounting Principles (C.A.P.) and a Committee on Accounting Terminology (C.A.T.) in 1938. Two years later the Commonwealth Institute's General Council published its first statement on accounting practice on cash discounts, without expressing its approval or disapproval of the statement (Zeff, 1973, pp. 29-30). The C.A.P. and the C.A.T. were replaced by an Accounting Research Committee (A.R.C.) in 1948, with a view to coordinating the activities of the State Research Committees (Zeff, 1973, p. 32).

In 1944 the General Council of the I.C.A.A. considered issuing formal guidance to members. The old guard within the Council resisted any pronouncement by the Institute and, if there had to be any pronouncement, they wanted the I.C.A.E.W. ones. Contrary to this attitude, affirmative response was received from other quarters within the Institute (Zeff, 1973, pp. 2-3).

The first technical committee of the I.C.A.A. was formed in 1944 with its first set of recommendations being issued in 1946. Although these recommendations were not prompted by any local event of significance, they were based on the I.C.A.E.W. recommendations of 1940's which were the outcome of criticism of the accounting and auditing profession and their practices in the late 1920's in Britain, and the epic British case of the Royal Mail Packet Co. of 1931 which intensified the ongoing criticism (Edwards, 1976, pp. 296-303 and Jager, Taylor and Craig, 1979, p. 207).

The 1946 recommendations placed emphasis on specification of items in statements, classification of items and the standardization of terms. Therefore, they dealt mainly with the form of the financial statements (Graham, 1978, p. 56 and Craswell, 1986, p. 94). By 1948 the I.C.A.A. had issued a total of seven recommendations, all based on their I.C.A.E.W. counterparts (Zeff, 1973, p. 1973, p.4 and Evans, 1974, p. 64).

Between 1946 and 1947 C.A.P. of C.I.A. reviewed the I.C.A.E.W. and I.C.A.A. pronouncements and prepared various draft pronouncements, none of which was approved by the C.I.A. General Council (Zeff, 1973, pp. 31-32).

1944 is seen by many (For example, see Graham 1978, p. 56) as the start of an organized approach to technical development by the profession. However the formation of the I.C.A.A. in 1928 and the founding of the A.S.A. in 1952 are also significant developments in organizing for such development. As we shall see later the development of professional accounting standards in Australia has been solely under the imprimatur of these two bodies. The A.S.A. and the I.C.A.A. are the result of mergers between various accounting bodies, and a further merger between the Institute and the Society is seen by, for example Zeff (1973, p. 66),[122] as a step towards consolidation of the profession's position as an accounting standards supplier.

---

122   Also see Balmford, 1977, p. 547.

In 1948 there was some concern about non-compliance with the 1946-48 recommendations, which in any case were not binding on the members (Miller, 1978, p. 97). Such non-compliance did not bring about any immediate reaction from the Institute. It can be inferred that this was because it did not create a major crisis nor could it be correlated with any crisis requiring immediate change.

Formative Stage:

However, in 1949 a number of accountants recognized that there was confusion both within and without the profession as to the standards which were to govern practice and it was expected that the accounting profession should take steps to resolve the confusion (Birkett and Walker, 1971, p. 98). In the Second Australian Congress of Accounting all aspects of the profession were reviewed. Among other things, the promulgation of authoritative standards of accounting and auditing was seen as a necessary condition of professional status. It was expected that general acceptance could be achieved from wide dissemination and discussion of proposed standards, self imposed discipline of accountants in following them and from voluntary acceptance. Compulsion, regimentation and legislative sanction were to follow general acceptance. The need for an organizational machinery for standard-setting was realized. There was unanimous agreement that accounting provides an historical record of stewardship based on historical cost. Therefore, it provided historical truth. There were also discussions for the integration of the professional bodies (Birkett and Walker, 1971, pp. 98-101).

Confusion and public criticism of accounts and accountants continued into the 1950's. The initial response by the profession was to accept responsibility to educate the public. The acceptance of increased responsibility led to a demand in 1950 by certain influential members of the I.C.A.A. for a research department within the I.C.A.A. During the period 1950-54 considerable demand was placed by I.C.A.A. members for guidance on accounting principles and certain State councils and influential members demanded an organizational set-up for developing accounting principles (Zeff, 1973, p. 6 and Graham, 1978, p. 56). This demand was met six years later in 1956 through the creation of the Australian Chartered Accountants Research and Service Foundation (A.C.A.R.S.F.). This foundation published seven technical bulletins in the years 1957 to 1963. In the mean time, in 1957 some members became concerned about non-compliance by companies with I.C.A.A. recommendations, whereas others, in 1959, still debated whether to have the Institute's own standards or to adopt those issued in the U.K.

Around 1957-58 demand was placed by various quarters of the I.C.A.A., for example, by the South Australian State Council and Sir Alexander Fitzgerald, for revising the 1946-48 recommendations. In 1958 I.C.A.A. General Council resolved to revise those recommendations (Zeff, 1973, p. 7).

In the 1950's the A.S.A. also responded to the criticisms of the profession. The C.I.A. undertook to form a Joint Committee of Accountancy Bodies in Australia to which four major bodies other than the I.C.A.A. joined (Zeff, 1973, p. 32). In the period 1951-53 the General Council of the C.I.A., later the A.S.A., sought ways of conducting accounting research and publicizing the results (Zeff, 1973, p.33).

The Society published an interim report on "Accounting Terminology" in 1953. The next year it appointed a full-time research officer and the year after that it started producing "Statements of Accounting" and "Technical Bulletins". Within the period 1956 to 1965 the Society published nine Statements on Accounting Practice (Zeff, 1973, p. 35).

By the end of the 1950's the professional accounting bodies had barely started establishing the machinery necessary for the preparation of standards. In fact, hardly any progress was made towards establishing compulsory professional standards. Efforts had only been made in setting guiding principles based on what accountants regarded as best practice which the members would apply with their own best judgment (Evans, 1974, p. 64).

Turning Point:

The decade of 1960's saw another turning point in the history of accounting regulatory policies in Australia. Similar to the 1890's which saw a shift from dependence on case laws to statutory laws, in the 1960's attention of the regulators and the critics shifted from the statutory laws to the professional accounting standards. The basic reason for such a shift was the nature of the events that followed the company collapses of the sixties (see Appendix 1). The Inspectors' reports of the liquidated companies revealed that even though the letter of the law as laid down in the statutes was followed, some thing more important was missing - that is the essential ingredient of "truth and fairness" - the spirit required by the Companies Act, but not defined in that Act (For example, see Baxt, 1970, p. 549).

Until such revelations were made, the accounting regulations set by the legislature and the stock exchanges provided for only the form and the amount of disclosure. They depended on the accounting profession to provide guidance in the area of measurement techniques. Appendix 1 shows that inspectors' reports of the companies which collapsed in the early sixties were mainly issued between 1963 and 1967. Apart from fraud, willful misrepresentation and deficiencies like the absence of "true and fair" disclosure to debenture holders, the accounting and audit practices and principles adopted by accountants and auditors were found to be deficient. (Chambers, 1973, p. 155, Evans, 1974, p. 64 and Jager, Taylor and Craig, 1979, p. 211). Those reports highlighted the practices adopted by the auditors and accountants and, in some cases, were the reason for heavy penalties for the auditors of liquidated companies (see Craswell, 1983, Table 7.1., p. 181). Some reports also demanded immediate steps to correct the anomalies. One such demand was made in the case of Reid Murray Holdings Ltd. (Murray and Shaw, 1966):

> In my opinion the investigations have shown that the practices accepted by accountants in 1961 in the preparation of company accounts were inadequate to prevent the presentation of misleading accounts and has shown further that the whole question of how company accounts ought to be prepared and presented required urgent and critical examination. (p. 122)

Criticism of the accounting principles and methods was not limited to that from the inspectors. Due to the enormity of the losses suffered, it spread through out the community including academics, stock exchanges and the press (Birkett and Walker, 1971, pp. 108-110). This was followed by the criticisms by the legislators and enforcers of legislation, like that by the Victorian Parliament in 1963, the N.S.W. Attorney-General in 1965 and the N.S.W. Registrar of Companies in 1967 (see Appendix 1).

The instances of demand for the restoration of order in the accounting profession and for the promulgation of accounting standards, and the subsequent reaction of the professional accounting bodies in the 1960s has been discussed in detail by Birkett and Walker (1971). From their account of the situation in the sixties, it is understood that the barrage of criticisms by the financial press in 1963 was initially aimed at the fraud and misinformation by company directors, accountants and auditors. With the revelations made by the company inspectors, criticism by the press, academics and stock exchange officials shifted to the accounting methods used by the liquidated companies. When the profession failed to recognize its short comings and defended itself by arguing that only a small section of the accounting and auditing profession was involved in the collapses, it was again stormed with criticisms.

Dissatisfaction with the conduct of the Institute and the profession generally was voiced in the Victorian Parliament. The absence of professional self-regulation was pointed out and threats of government legislation to register accountants were made (Appendix 1). Due to continuing failures, in 1964, the Attorney-General of N.S.W. threatened to take action; shareholders with a view to protect themselves formed the

Australian Shareholders Association; and the I.C.A.A. hired public relations consultants to improve its image.

It seems the attention during this period of company failures, was focused on the profession because the community felt that the profession was best suited to resolve the problems of accounting and auditing. Prior to that period, accounting regulations in respect of form, amount and timing of disclosure, were provided by the legislatures and the stock exchanges. The accounting profession was left to deal with the issues of accounting methods and principles (For example, see Evans, 1974, p. 75). Since the inspectors were revealing problems with accounting methods and principles, amongst other things, it was to be expected that the community and other regulators would look towards the accounting profession to resolve those issues.

As for the response to the criticisms, initially (from 1963 to 1965) the elite of the Institute, like R.A. Irish of the I.C.A.A., defended the profession asserting that the members possessed a high degree of competence and integrity and the whole profession should not be blamed for a few "bad apples" (Birkett and Walker, 1971, pp. 108-110 and p. 116). Such defensive tactics at times turned into an offensive. For example, as late as 1967, the I.C.A.A. responded to the criticisms by accusing the critics of the profession of being ill-qualified and ill-informed (Birkett and Walker, 1971, p. 123).

Members of the accounting profession who found themselves as the eventual victims of this disclosure dilemma, started expressing their concern. In 1964 a majority of the I.C.A.A. conference participants showed a shift from the stance adopted in 1949, by recognizing that historical cost accounting was deficient. The next year, in the third I.C.A.A. conference, there was unease over the company failures and the inspectors' criticism of the profession and their methods. This was followed by a joint statement by the I.C.A.A. and the A.S.A. recognizing the need for the determination of accounting principles (see Appendix 1).[123]

According to the evidence gathered in Appendix 5 it can be inferred that the professional bodies were quite slow and cautious in responding to the criticisms. Up until the fifties the A.S.A. and the I.C.A.A. had taken some initiative to guide their members. This was done through recommendations and supplementary guidance materials which were not compulsory in terms of compliance. At the start of the sixties the professional regulatory mechanism was in its formative stages. The Institute and the Society, although following separate paths, were moving in the same direction. The actions taken in early sixties by those bodies were not responses to the company collapses but were the on-going activities of the fifties.

Until 1964 the I.C.A.A. had adopted the *ad hoc* approach in the complex and controversial area of accounting principles. The committees in Sydney and Melbourne were sitting in judgment on each other and could not agree on generalities or specifics. And the approach used had been changed after every half-yearly meeting of the General Council (Zeff, 1973, p. 11). Accounting principles of the day were based largely on (1) the office practice of each of the many firms of practicing accountants, and (2) the opinions held by the company directors and accountants employed in commerce and industry (Zeff, 1973, p. 5). The work of the committees was done by busy practitioners without the aid of technical staff within the Institute (Zeff, 1973, p. 9). In 1964, realizing the ineffectiveness of this *modus operandi*, the General Council appointed a standing committee to propose recommendations on accounting principles (Zeff, 1973, p. 11).

---

123   Also see Jager, Taylor and Craig (1979, para 220 and 221, p. 211) for a brief account of the company failures prompting concern and action by the accounting profession.
          The number of companies on register in 1987 in N.S.W. alone was 295,507 (N.S.W. C.A.C. Annual Report 1987).

Later in 1964 the Committee on Accounting Principles and Audit Practice (C.A.P.A.P.) was formed by the Institute to consolidate the function of proposing accounting and auditing pronouncements. In the same year the A.S.A. and the I.C.A.A. discussed the possibility of a joint Accounting Research Foundation (A.R.F.) (Zeff, 1973, p. 11), but the I.C.A.A. continued to issue its own "Recommendations on Accounting Principles" - this time based on the I.C.A.E.W. recommendations of 1958-60. In 1965 it published its "Statements on Accounting Principles and Recommendations on Accounting Practice".

The company collapses of the sixties, with their detailed investigations, had damaging implications for the profession. The reaction of the A.S.A. seemed to be more aggressive than that of the I.C.A.A. (Also see Zeff, 1973, p. 12). There were signs within the A.S.A. towards recognizing the connection between company failures and accountants. The Society set up a committee in 1964 to study the findings of company inspectors. It later published, in 1966, a report called "Accounting Principles and Practices Discussed in Reports on Company Failures". Professional deficiencies were recognized in the following areas:

a.   The formulation, promulgation and regular review of accounting principles.
b.   Adherence to accounting principles by members.
c.   Audit of accounts.
d.   Relationship between management and accountant.
e.   Adequacy of the form and content of published financial statements (see Appendix 5).

This report also acknowledged that financial statements prepared in accordance with generally accepted principles were capable of misleading those who make use of the information contained in the statements and who are not aware of the technical limitations of the statements. It also accepted the accounting profession's general responsibility to ensure that published financial statements provide information that is not irrelevant or misleading (Ryan, 1967, p. 105 and Baxt, 1970, pp. 549-550).

In 1966 the Accounting and Audit Research Committee of the A.R.F. recognized the poor publicity received by the profession due to company failures and asserted the need to improve the standing of the profession. The methods suggested by the Committee and its parent bodies, the A.S.A and the I.C.A.A., included higher educational qualifications for entry into the profession, such as university graduation, standards for accounting and auditing, disciplinary measures for the members and one national accountancy body with statutory backing. The A.S.A. also asked its members to procure professional indemnity insurance.

In the meantime the inspectors continued their criticism of unresolved technical issues in accounting. The Victorian Chamber of Manufacturers pointed out the overall decline of ethical standards in accounting and auditing (Birkett and Walker, 1971, p. 122). Others like Mr. Ryan, N.S.W. Registrar of Companies looked at aspects other than a simple criticism of the accounting profession and the principles governing their practice. Ryan was critical of the unspecified "true and fair" criteria of reporting under the Companies Act (Birkett and Walker, 1971, p. 124). He suggested that a statutory body be constituted under the Companies Act and authorized to make regulations as to the form and content of accounts and as to the accounting principles to be applied in their preparation; such a body, he said, was to be constituted of representatives of the legal, accountancy and secretarial professions and representatives of government. The regulations made by such a body would be subject to disallowance by Parliament in the same manner as other regulations made under the authority of an Act of Parliament (Ryan, 1967, p. 106).

In 1967 the Company Law Advisory Committee (Eggleston Committee) was established to review existing provisions of the law. Its first interim report dealt with disclosure of information in accounts and reports of directors and powers, duties and responsibilities of auditors. It also raised the issue of an Australian Companies Commission which, among its other duties, would be able to alter statutory requirements for company accounts, group accounts and directors' reports.

Meanwhile, there was growing dissatisfaction within the ranks of the profession regarding contemporary accounting practices and increasing concern about statutory involvement in the development of accounting practice (Appendix 1).

In the 1960's, a fundamental but subtle change occurred in the composition of the Institute's General Council. The State Councils increasingly nominated more younger and progressive members to the General Council. This change was essential because of the fact that the accounting function was becoming more demanding and variegated. The changed attitude of the General Councillors brought with them a conviction that the Institute should play a more central and active role in the advancement of professional standards (Zeff, 1973, p. 12).

Although, the joint A.R.F. was incorporated in 1966, the I.C.A.A. kept reorganizing its own regulatory mechanism. The same year the General Council of the I.C.A.A. appointed a Development and Planning Committee to make a comprehensive review of the Institute's committee structure and mode of operation (Zeff, 1973, p. 12). On that committee's recommendation a Research Committee and a Technical Committee was created (Zeff, 1973, p. 13). Those committees started publishing their own exposure drafts on accounting and auditing and on that basis the I.C.A.A. kept issuing pronouncements. In 1969 the Institute replaced the committees with the Accounting Principles Committee which issued five draft statements between 1969 and 1970. This committee was converted into the Accounting Standards Committee in 1972 and then in 1974 it was merged with the Australian Accounting Standards Committee (see Appendix 5).

Simultaneously the A.S.A. was also actively pursuing to organize its standard-setting mechanism and prepare acceptable accounting pronouncements. In 1967 it issued its first General Council approved authoritative pronouncement (Zeff, 1973, p. 38). Between 1968-71 the Society's Research and Technical Committee issued a number of exposure drafts none of which could take the shape of authoritative pronouncements (Zeff, 1973, pp. 39-40).

Responding to the criticisms emanating from company failures the A.R.F. conducted a survey in 1968 to identify the perceived deficiencies of financial statements. In 1970 the Foundation published "A Statement of Australian Accounting Principles" and between 1970 and 1973 the A.S.A. and the I.C.A.A. jointly issued/endorsed four accounting standards (see Appendix 5).

To strengthen the position of the profession (which could also improve its standard-setting mechanism) the A.S.A. and the I.C.A.A., in 1968, once again discussed the integration of the two bodies. Although the discussion failed in 1969, the A.R.F. was reconstituted to suit the needs of both bodies (see Appendix 5). By March 1974 the structure of the Foundation was expanded to embrace joint technical activities. A Joint Standing Committee composed of the Executives of the Institute and the Society was created to administer the Foundation. The activities of the Foundation would be undertaken by four joint committees, namely Accounting Standards, Accountancy Research, Taxation Research and Legislation Review (The Australian Accountant, April 1974, p. 178 and Balmford, 1974, p. 6).

Company collapses, involving accounting and disclosure methods, continued into the late sixties. The situation worsened with the speculative mining boom and the collapses that followed it. The money market squeeze of 1970 added fuel to the situation which saw further company collapses. The accounting profession was further stimulated by the malpractice revealed by the Rae Committee investigation of securities markets following the boom and the bust in mining securities of 1970. Once again the measurement techniques and the quality of financial reporting was questioned (see Appendix 1). The reaction of the profession to such developments was to increase its efforts towards the development of accounting standards and the strengthening of the means of enforcing those standards (Gibson, 1979, p. 29).

Summing up, the events of the 1960's brought about another turning point in the history of accounting regulatory policies. Although considerable amount of statutory and stock exchange disclosure requirements existed, the company collapses helped unveil a major loop-hole in the provisions of the Companies Act. It was regarding the criterion of "true and fair" disclosure, which was considered insufficient for ensuring the quality of financial disclosure. Although some, like Ryan (1967), did point out this deficiency in the Act, most of the criticisms of improper reporting by companies were directed towards the accounting profession. This was because the members of the profession until that time were seen to be responsible for the maintenance of the quality of financial information.

First, the profession was reluctant to accept responsibility for the allegations made against it, but when the criticisms came close enough to threaten the profession's status as a profession the two major bodies, the A.S.A. and the I.C.A.A., started acting. Their reaction, among other things, was to satisfy the demand for adequate measures for "true and fair" reporting by organizing its standard-setting mechanism and supplying accounting standards.

The A.I.M. Annual Report Award:

Until now, in this chapter, we have discussed the modes of regulation through directives in the case of financial disclosure regulations in Australia. The other type of regulation, as mentioned earlier, is regulation through incentives. The only example of this type is the Annual Report Award instituted by the Australian Institute of Management (A.I.M.). Australia was one of the first countries to introduce awards for Annual Reports, after the United States which announced its first awards in 1941 (A.I.M., 1987, p. 2).

The A.I.M. award was introduced in 1950 (Gibson, 1971, p. 202, A.I.M., 1987, p. 2). At first it was confined to companies listed on the Australian stock exchanges. In 1957 its scope was enlarged to include unlisted organizations, like government and semi-government bodies, charitable institutions, and sporting clubs (A.I.M., 1983, p. 4).

Initially, the stated aim of the Award was "to encourage companies to make the Annual Reports speak for industry" (A.I.M., 1983, p. 4). During the course of the Award, it has been necessary to alter its nature, the methods of classification and the criteria to be met to meet changing requirements (A.I.M., 1987, p. 2). In 1969, separate criteria were developed against which the "Listed and Unlisted" company reports were evaluated (A.I.M., 1987, p. 2). In the same year separate criteria were also developed for the different categories of unlisted organizations. In 1973 the listed companies' reports were classified in accordance with the industry or type of operation in which the organizations were primarily engaged (A.I.M., 1983, p. 4).

In 1974, general and specific criteria were published for the guidance of those preparing reports. These criteria were expanded and included in the 1975 Adjudicators' Report as the basis for the evaluation of future annual reports. Modifications have been made to the criteria as and when it has been necessary (A.I.M., 1983, p. 4).

Since 1966 the half yearly/interim reports have been taken into account to judge the annual reports (A.I.M., 1965, p. 2).

The most recent set of objectives of the Award are:

- To encourage the presentation of adequate financial and other information vitally needed by shareholder, members, employees, and the general public, in a form which can be readily understood.

- To create public awareness of the purposes of enterprises and their achievements.

- To encourage the development of valid and objective measures of performance and to promote a better understanding of the results achieved.

- To establish a better relationship between management, members and employees by disseminating facts and financial results about their own organization. (A.I.M., 1987).

The annual reports are evaluated on their success in meeting A.I.M.'s established standards of criteria as set out in the Annual Report Handbooks of the Institute and is made without assessing the profitability, worth or potential of the enterprise (A.I.M., 1987). The criteria for reporting includes specific requirements for the disclosure of financial information (For example, see A.I.M., 1987, pp. 34-35, pp. 40-41, pp. 42-43, and p. 45), but no standard accounting methods are specified or suggested in the Award's requirements.

Despite its high ideals, the award has many weaknesses as a regulatory form. First its requirements have not been imposed on the organizations it purports to encourage to report. It is up to the companies to submit their annual reports for adjudication and till now the maximum number of companies that have submitted their reports in a year has been only 428 (A.I.M., 1983), which is a fraction of the total number of listed and unlisted companies/organizations throughout Australia. Again, since 1983 the number of organizations submitting their reports for the award has been falling continuously, and has dropped from 428 in that year to 348 in 1987 (A.I.M., 1983, 1984, 1985, 1986, and 1987). This continuous decline indicates a diminishing popularity of the Award.

Second, it has promoted matters of typographical and illustrative presentations rather than the substance of financial measurement and disclosure (Gibson, 1971, p. 203). For example, the adjudicators of the Award in 1987 noted that:

> There were a significant number of reports which included extremely abbreviated Balance Sheets, Profit and Loss Accounts and Sources and Applications of Funds. ... Major balance sheet changes in some instances were poorly covered by way of a very brief explanation. A consistent complaint by the examiners for many years has been in relation to Profit and Loss Accounts which do not show material and labour costs. This item has been included in the A.I.M.'s criteria for many years, but is generally ignored. (A.I.M., 1987, p. 16).

But, there have been specific items of reporting which are exceptions to those drawbacks. For example, the award has had a significant effect on overcoming the reluctance by the directors of Australian companies to disclose a vital item, like sales turnover (Gibson, 1979, p. 28).

From this brief profile of the A.I.M. Annual Report Awards we can infer that it is a weak mode of regulation of the form of company financial disclosure and plays a negligible role in the regulation of company accounting methods. Since it is a form of regulation through incentive it lacks the coercive strength possessed by other forms of disclosure regulation.

Conclusion:

The events which led to the demand for and supply of accounting regulation before the 1970s created three different cycles of accounting regulatory policies for company financial disclosure. The first cycle lasted up to the 1890s. During this period demand was placed on the courts to decide what should be the quantity and quality of information to be disclosed by the companies. In the same period the legislature, as the creator of the company form of organization, maintained a low profile in legislating for company financial disclosure.

In the second cycle, the events of 1890s prompted legislative action in Victoria which eventually spread to other states of Australia and finally took the shape of uniform legislations between 1961 and 1963. Although the review in this chapter lacks finer details, in certain instances it has been noted that the leglative requirements for financial disclosure were supplied by the legislators in pursuing their own interests through the satisfaction of demands of important interest groups, of which one could be noted as the accounting profession. Since it is beyond the scope of this thesis, no further attempt is made to analyze this regulatory period in greater detail.

The courts did not cease ruling on company disclosure issues, but their role shifted more towards interpreting the "letter and spirit" of the company legislation and providing answers to issues not dealt with by the legislature. For example, the courts have relentlessly pondered upon the issue of "true and fair", a criterion set under company legislations but never defined (Baxt, 1970, pp. 543-48 and Wolnizer, 1985, pp. 146-54).

Meanwhile, the organized capital markets in the form of stock exchanges were developed, with which came the listing requirements for companies wishing to list in those exchanges. Such requirements emphasized the amount, timing and frequency of disclosure. Listing requirements were supplied to maintain the competitive nature of the exchanges, which was primarily in the interest of the members of those exchanges. For financial disclosure, those requirements worked as a supplement to the statutory requirements and at times provided guidance for the development of statutory requirements.

The third cycle commenced with the events of the 1960's. Those events revealed a major area of deficiency in company financial reporting - that of methods and principles employed in financial disclosure. Until that time the aforementioned sources of disclosure regulation had not ventured, in depth, into this area. The courts only made attempts to resolve problems in certain specific issues brought before them, which was far from a systematic approach to resolving problems of accounting methods. It seems that accountants and auditors, as professionals, were entrusted with the responsibility of the selection and adoption of methods and principles of accounting measurement and advising the company directors in that respect. Consequently the accounting and auditing profession was seen to be responsible for failing to provide adequate measures when certain company accounting anomalies were revealed from the company failures of the sixties. The bodies representing the profession were at first slow to recognize their responsibility, but as the criticism against the profession geared up so did their response to such criticism. First they challenged the criticism of the critics. When the deficiencies in methods and principles were thoroughly scrutinized and publicly revealed, the status of their members as professionals was threatened. This prompted the A.S.A. and the I.C.A.A. to intensify their quest for resolving the problem which eventually led to the development of accounting standards.

By the turn of the decade, around 1970, the attention of the critics of company financial disclosure was diverted towards the accounting profession and their professional bodies, the A.S.A. and the I.C.A.A. Those bodies gained importance and joined the ranks of financial disclosure regulators by organizing to supply the required regulations. Due to the circumstances of the crisis to which they were responding they assumed the responsibility of supplying, mainly, accounting measurement standards and supplementary pronouncements.

Meanwhile, the A.I.M. Annual Report Awards, as means of regulation through incentive, have received considerably less attention compared to the other sources. Therefore no further discussion will be conducted regarding that Award.

From this chapter certain aspects of the regulatory model described in Chapter 5 are reinforced, It seems that there is evidence of those aspects existing in real regulatory situations. It is evident that the regulatory process for company financial disclosure regulations is dynamic and the policies adopted can change. The changes that occur are initiated by events and crises capable of revealing deficiencies in existing regulatory policies. Depending on the intensity and direction of demand the sources of regulation respond by providing the desired form of disclosure rules. Along with the nature of policy there can be shifts in the degree of attention paid to the various sources by the demanders. Such shifts are dependent on the desired nature of regulation.

Furthermore, there are two other important points that can be noticed from the review of financial disclosure regulatory policies in Australia. First, the various important sources of regulation, over the years, have assumed responsibility of providing separate modes of regulation, in turn supplementing the efforts of the other sources. This again is the outcome of the varying nature of events and crises faced in the area of company financial disclosure for which, from time to time, different sources of regulation were called upon to regulate. Second, during the later part of the period under review, that is by around 1970, the professional accounting bodies and their form of regulation had gained considerable importance. The courts had shifted more towards the interpretation of the law and, due to their institutional structure and limited capacity as lawmakers, they could not use a more comprehensive and systematic approach for providing disclosure and measurement rules. The stock exchanges, around the same time, had taken the role of supplementing existing statutory requirements. The legislature, although remaining active in providing disclosure requirements, seemed less intent on providing for measurement rules. As a result, we can infer that on the one hand the accounting bodies gained prominence in the supply of measurement requirements and on the other hand the legislature maintained its coercive influence by providing disclosure regulations regarding the form of disclosure.

Chapter 7

PROFESSIONAL ACCOUNTING BODIES AND ACCOUNTING STANDARDS

Introduction:

The review of the nature of the sources of company financial disclosure regulations in Australia in Chapter 6 explained why the accounting bodies, by the 1970's, gained prominence as a source of rules regarding accounting methods amongst all other forms of disclosure regulation. We now further analyze the reasons for the role of the accounting bodies in setting accounting standards.

In section 2 of this chapter we establish that issuing accounting standards and pronouncements is a mode of professional development and has been used simultaneously with other modes for improving the image of the profession. It is also shown that the importance of the standards has grown within the profession over the years.

Section 3 contains an analysis of the attention that has been paid to accounting standards as a form of regulation with increasing scrutiny of the responsibilities of accountants and auditors and their modes of practice. This analysis is based on the frequency with which certain classes of accounting literature have been published in Australia. In Section 4 the supply of accounting standards is studied as a response to that scrutiny in the literature.

Section 5 reviews the recognition received by the accounting standards as regulations and the professional accounting bodies as regulators.

In Section 6 we draw conclusions regarding the origin of accounting standards and its gradual transformation into a form of company financial disclosure regulation.

Accounting Pronouncements and Professional Development:

Willmott (1986) studied the emergence, development and role of accountancy bodies in the U.K. He argued that professional associations were primarily, but not exclusively, political bodies whose purpose was to define, organize, secure and advance the interests of their members, generally, and the vocal and influential members, in particular (p. 556). He asserted that to organize was the most fundamental aim of the professional association (p. 559). The founding of professional associations, he continued, was motivated by an altruistic desire to improve the quality and reliability of professional conduct (p. 260). He noted that the establishment of professional bodies offered the organizational means of regulating both the quality and flow of "professional" services, thereby limiting labour supply and raising its market value (p. 569). He explained that such bodies offered an opportunity to use the collective, monopoly of power of the membership to influence the demand side of the equation (p. 560). Those monopolies, he argued, were all the more effective for being hidden by a cloak of gentlemanly conduct, specialist expertise and state legitimization (p. 563). He elaborated that to maintain their position within the structure of power relations, the professional bodies sought recognition and confidence not only of the clients but also, and crucially of the state. State recognition, he noted, was normally obtained through incorporation (p. 560). He argued further, that such bodies may become institutionalized as law-proposing mechanisms in their own fields (p. 561).

Buckley (1980), with a similar self-interest view of the profession, argued that the accounting profession employed a rule-making apparatus to enhance the price of its products through (1) restricting entry, (2) restraining supply and (3) increasing demand. He noted that for those reasons the control of the policy function has been the critical variable in shaping the destiny of the profession.

Buckley's (1980) and Willmott's (1986) arguments, as discussed in Chapter 3, form an essential part of the model adopted for this thesis. In this Chapter it is explained with relevant evidence, that the basis of professional accounting standard-setting is the enhancement and protection of the interests of the professional accountants who are members of the bodies issuing such standards, and the standards, in fact, were initiated to achieve such goals. Circumstances, as shown in the last chapter and as analyzed further in this chapter, have provided added importance to accounting standards. Although accounting standards are now widely accepted as a form of company financial disclosure regulation, it is explained here that the profession sees standardization of accounting methods as an avenue for improving the image and status of the profession. Richardson (1988, p. 381) also argued from a similar perspective suggesting that the accounting profession gained rewards by standardizing their knowledge and institutionalizing training of practitioners, while simultaneously maintaining autonomy in practice.

To strengthen the aforementioned theoretical base further, we briefly look at the origins and development of professional accounting pronouncements in the United States. The United States scenario is a logical choice because of its long history of accounting research and professional pronouncements and in some respects, as is discussed later, its early history of the evolution of accounting pronouncements is similar to that of the early Australian developments.

United States:

Carey (1969) provided an elaborate description of the development of the accounting profession in the United States. Before he entered into his discussion he distinguished a profession from other pursuits and categorized it as a "body of specialized knowledge" (p. 3). His narration of the history of the accounting profession in the United States indicated that the primary ingredient for the creation of an accounting profession was the specialized knowledge that a small group of pioneers of the profession possessed. The next step was that of organization through which various professional bodies were created. Initially the individual members and then the accounting bodies sought recognition by the community through advertisements and other types of publicity. It was followed by a demand for legal recognition and backing. The first C.P.A. law was passed in 1896 in the State of New York which was swiftly followed by other states (pp. 44-45). As the struggle for achieving a professional identity continued the profession used various other methods of improving the status of the infant profession. It must be noted here that in addition to the profession's own efforts there were various other environmental variables which were also responsible for the rapid rise of the American accounting profession. Carey (1969) discussed most of them, for example the evolution of the corporate form, the industrial revolution and increase in internal and external trade (Chapter 2). He explained the development as follows:

> Economic and social change created the *need* for an accounting profession - but accountants themselves *created* the profession by constantly raising the standards of performance, by improving their education and training, by enlarging the scope of their services, and by accepting heavier responsibilities [Emphasis provided] (p. 4).

Amongst the modes of professional development adopted by the American accounting profession a review of the works by Carey (1969 and 1970) and Previts and Merino (1979) revealed that the following were commonly used:

(1)   Organizing and re-organizing the Profession.
(2)   Seeking community and legal recognition.
(3)   Education.
(4)   Professional and ethical standards.
(5)   Technical standards (accounting pronouncements, etc.).
(6)   Congresses and conventions.
(7)   Integration.
(8)   Advertisement and publicity.
(9)   Professional literature.

As seen above, technical standards (precursor's of accounting standards), were used as one of the means of professional development. Keeping in view the specialized knowledge the profession possessed, its members continuously strived to develop their expertise using the various methods which included accounting pronouncements. Carey (1969) in this respect added:

> To secure public confidence, the public accountants had to develop professional organizations, to formulate technical and ethical standards, to establish a system of training their successors, and to acquire symbolic evidence of competence and responsibility (pp. 5-6).

In this respect he noted that:

> The certificate of incorporation of the American Association (*The American Association of Public Accountants*) included as one of its objectives "establishing a high standard of professional attainments through general education and knowledge otherwise." (pp. 40-41)

From Carey's (1969) review of the Profession's history (that of U.S. extensively and Britain briefly) it is found that both the British and the U.S. accounting bodies initially adopted the approach of enlightening the members through lectures. Lectures were delivered to students and in conferences by the leaders of the profession mainly on contentious topics (p. 21 and p. 75). Other forms of maintaining a certain level of expertise were also adopted mainly in the area of education, such as introducing minimum education standards, examinations and the production of instructive literature (For example, see pp. 40-43 and p. 48). Later the American Association realized that the lack of technical standards and the need for uniformity were pressing problems. This led to the introduction of technical meetings (p. 48). In times of controversy regarding accounting methods suggestions for an accounting court were made on several occasions. On the other hand uniformity through consensus seemed to be a simple solution in the eyes of both the accountants and the government officials (Previts and Merino, 1979, p. 185).

The demand for "uniform accounting" came from both within and outside the profession. Previts and Merino (1979) explained this as follows:

Uniform Accounting was the culmination of a trend which began around the turn of the century, namely, to look upon uniformity as a panacea for accounting problems. Accountants themselves had contributed to the growing "faith" which politicians placed in uniformity. (p. 185)

From Previts and Merino's (1979) explanation one important aspect of "Uniform Accounting" is revealed. The quest for uniformity which subsequently led to the publication of a document called *Uniform Accounting* by the American Association was the point of origin for authoritative accounting pronouncements issued by the Profession. Although the Association issued the *Uniform Accounting* in response to pressure from governmental sources and certain segments of the profession itself, most practitioners differed in principle from that document, and it failed to achieve its purpose of guiding the profession (pp. 188-190).

Meanwhile there were other moves within the American Association to achieve uniformity. In the 1910s attention was paid to accounting terminology, but with little success. (Carey, 1969, pp.76-77).

The use of accounting pronouncements to guide or enlighten the profession was not given too much attention again till about the mid-thirties. Only pronouncements like the "Verification of Financial Statements" in 1929, were issued by the A.I.A. (Dean, 1985) - which can be classified as auditing pronouncements. The demand for accounting pronouncements increased with the demand for audited financial statements under the New York Stock Exchange requirements and the Securities and Exchange Act (Zeff, 1979, p. 209). Chatov (1975) noted the importance of the Securities and Exchange Act in influencing the fortunes of the Profession:

The accountants played a crucial role between June, 1933, and June 1934. Compared with their relative exclusion from the deliberations prior to passage of the Securities Act, their new involvement was incredible. Before the acts accountants were weak auxiliaries in the financial system. Subsequently, they were the fulcrum in the critical battle over the determination of financial standards. (p. 39).

Chatov (1975) summarized this role of the accountants in financial accounting standard-setting as follows:

Both accountants and their corporate clients worked hard and successfully to keep the SEC from exercising financial accounting controls. Between 1938 and 1972, the A.I.C.P.A. had *de facto* authority over generally accepted accounting principles, but desire of its members to avoid limitations on their freedom to choose among accounting alternatives guaranteed that the A.I.C.P.A. would do a mediocre job at best in its attempt to develop effective principles. After the A.I.C.P.A. failure became completely evident, authority for the development of accounting principles, now institutionalized in the private sector, did not revert to the SEC. Instead, the authority was assumed by a new group (the F.A.S.B.) composed of representatives from self-selected private organizations.

Corporate financial reporting standards presently are administered by a three-tiered organization drawn exclusively from accounting practitioners, industrial corporations, financial analysts, and accounting "educators." ...

Accountants now quite clearly share authority for setting financial standards with people from the financial and corporate sectors. (pp. 4-5)

Our brief review of the history of the inception of accounting standard-setting in United States indicates that the accounting practitioners took a pioneering role in the evolution of accounting pronouncements and the reason for this kind of involvement was to develop standard practice to enhance the reputation of a rapidly growing profession. It was in response to the demand from within to develop the special expertise that the profession possessed. Later the profession also responded to crises involving financial disclosure before and after the "great crash" by issuing accounting pronouncements. The purpose now seemed to be to maintain its identity as a profession.

The continuing interest and struggle to keep the standard-setting process within its control was in the profession's own interest. The profession saw the accounting expertise as an essential skill for the maintenance of a professional identity and the development of the standards as the development of that expertise. Therefore, the active role of the profession in the standard-setting process was clearly a ploy to safeguard the profession's own image which its pioneers had worked hard to achieve.

Australia:

Having seen the interest and the role of the profession in accounting standard-setting in the United States we now venture into a detailed analysis of the nature of involvement of the Australian accounting profession in accounting standard-setting in Australia.

Carrington (1973), in reviewing the Australian accounting profession, provided two reasons for the creation of an accounting profession:

The first of these conditions was the demand by the community for certain *scarce skills* involving personal judgment and its recognition that a particular group of people were the most favourable source of the knowledge and services required. The particular skills of financial recording, analysis and management were rendered relatively more scarce by a sharp rise in the demand, due to changes in industrial organization and activity. These same circumstances led the individual possessors of skill and knowledge to find it more beneficial to accept the discipline of professional membership than to "go it alone", thus meeting the second requirement for existence of a profession. Their motives might have included an altruistic wish to see the public enjoy high and responsible services, a desire to avoid discredit from the activities of those insufficiently qualified, a desire for public recognition, and even the aim of avoiding undue competition. In return they accepted ethical standards, improved their methods and encouraged education and training.

The profession arose, therefore, not so much from a deliberate fulfillment of some plan of its members, but rather as a logical consequence of broader economic and social developments (p. 4). [Emphasis added]

The role of the professional accounting bodies and their various methods of professional development is very much in the interest of its members. Parker's (1961) narration of the inception of professional accounting bodies in Australia clearly indicates this. Describing the creation of the first accountancy body in Australia - the Adelaide Society of Accountants, he found that the first set of objects of that Society referred to the fact that the Society's purpose was to gain recognition for the profession, and to protect and enhance the interests of its members.

Tables 7.1 and 7.2 show the use of different modes of professional development adopted by the Australian accounting profession (that is the A.S.A. and the I.C.A.A.). If these modes are compared with those used by the American Profession as described by Carey (1969) and Previts and Merino (1979) and listed earlier in this section, we find close similarities between the Australian and American development. The years accounted for in the two tables are 1953 to 1986 for the A.S.A. and 1936 to 1986 for the I.C.A.A., that is, from the first available annual reports of each body. These tables are based on a broad review of annual reports of those years, except where the annual reports are unavailable. The numbers 1 to 5 marked against the various modes in different years indicate the position in which the item was discussed in the annual report. For example, 1 indicates that the item was the first amongst all items discussed in the report, 2 indicates that it was the next item and 3 signifies the third position of the item. Apart from the notations of 1 to 5, X's have been marked against the modes. These X's signify that the item was discussed but it was not one of the first five discussed in the report.

The reason for the use of notations from 1 to 5 is to show, in a systematic fashion, that the item appears to have been given greater priority by the professional bodies in comparison with other issues. Although the position of the mode on various occasions is assumed to reflect its importance to the professional body, some items consistently occupied the same position till a major change was made in the format of the reports. Therefore, even if the position of the item discussed on many occasions may signify the priority of that item in the agenda of the professional body, it may not be so for all years. To that extent the weighting is arbitrary.

In the case of the A.S.A., out of the 34 annual reports reviewed, accounting pronouncements were discussed in 25 of the reports, Within those 25 reports it occupied a position between 1 to 5 in 11 years. It is interesting to note, that out of those 11 years 10 were in the 1960's and the 1970's. In the same twenty year period accounting pronouncements were discussed in the reports in all but 4 years. We shall also see later that in these two decades accounting standards were closely scrutinized in the accounting literature.

For I.C.A.A. 51 annual reports were reviewed, out of which there were discussions on accounting pronouncements in 31 reports. In 28 of those reports accounting pronouncements were placed in one of the first five positions. 17 of those 28 occurred in the twenty years period of 1960's and 1970's. It was also discussed in the remaining 3 years of the 20 years period.

Although the issue of accounting pronouncements in Australia received prominence in 1944 when the I.C.A.A. first entertained the idea of issuing recommendations (See Zeff, 1973, p. 2), some thought was already being given to achieving uniformity in accounting principles and accounting terminology. On two separate occasions in 1936 and 1937, Sir Alexander Fitzgerald voiced the need for the opinions of the accounting bodies on general principles which would be of universal application. In 1937 a special committee of the Commonwealth Institute of Accountants, entrusted with the task of recommending on the various means of developing the Institutes activities, recommended that the General Council set up committees on accounting principles and terminology. It was contemplated that on the basis of research conducted by State committees the General council would issue authoritative statements (Zeff, 1973, p. 29).

TABLE 7.1: MODES OF DEVELOPING THE ACCOUNTING PROFESSION USED BY THE A.S.A.

Mode of Professional Development	1953	54	55	56	57	58	59	1960	61	62	63	64	65	66	67	68	69
Organization	1		1	1	1	1	1						1	1	2		
Registration & Status	2	1	2	2	2	2				1	X	3					
Education and Professional Development	3	3	3	3	3	4	2	2	1	1	2	3	4	2	3	3	2
Publications	5	5	5		X	X	4	5	4	3	4	5				5	5
Professional Conduct	X	X	X	X	X	X	5	X	5	4	X	2	X	X			X
Involvement in Company and Other Legislations	X	X	X					X	X	5	X		X	X	5	X	4
Accounting Pronouncements Recommendations & Standards					X	X		4	3	X		5		2	4	X	
Code of Ethics & Auditing Standards																	

Source: Extracted from A.S.A. Annual Reports

TABLE 7.1: MODES OF DEVELOPING THE ACCOUNTING PROFESSION USED BY THE A.S.A. [Continued]

Mode of Professional Development	Year																
	1953	54	55	56	57	58	59	1960	61	62	63	64	65	66	67	68	69
Mandatory Accounting Standards																	
Self-Regulation																	
Co-Regulation																	
Inflation Accounting																	
Other Research in Accounting, Auditing, Etc.	4	4	4	4	5	5	3	3	2	2	3	4		3	4	4	3
Conventions & Congresses	X	2		5	4	3		1					5	5			
Integration & Co-ordination with Other Accountancy Bodies											1	1			2	1	1
Publicity & Advertising																	
Specialization																	
Indemnity Insurance & Limiting Professional Liability																	

TABLE 7.1: MODES OF DEVELOPING THE ACCOUNTING PROFESSION USED BY THE A.S.A. [Continued]

Mode of Professional Development	1970	71	72	73	74	75	76	77	78	79	1980	81	82	83	84	85	86
Organization		1					1			1			X				
Registration & Status				4	2	2	X				4						
Education and Professional Development	1	3	3	1	1	5	X	2	X	4	2	2	X		1	1	2
Publications	X	4	X	5	4	X			X	5		X	X	X	4		3
Professional Conduct	5	5		X	5	X					5	5	X	X	X	5	5
Involvement in Company and Other Legislations	4	X	5	4	X	3	5						X		4		
Accounting Pronouncements Recommendations & Standards	3	X	X	3	3	4		4	X	X	X	X	X	X	5	X	X
Code of Ethics & Auditing Standards																	

TABLE 7.1: MODES OF DEVELOPING THE ACCOUNTING PROFESSION USED BY THE A.S.A.
[Continued]

Mode of Professional Development	1970	71	72	73	74	75	76	77	78	79	1980	81	82	83	84	85	86
Mandatory Accounting Standards										X		3	4	4	2		
Self-Regulation									3		2						
Co-Regulation														3	5	3	
Inflation Accounting						2	3		1	x							
Other Research in Accounting, Auditing, Etc.	2		X					1									
Conventions & Congresses							2						1			2	
Integration & Co-ordination with Other Accountancy Bodies		X	1				1	4	3	2	X		1	1			
Publicity & Advertising		2	2						4	3	X	X		5	2	4	4
Specialization								5	5	2	X		3	1	3	3	1
Indemnity Insurance & Limiting Professional Liability																	

Table 7.2: Methods of Professional Development
Adopted by the I.C.A.A.

Mode of Professional Development	Year																
	1936	37	38	39	1940	41	42	43	44	45	46	47	48	49	1950	51	52
Organization	3	1			1	1	1	1	N.A	1	1	2	3	N.A	1	3	2
Registration & Status				X			4		N.A	4				N.A	X		
Education and Professional Development				4	X	3	2	4	N.A	2	3	X	1	N.A.		1	1
Publications	2		1		5	4	3	3	N.A	X	5	3	2	N.A	4	X	4
Professional Conduct			2	3	3				N.A.						N.A.	X	X
Involvement in Company and Other Legislations					2	2	2	2	N.A	5			4	N.A	5	X	3
Accounting Pronouncements Recommendations & Standards								N.A	3		2	4			N.A.		
Code of Ethics & Auditing Standards				1	4		4		N.A.			5	5		N.A.		2

Source: Extracted from I.C.A.A. Annual Reports

Table 7.2: Methods of Professional Development
Adopted by the I.C.A.A.
[Continued]

Mode of Professional Development	1936	37	38	39	1940	41	42	43	44	45	46	47	48	49	1950	51	52
Mandatory Accounting Standards								N.A.						N.A.			
Self-Regulation								N.A.						N.A.			
Co-Regulation								N.A.						N.A.			
Inflation Accounting								N.A.						N.A.			
Other Research in Accounting, Auditing, Etc.					5			N.A.			4	1	X	N.A	3	4	5
Conventions & Congresses	1		3					N.A.						N.A	2	X	
Integration & Co-ordination with Other Accountancy Bodies								N.A.						N.A.			
Publicity & Advertising								N.A.						N.A.			5
Specialization								N.A.						N.A.			
Indemnity Insurance & Limiting Professional Liability					5			N.A.						N.A.			

Table 7.2: Methods of Professional Development
Adopted by the I.C.A.A.
[Continued]

Mode of Professional Development	1953	54	55	56	57	58	59	1960	61	62	63	64	65	66	67	68	69
Organization	3	4			3	2	2				X	X	X	2	1		
Registration & Status			X								X						
Education and Professional Development	2	1	1	1	1	1	1	1	1	1	1	1	1	1	X	X	X
Publications	4	4			2	3								4			X
Professional Conduct	X	X	X	X	X	X	X	X	X	X	X	X	X	X	4	4	4
Involvement in Company and Other Legislations	X		2	4	4	X	X	5	5	4	5	5	3	5	X	X	X
Accounting Pronouncements Recommendations & Standards					5	5	5	4	3	3	3	3	X	X	2	3	3
Code of Ethics & Auditing Standards		2					X	X	X	X		X	X		3	5	5

Table 7.2: Methods of Professional Development
Adopted by the I.C.A.A.
[Continued]

Mode of Professional Development	1953	54	55	56	57	58	59	1960	61	62	63	64	65	66	67	68	69
Mandatory Accounting Standards																	
Self-Regulation																	
Co-Regulation																	
Inflation Accounting															X		
Other Research in Accounting, Auditing, Etc.	5	5	5	2	X	4	3	3	2	2	2	2	4	X	X	X	X
Conventions & Congresses	1		3		X	X	X	X	5	X	X		2	3	5	1	1
Integration & Co-ordination with Other Accountancy Bodies														5	X	2	2
Publicity & Advertising		3	3	5	X						X		X	X			
Specialization																	
Indemnity Insurance & Limiting Professional Liability							4		2	4		4	4				X

Table 7.2: Methods of Professional Development
Adopted by the I.C.A.A.
[Continued]

Mode of Professional Development	Year																
	1970	71	72	73	74	75	76	77	78	79	1980	81	82	83	84	85	86
Organization	2	3	1	1	1	5	5									5	3
Registration & Status		X			X	X	X	X	2		2	X	5	X	5	X	X
Education and Professional Development	3	1	2	4	5			X	X	X	X	X	X	3		4	X
Publications	X	X	5	X	X			X		X	X	X	X	5		X	X
Professional Conduct	X				X	X	X	X	X		X	5	3	X			
Involvement in Company and Other Legislations		5	3		4	3	3	5			X	1	2	2	3		4
Accounting Pronouncements Recommendations & Standards	4	2	4	3	2	2	1	3	5	X	5	3	1	4		1	
Code of Ethics & Auditing Standards					3		2	4	X	5	3	X	X	X		X	X

Table 7.2: Methods of Professional Development
Adopted by the I.C.A.A.
[Continued]

Mode of Professional Development	1970	71	72	73	74	75	76	77	78	79	1980	81	82	83	84	85	86
Mandatory Accounting Standards									3						1	2	1
Self-Regulation																	
Co-Regulation									4								
Inflation Accounting								1	2	3		4	4	X			
Other Research in Accounting, Auditing, Etc.	X	X					4	2	X	4		X		4	2	3	X
Conventions & Congresses				2		1			1			X	X	X	X	X	X
Integration & Co-ordination with Other Accountancy Bodies	1		X		4	X	X	X	1			1	2	X			
Publicity & Advertising	X	X			5	X		X	X	X	X	X	X	1	4	X	5
Specialization															X		
Indemnity Insurance & Limiting Professional Liability	5	4									X	X	X	X	X		2

Two aspects were important in this inception of the idea of authoritative accounting pronouncements. First, it was part of a remedial programme with the objective of improving the image of the profession or in other words accounting pronouncements were adopted for the purpose of professional development. Second, it was to first achieve consensus on principles applied universally and then issue opinions (Zeff, 1973, p. 29). Therefore the C.I.A. was interested only in guiding its members by informing them about accounting principles of universal application, rather than applying pronouncements for company financial disclosure regulation.

Feller (1974) also asserted that it was not the purpose of the professional accounting pronouncements to lay down the law or to wield authority. They were a response of the profession to challenges presented by the developments in the economic, social and political environment (p. 392).

Although the Commonwealth Institute did proceed with accounting research of its own and also reviewed the I.C.A.E.W. Recommendations, it did not issue any authoritative pronouncements. It did embark upon improving the skills of its members by using other modes of informing the members, such as research lectures, formation of State research committees and publishing of technical papers in The Australian Accountant (Zeff, 1973, pp. 30-33). After the creation of the A.S.A., the various modes of determining and disseminating the universal or preferred accounting practices continued but the performance of the Society in issuing accounting pronouncements remained low. In fact, the A.S.A. issued only one authoritative pronouncement before combining its efforts with the I.C.A.A. (See Table 7.4.).

The A.S.A. and its predecessor the C.I.A. did not issue many authoritative pronouncements. Nevertheless the objective of all the other efforts related to pronouncements, like research lectures and bulletins, remained the same as that adopted at the A.S.A.'s inception - the development of the professional skills and the improvement of image of the profession. For example Zeff (1973) commented as follows about the research lectures:

> The lectures were viewed as an effective means of stimulating accounting research and of publishing the results for the *benefit* of the profession (p. 40). [Emphasis added]

The I.C.A.A., amidst controversy regarding whether to issue pronouncements (its own or the I.C.A.E.W.'s),[124] also issued pronouncements to guide and enlighten its members (Zeff, 1973, p. 2) rather than with an objective of regulating company financial disclosure. The purpose of the guidance initially was to inform the members regarding the best practice (Evans, 1974, p. 64). Jager, Taylor and Craig (1979) had this to say regarding the Institute's Recommendations:

> These recommendations could be regarded as the result of the movement from within the accounting profession for reform, which had steadily been gaining momentum over two or three decades (p. 205).

The early beginnings of the use of accounting pronouncements in Australia is quite similar to those of the United States. The purpose of issuing pronouncements in Australia was also to enhance the image of an evolving profession. Similar to the American experience the Australian accounting bodies initially paid less attention to the development of pronouncements than to

---

124   See previous chapter or Zeff (1973, p. 2).

other matters (See Tables 7.1 and 7.2), and like their American counterparts they started paying more attention to the pronouncements after anomalies in company financial reporting was detected in certain major company failures. This later observation of the Australian Profession reacting to a certain crisis and the eventual upgrading of professional accounting pronouncements to instruments of company financial disclosure regulation is analyzed further in the next few sections.

Accounting Literature and Accounting Standards:

In this section the nature of attention paid to accounting pronouncements in Australia since 1945 is analyzed. In the previous section we found that accounting pronouncements had roots in developing professional accounting practices. The following analysis is in the light of attention paid to various forms of professional development techniques used by the Profession.

Data:

The accounting profession applied various modes of professional development for its members, some of which were also used to counter the criticisms of the sixties. Headings of columns 5 to 15 in Table 7.3.A. provide the names of those major methods.

The data in Table 7.3.A. cover a time period from 1945 to 1986 and include literature from professional, academic, financial and the general press. It has been compiled from the annual indexes of literature published by the Australian Public Affairs Information Service (A.P.A.I.S.). The A.P.A.I.S. indexes have been chosen in preference to the Accountants Index, published in the U.S., because it includes information about the Australian financial and general press, for example the Australian Financial Review, the Business Review Weekly and the Sydney Morning Herald, in addition to that of the professional and academic literature. It is felt that such publications either play a significant role in forming the opinion of the public or are used by interested parties to voice their own opinion. Again, A.P.A.I.S. indexes cover a longer time period than other comprehensive indexes like the Australian Business Index.[125]

The choice of the period 1945 to 1986 has some significance attached to it. Apart from 1946 being the year from which A.P.A.I.S. indexes commenced publications, it was the year preceding the year, that is 1946, in which the Australian accounting profession issued its first set of pronouncements. If there was a major demand for those pronouncements within Australia there could have been some exchange of ideas through the accounting literature in 1945. Again, 1986 is the year after the last year selected for this study, that is 1985. 1986 has been included to include any literature concerning the creation of the A.S.R.B. and mandatory accounting standards which may have overflowed from previous years' debates.

Although certain precautions have been taken in the preparation of the table, there may be some errors of compilation still remaining. For example, multiple listings of the same literature under various headings had to be identified and eliminated, but it cannot be guaranteed that all have been dealt with. Again frequent changes in the categories used for indexing created a problem and necessitated reclassification according to the categories in the Table. In addition, some cases of misclassification, between years and between classes, were also

---

125   The Australian Business Index commenced publication from January, 1980.

identified in the A.P.A.I.S. indexes, and these have been reclassified.

Apart from the remaining errors that could exist in the Table, there are other limitations of this table. First, all items in the table have been given a weight of one, which is contrary to the fact that all publications may not have the same degree of influence on the readers. The influence of the publication, amongst other things, may vary with the importance of the author or the institution he or she represents, the type of market that publication caters to and the timing of the publication. As it is quite difficult to assess the influence of each item of literature, all items have been given the arbitrary, equal weight of one.

Second, the items which dealt at length with two or more subjects have been counted for in more than one column, to account for all subjects it dealt with.

Third, no distinction is made for whether the item was for or against a certain issue/method because in many cases the author made no such distinction or it was difficult to determine a clear distinction. Consequently, the figures only represent the general nature of attention paid to a topic in a particular year.

Finally, an attempt was made to keep the classifications of this table similar to those of Tables 7.1. and 7.2., but due to the varying nature of classifications in the A.P.A.I.S. indexes and the annual reports of the accounting bodies, this was not completely possible.

Table 7.3A: Frequency of Accounting Literature Regarding Criticisms of
Professional Development Methods of the Accounting Profession

Year Company Failure & Accounting	Responsibility & Liability of Accountants & Auditors	Total of Methods	Accounting Principles	Accounting Standards	Total Professional Accounting Pronouncements [col.5 + col.6]	Mandatory Standards	Auditing Standards
1	2	3	4	5	6	7	8	9
YR	COFAIL	RESP	MTHD	PRIN	STD	PRO	MSTD	AUSTD
1945	0	0	0	0	0	0	0	0
1946	0	0	0	0	0	0	0	0
1947	0	0	0	0	0	0	0	0
1948	0	1	5	2	0	2	0	0
1949	0	0	0	0	0	0	0	0
1950	0	0	0	0	0	0	0	0
1951	0	1	3	1	0	1	0	0
1952	0	1	12	1	0	1	0	0
1953	0	1	11	1	0	1	0	0
1954	0	1	8	3	0	3	0	0
1955	0	0	3	0	0	0	0	0
1956	0	0	5	0	0	0	0	0
1957	0	0	0	1	0	1	0	0
1958	0	0	1	0	0	0	0	0
1959	0	1	1	0	0	0	0	0
1960	0	0	1	0	0	0	0	0
1961	0	0	0	0	0	0	0	0
1962	0	1	0	0	0	0	0	0
1963	0	5	2	2	0	2	0	0
1964	3	0	2	3	0	3	0	2
1965	2	2	4	1	0	1	0	8
1966	4	5	3	3	0	3	0	0
1967	0	2	8	0	0	0	1	1
1968	0	4	14	0	1	1	1	3
1969	1	4	7	6	0	6	1	1
1970	0	2	9	0	0	0	1	0
1971	0	1	12	5	1	6	0	0
1972	1	5	10	0	3	3	1	0
1973	2	8	27	5	2	7	1	1
1974	1	6	14	0	10	10	2	3
1975	1	12	50	0	22	18	0	3
1976	0	10	40	0	12	12	1	2
1977	1	13	24	0	18	18	2	2
1978	1	7	17	3	11	14	2	1
1979	0	13	39	0	10	10	4	5
1980	3	10	27	0	8	8	0	2
1981	2	17	38	0	4	4	4	0
1982	0	13	35	2	15	17	9	3
1983	0	7	18	0	7	7	3	7
1984	0	9	25	1	7	18	6	12
1985	0	14	23	2	10	12	6	4
1986	0	7	16	0	24	24	5	1

Source: A.P.A.I.S. Index

Table 7.3A: Frequency of Accounting Literature Regarding Criticisms of
Professional Development Methods of the Accounting Profession
[Continued]

Year	Accounting & Companies& Acts	Education & Qualification	Registra & Status& Coordinatio&	Integration	Indemnity Insurance Limited Liability	Advertisement & Publicity
1	10	11	12	13	14	15
YR	COACT	EDU	REG	INT	INDM	ADV
1945	0	0	0	0	0	0
1946	0	0	0	0	0	0
1947	0	0	1	0	0	0
1948	4	0	1	0	0	0
1949	2	0	1	0	0	0
1950	0	0	3	0	0	0
1951	0	0	1	0	0	0
1952	3	2	3	1	0	0
1953	2	1	0	0	0	0
1954	3	1	1	0	0	0
1955	0	0	0	0	0	0
1956	0	5	3	0	0	0
1957	0	0	2	0	0	0
1958	1	0	3	0	0	0
1959	1	0	3	0	0	0
1960	3	1	4	0	0	0
1961	4	0	1	0	0	0
1962	0	1	2	0	0	0
1963	1	3	2	0	0	0
1964	6	2	1	0	0	1
1965	1	8	3	0	0	0
1966	3	7	2	1	0	0
1967	4	8	2	0	0	0
1968	2	4	0	1	0	0
1969	3	5	3	2	0	0
1970	4	2	7	0	1	0
1971	9	4	1	1	0	0
1972	8	3	3	0	0	0
1973	1	10	5	0	0	0
1974	4	16	3	1	0	0
1975	4	12	2	1	0	0
1976	6	8	3	0	0	0
1977	1	3	1	1	0	0
1978	0	5	4	3	0	0
1979	2	10	9	0	1	1
1980	4	7	11	1	4	3
1981	4	13	7	13	0	0
1982	6	13	11	2	1	2
1983	6	10	15	0	0	4
1984	4	8	10	1	0	15
1985	5	11	10	1	0	6
1986	5	8	4	0	4	4

Analysis:

A simple glance at the figures in Table 7.3.A. tells us that there has been a remarkable jump, since 1960s, in the types of literature that have been accounted for in that table. Basically two kinds of literature have been dealt with. Columns 2, 3 and 4 represent those items which dealt with a critique/analysis/discussion on company failures and accounting; the responsibilities and liabilities of the profession and its members; and various accounting methods.

The second kind of literature, from columns 5 to 15, dealt with the means that were adopted or examined by the accounting profession or others for resolving the problems faced by the profession. The classes that have been accounted for are those which have received at least a reasonable amount of coverage and attention in the literature or in the annual reports.

Initially the intention here was to identify the correlation between the criticisms arising from company failures in the accounting literature in Australia with the attention paid to various methods of professional development in accounting in the literature, thus revealing the methods which received greater attention. From column 2 of Table 7.3.A. it can be seen that, although company failures did begin to receive attention in the 1960s, literature dealing specifically with failures was scanty and intermittent and mitigated against a feasible analysis. In fact there is another class of literature in accounting which can act as an indicator of the attention paid toward the accounting profession. This is the literature on the responsibilities and liabilities of accountants and auditors (Col. 3) under various conditions. A cursory look at column 3 of Table 7.3.A. tells us that even though there has been little literature directly on company failures, there has been a significant amount of literature on responsibilities and liabilities of accountants and auditors, specially since the sixties. Since discussions relating to responsibilities and liabilities of accountants have often led to the examination of various modes of professional development (For example see Birkett and Walker, 1971, p. 99), this latter class of literature has been taken as a proxy for the growing attention paid to the profession generally, from both within and without the profession. Again accounting methods have been a major issue for the criticism of the Profession, for which the literature in that area has been included in the analysis (Col. 4).

Carrington (1973) in this respect, recognized the relationship between the dissatisfaction with accounting reports and practitioners' liability on the one hand and the demand for accounting standards. He stated:

> A great deal of stress is currently being laid on the need for authoritative accounting standards or principles as a means of overcoming public dissatisfaction with accounting reports and reducing the auditors liability by providing authoritative backing for individual practitioners as to appropriate procedures.

As noted in the previous chapter anomalies in techniques have led to greater criticism of the profession. Carrington (1973) stressed this point further:

A combination of two unfortunate features of present accounting practice provides the strongest case for accounting standards. These are wide variety of possible alternatives which can be used in matters of accounting procedure and the limited and sometimes non-existent, disclosure to the recipients of reports regarding the methods selected or the significance of a particular choice in terms of the results produced (p. 9).

Attention has been paid to accounting practices and methods in the literature. The amount of discussion on the different methods has, again, been taken as proxy to represent the general nature of attention paid on accounting methods.

Table 7.3.A. (Tables 7.3.BA. through 7.3.BD.) has been prepared to provide Spearman's correlation matrices for correlation between the annual frequency of literature in the various groups identified in Table 7.3.A.

Spearman's correlation technique has been used because it is a non-parametric technique, thereby being suitable for discrete variables as opposed to continuous variables (Huck, et al, 1974, p. 31). In this analysis we are using the frequency of literature in each year as an indicator of importance that had been placed on various issues in those years rather than as a measure which can assume any numerical value on a continuous scale. This is because literature vary in importance and as issues discussed in such literature flow from one year to the other with varying time lags between the emergence of an issue and the publication of literature on such issues it is difficult to provide the exact measure of importance placed on an issue in the literature on a continuous scale. Hence the choice of a non-parametric technique instead of a parametric technique.

Table 7.3.B.: The Spearman Correlation Coefficient Matrix for All Variables of Table 7.3.A.

Table 7.3.BA.: For All Years

Variables	COFAIL	RESP	MTHD	PRIN	STD	PRO	MSTD	AUSTD	COACT	EDU	REG	INT	INDM
RESP	.3944*												
MTHD	.3103	.8850**											
PRIN	.2416	.1205	.1092										
STD	.2033	.7927**	.7987**	-.1317									
PRO	.4015*	.8288**	.8182**	.3564	.8312**								
MSTD	.1340	.7247**	.7017**	-.0089	.7030**	.6511**							
AUSTD	.3037	.6728**	.6677**	.0651	.6721**	.6879**	.6486**						
COACT	.1573	.4727**	.5427**	.1150	.4906**	.5032**	.5217**	.3903*					
EDU	.4320*	.8432**	.8283**	.1329	.6872**	.7334**	.7539**	.7431**	.5401**				
REG	.1847	.5931**	.5374**	.0037	.4545*	.4268*	.5560**	.4603*	.3679*	.6340**			
INT	.4380*	.5832**	.5537**	.2981	.5493**	.5927**	.4050*	.3800*	.2814	.5399**	.2882		
INDM	-.0245	.3629*	.3643*	-.1570	.3966*	.3123	.2773	.2558	.2798	.2905	.4778**	.0668	
ADV	-.0135	.4460*	.4320*	.0732	.5256**	.5262**	.5504***	.6282**	.4746**	.4573*	.5590**	.1745	.5412***

* - Significance level .01;   ** - Significance level .001;   "." is printed if coefficient cannot be computed.
Note: All abbreviated variable names are explained in Table 7.3. column headings.

Table 7.3.B.: The Spearman Correlation Coefficient Matrix for All Variables of Table 7.3.A.

Table 7.3.BB.: For Years 1945 to 1959.

Variables	COFAIL	RESP	MTHD	PRIN	STD	PRO	MSTD	AUSTD	COACT	EDU	REG	INT	INDM
RESP	.	.7340**											
MTHD	.	.7369***	.6184*										
PRIN	.												
STD													
PRO	.	.7369***	.6184*	1.0000**	.								
MSTD						.							
AUSTD							.						
COACT	.	.6683*	.6048*	.5809	.	.5809	.	.					
EDU	.	.3643	.7559**	.3628	.	.3628	.	.	.3546				
REG	.	.0495	.0910	-.0673	.	-.0673	.	.	.1222	.2056			
INT	.	.3273	.4485	.2471	.	.2471	.	.	.3702	.4770	.3241	.	
INDM	.		.	.	.	.	.	.	.	.	.	.	.
ADV	.		.	.	.	.	.	.	.	.	.	.	.

* - Significance level .01;   ** - Significance level .001;   "." is printed if coefficient cannot be computed.
Note: All abbreviated variable names are explained in Table 7.3. column headings.

Table 7.3.B.: The Spearman Correlation Coefficient Matrix for All Variables of Table 7.3.A.

Table 7.3.BC. For Years 1960 to 1980

Variables	COFAIL	RESP	MTHD	PRIN	STD	PRO	MSTD	AUSTD	COACT	EDU	REG	INT	INDM
RESP	.2150												
MTHD	.0878	.8327**											
PRIN	.5023	-.0937	-.1065										
STD	-.0322	.7188**	.8110**	-.3201									
PRO	.3496	.7796***	.7616**	.2265	.7851**								
MSTD	.1110	.6064*	.6613***	-.1905	.4839	.4521							
AUSTD	.2688	.4733	.5738*	-.1399	.4842	.5135	.5034						
COACT	.0939	-.2385	.0649	-.1251	.0966	-.0370	.1750	-.1309					
EDU	.3235	.6645**	.7046**	.1107	.4136	.5821*	.6531**	.6562**	-.0077				
REG	.0354	.3015	.2594	.0069	-.0214	.0585	.3216	.0471	-.1831	.3167			
INT	.2895	.3104	.3310	.3330	.4517	.5874*	.1297	.1779	-.1134	.2793	-.2143		
INDM	-.3137	.1599	.2026	-.2616	.0317	-.0584	.1474	.0752	.0147	.0290	.5305*	-.2655	
ADV	.1098	.0145	.0434	.0491	.0317	.1606	.1474	.3610	.1173	.0290	.0737	-.2655	.4444

* - Significance level .01;   ** - Significance level .001;   "." is printed if coefficient cannot be computed.

Note: All abbreviated variable names are explained in Table 7.3. column headings.

Table 7.3.B.: The Spearman Correlation Coefficient Matrix for All Variables of Table 7.3.A.

Table 7.3.BD. For the Years 1970 to 1986.

Variables	COFAIL	RESP	MTHD	PRIN	STD	PRO	MSTD	AUSTD	COACT	EDU	REG	INT	INDM
RESP	.1341												
MTHD	.1611	.7811**											
PRIN	-.0971	-.0910	-.1013										
STD	-.1535	.4508	.4012	-.2184									
PRO	-.1745	.4125	.3717	-.0238	.9722**								
MSTD	-.3092	.4346	.2996	.0595	.2760	.2854							
AUSTD	-.3394	.3960	.4065	-.0546	.3685	.4053	.5226						
COACT	-.4853	-.2687	-.2315	-.0265	-.0972	-.159	.1844	-.0778					
EDU	.0685	.4985	.5120	.0152	.2104	.1949	.7178**	.4750	-.0013				
REG	-.1822	.2918	.1658	.0498	-.1558	-.1558	.3735	.4653	.0297	.2920			
INT	.3235	.3914	.1835	.3201	.2053	.2238	.1308	0	-.2017	.3146	.0172		
INDM	-.1680	.0230	0	-.2552	.2070	.1687	.0742	-.0348	-.0039	-.1115	.4071	-.1974	
ADV	-.4469	.2506	.0680	.0579	.2026	.2488	.5607*	.6487*	.1980	.1941	.7318**	-.0577	.3638

* - Significance level .01;   ** - Significance level .001;   " . " is printed if coefficient cannot be computed.
Note: All abbreviated variable names are explained in Table 7.3. column headings.

The four tables Table 7.3.BA. to Table 7.3.BD. provide correlation matrices for four periods. Table 7.3.BA. provides correlation coefficients for the years 1945 to 1986, that is all the years under consideration. Table 7.3.BB. provides correlation coefficients for the pre 1960's period of 1945 to 1959. Table 7.3.BC. provides correlation coefficients for the years 1960 to 1980 - a period within which accountants and accounting methods received considerable public attention. Finally, a correlation matrix has been computed for the years 1970 to 1986 to analyze the situation in a period when mandatory/legislatively backed standards were demanded. The breakdown of the 41 year period of 1945-86 to smaller periods can provide necessary insight into the trend in the scrutiny of the various areas of accounting in the literature under changing circumstances.

For the purposes of our analysis we will consider as highly significant only those correlation coefficients that are significant at .001 level of significance. When interpreting the correlation coefficients it is essential to remember that a high correlation does not necessarily indicate that a causal relationship exists between the two variables. The cause of the high correlation between two variables may be a third variable in some cases.

The findings in Table 7.3.BA. reveal that for the 41 year period accounted for the correlation coefficient for the Responsibilities and Liabilities of accountants and auditors literature and the Accounting Methods literature is highly significant. The same is true for crisis and non-crisis periods as shown in Tables 7.3.BB. to 7.3.BD. This indicates that the scrutiny in the literature on Responsibilities and Liabilities and Accounting Methods go "hand-in-hand", even under changing circumstances. Under the 41 year time span accounted for in Table 7.3.BA. the importance placed on these two areas seem to have drawn attention to various modes of professional development. This is indicated by the high correlation between these two variables and Accounting Standards, Accounting Pronouncements and Mandatory Standards; Auditing Standards; Accounting and Companies Acts; Education and Qualification; Registration and Status; and Integration and Coordination between accounting bodies. This is consistent with our earlier discussion in this and the previous chapter that scrutiny of accountants and accounting methods had led to (or can lead to) the assessment of professional development methods from both within and outside the profession.

If we see Table 7.3.BB. to 7.3.BD. the latter observation is not true in all circumstances. Table 7.3.BB. shows a high correlation between Responsibilities and Liabilities literature and that on Accounting Principles. As accounting standards was virtually a non-existent term between 1945 and 1959 and as no literature could be located on that subject, the correlation coefficient between Total Pronouncements and Responsibilities and Liabilities is the same as that for Accounting Principles. The observation made here leads us to believe that accounting principles which were issued solely by the profession were discussed in the literature simultaneously with the issues on accountants and auditors liabilities. On the other hand more attention seems to have been placed on Education and Qualifications in relation to the frequency of literature on Accounting Methods in the 1945-59 period (See the correlation coefficient for these to variables).

The correlation coefficients in Table 7.3.BC. indicate that in the 1960-80 period attention moved from accounting principles to accounting standards. As the correlation between the Responsibility and Liabilities and Accounting Methods literature on the one hand and the Principles literature slid to negative values, that with Accounting Standards became highly significant. This conforms to our observations in Chapter 6 and also in Chapter 8 that within this period there was a shift from demands for broad accounting principles to more enforceable accounting standards. But, as a whole, accounting pronouncements remained high on the agenda in the literature. Another mode of professional development that also received considerable attention in this period was Education and Qualifications (See its correlation coefficients with Responsibilities and Liabilities and Accounting Methods). Mandatory Standards also received significant attention in relation to Accounting Methods. This as we shall see in Chapter 8 is conformity to the fact that in the earlier stages of the demand for mandatory standards, such demands were placed in the light of poor performance of the accounting profession to prepare accounting standards to combat the wide spread misuse of accounting methods.

Table 7.3.BD. which has been constructed mainly to study the correlation between Mandatory Standards on the one hand and Responsibilities and Liabilities and Accounting Methods on the other, between 1970 and 1980. There seems to be no significant correlation in this case. The major reason that can be forwarded at this stage and has been discussed in Chapter 8 was that mandatory standards as an issue gained importance from mid-1970 onwards because of claims of non-compliance with professional accounting standards by companies and the lack of the power of the accounting profession to enforce their standards.

There are some other correlation coefficients, specially in Table 7.3.BA., that are highly significant. All these coefficients are for correlation between modes of professional development. Some of these, like that between Accounting Principles or Accounting Standards and Accounting Pronouncements are inevitable because the first two are the components of the latter. Others like that between Auditing Standards and Accounting Pronouncements or Standards may be because they are complimentary modes of professional development. Whereas others are high simply because they represent the correlation between variables which are highly correlated to a third variable such as Responsibilities and Liabilities or Accounting Methods. What ever their cause may be those issues are out of our scope of discussion.

The increased frequency of literature on accounting pronouncements and the higher correlation between that frequency and those of Accountants and Auditors Responsibilities and Liabilities and Accounting Methods in the 1960-80 period indicate that accounting pronouncements did receive enhanced attention during the period of crisis and the years immediately preceding it, as noted in Chapter 6. Again the amount of discussions on Accounting Pronouncement in the literature seems to be closely related to the amount of Accounting Methods literature and the latter is correlated to Responsibilities and Liabilities literature. The correlations are higher for the years 1960 to 1980. This indicates that the discussion on methods could have led to increased attention on accounting pronouncements but it also indicates that this increased attention could also have been brought about by the focus on the accountants and auditors Responsibilities and Liabilities due to increased criticism of their accounting methods. In our review of the inception of the accounting pronouncements as financial disclosure regulation in the previous chapter, we noted this last finding. Literatures like that of Birkett and Walker (1971) and Zeff (1973) have mentioned that the professional bodies, specially the I.C.A.A., responded to the criticism of professional methods only when the members started feeling threatened by such criticisms. The substantive strength of the correlation coefficients of Accounting Pronouncements with Responsibilities and

Liabilities and Accounting Methods, in the pre and post 1960 periods, compared to that of most other modes of professional development, indicates that accounting pronouncements received greater attention than the other modes which had been adopted by the Australian profession for professional development.

As noted earlier, in the period prior to 1960's accounting standards were given hardly any attention. Discussions on pronouncements were restricted to accounting principles. This was complemented by literature on education and qualification of members and participation of accounting bodies in the preparation of Companies Acts. This implies that the profession bodies and their critics were keen in resolving issues of professional development through methods other than accounting standards. A similar picture is provided by Tables 7.1. and 7.2. An inference that can be drawn is that in the period prior to 1960, as attention was on various other methods of professional development, very little attention was paid to accounting standards by the profession. This will be discussed further in the next section.

These observations suggest why the profession did not venture too much into accounting standards in particular or in the domain of accounting pronouncements, generally, before the 1960's. In the light of the theoretical model (Chapter 3), we can simply deduce that between 1945 to 1959 there was insufficient demand for them as modes of professional development or as a form of company financial disclosure regulation. Our observations show that the company collapses of the sixties and early seventies did lead to greater focus on accounting methods (Column 4) and accountants and auditors responsibilities and liabilities (Column 3). The close relationship of the attention paid to accounting pronouncements generally and accounting standards in particular support our contention of Chapter 6 that crises of the sixties and early seventies led to greater emphasis on professional accounting standards.

The shift in the literature from recommendations and principles to accounting standards and mandatory accounting standards implies that the accounting pronouncements that were once adopted as a means of guiding the profession, started being regarded as a mode of company financial disclosure regulation. More concrete evidence is provided for this observation in the next section.

Professional Accounting Pronouncements:

In this section the activities of the profession in terms of producing accounting standards is analyzed.

Data:

Table 7.4. shows the number of authoritative pronouncements issued by the accounting bodies since the first set of recommendations issued by the I.C.A.A. in 1946. In that table various forms of authoritative pronouncements issued by the profession have been accounted for. The criterion for recognizing them as authoritative is that they have either received approval of the National Councils of one of the accounting bodies or both the National Councils.[126]

---

126   A.S.R.B. Approved Accounting Standards accounted for in Table 7.4., although more authoritative than professional accounting pronouncements, have not been discussed in this chapter because they are not professional standards.

Table 7.4. Authoritative Pronouncements issued annually by the Accounting Profession

Year	Recommendations Statements on accounting of the ICAA		Pronouncements issued by the ASA*	Statements on Accounting Practice issued by the ICAA (D1)		Australian Accounting Standards (DS/AAS) issued by the ICAA & ASA		Approved Accounting Standards issued by the ASRB	Provisional Accounting Standards & Statements of Accounting Practice of the ICAA & ASA		Total of issues, amendments & withdrawals
	Issued	Withdrawn		Issued	Withdrawn	Issued	Amended		Issued	Amended	
1	2	3	4	5	6	7	8	9	10	11	12
1945											0
1946	6										6
1947											0
1948	1										1
1949											0
1950											0
1951											0
1952											0
1953											0
1954											0
1955											0
1956											0
1957											0
1958											0
1959											0
1960				1							1
1961											0
1962											0
1963	1	1		2							4
1964	1			1							2
1965											0

*Between 1956 and 1965 the ASA States and individual project committees prepared nine practice bulletins. Since these bulletins were not submitted to the General Council for approval they are not considered authoritative enough to have similar effect as pronouncements or recommendations or standards.

**Drafts or redrafts have not been considered in this table as authoritative pronouncements, but amendments and withdrawals are considered equal in importance to the issue of new pronouncements, recommendations and standards.

***Column 7 includes standards reissued by the Profession after approval by the ASRB

****ASRB 1002 was issued, revoked and reissued again in the same year, and has been accounted for both issues.

Table 7.4. Authoritative Pronouncements issued mainly by the Accounting Profession [Continued]

Year	Recommendations Statements on accounting of the ICAA		Pronouncements issued by the ASA¹	Statements on Accounting Practice Issued by the ICAA (D1)		Australian Accounting Standards (DS/AAS) issued by the ICAA & ASA		Approved Accounting Standards issued by the ASRB	Provisional Accounting Standards & Statements of Accounting Practice of the ICAA & ASA		Total of issues, amendments & withdrawals
	Issued	Withdrawn		Issued	Withdrawn	Issued	Amended		Issued	Amended	
1	2	3	4	5	6	7	8	9	10	11	12
1966											0
1967			1								1
1968											0
1969				1							1
1970				5	1						6
1971				1							1
1972				1		1					2
1973					1		1				2
1974						4	1				5
1975											0
1976						2	1		2		5
1977							2			2	2
1978					1						3
1979											0
1980											0
1981						1	1				2
1982						4	2				0
1983						4	1			2	8
1984						3	1				5
1985						6		3			4
1986								7			6
Total	8	2	1	12	3	25	10	10	2	4	67

Sources: Zeff (1973), Graham (1978), ICAA Members Handbook (Updated upto December 1986), Craig Craswell (1986) and ASRB Releases (Handbook, updated upto July 1987)

Basically there have been the following seven kinds of professional accounting pronouncements:

(1)   Recommendations on Accounting Principles, issued by the I.C.A.A. (Column 2 and 3).

(2)   Statements of Accounting Principles and Recommendations on Accounting Practice, issued by the I.C.A.A. (Column 2 and 3).

(3)   Accounting Pronouncements issued by the A.S.A. (Column 4).

(4)   Statements on Accounting Practice issued by the I.C.A.A. (Column 5 and 6).

(5)   Statements of Accounting Standards issued by the I.C.A.A. (Column 7 and 8).

(6)   Australian Accounting Standards issued jointly by the A.S.A. and the I.C.A.A. (Column 7 and 8).

(7)   Provisional Accounting Standards and Statement of Accounting Practice issued jointly by the A.S.A. and the I.C.A.A. (Column 10 and 11).

The recommendations, statements or pronouncements accounted for in columns 2 and 4 are those that were issued by the A.S.A. and the I.C.A.A. basically to guide their members and were not for mandatory compliance by their members (For example, see Craswell, 1986, pp. 106-7). The next series of accounting statements issued by the I.C.A.A. called "Statements on Accounting Practice" are accounted for in column 5. In terms of compliance they carried similar authority to that of its predecessors (For example, see Craswell, 1986, p. 106). Column 7 and 8 accounts for the accounting standards, currently known as Australian Accounting Standards, issued and amended jointly by the two accounting bodies. They require compliance by the members of the two bodies (See APS1 issued jointly by the two bodies).[127] Provisional Accounting Standards issued and amended by the two bodies are accounted for in Columns 10 and 11. Conformity to these standards is not compulsory. Withdrawal of certain pronouncements have also been taken into account in Columns 3 and 6, as it is also seen as a major decision on the part of the accounting bodies with respect to accounting pronouncements.

At the outset it must be noted that Table 7.4. has severe limitations in providing a detailed picture of the efforts of the Profession to issue accounting pronouncements. Since it is not the purpose here to discuss in detail the various steps taken by the Profession to develop various standards over the time period covered in Table 7.4., only a broad idea of the extent of the Profession's efforts is provided here. To do this Tables 7.5. and 7.6. have been constructed. Those tables broadly quantify the effort of the professional bodies (Table 7.5. for the A.S.A. and Table 7.6. for the I.C.A.A.). They take into account the the amount of expenditure incurred by the two professional bodies on accounting, auditing, ethical and other related pronouncements, and related research and committee activities.

The amount spent on accounting pronouncements could not be shown separately due to non-availability of properly classified information.

---

127   Craswell (1986), pp. 109-115 described the range of conformity rules that preceded APS1.

Table 7.5: A.S.A.'s Expenditure on Pronouncements

Year	Number of Members in Nearest Thousands	Subscription & Other Reciepts from Members	Pronouncements & Standards Expenditure	Reciepts per Member (Col. 3 by Col. 2) Nearest cent	Pronouncements Expenditure per Member (Col. 5/Col. 2) Nearest cent	Percentage of Membership Reciepts spent on Pronouncements
1	2	3	5	6	7	8
1956	21	54	2	2.57	0.10	3.89%
1957	21	66	1	3.14	0.05	1.59%
1958	22	68	2	3.09	0.09	2.91%
1959	22	70	1	3.18	0.05	1.57%
1960	23	95	3	4.13	0.13	3.15%
1961	24	97	2	4.04	0.08	1.98%
1962	24	100	1	4.17	0.04	0.96%
1963	25	104	2	4.16	0.08	1.92%
1964	26	111	N.A.	4.27	N.A.	N.A.
1965	27	321	10	11.89	0.37	3.11%
1966	28	333	N.A.	11.89	N.A.	N.A.
1967	29	349	10	12.03	0.34	2.83%
1968	30	476	10	15.87	0.33	2.08%
1969	32	503	20	15.72	0.63	4.01%
1970	33	643	20	19.48	0.61	3.13%

Table 7.5: A.S.A.'s Expenditure on Pronouncements [Continued]

Year	Number of Members in Nearest Thousands	Subscription & Other Reciepts from Members	Pronouncements & Standards Expenditure	Reciepts per Member (Col. 3 by Col. 2) Nearest cent	Pronouncements Expenditure per Member (Col. 5/Col. 2) Nearest cent	Percentage of Membership Reciepts spent on Pronouncements
1	2	3	5	6	7	8
1971	35	679	N.A.	19.40	N.A.	N.A.
1972	36	850	7	23.61	0.19	0.80%
1973	38	885	14	23.29	0.37	1.59%
1974	39	1,062	10	27.23	0.26	0.95%
1975	40	1,680	91	42.00	2.28	5.43%
1976	42	2,125	141	50.60	3.36	6.64%
1977	43	2,278	152	52.98	3.53	6.66%
1978	43	2,733	125	63.56	2.91	4.58%
1979	44	2,887	167	65.61	3.80	5.79%
1980	45	3,312	178	73.60	3.96	5.38%
1981	46	3,910	178	85.00	3.87	4.55%
1982	48	5,086	246	105.96	5.13	4.84%
1983	50	5,434	284	108.68	5.68	5.23%
1984	52	7,173	334	137.94	6.42	4.65%
1985	53	8,229	393	155.26	7.42	4.78%
1986	54	9,715	514	179.91	9.52	5.29%

Source: Extracted from A.S.A Annual Reports.

Table 7.6: I.C.A.A.'s Expenditure on Pronouncements

Year	Number of Members in Nearest Thousands	Subscription & Other Receipts from Members	Pronouncements & Standards Expenditure	Receipts per Member (Col. 3 by Col. 2) Nearest cent	Pronouncements Expenditure per Member (Col. 5/Col. 2) Nearest cent	Percentage of Membership Reciepts spent on Pronouncements
1	2	3	5	6	7	8
1956	4	27	1	6.75	0.25	3.70%
1957	4	28	0	7.00	0.00	0.00%
1958	4	28	0	7.00	0.00	0.00%
1959	4	29	N.A.	7.25	N.A.	N.A.
1960	4	43	N.A.	10.75	N.A.	N.A.
1961	4	44	1	11.00	0.25	2.27%
1962	4	45	2	11.25	0.50	4.44%
1963	5	47	0	9.40	0.00	0.00%
1964	5	49	0	9.80	0.00	0.00%
1965	5	50	0	10.00	0.00	0.00%
1966	5	154	20	30.80	4.00	12.99%
1967	5	160	20	32.00	4.00	12.50%
1968	5	164	0	32.80	0.00	0.00%
1969	5	264	33	52.80	6.60	12.50%
1970	6	275	34	45.83	5.67	12.37%

Table 7.6: I.C.A.A.'s Expenditure on Pronouncements [Continued]

Year	Number of Members in Thousands	Subscription & Other Reciepts in Nearest Thousands Members	Pronouncements & Standards Expenditure	Reciepts per Member (Col. 3 by Col. 2) Nearest cent	Pronouncements Expenditure per Member (Col. 5/Col. 2) Nearest cent	Percentage of Membership Reciepts spent on Pronouncements
1	2	3	5	6	7	8
1971	6	288	23	48.00	3.83	7.98%
1972	6	394	20	65.67	3.33	5.07%
1973	7	424	20	60.57	2.86	4.72%
1974	7	440	56	62.86	8.00	12.73%
1975	8	696	91	87.00	11.38	13.08%
1976	8	831	108	103.88	13.50	13.00%
1977	9	1,101	189	122.33	21.00	17.17%
1978	10	1,516	145	151.60	13.18	8.69%
1979	11	1,741	186	158.27	16.91	10.68%
1980	11	1,999	320	181.73	29.09	16.01%
1981	12	2,426	278	202.17	23.17	11.46%
1982	13	2,774	445	213.38	34.23	16.04%
1983	13	3,272	538	251.69	41.38	16.38%
1984	14	3,726	731	266.14	52.21	19.62%
1985	15	4,220	697	281.33	46.47	16.52%
1986	16	5,158	750	322.38	46.88	14.54%

Source: Extracted from I.C.A.A Annual Reports.

Features of major interest in Tables 7.5. and 7.6. are in columns 4, 6 and 7. Column 4 provides the total expenditure, in nearest thousands, incurred on pronouncements and standards of all kinds (accounting, auditing, etc.) issued by the two bodies. It is shown later in this section that there is ample reason to believe that most of these expenditures were incurred on accounting pronouncements. One important aspect of the expenditures accounted for in Column 4 is that they are not the exact amounts of pronouncement related expenditures. The figures are the best possible estimates that could be acquired from those reports. They include expenditures incurred directly by the two bodies and their contributions to the A.A.R.F. Since the classifications of expenditure vary between the A.S.A. and I.C.A.A., the estimates for the two bodies may not have exactly the same bases of calculations.

Columns 6 and 7 provide information regarding per member expenditures on pronouncements and percentage of membership receipts spent on pronouncements, respectively.

In Tables 7.5. and 7.6. the data is for the period 1956 to 1986. Figures before that period are unascertainable from the annual reports of the two bodies. In addition, some problems were faced in extracting data from the annual reports. These problems were mainly with respect to adjustments for changing classifications of accounts and change to decimal system (Pounds to Dollars) in 1965-66. Again zeros do not represent exact zero figures. Since figures have been rounded to the nearest thousand, a zero means that the figure was less than $500 for that year. In case of "N.A." the figures were not available or not ascertainable from the annual reports. Finally, as the calculations of columns 5, 6 and 7 are based on the rounded figures of columns 2, 3 and 4, there may be minor rounding errors. Since we are interested in ascertaining the general nature of receipt and expenditures, such errors are acceptable.

To show that the professional bodies have been exerting more of their efforts on accounting pronouncements than on auditing or other statements an investigation is conducted into the A.A.R.F.'s structure, organization and staffing; and accounting and auditing exposure drafts, guidance releases and related technical publications. These data have been directly procured from the Foundation and cover the period from January 1971 to February 1988. Their purpose here is to illustrate the extent of attention paid to accounting pronouncements compared to other pronouncements and research activities during and after the 1970's. A detailed account of the efforts made by the professional bodies prior to 1973 has been made by Zeff (1973). Since accounting pronouncements are generally more contentious and more difficult to agree upon than, for example auditing standards (See Moonitz, 1974), there is substantial cause for believing that they attract more funds for issuing pronouncements than the other pronouncements.

Analysis:

Table 7.4. (column 13) shows that after the initial issue of authoritative pronouncements in 1946 and 1948 by the I.C.A.A. there was eleven years of silence. The professional bodies started issuing or taking other major decisions regarding pronouncements, like withdrawal and amendments, in 1960. Their activities peaked in 1963 and 1970, and continued more steadily into the seventies. The first pronouncement in the series of pronouncements later to be called Australian Accounting Standards was issued in 1972.

It is noted from Table 7.4. that the number of standards produced by the profession increased progressively from the sixties and gathered greater momentum in the seventies. Simultaneously the influence of the pronouncements was progressively increased by the accounting bodies. Craswell (1986) noted that from the inception of the recommendations till 1971 the application of the pronouncements were not compulsory for the members of the accounting bodies. The changes in the title of the pronouncements from time to time were not always accompanied by changes in the authoritativeness of the rules. For example, the change from "Statements on Accounting Principles and Recommendations on Accounting Practice" to "Statements on Accounting Practice" was because the previous title was too long (p. 106).

With the issue of Statement K1 by the I.C.A.A. in 1971 and the substitution of the term "recommendations" and "statements of accounting practice" by the term "standards of accounting practice" the status of the pronouncements were enhanced from instruments of "guidance" to "benchmarks" of accounting practice. The four versions of Statement K1 of the I.C.A.A., the Statement 300 of the A.S.A. and finally the APS1 jointly issued by the two bodies, elevated the status further eventually making it compulsory for the members of the two bodies to comply with or support the standards or else disclose all deviations from the standards[128] (Craswell, 1986, pp. 105-115).

Since Table 7.4. provides only a broad idea of the major decisions regarding issue, amendments and withdrawal of accounting pronouncements, we have to look at Tables 7.5. and

---

128   APS1 sets out certain requirements which are to be fulfilled by the members in such cases.

7.6. to get an idea of the extent of resources expended on accounting pronouncements by the professional bodies.

Tables 7.5. and 7.6. reveal that the number of members in the A.S.A. and the I.C.A.A. has steadily increased (Column 2). The total amount of subscription and other receipts from members has risen considerably (Column 3). The contribution of individual members has also grown rapidly in the same period (Column 5).

The total expenditure on pronouncements has also increased enormously over the years (Column 4). The pronouncements expenditure per member rose almost 95 times for the A.S.A. and almost twice that rate in the case of the Institute (Column 6). Up until around early 1970's the two bodies spent intermittently on pronouncements and the level of expenditure was low. From around mid seventies both accounting bodies started to spend more steadily. The expenditure has also been growing since then.

Column 7 of Table 7.5. and Table 7.6. is important because it reveals the proportion of the per members receipt that is spent on pronouncements. The percentage of membership receipts spent on pronouncements has grown steadily since early seventies, especially for the I.C.A.A. it has grown almost four times between 1972 to 1984. An increasing proportion of receipts being spent on pronouncements indicates that the professional bodies are emphasizing pronouncements more than other modes of professional development as a whole.

In the case of the I.C.A.A., even though the per member average receipt was higher than the A.S.A.'s, the proportion of expenditure on pronouncements was considerably higher than that of the Society's. The reasons for this are that the Institute's membership is much smaller than the Society's and the total amount spent by the Institute on pronouncements in most years was also greater than the Society's. One reason for the latter could be that the I.C.A.A. has been more active on its own in the area of ethical and auditing standards (See Table 7.2.). Another reason, of course, is that in the later years the Institute has disclosed most of its professional development committees' expenditure with the expenditure on technical pronouncements, whereas A.S.A. has not pursued that policy.

To get an idea of the proportion of professional bodies' resources being spent on developing and issuing accounting pronouncements A.A.R.F.'s recent structure and activities were analyzed. Although this analysis is limited to the data of the A.A.R.F. starting from the seventies, we find certain interesting aspects of the activities of the accounting bodies in the area of pronouncements.[129] For example, Table 7.7. shows that a majority of the Technical Staff of the jointly funded A.A.R.F. deal with accounting research.

It must be noted here that research on the development of accounting and auditing standards may be complementary in some cases because accounting standards have audit implications and vice versa. Therefore a demarcation between accounting and auditing standard-setting activities may not be as distinct as is portrayed in the following tables. The purpose here is to give a broad idea of the Foundation's activities. Moreover, as Moonitz (1974) pointed out, accounting standard-setting activities take more

---

129   Since Tables 7.7 to 7.9 do not take into account items like additional staffing through employment of paid or un-paid expertise, from time to time, and the amount of time spent on the preparation of each publication, the tables only provide a broad idea of the Foundations activities.

time and effort than auditing standards due to their wider
implications.

Table 7.7.: Staffing Levels of the Three Broad Areas of A.A.R.F.'s
Activities (Excluding the Director) as in July 1987.

Activities	Number of Staff Members	Percentage
Accounting	6.5*	59%
Auditing	2.5*	23%
Law Review	2	18%
Total	11	100%

*There was one Project Manager dealing with both accounting and
auditing research. Therefore, 0.5 has been assigned to both the
areas.

A further analysis reveals, that in terms of background or
ancillary activities required prior to the development and release
of pronouncements the A.A.R.F. has produced more in the area of
accounting than for auditing. Table 7.8. provides some idea of
those activities, like the number of exposure drafts, guidance
releases and technical papers issued by the A.A.R.F. since 1970 in
the areas of accounting and auditing.

Table 7.8.: Number of Exposure Drafts, Guidance Releases and Technical Papers issued by the A.A.R.F. since 1970.

Activities	Exposure Drafts		Guidance Releases		Technical Papers	
	No.	%	No.	%	No.	%
Accounting	43	61%	8	67%	35	80%
Auditing	27	39%	4	33%	9	20%
Total	70	100%	12	100%	44	100%

Information compiled in Table 7.9. shows that in the post crisis period of 1971 to 1980 the A.A.R.F. was even more involved in the preparation of accounting standards compared to auditing standards. In that period it produced a higher percentage of accounting exposure drafts than that produced in the period covered by Table 7.8.

Table 7.9: Number of Exposure Drafts, Guidance Releases and Technical Papers issued by the A.A.R.F. from 1970 to 1980.

Activities	Exposure Drafts		Guidance Releases		Technical Papers	
	No.	%	No.	%	No.	%
Accounting	17	89%	0	0%	20	76%
Auditing	2	11%	0	0%	6	24%
Total	19	100%	0	0%	26	100%

Our findings in this section indicate that the profession did respond to the scrutiny it faced during and after events involving company financial disclosure. Its response is evidenced from the enhancement in the number and authority of accounting pronouncements; the increase in the expenditure incurred on pronouncements; and the increase in the amount of background activities, like exposure drafts, research, etc.

Dependence on Professional Accounting Standards:

In this section, professional accounting standards are shown to have become the most prominent form of accounting regulation amidst all other forms of such regulation. This is because sources of other forms of regulations are relying increasingly on the accounting profession and its standards to provide specificity to their own rules. In this respect it is pointed out in the following discussion that in those other forms of regulation, the rule makers have rarely made explicit provisions for the recognition of the professional accounting standards, but they have on many occasions supported or approved the use of professional standards.

Professional accounting standards are those standards which are determined by the A.A.R.F. and approved by the National Council of the I.C.A.A. and the A.S.A. Auditors and accountants, who are members of these two bodies, and are entrusted with the authentication or preparation of company accounts, are expected by their respective bodies to conform to the standards or disclose and explain any non-compliance with the standards (APS 1). These standards whilst mainly concerned with the measurement of material figures in the accounts may also deal with the form of disclosure.

Courts and Governments:

The Australian Companies Act of 1981 (with subsequent amendments) has extensive financial disclosure requirements[130] which the company directors have to follow. Although the Act

---

130   See Australian Companies Act 1981, Sub-Sections 267(1) and 269(8), Section 275 and Schedule 7.

does not explicitly provide support or recognition to the professional accounting standards, the legislators and the enforcers of companies law - the courts, the N.C.S.C. and the C.A.C.s, on various occasions have recognized the importance of such standards and their improvement. For example Graham, Jager and Taylor (1984), did not regard the requirements of the Act as a complete code of company accounting, but they felt that on the matters on which the Act did pronounce, its authority was paramount (p. 5). In this respect, Peirson and Ramsay (1983) noted that the Companies Act _did not_ legislate accounting measurement standards and cases decided by the courts had not established any general accounting standards in order to produce a true and fair view.[131]

The Courts, apart from dealing with the common law liabilities of auditors and directors, are also concerned with the interpretation of the provisions of the Act. In this respect Graham, Jager and Taylor (1984) stated that due to the non-specificity of the provisions of the Act, questions arising with respect to what is a "true and fair" view of the profit or loss or state of affairs of the company are dealt with by resorting to general commercial and accounting usage and custom. Sources of evidence regarding such usage and custom are the opinions of the practitioners, published articles and textbooks, and more recently and increasingly, the pronouncements and publications of the leading accounting bodies (p. 5). The dependence on accounting practices by courts, in the absence of statutory requirements was upheld in *Lothian Chemical Co. Ltd. V Rogers* (1926) (See Table 6.3.). In that case it was held that where the ordinary principles of accounting are not invaded by

---

131   Sub-section 269(8) of the Act broadly states that the accounting reports presented must show a "true and fair view" of the company's profit or loss and the state of affairs.

the statute they must be allowed to prevail. The authoritative importance of the practitioners and the accounting bodies in defining the "true and fair" provisions of the Act by the courts has also been identified by Mannix and Mannix (1982, p. 31). Although courts normally depend on established practice, there have been cases in the past where the courts ruled differently (as for example *Lee V Neuchatel Asphalt Co.* (1889) and *Phillips V Melbourne and Castlemaine Soap and Candle Co.* (1890) in Table 6.3.). In other cases, like *Re City Equitable Fire Insurance Co. Ltd.* (1925) case, the *Royal Mail* (1931) case and the *Re Press Caps Ltd.* (1949) case the dicta or judgments challenged the efficacy of the extant accounting practice. In addition, in *FCT V Flood Pty Ltd.* (1953) (a taxation case) the High Court of Australia clarified the position and authority of the courts by ruling that although courts will refer to generally acceptable accounting principles, it is the court which makes the final decision on the issues in dispute.[132]

More recently, the difficulties involved in providing specific measurement rules and defining the "true and fair" requirement have been recognized by the legislators (For example, see Ryan, 1967 and 1974 and F. Walker, 1980 and 1981b). The legislatures of most Western countries, including Australia, have abdicated the role of setting company accounting standards and the professional accounting bodies have moved progressively to acquire this legislative responsibility (F. Walker, 1980, p. 12). Frank Walker, the former attorney-general of N.S.W., who in 1977 was a strong proponent of government intervention in the

---

132   Wolnizer (1985) provided evidence of court rulings in Australia, U.K. and U.S.A. where the courts overruled the technical meaning of "true and fair affairs" as provided under extant generally accepted accounting principles and ascribed it its ordinary and natural meaning (pp. 146-154).

accounting standard-setting process, by 1981 accepted that the accounting profession was best qualified for standard-setting and proposed a standard-setting process where the Government would only play a supervisory role (F. Walker, 1981b). The Australian Financial Systems Report of the Committee of Inquiry (1981) also highlighted the role of the profession in standard-setting under the supervision of the Government and recommended that:

> The two professional accounting bodies should continue to be responsible for the design and development of accounting standards (p. 372).

The Legislature has, in principle, conferred the legislative function of providing specificity to the accounting requirements of the Act to the accounting profession (Ryan, 1974). Explaining this situation Ryan (1974) stated:

> It is a legislative function of an ambulatory nature: what is "true and fair" at any particular point of time will correspond with what professional accountants as a body conceive to be proper accounting principles. The evolution, development and general acceptance of those principles will cause the concept of what is "true and fair" to shift accordingly (p. 15).

The failure of the legislature and the courts to specify the measurement rules and their implicit acceptance of the accounting profession to provide such rules has led the company law enforcing agencies to accept the importance of professional accounting standards in defining the term "true and fair". In 1976 the N.S.W. C.A.C. explicitly stated in its Annual Report its policy as follows:

The Commission has adopted the policy that non-compliance
with the accounting standards promulgated by the Institute of
Chartered Accountants in Australia and the Australian Society of
Accountants is prima facie evidence that the accounts may not
show a true and fair view. Explanation is therefore sought from
directors in cases where non-compliance with a standard is
apparent from an examination of the accounts if the reason for
non-compliance and the financial effect thereof are not disclosed
in the note to the accounts or directors' report. A similar inquiry
is made of the auditor of the company if his report is not
qualified in such circumstances.[133]

In this respect Morley (1979) pointed out that the drafting
was very careful - the Commission did not state that accounts must
comply with the standards in order to show a true and fair - but it
did imply that a reader of the accounts should be made aware of
non-compliance and be able to reconstruct the accounts and adjust
them to achieve compliance with the accounting standards should
he so desire (p. 31). The other State C.A.C.s have adopted a
similar policy (Australian Financial Systems, Report of the
Committee of Inquiry, 1981, p. 370).

There have been other important instances where the
Government has adopted the view that the profession should take
the lead. One such instance was the drive for current cost
accounting. Balmford (1977) stated that the profession took the
C.C.A. problem so seriously that it requested the Commonwealth
Government to sponsor the C.C.A. Steering Group, but despite its
interest, the Government took the view that it was preferable for
the profession to take the lead (p. 552).

---

133   Also see Balmford (1977, p. 551), Miller (1978, p. 92), Morley (1979, p.
       31) and Australian Financial Systems, Report of the Committee of Inquiry
       (1981, p. 370).

In Australia the concept of co-regulation is not restricted to accounting, but is also found in other areas. Masel (1983, p. 542) (Former Chairman of the N.C.S.C.) mentioned that governments (in Australia) recognized the advantages of co-regulation. That is governments were prepared to delegate authority to professional and other associations for the purpose of carrying out certain regulatory functions. Such dependence of the government on the accounting profession has been explained by Willmott (1986), as an outcome of a process whereby the professions and the state have to support and/or restrict each others activities for their own survival (pp. 563-564).

The A.A.S.E.:

The listing requirements of the Australian Associated Stock Exchanges (A.A.S.E.) are silent in respect of measurement methods employed in the preparation of company accounts. The stock exchange requirements have followed a trend towards greater, more frequent and timely disclosure, but little effort has been made to develop standards for the calculation of accounting figures in the financial statements.

There are two reasons to believe that the stock exchanges tacitly accept the usage of accounting standards in the preparation of financial statements required by them. First, in 1974 the A.A.S.E. expressly recommended to the listed companies under its Official Listing Requirements, that they conform with the professional accounting standards or explain the departure from such standards. If the departure was significant, they were expected to disclose the financial effect of the departure or provide a reason for not disclosing the financial effect (Balmford, 1974, p. 7).

Second, the A.A.S.E. listed companies are incorporated under the Companies Act and have to abide by the requirements of the Act. As seen earlier, legislators, courts and the enforcers of companies law all see adoption of the professional accounting standards, *prima facie*, as the best available means of determining a "true and fair" view of company accounts. This indicates that all listed companies as companies incorporated under the Companies Act are expected to follow the professional accounting standards, even without the recommendations of the A.A.S.E.

Moreover, the A.A.S.E. and its constituent exchanges, when considering changes in the financial disclosure provisions of its listing requirements, have customarily sought the views of the accounting profession. Some important instances of such communications and the growing liaison between the stock exchanges and the profession has been noted by Zeff (1973, pp. 50-51).

The A.I.M. Annual Report Award:

The Australian Institute of Management recognizes the Australian Accounting Standards issued by the professional bodies for the purposes of the Award. The criteria set for financial statements of competitive business enterprises by the Institute in 1987 confirmed this:

> Accounts should comply with the Seventh Schedule of the appropriate Companies Code and with the statements of Accounting Standards issued by the Australian Society of Accountants and the Institute of Chartered Accountants in Australia. Compliance with the Statement of Accounting Practice dealing with current cost accounting is desirable. Noncompliance or departure from the standards should be fully explained in the Accounts and the Director's Report, particularly when the auditors qualify their report (A.I.M., 37th Annual Report Award Handbook and Report of the Adjudicators 1987, pp. 34-35).

This criterion is also maintained for Government business enterprises:

> Adequate explanatory notes accompanying the financial statements including a statement of significant financial and accounting policies in compliance with accounting standards issued by professional accounting bodies, and a statement of whether Australian Accounting Standards are observed and if not, why not (A.I.M., 37th Annual Report Award Handbook and Report of the Adjudicators 1987, p. 40).

The obvious conclusion here is that the A.I.M. expects its Annual Report Award participants to conform to the professional accounting standards.

Conclusion:

The analysis in this chapter supports the proposition that professional accounting pronouncements, later to be known as standards, were a means of guiding and developing the skills of accountants and auditors, in particular, and the image of the profession, in general. Having received considerable attention in the past, specially in the sixties and the seventies, the accounting profession responded by issuing an increasing number of accounting standards with increasing authority. On the one hand the standards have become one of the significant means by which the accounting profession can, at least, be seen to be keeping its "house in order;" and on the other hand it is being seen as a means of company financial disclosure regulation. That conforms with Wells (1978, p. 4), that like any other profession, traditionally, regulation of accounting profession has come from within in order to self-discipline the profession. The purpose of that, according to Wells, was to maintain or enhance the recognition and status enjoyed by its members.

The professional accounting standards and the profession as a whole, though often criticized, have received the recognition of the other sources of regulation - the courts, the legislators, the stock exchanges and the A.I.M.. This recognition has been mainly in the area of providing measurement requirements. Other requirements, mainly those of form, timing and frequency of disclosure are still provided by the legislature and the A.A.S.E., and in the case of interpretation of requirements and unspecified circumstances the courts provide the requirements.

Consequently, the evidence and arguments in this chapter suggest that, by around late 1970's and early 1980's, professional accounting standards and the accounting bodies were firmly entrenched as a form of company financial disclosure regulation and rule-makers, respectively.

The following quotes, one in the beginning of the seventies and the other in late seventies sums up this conclusion:

> In the early sixties, the profession in general and the auditors in particular were under attack in the soul-searching aftermath of numerous company failures. Whilst much of the criticism was unwarranted, the profession has, nevertheless, emerged from the ordeal stronger and better equipped to meet the demands of all those whom it serves (Savage, 1970, p. ii).

> Australian accounting standards are here to stay and will play an increasingly important part in the work of all accountants (Faggotter, 1978, p. 181).

Chapter 8

TOWARDS MANDATORY ACCOUNTING STANDARDS IN A CHANGING REGULATORY ENVIRONMENT

Introduction:

It was established in chapters 6 and 8, that by the end of the 1970's and into the early 1980's professional accounting standards received recognition from various sectors as company financial disclosure regulation and the professional accounting bodies as accounting standard setters. We now proceed into an investigation of the activities in the 1970's which led to the concept of co-regulation in accounting standard-setting.

In this respect we first study the changing company regulatory environment in the seventies. This is done in Section 2 where we look at the reason for and the nature of co-operation between the States and the Commonwealth for regulating companies.

The shift towards mandatory standards, in the light of deficiencies of professional accounting standards and the weaknesses of the standard-setting and enforcement system adopted by the accounting profession, is discussed in Section 3.

Section 4 looks at co-regulation and illustrates the manner of co-regulation adopted for the regulation of companies and the securities market in Australia. In that perspective we review the introduction of the concept of co-regulation into the area of accounting standard-setting as a means of developing mandatory standards.

Finally, Section 5 summarizes and evaluates the nature of the environmental setting prior to the demand for and supply of an organization capable of providing mandatory standards.

Co-operation for Company Regulation:

In Chapter 6 it was mentioned that attempts to achieve uniformity between company legislations of the Australian States was made in the late 1950's and Acts were later passed by those States in 1961 and 1962. Although various differences remained between the legislations, the main object of uniformity was achieved in the broad sense (CCH, 1986, p. 5).

The Advisory Committee on Company Law (Eggleston Committee), set up in 1967 in response to the crisis prevailing due to company collapses, made extensive recommendations for reform to the State Parliaments in 1970. Bills presented on that basis had a turbulent passage and were accepted in all States, except Tasmania, between 1971 and 1973 (CCH, 1986, p. 5).

Various minor amendments followed the Acts and in 1974 Queensland, N.S.W. and Victoria ratified the Interstate Corporate Affairs Agreement. To overcome the difficulties of general administration of companies laws the three States agreed to make it easier for their Companies Offices in the administration of the Acts. Accordingly a company complying with the requirements and formalities in one of the signatory States was allowed to operate in the other two States without undergoing the same requirements and formalities (CCH, 1986, pp. 5-6).

Western Australia joined the agreement in 1975. Bills were introduced in the Parliaments of the participating states in 1975 and by the passing of 1976 Acts their company law and practice became virtually uniform. Although South Australia amended its Companies Act in 1979 to bring uniformity with that of other four mainland states, it never joined the Agreement (CCH, 1986, p. 6).

The State legislative activities during the years 1972-75 was, in a large part, a response to the Whitlam Government's decision to proceed with the introduction of a national companies legislation by the Federal Government. The Whitlam Government's decision followed a shift in the High Court's attitude to the power of the Commonwealth with respect to corporations (CCH, 1986, p. 6).

In Australia the regulation of companies is the province of the State Parliaments. The Federal Constitution does not provide the Commonwealth with the direct power to create companies. Sec. 51(xx) of the Constitution empowers the Commonwealth Parliament to make laws only with respect to "foreign corporations, and trading and financial corporations formed within the limits of the Commonwealth" (CCH, 1986, p. 6). The powerlessness of the Commonwealth has been tested in the courts on various occasions and difficulties in interpreting Sec. 51(xx) have been expressed by the High Court (CCH, 1986, pp. 6-7).

The Rae Report of 1974 did more than anything else to focus attention on the weaknesses and inadequacies of the operation of the Australian securities industry in the heady days of the sixties mining boom. It recommended a national approach to company regulation through the establishment of a national commission:

Our recommendation is that the new national regulatory body be established by the Federal Government ... In our view time has come for the Federal Government to step in and to assume the responsibilities for seeing that the securities market is properly regulated (The Report of the Senate Select Committee on Securities and Exchange, 1974, p. 494).

The Report further added:

The legislative action should be in pursuance of two broad, sometimes conflicting, objectives of national policy:

(i)   The first is to maintain, facilitate and improve the performance of the capital market in the interests of economic development, efficacy and stability.

(ii)   The second is to ensure adequate protection of those who invest in the securities of public companies and in the securities market (The Report of the Senate Select Committee on Securities and Exchange, 1974, p. 494).

The Committee based its recommendations on the following issues:

One of the main themes of this Report ... is that the securities market is largely an interacting national market.

A second reason for our conclusion about the inadequacy of State regulation is that there is a substantial lack of national uniformity in:

(i)   the relevant law;
(ii)   the administrative practice in respect to the law;
(iii)   the quality of its administration.
(The Report of the Senate Select Committee on Securities and Exchange, 1974, p. 481).

That report also drew attention to some shortcomings in accounting standards and company disclosure (Morley, 1979, p. 35).

In response to the Rae Report, in 1976 the Commonwealth Government released a proposal for a "national" cooperative scheme for the regulation of companies and securities in Australia. Despite controversies and the debate that followed the proposal, the Scheme was adopted by the Commonwealth and the six states in 1977. Northern Territories joined it in 1986 (CCH, 1986, pp. 2-3). Briefly, the parties concurred on the need for:

- uniform legislation;
- uniform administration
- a cooperative approach;
- minimum procedural requirements; and
- adequate processes of law reform.

The expected objectives of the parties to the scheme are:
- to promote commercial certainty;
- bring about a reduction in business costs;
- increase capital market efficiency; and
- maintain the confidence of investors in the securities market through suitable provisions for investor protection (CCH, 1986, p. 3).

The institutional framework of the Scheme consisting of the Ministerial Council, the N.C.S.C., the C.L.R.C. etc., has been discussed in Chapter 4. The substantive legislation composing of the various Acts and State Codes have also been briefly reviewed in the same chapter.

What makes the Cooperative Scheme important is that, given the constitutional predicament, the creation of a cooperative scheme required the development of some procedure by which one set of statutory provisions could apply right across the country. The legislative device adopted was that the Commonwealth enacted the laws which applied only to the Australian Capital Territory, and each state adopted it by means of Application of Laws legislation passed in the respective states (CCH, 1986 p. 13). In the case of company financial reporting, this means that a single set of legislative requirements replaced a situation where each state had its own requirements.

As far as accountants and their professional bodies are concerned the advantages of this scheme are as follows:

1.   One set of company laws through out Australia.
2.   A national scheme for the registration of auditors and liquidators.
3.   A single set of financial reporting requirements to deal with.
4.   A single mechanism to deal with when it comes to the affairs regarding development of statutory requirements of accountants, auditors and company financial disclosure.

As for the politicians in the States and the Commonwealth they satisfied the demand of their constituencies for greater investor protection through uniform regulation by hardly giving up any of their authority. The State Governments although in practice have allowed the Commonwealth Government to enact laws regarding companies and securities, they have not given up the authority to do the same themselves. On the other hand the Commonwealth gained authority under the formal agreement of the Scheme to enact laws regarding companies and securities which were applicable throughout the country, without undertaking the effort and cost of amending the Constitution.

Mandatory Accounting Standards:

Although from the previous chapter it seems that professional accounting standards gained considerable attention and recognition in the community, at the same time its weaknesses were also being revealed. The weaknesses were of two kinds. First, there were deficiencies in the enacted standards and then there were those with respect to the process of standard-setting and enforcement. This led to an aura of non-acceptance and non-compliance both within the professional circles and outside the profession, which induced calls for government intervention in standard-setting or government support for professional standards. A review of literature revealed the following major forms of criticisms that were used for demanding mandatory accounting standards. By mandatory accounting standards it is commonly meant those standards that have the coercive backing of the government or the legislature. Accordingly, any serious involvement of the government or the legislature in defining standards could mean the provision of legal backing to the standards. Therefore, in our discussion any form of government involvement in standards is implied to mean some degree of mandatory compliance by companies.

Quality and Uniformity of Financial Disclosure:

It has been generally argued that the professional accounting standards have failed to achieve the objective of enhancing the quality and uniformity of reporting. Amongst the first to suggest the use of mandatory accounting standards was Ryan (1967), the former Registrar of Companies. Government company regulators have shown keen interest in company financial reporting since the company collapses of 1960s. Ryan at an accounting convention in 1967 analyzed the financial reporting criterion of "true and fair" view of the Companies Act. He found it to be an ambiguous term (See Ryan, 1967 and 1974; and Morley, 1979, p. 35). In his critique of the "true and fair" view of reporting he urged the accounting profession to prepare an identifiable code of "generally acceptable accounting principles". If the profession failed to assure such a commitment, he suggested the formation of a statutory body capable of producing accounting regulations (p. 106). This proposition was reinforced by him in a 1973 conference (Ryan, 1974).

Ryan's 1967 call for the development of accounting principles was made as a solution to the vagueness in the statute (Ryan, 1967). It can be noted that his appeal was made in an effort to motivate the profession to do something about the lack of definition of a statutory requirement of "true and fair" reporting. It was well ahead of the progress in professional standard-setting that the profession made in the seventies.

A similar view was also expressed by Chambers in 1969, which was reported by Mathews (1969), as follows:

> Professor Chambers' point on seeking legislation to back up professional bodies' pronouncements was ... to prevent the use of numerous valuation rules that have no basis in theory or in logic (p. 632).

Meanwhile the profession itself was aware of the threat of legislative intervention in standard-setting if it failed to provide standards which improved uniformity in accounting practice. An Editorial in The Chartered Accountant in Australia had this comment on that issue:

> Given the need to reduce the wide range of acceptable
> alternatives which practice hitherto has allowed the accountant,
> the development of accounting standards by the profession is an
> urgent problem. The possibility of legislative action in the event
> of failure to define standards is an ever present possibility in
> Australia and elsewhere, however expensive and ineffective in
> the long term such a policy might prove (The Chartered
> Accountant in Australia, April, 1974, p. 3).

The idea of substituting the term "true and fair view" by
accounting principles seems to have been borrowed from the
auditors themselves. Irish, a leading auditing expert in Australia,
authenticated this perspective in the following manner:

> the phrase 'true and fair' is a technical and legal term which
> must be interpreted according to generally accepted principles of
> accounting (Irish, 1972, p. 1).

The Implication is, that if there is compliance with generally
accepted accounting principles, then a "true and fair" view is
presented (Henderson, 1985, p. 50).

The scepticism about accounting in the 1960s and 1970s
led to a wide spread belief amongst non-accountants that the
diversity of available, generally accepted accounting principles and
the lack of criteria which for choosing which procedure was
appropriate in the circumstances, led to non-comparability of the
financial statements of different companies and an opportunity to
manipulate reported profits and financial position. Whether or not
this belief was justified, it was strong enough to cause the
accounting profession to embark on a programme of preparing and
issuing financial accounting standards (Henderson, 1985, p. 50).

An argument for mandatory standards, made well after the
profession had taken some major steps in standard-setting and had

issued a number of accounting standards, was placed by the N.S.W. Accounting Standards Review Committee (Chambers, et al, 1978). The Committee argued that the profession's standards were inappropriate and incapable of producing a "true and fair" view. They were critical of the mode of standard-setting used by the profession and pointed out that standards were not based on any explicit definition of "true and fair", "profit and loss" or "state of affairs". They found the historical cost concept, on which the standards were based, as weak and inconsistent with the spirit of "true and fair" reporting. This led them to believe that professional standards were incapable of improving the quality of company financial information.[134] They recommended that the legislature clarify the meaning of "true and fair" and that a national body be created to set priorities for the professional standard-setting process. This in essence meant that if the profession prepared standards within those priorities, those standards would indirectly receive legislative support. The Committee had stopped short of expressing this view.

Compliance with Professional Accounting Standards:

Another area of criticism was compliance of non-members of the accounting bodies in addition to that of the members of those bodies with professional accounting standards.

In 1970, the importance of adequate company reporting was reinforced with the creation of a separate Corporate Finance and Accounting Division in the newly established Corporate Affairs Commission in N.S.W. Initially, its functions comprised of

---

134   Around the same time others (For example, see Whittred, 1978) also criticized the quality of professional accounting standards.

examination and review of companies financial documents and matters pertaining to the accounts and audit provisions of the Companies Act (Report of the Registrar of Companies, December 31, 1970). Subsequently, the functions of this Division were increased beyond routine checks of company disclosure. It later encompassed the analysis of financial viability of companies and their compliance with professional accounting standards (Morley, 1979, p. 35).

With the increase in the development of accounting principles by the accounting profession in early 1970s (see Table 7.4.), conflicts arose between the company directors and auditors as to the application of appropriate principles. Towards the end of 1972 the Commissioner of the N.S.W. C.A.C. raised the possibility of approaching the Supreme Court in respect of those conflicts. This made the accountancy bodies to actively review its principles and resolve the contentious issues. Noting the steps being taken by the accounting profession, the C.A.C. withheld further action on those issues (The Report of the Corporate Affairs Commission, December, 31, 1973, p. 2).

As a result of the well publicized company failures of 1970s the professional accounting bodies in Australia were once again the subject of strong criticism. This time it was mainly for their inability to issue and enforce accounting standards (Jager, et al, 1979, p. 213).

In 1975, the N.S.W. Corporate Affairs Commission commenced examination of selected financial statements for compliance with local accounting standards (The Report of the Corporate Affairs Commission, December, 31, 1979, p. 10). In 1976 the Commission announced its policy that non-compliance with the accounting standards issued by the Australian accountancy bodies (the I.C.A.A. and the A.S.A.) by a company would be prima facie evidence that the accounts may not show a true and fair view. A panel had been established with representatives from the Commission and the Joint Accounting Bodies, to review instances of non-compliance with standards, particularly by public companies, with a view to establish the extent of non-compliance. The result of the examination provided evidence in support of the view that the procedures for establishing and enforcement of standards were inadequate. The view when conveyed to the Attorney-General, Mr. F. Walker, led to suggestions for government involvement in establishing accounting standards with statutory recognition. In this respect the Business Review Weekly reported:

> More than 40 percent of the accounts appeared to have failed to comply with one or more of the accounting standards ... a level of compliance which helps explain the N.S.W. attorney-general's doubts as to whether the accounting profession is equipped to develop and monitor compliance with appropriate standards (Business Review Weekly, December 31, 1981, p. 45).

Frank Walker, the Attorney-General of N.S.W. at that time, expressed his doubts regarding the profession in the following words:

> When I became Attorney-General for N.S.W. in 1976, I found the Corporate Affairs Commission labouring under great difficulties trying to bring to book those responsible for the failure of major corporations.
>
> I was shocked to discover important prosecutions failing through lack of certainty as to what were proper accounting standards.

Towards Mandatory Accounting Standards

> Like many non-accountants, I had great difficulty comprehending a concept which suggests that truth and fairness can be achieved by application of a variety of principles - one which can point to a loss of $3 million while another, in the same set of circumstances, justifies the announcement of a profit of $100,000.

> I (also) took every opportunity to sound a clear warning to the accountancy profession, either to put its house in order or face the prospect of greater Government involvement in the regulation of the profession (F. Walker, 1981a, p. 235).

In 1977 Mr. Walker emphasizing the need for Government involvement, appointed an Accounting Standards Review Committee. That Committee was also critical of the existing accounting standards and endorsed the need for statutory backing of appropriately designed standards (The Report of the Corporate Affairs Commission, December, 31, 1979, p. 10; also see Jager et al, 1979, p. 213)).

Regarding the Profession's efforts, it was argued that compliance with accounting standards had not been enforced by the accounting bodies (For example, see Peirson and Ramsay, 1983, p. 296). Statement APS1 through which the professional bodies enforced its accounting standards on its members, could not enforce the standards on non-member directors of companies. Again, the enforcement mechanism applied against members was mandatory disclosure of non-compliance with standards rather than mandatory compliance. This, Peirson and Ramsay (1983, p. 296) argued, did not assure compliance by the members with the standards, even though they may be complying with APS1. Lastly, there had been no disciplinary action by the bodies against members for non-compliance with APS1 (Peirson and Ramsay, 1983, p. 296).

During the later half of the seventies, compliance with the accounting standards by the companies and the profession's strength to enforce the standards were investigated. Ramsay (1982) revealed that there was a high degree of compliance with APS1, specially by the management of companies. The same research also indicated that such compliance with APS1, on the other hand, showed that most managements disclosed non-compliance with accounting standards. This clearly indicated that most managements did not comply with professional accounting standards. Such non-compliance had also been revealed by the N.S.W. Corporate Affairs Commission (See Morley, 1978, and R. Walker, 1987, p. 270). In addition to this, Morley (1978) provided evidence of company directors expressly rejecting the N.S.W. Corporate Affairs Commission's instructions to comply with the Profession's accounting standards, on the grounds that they were neither generally accepted nor did they have the force of law (pp. 33-34). Non-compliance with professional accounting standards, therefore, became a major issue of concern and a common subject for the criticism of the Profession's capacity to regulate company financial disclosure.

Apart from APS1 and its predecessors, the various versions of I.C.A.A. Statement K1 and A.S.A. Statement 300, which had jurisdiction only over the accounting bodies' members, the profession also attempted to impose its standards over the preparers of financial statements. This they tried through the Principal Accounting Officer (P.A.O.) provision of the Companies Act. The 1971 amendments to the Uniform Companies Act (1961) imposed an obligation on principal accounting officers of the company to state whether, to the best of their knowledge and belief, the accounts gave a true and fair view of the matters required to be dealt under that section. With the introduction of conformity rule of the Institute (Statement K1) any member of the

Institute holding the P.A.O. position was expected to disclose non-conformity with accounting standards. With the recognition of the professional accounting standards by the N.S.W. C.A.C. in 1977 and the A.A.S.E. in 1974 it became obligatory for the P.A.O.s to comply with accounting standards. This P.A.O. provision was later omitted from the Act of 1981. The Companies Act now requires only the directors (apart from the auditor's report, Section 285) of a company to express an opinion regarding the "true and fair" view of financial statements (Section 269). Despite this elaborate arrangement, compliance with professional accounting standards remained an unsolved problem[135] nor were those provisions capable of significantly improving the quality of reported information (Edwards, 1979).

In the later half of the seventies the profession started responding to the lack of acceptance and compliance to its standards by the company directors. Its main response was to attribute non-compliance to the difficulty of imposing the Profession's standards on the directors. To alleviate the situation it suggested that the standards should receive automatic statutory backing (Bishop, 1978, p. 3 and The Report of the Professional Standards Review Committee, 1979).

The Need for Participation:

Another contentious issue was the Profession's moral right to issue accounting standards. Back in 1969, when it was asked in an accounting conference, who should set accounting standards, there was an overwhelming consensus within professionals, academics and others that standard-setting should remain as a responsibility of the profession, with a view to maintaining a flexible process to

---

135   Also see McKeon (1976), p. 423.

adapt to changing needs (Mathews, 1969, p. 632). But soon some advocates of government intervention started arguing that accounting standards should have the effect of law and as public interest was at stake it would be wrong to leave the setting of standards to non-public organizations, such as the accounting bodies (Feller, 1974, p. 393 and Peirson and Ramsay, 1983, pp. 296-97). In this respect the former Attorney-General of N.S.W., Mr. Frank Walker, emphasizing the participation of government and other interests in the approval of standards, asserted that

> whilst accountants are unquestionably qualified to evolve accounting standards a truly representative body should make the final determination of the value of any standard before it is imposed (F. Walker, 1981b, p. 23).

He further stated:

> Government, commerce and industry, indeed all consumers of accounting services, have a right to say before they find themselves forced to comply with a standard that could be onerous, costly or dangerously inflexible (F. Walker, 1981b, p. 23).

His suggestion was based on his experience with C.C.A. In 1977 he was approached by deputations from company directors and some accountants seeking to stop the introduction of C.C.A. by the professional bodies. He felt that the introduction of C.C.A. would be a major economic decision, therefore the decision to introduce it could not be left in the hands of the profession without reference to government and consumers of accounting services (Peirson and Ramsay, 1983, pp. 296-7). Consequently, he suggested a mode of self-regulation where the profession would prepare standards with the participation of other interest groups and under the supervision of the government (F. Walker, 1981b, also see F. Walker, 1980, pp. 13-15).

The Trend Towards Mandatory Accounting Standards:

Table 8.1. summarizes the nature of some of the arguments placed in favour of or against government or legislative intervention in accounting standard-setting. The Table illustrates the trend towards mandatory accounting standards in the 1970s or more specifically before the formal recognition for the need for such standards by the State and Commonwealth Governments in the Ministerial Council Resolution, 23 May, 1980 (N.C.S.C. Release 401, 1981, p. 1). Accordingly, the Table encompasses only those items in the accounting literature that were published before or in 1980.

From the table we can infer that in the early stages of the demand for mandatory accounting standards the demand came mainly from the government sector, for example by Government committees, corporate affairs officials and legislators. A few academics were also in the forefront in recommending government involvement. Sources from the profession or close to the profession initially rejected the idea of government involvement but later took the lead for demanding legislative support for their standards.

The reasons for the call for government intervention were first due to the lack of quality and uniformity of disclosure - which, as we can see in columns 4 and 5, was initially due to the absence of the definition of "true and fair" in the Companies Act and then, after the issuing of some professional accounting standards, due to the deficiencies of those standards *per se*.

Table 8.1: Early Attention Towards Mandatory Accounting Standards

Source (Chronologically)	Type of Source:	Mandatory Standards:	Reasons for Mandatory Standards	
	Government (G) Profession (P) Academics (A) Others (O)	Yes (Y) No (N)	Lack of Definition of true and fair	Lack of Quality of Professional Standards
1	2	3	4	5
Ryan (1967)	G	Y	X	
Harrowell in Mathews (1969)	P	N		
Chambers in Mathews (1969)	A	Y	X	
Company Law Advisory Committee (1970)	G	Y	X	
Ryan (1972) in Ryan (1974)	G	Y	X	
Riley (1973)	O	N		
Ryan (1974)	G	Y	X	
Corporations and Securities Industries Bill (1974)	G	Y	X	X

Table 8.1 (Continued): Early Attention Towards Mandatory Accounting Standards

Source (Chronologically)	Reasons for Mandatory Standards		Form of Government Intervention		
	Lack of Compliance	Community Participation	Government Prepared	Government Support for Professional Standards	Judicial Intervention or Tribunal
1	6	7	8	9	10
Ryan (1967)			X		
Harrowell in Mathews (1969)					
Chambers in Mathews (1969)				X	
Company Law Advisory Committee (1970)			X		
Ryan (1972) in Ryan (1974)	X				X
Riley (1973)					X
Ryan (1974)				X	
Corporations and Securities Industries Bill (1974)			X		

Table 8.1 (Continued): Early Attention Towards Mandatory Accounting Standards

Source (Chronologically)	Type of Source:	Mandatory Standards:	Reasons for Mandatory Standards	
	Government (G) Profession (P) Academics (A) Others (O)	Yes (Y) No (N)	Lack of Definition of true and fair	Lack of Quality of Professional Standards
1	2	3	4	5
Frank Walker in 1977 in Walker (1981) also in Balmford (1977)	G	Y		
Hutcheson (1977)	O	N		
Taylor (1977)	A	Y		X
NSW Accounting Standards Review Committee (1978)	G/A	Y	X	X
Bishop (1978)	P	Y		
Studdy (1979)	P	Y		X
Report of the Professional Standards Review Committee (1979)	P	Y		
Winsen (1980)	A	N		

Table 8.1 (Continued): Early Attention Towards Mandatory Accounting Standards

Source (Chronologically)	Reasons for Mandatory Standards		Form of Government Intervention		
	Lack of Compliance	Community Participation	Government Prepared	Government Support for Professional Standards	Judicial Intervention or Tribunal
1	6	7	8	9	10
Frank Walker in 1977 in Walker (1981) also in Balmford (1977)	X			X	
Hutcheson (1977)					
Taylor (1977)	X			X	
NSW Accounting Standards Review Committee (1978)				X	
Bishop (1978)	X			X	
Studdy (1979)	X	X		X	
Report of the Professional Standards Review Committee (1979)	X			X	
Winsen (1980)					

As discussed earlier, compliance (column 6) became a major issue in the later half of the seventies for demanding government support for professional standards. Community participation (column 7) did not seem to be a very popular issue compared to the other problems.

As for the form of government intervention there has always been a diversity of arguments between preparation of standards by statutory organizations and some form of government support for professional standards. The demand for government's involvement in the preparation of standards normally came from government sources, mainly in the first half of the seventies. With the increased activity of professional standard-setting those demands became less frequent. Another reason for the reduced attention toward standard-setting by government bodies may be the absence of a central government regulatory machinery for companies, at that time, which could create a body capable of enforcing standards throughout Australia. Occasional demands for judicial intervention and an accounting tribunal were also made.

The form of government intervention which started receiving greater attention during the later half of the seventies was government support for professional standards. Despite considerable effort by the accounting profession to develop standards and the recognition of the professional bodies as the main source of accounting standards, the profession failed to acquire adequate compliance by company directors. Therefore, it is not unusual that most such demand for government backing for professional standards came from the profession (see Column 9).

Co-regulation for Company Accounting:

After establishing the ground rules, through a single set of statutes and an institutional framework, for the regulation of companies, the next step was to resolve the intricate details of various areas of company regulation, for example transaction in securities and financial reporting. The premise chosen for the determination of rules in those areas was co-regulation. The concept of co-regulation developed out of the opposing systems of self-regulation versus government regulation.

Co-regulation is self-regulation with minimal government supervision and participation. Government involvement is only to the extent necessary to ensure that an essentially self-regulatory organization or profession effectively discharges regulatory functions. This minimizes bureaucratic interference and cost, and utilizes the profession's expertise and self-imposed standards (Vincent, 1981, p. 236). Another advantage of co-regulation, in its use of self-regulation, is its potential for establishing and enforcing ethical standards beyond those that any law can establish (Masel, 1983, p. 542).

Masel (1983) described co-regulation and the need for co-regulation in the following manner:

> It is a feature of a mixed economy that certain functions which are carried out by professionals are often regulated both by the self-regulatory organization, ... and by a government agency. This dual form of regulation - implying that governments should recognize self-regulatory organizations but should oversee their activities and stand ready to regulate directly where and as circumstances may require - is often termed "co-regulation" (p. 542).

He elaborated further that governments recognize professional associations carrying out regulatory functions which would otherwise be the responsibility of the government. Examples of co-regulation in Australia, other than in accounting, are that of stock exchanges, securities analysts, lawyers, engineers and architects. (Also see Masel, 1983, p. 542).

With the growing concern towards weaknesses of professional accounting standards and the Profession's process of standard-setting and enforcement, attention was focused on co-regulation as an alternate solution. Co-regulation in the accounting context was seen to have two aspects. One was that of the profession's internal by-laws, ethical rulings and auditing standards. These affected only the accountants and auditors who are members of the professional bodies. The other was that of the accounting standards. The nature of accounting standards was found to be such that they imposed obligations upon parties involved in a completely different way from the internal by-laws of accounting bodies, or even the business and listing rules of a stock exchange. Accounting standards imposed obligations upon third parties, namely preparers of or signatories to financial statements. Also a user of financial statements was concerned with accounting standards inasmuch as he/she knew that the auditor was required to make reference in his/her report to departure from accounting standards and would be particularly concerned in those cases where the auditor provided a qualified opinion (Masel, 1983, p. 543).

It is now generally recognized that the present legislative requirements provide broadly for a true and fair view in the company financial reports. Those provisions do not require uniformity of treatment of accounting methods between companies. Flexibility is permitted so long as the result gives a true and fair view. Moreover, it has long been recognized that it is impractical for legislation to seek to describe in detail all the requirements in order to ensure true and fair reporting. It is these considerations which have led to the acceptance of accounting standards developed principally by the accounting profession, with the object of supplementing the legislative requirements imposed upon the directors and the auditors (Masel, 1983, p. 543).

A serious weakness encountered by the private standard-setting agency is the lack of true authority to enforce accounting standards (as distinct from auditing standards), simply because something more than acceptance by individual members is required (Moonitz, 1974; Wells, 1978; and Masel, 1983, p. 543). To be effective, such standards require acceptance by preparers and users. In a democratic society, like Australia, where something more than voluntary acceptance by third parties is required, government authority is usually the only form of coercion. This signifies that if accounting standards are to be enforced against third parties, there must be a transfer of some part of the standard-setting process from self-regulatory organizations to a government authority (Masel, 1983, p. 543).

Masel (1983) felt that the Australian accounting bodies seemed to have recognized that government intervention was necessary because accounting standards set by them proved to be inadequate in terms of compliance. This, he noted, was expressed in their submissions, to the government, for legislative backing of standards. Non-compliance as he stated could be of two types - by the profession's own members and by the preparers of financial statements. He noted the presence of both, but it was the latter which, he felt, was outside the jurisdiction of the professional bodies. This was of concern for both the government and the professional bodies, and also to others in the community, like the academics (Masel, 1983, p. 543).

In Australia the debate as to the nature and extent of regulation of accounting has centred not so much upon whether or not such standards should pass wholly out of the realm of self-regulation, but rather upon the status to which such accounting standards should be accorded legislative support. This led to the formulation of a suitable political and administrative model for approval and enforcement of mandatory standards. That model necessitated the participation of others, specially the preparers of financial statements. The participation of those previously outside the standard-setting mechanism was felt essential due to the wider implications of accounting standards (beyond those of auditing standards). For acceptance of accounting standards by the parties outside the accounting profession it was essential to include others in the role of approving the standards (Masel, 1983, pp. 543-44).

In sum, the scheme for co-regulation provided the following environment for the establishment of mandatory accounting standards in Australia:

(1)   The use of coercive power of the government in supervising standard-setting and enforcing the standards.

(2)   The use of existing standard-setting facilities and expertise of the professional bodies.

(3)   The inclusion of outsiders affected by the standards or interested in standard-setting through the extension of the due process mechanism already adopted by the profession, that is to include the

opinion of others in the approval stage, specially the preparers of financial statements, to enhance acceptance of the standards.

Conclusion:

The review of the changing company regulatory system and the form of company financial disclosure requirements in the 1970's, discloses the occurrence of two major changes. First, there was a shift from a fragmented State based company regulatory system to a single States-Commonwealth cooperative system applicable uniformly to all States and Territories. Within the same period there was a growing concern regarding the profession based accounting standard-setting mechanism and increasing demands for government involvement.

Government involvement in standard-setting under the previous State based company regulatory systems was also demanded but not attempted. The cooperative scheme provided a single national regulatory system which seemed to provide improved grounds for government involvement with a view to correcting the anomalies in the professional standard-setting system. Despite the presence of various anomalies, non-compliance with professional standards received greater attention - specially in the later half of the seventies. The sources of such attention were the accounting profession and the enforcers of company regulations.

Meanwhile, the company regulators recognized the legislature's lack of capacity to define a "true and fair" view or specific accounting standards. In that light, the scheme which seemed to receive increased attention, for the removal of anomalies in standards, was a government-profession based co-regulatory scheme.

Chapter 9

THE CREATION OF THE A.S.R.B.
- THE ACTIVITIES AND EVENTS

Introduction:

Regulatory policy making as a process and the various elements within that process have been discussed in Chapter 5.

The A.S.R.B., the outcome of such a process, has been described in Chapters 2 and 3. In this and the following chapters some light is shed on the process of policy-making, that led to the Board's creation and the establishment of its functions. We have seen in the previous chapter that events in the 1970's shifted the focus from professional accounting standards to Government backed mandatory accounting standards. We now look at the developments which led to the creation of an organization capable of providing a certain form of mandatory accounting standards - the approved accounting standards.

Three stages are noted in the establishment of the Board's organization and functions. The first stage is dealt with in Section 2. It relates to the debate prior to the Ministerial Council for Companies and Securities resolution dated May 23, 1980, in which the Council formed the opinion that an A.S.R.B. was needed. Section 3 deals with the second stage which led to the formation of the Board with some tentative functions. In it the submissions and other literature which preceded the decision of the Council to create the Board are studied. The tentative functions and criteria for approving proposed standards were finalized in the third stage. Section 3 contains a study of that process.

The Inception of the Idea for a Board:

In Table 8.1., in the previous chapter, suggestions for various forms of government intervention in the development of accounting standards were identified and discussed. A number of those propositions suggested the creation of a new body for establishing legislatively backed standards. Such suggestions are identified here to explain why a separate body was demanded in spite of the existence of the profession sponsored standard-setting mechanism. Suggestions mainly included the creation of a statutory body (commission or authority), an independent board, an accounting tribunal or a profession sponsored board with government support for its standards.

Table 9.1. lists the following:

(1)   The sources which proposed a new body. All sources were either published or appeared in public documents of the Government or other organizations (Column 1).
(2)   The type of source - Government, Profession, Academics and others (Column 2).
(3)   Form of the proposed body (Column 3).
(4)   The composition of the proposed body - that is its membership (Column 4).
(5)   Their proposed functions (Columns 5 thru 9).

Looking at the sources in detail, we find that the first major thrust for the creation of a government sponsored body capable of developing or participating in the development of accounting standards, came from bureaucrats responsible for the administration of company law. Mr. Ryan, the former N.S.W. Registrar of Companies (later Commissioner and then the Chairman of N.S.W.

C.A.C.), suggested the creation of a statutory commission in N.S.W. in 1967 to combat the lack of statutory clarification of the "true and fair" reporting requirement[136] (Ryan, 1967, 106). This criterion, he felt, was ambiguous and found "to be not only wholly inappropriate as a criterion for the verification of accounts but a snare and a delusion to the uninformed" (Ryan, 1974, p. 8). He was looking mainly from the company regulator's view point of improving the verification of company accounts.

His first recommendation was the abandonment of the of the "true and fair" requirement in favour of the American formula, under which auditors reported their opinion that "the accounts present fairly the financial position of the company and the result of its operation in conformity with generally accepted accounting principles" (Ryan, 1967, p. 106). He qualified this recommendation by adding that the accounting profession should assure him that it could produce an identifiable code which answers to the description of 'generally accepted accounting principles'. Otherwise he proposed:

> that a statutory body be constituted under the Companies Act and authorized to make regulations as to form and contents of accounts and as to the accounting principles to be applied in their preparation; such a body to be constituted of representatives of the legal profession, accountancy and secretarial professions and representatives of government, and that the regulations made by such a body should be subject to disallowance by Parliament in the same manner as other regulations made under the authority of an Act of Parliament (Ryan, 1967, 106).

---

136   In Chapter 6 it had been mentioned that this criterion was introduced in Australia through the Victorian Companies Act in 1955 and the N.S.W. in 1961.

Table 9.1.: Demand for a Government Sponsored Accounting Standard-Setting Body in the Accounting Literature

Source (Chronologically)	Type of Source:	Form of Body	Membership
	Government (G) Profession (P) Academics (A) Others (O)	Statutory Body (SB) Independent Body (IB) Accounting Tribunal (AT) Profession Sponsored Board With Government Support (PSB)	Mainly Accountants (A) Mainly Non- Accountants (N) Broad Based (B)
1	2	3	4
Ryan (1967)	G	SB	B
Company Law Advisory Committee (1970)	G	SB	
Ryan (1974)	G	SB	
Corporations and Securities Industries Bill (1974)	G	SB	

Table 9.1. (Continued): Demand for a Government Sponsored Accounting Standard-Setting Body in the Accounting Literature

Source (Chronologically)	Prepare Standards	Review and Approve Standards - Professions only (PO) - Any source (AS)	Set Priorities for Standard Setting	Monitor Compliance	Set Conceputal Framework
1	5	6	7	8	9
Ryan (1967)	X				
Company Law Advisory Committee (1970)	X				
Ryan (1974)		X			
Corporations and Securities Industries Bill (1974)	X				

Table 9.1. (Continued): Demand for a Government Sponsored
Accounting Standard-Setting Body in the Accounting Literature

Source (Chronologically)	Type of Source:	Form of Body	Membership
	Government (G) Profession (P) Academics (A) Others (O)	Statutory Body (SB) Independent Body (IB) Accounting Tribunal (AT) Profession Sponsored Board With Government Support (PSB)	Mainly Accountants (A) Mainly Non- Accountants (N) Broad Based (B)
1	2	3	4
Frank Walker in 1977 in Walker (1981) also in Balmford (1977)	G	AT	B
NSW Accounting Standards Review Committee (1978)	G	IB	
Studdy (1979)	P	PSB	A
Report of the Professional Standards Review Committee (1979)			
Cook (1981)	G	IB	

Table 9.1. (Continued): Demand for a Government Sponsored Accounting Standard-Setting Body in the Accounting Literature

Source (Chronologically)	Its Proposed Functions				
	Prepare Standards	Review and Approve Standards - Professions only (PO) - Any source (AS)	Set Priorities for Standard Setting	Monitor Compliance	Set Conceputal Framework
1	5	6	7	8	9
Frank Walker in 1977 in Walker (1981) also in Balmford (1977)		X			
NSW Accounting Standards Review Committee (1978)		X	X	X	
Studdy (1979)	X				
Report of the Professional Standards Review Committee (1979)					
Cook (1981)		X			

Table 9.1. (Continued): Demand for a Government Sponsored Accounting Standard-Setting Body in the Accounting Literature

Source (Chronologically)	Type of Source: Government (G) Profession (P) Academics (A) Others (O)	Form of Body Statutory Body (SB) Independent Body (IB) Accounting Tribunal (AT) Profession Sponsored Board With Government Support (PSB)	Membership Mainly Accountants (A) Mainly Non- Accountants (N) Broad Based (B)
1	2	3	4
Frank Walker (1981b)	G	IB	B
Australian Financial System, Report of the Committee of Enquiry (1981)	G	IB	B
Joint Submission by Accounting Bodies (1982)	P	PSB	A
Prosser (1982)	P	PSB	A
Executive Director A.S.A. (1983)	P	PSB	A

Table 9.1. (Continued): Demand for a Government Sponsored Accounting Standard-Setting Body in the Accounting Literature

Source (Chronologically)		Its Proposed Functions			
	Prepare Standards	Review and Approve Standards - Professions only (PO) - Any source (AS)	Set Priorities for Standard Setting	Monitor Compliance	Set Conceputal Framework
1	5	6	7	8	9
Frank Walker (1981b)		PO	X		
Australian Financial System, Report of the Committee of Enquiry (1981)		PO			
Joint Submission by Accounting Bodies (1982)		PO			
Prosser (1982)		PO			
Executive Director A.S.A. (1983)		PO			

The noteworthy aspects of his proposed commission were that being a statutory body its standards would be backed by statute and hence be mandatory; it would be broad based with representatives from a variety of interest groups; and it would produce its own regulations.

Ryan's call for a statutory commission was at a time when the accounting profession had a weak programme of standard-setting. Indirectly, he threatened the profession to either gear-up its efforts to set standards or else the government would have to intervene and establish a statutory commission to set such standards.

In 1974 Ryan "revisited" the issue of "true and fair" view. He weighed the arguments for and against legislative recognition of the generally accepted accounting principles through the adoption of the above mentioned American formula. He found that there were two major arguments: (1) for the statutory prescription of standard accounting principles and practices; and (2) that considerable development of generally accepted accounting principles was still needed in Australia to accord statutory backing to such principles. Therefore, he accepted the status quo of maintaining the existing "true and fair" provisions. Alternatively, he also pointed out, the South African Institute of Chartered Accountants proposition for a broad based representative board called the Accounting Practices Board. That board was expected to review accounting standards and place the seal of general acceptance on the standards acceptable to it (Ryan, 1974, p. 16).

At this stage Ryan also moderated his previous (Ryan, 1967) proposals for direct government intervention. The reason for such moderation, as he put forward, was the impressive search and examination of principles and procedures by the accounting profession. He expressed his satisfaction by stating that: "This process seems to have proceeded at ever increasing tempo since 1967 when I first began to take a closer interest in the matter" (Ryan, 1974, p. 16). We have also seen in Chapter 7, that the professional accounting bodies accelerated their standard-setting efforts from early 1970's.

With the increase in the effort by those bodies the C.A.C. accepted the role of monitoring compliance with professional accounting standards in company financial statements (see Chapter 8). With the creation of the N.S.W. C.A.C. in 1970, a Corporate Finance and Accounting Division was created within the Commission to monitor the financial reporting of companies according to the disclosure provisions of the companies statutes. This division also closely followed the development of accounting standards by the accounting bodies. From Table 9.2. we can see that this division started with a small staff of nine in 1970. With the addition of analysis checks (financial analysis of statements) and compliance with standards tests to its initial function of disclosure checks, its strength rose to 37 in 1977.

After three years of monitoring compliance with the standards the Commission found that the professional bodies' procedures for establishing and enforcing accounting standards were inadequate, and in 1977 it conveyed its view to the N.S.W. Attorney-General, Mr. Frank Walker. The Commission also provided him with some suggestions as to how the present arrangements might be improved. Mr. F. Walker was already disturbed by the weak accounting provisions of the Companies Act and the unilateral involvement of the profession in accounting issues. He expressed his concern publicly in a press release in July, 1977 and canvassed the question of the establishment of an Accounting Standards Review Board (The Report of the Corporate

<u>Affairs Commission</u>, December 31, 1979, p. 10). Therefore, the idea of an A.S.R.B. was first conceived by the company regulators of N.S.W. in their bid to find a solution to the dilemma of monitoring company reporting under the "true and fair view" concept.

F. Walker's enthusiasm for a board stemmed from his efforts from 1976 to fulfill what he called his unpopular and incredibly difficult duty to prosecute white-collar criminals, mostly charged with financial mis-statements in the course of capital raisings. His first job was to get expert evidence about what form a true-and-fair set of accounts should have taken (Thomas, 1982, p. 59). He stated:

> To our chagrin we found a state of virtual anarchy existed on accounting standards.
>
> The lack of uniformity in the meaning of accounting terms and the infinite interpretations one can extract from financial statements provides endless difficulties for prosecutors of white-collar crimes (cited by Thomas, 1982, p. 59).

He felt that almost anything was possible in the way of manipulation of profit, secret reserves and asset valuations. His concern originated from the fact that companies were crashing only months after presentation of healthy and audited accounts. He was also irritated by the 1977 decision of the I.C.A.A. and the A.S.A. attempting to impose current cost accounting (C.C.A.) without reference to government or advice from customers, at a time when C.C.A. would have halved stated profits and shown many companies to be reporting losses, as well as disturbing the tax regime[137] (Thomas, 1982, p. 59).

At this point it was not very clear what the proposed board's functions would be or how it would operate. F. Walker saw such a board as being engaged principally on the task of reviewing and either endorsing or rejecting proposed standards. An endorsed standard would be given statutory recognition. He suggested that the board could comprise of five members experienced in industry, commerce, economics, law or public administration as well as consumer representation. F. Walker referred this proposal to the Attorneys-General of all States and the Commonwealth for their consideration, which indicated that the proposed board would be national in status (The Report of the Corporate Affairs Commission, December 31, 1978, p. 12). It may be recalled that at this stage there was no Commonwealth Companies Act, nor was there any regulatory mechanism for companies which covered all the territories and states of Australia. The Interstate Corporate Affairs Commission, which was the only interstate mechanism, comprised of four out of the six States - N.S.W., Queensland, Victoria and Western Australia (The Report of the Corporate Affairs Commission, December 31, 1978, p. 105).

---

137   This is contrary to Balmford's (1977) claims that the accounting bodies had in fact suggested to the Commonwealth Government to sponsor a C.C.A. steering group, but the Government took the view that it was preferable for the profession to take the lead (p. 552).

Table 9.2.: Staff Strength of the Corporate Finance and Accounting
Division of the N.S.W. Corporate Affairs Commission Compared
to Other Divisions of the Commission

Division/Branch	1970	1971	1972	1973	1974	1975
Legal Division	7 (3)	9 (3)	11 (4)	19 (6)	30 (8)	30 (8)
Administrative and Services Branch	66 (26)	75 (28)	73 (26)	78 (25)	81 (21)	85 (22)
Registration and Licensing Division	118 (47)	124 (45)	124 (45)	140 (44)	162 (42)	161 (40)
Corporate Finance and Accounting Division	9 (4)	9 (3)	14 (4)	15 (5)	28 (7)	30 (8)
Investigation and Prosecution Division	57 (23)	57 (21)	57 (21)	64 (20)	88 (22)	90 (23)
Total	257 (100)	274 (100)	276 (100)	316 (100)	389 (100)	396 (100)

Note: Figures in parentheses are percentages.

Table 9.2. (Continued): Staff Strength of the Corporate Finance and Accounting Division of the N.S.W. Corporate Affairs Commission Compared to Other Divisions of the Commission

Division/Branch	1976	1977	1978	1979	1980	1981
Legal Division	39 (10)	44 (11)	63 (14)	63 (14)	64 (14)	69 (12)
Administrative and Services Branch	89 (22)	86 (21)	81 (17)	72 (15)	86 (18)	98 (18)
Registration and Licensing Division	162 (41)	166 (41)	161 (35)	170 (36)	172 (36)	207 (37)
Corporate Finance and Accounting Division	36 (9)	37 (9)	37 (8)	31 (7)	30 (6)	37 (7)
Investigation and Prosecution Division	71 (18)	71 (18)	119 (26)	132 (28)	126 (26)	143 (26)
Total	397 (100)	404 (100)	461 (100)	468 (100)	478 (100)	554 (100)

Note: Figures in parentheses are percentages.

A further development in the area of accounting standards occurred in November, 1977, when the N.S.W. Attorney-General appointed an Accounting Standards Review Committee under the Chairmanship of Professor R.J. Chambers with a view to examining the extant professional accounting standards and considering any other standard coming to the attention of the Committee which could be considered to be in the interest of users of published accounting information. In March, 1978 a news item in The Chartered Accountant in Australia appeared in which it was mentioned that the I.C.A.A. and the A.S.A., after a discussion with the Attorney-General had resolved not to participate in the Committee's activities (p. 9). No reason for the non-participation was given.

The Review Committee reported in May, 1978. It pointed out the inappropriateness of existing standards and recommended statutory backing of properly designed standards (The Report of the Corporate Affairs Commission, December 31, 1978, p. 12). For designing appropriate accounting standards it suggested that the statutory prescription of the quality of accounts, the meaning of "true and fair view", be clarified and that the professional bodies be expected to devise auxiliary standards consistent with the requirements of the legislation. Accordingly, the standards proposed by the profession would be subject to review by an independent authority; and, if the authority found that the standards conformed with the spirit of the legislation, they could be endorsed for the purposes of practice under the provisions of the Companies Act (Chambers, et al, p. 145). In this manner, this Committee also recommended the creation of an independent body like the A.S.R.B.

The functions envisaged by the Committee for the proposed authority were:

(1)   To endorse or recommend to the appropriate
       Ministers standards which conformed with the
       requirements of the Act;
(2)   To recommend to the professional bodies matters
       on which standards should be developed;
(3)   To recommend to appropriate Ministers amendments to the
       legislation on its own initiative or on the basis of
       submissions received by it;
(4)   To investigate the degree of conformity with
       endorsed standards; and
(5)   To propose revisions to existing standards
       (Chambers, et al, p. 145).

Formation of standards by professional bodies and their
review and endorsement by the proposed authority was seen, by
the Committee as an appropriate way of engaging technical
expertise with due consideration of private and public interests
(Chambers, et al, p. 145).

Simultaneous to the efforts of the N.S.W. Government,
other State Governments and the Commonwealth Government were
also in search of solutions to the problems relating to the
regulation of companies, in particular, and the securities market,
in general. Addition of new laws and expansion of existing ones,
in the 1960s, have already been discussed in Chapter 6. In 1970 a
Commonwealth and States Company Law Advisory Committee
recommended the establishment of a 'Companies Commission'
with the power to alter or add to the provisions of the Act as to
form and content of a company's accounts (Companies Law
Advisory Committee, 1970, para 49).

Despite the constitutional problems discussed in Chapter 8,
regarding the lack of Commonwealth Government's authority to

enact a national Companies Act. the Whitlam Labour Government introduced a bill in the Commonwealth Parliament for a Commonwealth Corporations and Securities Industry Act in 1974. This bill as a whole showed a concern for accounting principles and their development. It stipulated that creation of a Corporations and Exchange Commission, which amongst its other duties, would be required to conduct research in relation to matters affecting the interests of investors in securities of prescribed corporations, including research into "the improvement of accounting principles and methods" (Paterson and Ednie, 1975, p. 49). The proposed Commission would also be empowered to prescribe accounting principles prepared by it (R. Walker, 1987, p. 270). This bill was not enacted because of a change in the Commonwealth Government from Labour to Liberal-National.

The I.C.A.A. and the A.S.A. objected to the standard-setting capacity of the proposed Commission. In a joint statement they argued that the Commission should accept the accounting standards developed by the A.A.R.F., as long as they were to the satisfaction of the Commission (The Chartered Accountant in Australia, May, 1975).

In 1974 the need for an Australian Securities Commission and a nationally uniform law was reiterated by the Senate Select Committee on Securities and Exchange. Although no mention was made about accounting aspects of company regulation in the recommendations (Report from the Senate Select Committee on Securities and Exchange, July, 1974, Chapters 15 and 16), the Commission did shed light into the shortcomings in accounting standards and company disclosure (Morley, 1979, p. 35, Also see Chapter 8).

In anticipation of a change towards Commonwealth legislations by the Labour Federal Government, in the early parts of 1970s, several States (N.S.W., Queensland and Victoria), all of them having non-Labour Governments, sought to find a solution to company law weaknesses without the participation of the Commonwealth Government. They formed the Interstate Corporate Affairs Commission (I.C.A.C.) in 1974 (Morley, 1979, p. 35).

In the same year an Accounts Sub-committee was formed within the I.C.A.C. to bring about greater uniformity in the company disclosure requirements between the participating States. With the severe reservations expressed publicly by the Victorian company law administrators in respect of tax-effect accounting standards, the professional bodies adopted the policy of referring the drafts to the I.C.A.C. (Morley, 1979, p. 35).

Once again the professional bodies were slow in responding to the criticism they faced, specially from that of the N.S.W. company regulators. In this respect on August 3, 1977, McKeon (1977a) wrote in the Australian Financial Review that:

> Amid growing criticism of accountancy standards and competence, two States have moved to bring the profession under closer government scrutiny and supervision. But while the accountants themselves show a seeming infinite capacity to debate such matters as the design of their letter heads, they are proving less diligent in tackling the serious fundamental problems facing the profession. (p. 2)

The two bodies, McKeon (1977a) added, had feared government interference for many years and senior councillors had, from time to time, warned of the need for members to keep their house in order. Many councillors would privately admit that the steps were not effective enough (p. 2). In this respect McKeon noted that

> they (the profession) have yet to make an official statement on the N.S.W. move, a move which reflects the disenchantment of the Corporate Affairs Commissioner, Mr. Frank J. O Ryan, with content and level of compliance with standards (p. 2).

McKeon(1977a) quoted many recent (around 1977) examples of questionable accounting practices and behaviour, some leading to convictions, and found that:

> Nothing has been published in recent issues of either the I.C.A.'s official journal, the Chartered Accountant in Australia, or in the A.S.A.'s official journal, The Australian Accountant, about surveillance measures (p. 3).

Accordingly, McKeon suggested that the profession should ensure that its rules were reasonable and in keeping with modern business practice. He added that non-compliance with internal rules and relevant outside legislation should be efficiently monitored (p. 6).

In addition to criticizing the profession's apparent lack of surveillance, McKeon, on August 4, 1977, in the Australian Financial Review illustrated the deep concern of government officials, academics and others with respect to the profession's ability to devise and implement appropriate accounting standards (McKeon, 1977b, p. 2)

A strong reply to the criticisms of the accountants came from Balmford (1977), a senior member of the accounting profession, in the October issue of the Australian Accountant. He mentioned that the stock exchanges within Australia and overseas had tended to accept the profession's efforts to develop standards and had encouraged or required compliance or disclosure of non-compliance with those standards (p. 553). He expressed satisfaction with the policy of compliance or non-compliance adopted by the accounting bodies and did not support the idea of total compliance with all standards under all circumstances (p. 554). He was critical of the N.S.W. C.A.C.'s surveys on compliance and emphasized that there cannot always be a black and white solution to every accounting problem (p. 554). He was also shocked by the calls for government intervention made by the N.S.W. Attorney-General. In this respect he wrote:

> The recent spate of corporate problems in New South Wales has naturally brought the subject into the political arena once again. Only recently we read of suggestions by the N.S.W. Attorney-General for the establishment of an Accounting Standards Review Board. One would have hoped that the problem would be left to the profession rather than seeking a "legislative framework" to ensure that "responsible standards" are adopted. Whatever one's views on government intervention in the area, the thought of standards on individual State basis appals me. If intervention is to come, let it be on a national basis (p. 555).

Pursuing the issue of government intervention he suggested that

> If that does happen, we can only hope that the profession will retain an active and effective role, for the expertise in the problems of accounting in the private sector lie in that sector and I don't believe that the motives of the profession in its attempts to improve accounting and reporting can be questioned (p. 555).

The profession's main public response was to attribute non-compliance to the difficulty of imposing the profession's standards on company directors. It was argued that the profession's standards should receive automatic statutory backing (R. Walker, 1987, p. 270). An authoritative attack on the criticisms of the profession came from the Professional Standards Review Committee of the I.C.A.A. This Committee commented that:

> After examining criticism of the profession made over recent years and conceding that some of the criticism made was justified or had prima facie validity, the Committee concluded that much of it should be rejected. Among such criticism was that made by persons not qualified to comment on accounting matters, criticisms based on inaccurate and misleading quotations, criticism which is emotional worded, and criticisms made on invalid opinions or assumptions (The Chartered Accountant in Australia, 1979, p. 65).

The Committee recommended that the Institute should pay greater attention to replying to such criticism. It also suggested that the Institute should initiate and increase measures to require, facilitate and monitor higher and stricter standards, particularly in relation to accounting for and auditing of listed companies. It strongly opposed the idea of Government involvement in standard-setting and recommended that the accountancy profession should retain the responsibility for preparing and issuing accounting standards. In doing so it suggested consultation with the Government, C.A.C.'s, stock exchanges and the Institute of Directors in Australia. It supported the existing policy of compliance adopted by the accounting bodies and recommended that the Institute should continue to seek statutory and stock exchange support for compliance with professional accounting standards. It also suggested that the Institute should strongly resist any Government involvement in the enforcement of standards. The Committee also made various other recommendations with respect to the discipline and professional standards of its members (The Chartered Accountant in Australia, 1979, pp. 65-66).

In March 1980 Frank Walker reiterated his intentions to establish the A.S.R.B. In a speech in an accounting seminar he argued for the formation of a five member review board with the power to review standards proposed to it by the accounting profession and others. He specifically mentioned that the board would not promote or develop its own standards. The board, he contemplated, would include members from industry, commerce, economics, law and public administration (F. Walker, 1980, p. 15). Whether his failure to include the accounting profession in his list of those eligible for membership was intentional or not, is not known.

Table 8.1. also lists some of the other critics, within the profession, of government involvement in accounting standard-setting. Most of those critics proposed statutory backing for professional accounting standards and not government involvement in the preparation of accounting standards.

The Creation of the Board:

On May 23, 1980 the Ministerial Council for Companies and Securities resolved that the establishment of an Accounting Standards Review Board should be considered by the N.C.S.C. (N.C.S.C. Release 401, 1981, p. 1).

The accounting bodies reacted, almost immediately, to the Ministerial Council resolution. On June 9, 1980, the A.S.A. communicated its views to the N.C.S.C. Executive Director with respect to the proposed board (Letter by the A.S.A. Executive Director, dated June, 9, 1980). The views of the Society were as follows:

(1)   It expressed its support for a national board with a broad based representative organization comprising of a significant number of non-accountants, but it

also indicated the need for a high proportion of representatives of the two accounting bodies. (From this proposition it is difficult to tell whether it was seeking a majority membership for the accounting bodies with some non-accountant members or not).

(2)   The Board's functions should be limited to reviewing professional accounting standards.

(3)   Once the standard was approved by the Board it should be endorsed. (It did not say by whom).

(4)   In case of disagreement with the whole or part of a proposed standard, the standard should be referred back to the profession.

(5)   The Board might recommend projects which need to be undertaken by the profession and assist in the determination of priorities.

(6)   The A.A.R.F. should continue to be charged with developing draft standards for consideration by the Board.

After mutual consultations through their Joint Standing Committee, the two accounting bodies, the A.S.A. and the I.C.A.A., wrote to the Chairman of the N.C.S.C. communicating their opinion about the proposed board (Letter by the Presidents of the A.S.A. and the I.C.A.A. dated August 14, 1980). Their views were as follows:

(1)   The Board should be the means for obtaining legislative backing for professional accounting standards.

(2)   Developing of accounting standards should be the responsibility of the A.A.R.F.

(3)   The Board should include a majority of accountants appointed from a list provided by the accounting bodies and the remaining members would represent the preparers, attestors and users of accounting information.

(4)   The Board should have the right to veto or send back proposed standards to the Foundation.

Meanwhile Frank Walker, the N.S.W. Attorney-General, started showing signs of moderation. He felt that the accountants were making satisfactory progress towards self regulation. The compromise was embodied in the term "co-regulation".[138] According to him the most appropriate form of regulation of the profession would be a blend of self-regulation, community participation and government supervision. This was supported by the A.S.A. Executive Director because of its similarity with the stock exchange regulations which were backed by the statute and the N.C.S.C. (Business Review Weekly, May 16, p. 46, May 23, and June 13, p. 45, 1981).

On the other hand amongst the politicians there were those who completely opposed the need for the creation of a regulatory Accounting Standards Review Board. This was emphasized by the

---

138   See Chapter 8 for a detailed discussion on co-regulation.

Commonwealth Business and Consumer Affairs Minister, Mr. John Moore, at an A.S.A. convention. He stressed deregulation of business and the private sector, and added that intervention was needed only to remove distortions in the market (Business Review Weekly, May 16, 1981, p. 46).

In the mean time, the Final Report of the Committee of Inquiry into the Australian Financial System (Campbell Committee Report) was published in September 1981. The Committee studied the problems of company reporting and standard-setting and weighed the "pros and cons" of having a standards review board. After studying the situation the
Committee recommended that:

(a)   The two professional accounting bodies should continue to be responsible for the design and development of accounting standards.

(b)   An Accounting Standards Review Board should be established with responsibility for deciding on the adoption of accounting standards, having regard to the needs of different users; the N.C.S.C., professional accounting bodies and other interested parties should be represented on the Board.

(c)   Accounting standards recommended by such a board should be given legislative support (Australian Financial System, the Final Report of the Committee of Inquiry, 1981, p. 372).

The N.S.W. C.A.C., having to continue to examine company documents under the Co-operative Scheme, kept monitoring compliance with accounting standards under its previously adopted policy of using compliance as an indicator of "true and fair" reporting. In 1980 the Corporate Finance and Accounting Division of the Commission was further strengthened through a partial restructuring (The Report of the Corporate Affairs Commission, December 31, 1980, p. 17). Through such efforts, the Commission noted insignificant improvement in the extent of compliance by companies. In 1981 the Chairman of the C.A.C., Mr. J.C. Cooke showed concern regarding this vexed issue. In doing so he supported the idea of establishing an A.S.R.B. as envisaged by the Ministerial Council. His views regarding the functions of the Board were not quite similar to those being suggested by the accounting profession, but more in line with that of F. Walker (1980, p. 15). He expected it to be capable of reviewing standards proposed mainly by the profession and also those proposed by others. He also contemplated that the standards approved by the Board would be mandatory for compliance by both the members of the profession and those involved in the preparation of company accounts (Cooke, 1981, pp. 548-9). Thus making it possible for non-professional accounting standards to be imposed on the profession.

Meanwhile Frank Walker, the N.S.W. Attorney-General, continued his campaign for an A.S.R.B. under his, now well known, notion of "co-regulation". Although he commended the efforts and skills of the accounting profession in setting standards, he emphasized the need for non-professional and government participation in the final approval of standards for imposition on the companies. He warned that unless the profession took a stand soon for a broadly represented review body his hopes would be dashed in favour of the status quo or regulation by bureaucrats (F. Walker, 1981b).

Prior to another meeting of the Ministerial Council (that of November 19, 1981) where the A.S.R.B. was expected to be discussed again, the powerful industrial group, The Australian Industry Development Association (A.I.D.A.) attacked the establishment of the Board. The Association, composed of Australia's top 50 companies, was critical of the fact that the proposal for an A.S.R.B. drawn up by the N.C.S.C. was not opened for public discussion before being submitted to the Ministerial Council. It felt that accounting standards and its development and review were of considerable importance to the business community and that the community should be allowed to comment on the proposal. It felt that although the accounting bodies had given their indication of acceptance for the Board there was serious equivocation within the profession. The creation of the Board was seen by the Association as a further incursion of the bureaucracy in the administration of business and it favoured leaving standard-setting to the private sector. It communicated its view, specially regarding the lack of due process in the creation of the Board, to the Ministerial Council before the above mentioned meeting (The <u>Australian Financial Review</u>, November 16, 1981, p. 1 and p. 35).

Subsequently, the Council decided that comments of interested persons should be sought on the recommendations made by the N.C.S.C. for an A.S.R.B. Written submissions were invited by the Commission on November 26, 1981 (<u>N.C.S.C. Release 401</u>, 1981, p. 1).

The N.C.S.C. in its invitation for submissions provided the following reasons for the establishment of an A.S.R.B.

> Company law in Australia requires the directors of a company to cause a profit and loss account and balance sheet to be made out for each financial year; to state whether in their opinion the profit and loss account gives a true and fair view of the profit or loss of the company for that financial year and the balance sheet is drawn up so as to give a true and fair view of the state of affairs of the company at the end of that financial year; and to cause an auditor's report to be attached to or endorsed on those accounts.

The law is silent concerning the standards to be applied to determine compliance with the concept of a "true and fair view". However in considering what is "true and fair", the courts have had regard to accountants' evidence on accounting principles and conventions.

The accounting profession has attempted to set standards but have encountered difficulties with the acceptance of such standards by business community. There are also philosophical problems with the present method of policing such standards. Implicit within any proposal to establish a standards review board is the necessity for standards to be set and accepted by the professional and business community to warranting legislative support.

The business community could be expected to resist the imposition of standards set unilaterally either by government or by the accounting bodies.

The establishment of an independent board, with appropriately representative membership, to review standards set by the accounting profession and, if thought fit, to recommend their endorsement by the N.C.S.C., is proposed as the most satisfactory means of ensuring that standards are set and accepted in a manner warranting legislative support. (N.C.S.C. Release 401, 1981, pp. 1-2).

The reasons put forward by the N.C.S.C. for recommending an A.S.R.B. seemed similar to those expressed by the N.S.W. company regulators. The contentious issue, which it saw needed resolution through legislatively supported standards, was the concept of "true and fair view". In doing so, the N.C.S.C. claimed that the proposed board would be consistent with that recommended by the N.S.W. Accounting Standards Review Committee in 1978 (N.C.S.C. Release 401, 1981, p. 2). Actually that was not the case, because that committee had recommended that the statutory prescription of "true and fair view" should be clarified and that a national authority be appointed and delegated the task of ensuring that standards proposed for adoption by the professional bodies conformed with the requirements of the Companies Act (Chambers, et al, 1978, pp. 144-5). In N.C.S.C.'s recommendation for an A.S.R.B. there was no mention about clarification of the "true and fair view" requirement by the legislature, rather it adhered to the concept of preparing standards to clarify what is "true and fair view". Accordingly, we can also add that those recommendations did not provide for a term of reference on the basis of which the proposed board would review proposed standards. Rather it expected the Board to review standards without a term of reference in order to obtain a meaning of the statutory term the "true and fair view".

The N.C.S.C. also proposed some major functions for the Board. It proposed that the principal functions would be
(1)   To approve priorities proposed by the accounting bodies for the formulation of accounting standards;
(2)   To review those standards; and
(3)   To recommend standards considered suitable for endorsement by the N.C.S.C.

The Board would not be empowered to initiate, suspend or halt projects already approved, to revise priorities or to alter proposed standards unilaterally. Unapproved standards would be returned to the accounting bodies for reconsideration (p. 2).

A standard approved by the Board would be considered as generally acceptable and its application in the preparation of company accounts would be considered as the fulfillment of the "true and fair" reporting requirement. All departures from the standards would have to be disclosed and endorsed by the company auditor. The N.C.S.C. proposal also approved of the efficacy of the professional bodies' standard-setting process and found it to be unnecessary for the Board to duplicate this process (p. 2).

The N.C.S.C. proposed a membership of seven, the members being expected to be of high professional, business and/or academic standing and authority. Out of the seven, four members including the Chairman would be appointed by the Ministerial Council, one member would be nominated from each of the two accounting bodies and the N.C.S.C. (p. 3).

With only a few exceptions, the N.C.S.C. recommendations regarding the organization and functions of the Board were consistent with the views expressed earlier by various important sources, as enumerated above. Although the extent of the effective participation by the various parties behind the scenes is not known, the sources and their opinion, discussed earlier, are considered important because they were expressed publicly and reported by the media. And of course the accounting bodies, the State and Commonwealth Ministers, the C.A.C.'s, the A.I.D.A. etc., who participated up to this stage of the Board's creation could be considered as important representatives of interest groups in the community.

The N.C.S.C. Release 401 recommendations were based on the earlier calls for an A.S.R.B. as envisaged by the N.S.W. Corporate Affairs Commissioner and the State's Attorney-General. The Board would be delegated the task of authorizing a set of standards capable of clarifying the undefined concept of "true and fair view" adopted in the Companies Act. In doing so it would facilitate the C.A.C.'s task of examining the company accounts under the "true and fair" criteria.

The Commission's recommendations did not conform with the N.S.W. Accounting Standards Review Committee's recommendations as regards the power of the board to recommend priorities to the accounting profession for setting standards. In those recommendations the Commission also did not clearly identify the benefits of having a Board in the securities market context. It emphasized the importance of the concept of "true and fair view" and the need for having legislatively backed standards, but it did not say how the enhancement of the status of accounting standards to legislatively backed standards could bring about greater truth and fairness in the accounts. As already mentioned, the Commission did not expect the A.S.R.B. to define what is "true and fair" and approve standards on that basis. Rather it expected that the Board would establish a conceptual framework institutionalizing the notion of due process for the approval of every proposed standard.

In its recommendations, the N.C.S.C. did adopt the profession's proposition of limiting the function of the Board as a review board. The recommendations also adopted the profession's mode of compliance with room for disclosed non-compliance. The accounting bodies suggestion for the profession to remain as the sole source of proposed standards and that the Board should return the standards in full to the profession, if rejected, were also incorporated in the N.C.S.C. proposals. In that manner the Board would be capable of providing legislative backing to only the professional accounting standards, as demanded by the profession.

One important and controversial addition in the Commission's recommendations was the additional step of endorsement of the standards by the N.C.S.C. after approval by the A.S.R.B. (N.C.S.C. Release 401, 1981, p. 2 and p. 4). This was never mentioned by any one and was the Commission's own proposition.

Twenty four written submissions were received in response to the N.C.S.C. Release 401 recommendations. The opinion of the respondents are summarized and tabulated in Table 9.3. The N.C.S.C.'s response through the incorporation of those views in its Release 405 of December 3, 1982, are listed in the last column of Table 9.3. The respondents have been grouped in four groups in that table. There was no specific response by a clearly identifiable user of accounting information. The responses received were varied. Some were in agreement with the Release 401 recommendations and some provided alternative or opposing views to those recommendations. All such views are listed in the table.

The recommendations of Release 405 of the Commission seem to have incorporated those responses (See Table 9.3.). Although no hard and fast rule was adopted in accepting a respondent's suggestions, in most cases the N.C.S.C. accepted the criteria which received greater support from the respondents as compared to those which received lesser support (See the last column of Table 9.3.). In other cases the Commission deduced additional requirements for the Board. For example, in order to promote public confidence in the Board, it recommended that the Board should be empowered to review overseas standards and sponsor the development of its own standards. It also proposed that the Board should be allowed to have public exposure and public hearings with regards to its deliberations (N.C.S.C. Release 405, 1982, para 51 and paras 53-56).

Amongst its major recommendations the Commission reiterated the policy of creating an independent board with the objective of providing statutory backing to accounting standards.

The statutory backing would be in terms of statutory recognition of standards approved by the Board rather than statutory prescription. This would provide for mandatory standards with room for disclosed non-compliance only when departure from standards was necessary to provide the "true and fair view". The Commission still suggested that it be empowered to endorse or disallow the Board's approved standards, but its power to appoint a member of the Board was not included in this set of recommendations (N.C.S.C. Release 405, 1982, para 3).

Regarding its interest in having the right to disallow approved standards the Commission informed that it derived its interest in the standard-setting process from its overall responsibility for policy and administration relating to companies and regulation of the securities industry. And, that appropriate standards would facilitate in its objective of improving the efficiency of securities markets (N.C.S.C. Release 405, 1982, paras 4, 5 and 63 to 66).

As for the source of proposed standards, its recommendations were expanded, over those of Release 401, to make provisions for reviewing standards from other sources in addition to that of the Australian accountancy bodies. That would include standards of other countries and standards prepared under the Boards own sponsorship (N.C.S.C. Release 405, 1981, para 45).

Although the Commission still expected the Board to have a broadly representative organization, it specified that the members would have appropriate technical qualifications. The Commission also stipulated that the Board would be empowered to set priorities for standard-setting by the profession or any other source (N.C.S.C. Release 405, 1981, paras 48 and 50).

Table 9.3.: The Profile of the Submissions in Response to the Ministerial
Council Resolution, May 23, 1980

Respondents

Response (Agreed with NCSC Release 401 or Proposed) (Policy Issues)	Preparers of Financial Statements	Professional Bodies Firms and Individuals
Standards with Legislative Backing		
- Yes with Room for Disclosed Departures	6 (64)	3 (60)
- No	4 (36)	2 (40)
- Prescribed by Law	1 (9)	0 (0)
Type of Organization:		
- Accounting Profession Sponsored Body	2 (18)	1 (20)
- Government Sponsored Body	1 (9)	0 (0)
- Independent of Above Two	6 (55)	0 (0)
- None of the Above	1 (9)	0 (0)
Participation:		
- Mainly from the Accounting Bodies	2 (18)	1 (20)
- No Majority for the Accounting Bodies	0 (0)	0 (0)
- Wide Participation	5 (45)	0 (0)

Notes:
1. Figures without parentheses represent actual number of submissions.
2. Figures within parentheses are submissions as a percentage of the total number of submissions for that group. These percentages have been used in the statistical calculations of Chapter 10.
3. In the case of N.C.S.C. recommendations based on those submissions a "Y" represents that the particular response was recommended to the Ministerial Council and an "N" indicates that the response was not recommended to the Council. Since we do not know whether the N.C.S.C. commissioners voted on each issue before such recommendation and as it is not possible to exactly weigh each recommendation, a "Y" has been assigned an arbitrary weight of 100% and an "N" a weight of 0%.

Table 9.3. (Continued): The Profile of the Submissions in Response to the Ministerial Council Resolution, May 23, 1980

	Respondents			N.C.S.C.
	Academics	Others	Total	Recommendations (Release 405)
Standards with Legislative Backing				
- Yes with Room for Disclosed Departures	3 (50)	2 (100)	15 (63)	Y (100)
- No	3 (50)	0 (0)	9 (37)	N (0)
- Prescribed by Law	0 (0)	0 (0)	1 (4)	N (0)
Type of Organization:				
- Accounting Profession Sponsored Body	0 (0)	0 (0)	3 (13)	N (0)
- Government Sponsored Body	1 (17)	0 (0)	2 (8)	N (0)
- Independent of Above Two	1 (17)	1 (50)	8 (33)	Y (100)
- None of the Above	2 (33)	1 (50)	4 (17)	N (0)
Participation:				
- Mainly from the Accounting Bodies	2 (33)	0 (0)	5 (21)	N (0)
- No Majority for the Accounting Bodies	1 (17)	0 (0)	1 (4)	N (0)
- Wide Participation	1 (17)	1 (50)	7 (29)	Y (100)

Table 9.3. (Continued): The Profile of the Submissions in Response to the Ministerial Council Resolution, May 23, 1980

	Respondents	
Response (Agreed with NCSC Release 401 or Proposed) (Policy Issues)	Preparers of Financial Statements	Professional Bodies Firms and Individuals
Membership Qualities:		
- Technical Accounting Skills	7 (64)	3 (60)
- Fewer Government Appointees with Unspecified Skills	4 (36)	0 (0)
Functions:		
- Review of Standards	5 (45)	2 (40)
- Tribunal for Resolving Disputes	0 (0)	1 (20)
- Setting Priorities for the Profession's Standard-setting	2 (18)	1 (20)
- Establishing a Conceptual Framework	0 (0)	0 (0)
Purpose of having an A.S.R.B. or any other form of Government Involvement:		
- Define/State the "True and Fair" Requirement	2 (18)	2 (40)
- Improve the Quality of Reporting	3 (27)	1 (20)
- Enhance Compliance with Accounting Standards	6 (55)	4 (80)
Stated or Implied Objective:		
- Achieve Public Interest	2 (18)	1 (20)
- Satisfy Private Interests	5 (45)	0 (0)

Table 9.3. (Continued): The Profile of the Submissions in Response to the Ministerial Council Resolution, May 23, 1980

	Academics	Respondents Others	Total	N.C.S.C. Recommendations (Release 405)
Membership Qualities:				
- Technical Accounting Skills	3 (50)	0 (0)	13 (54)	Y (100)
- Fewer Government Appointees with Unspecified Skills	0 (0)	0 (0)	4 (17)	N (0)
Functions:				
- Review of Standards	1 (17)	0 (0)	8 (33)	Y (100)
- Tribunal for Resolving Disputes	0 (0)	0 (0)	1 (4)	N (0)
- Setting Priorities for the Profession's Standard-setting	2 (33)	0 (0)	5 (21)	N (0)
- Establishing a Conceptual Framework	3 (50)	0 (0)	3 (13)	N (0)
Purpose of having an A.S.R.B. or any other form of Government Involvement:				
- Define/State the "True and Fair" Requirement	3 (50)	0 (0)	7 (29)	0 (0)
- Improve the Quality of Reporting	2 (33)	1 (50)	7 (29)	Y (100)
- Enhance Compliance with Accounting Standards	0 (0)	1 (50)	11 (46)	Y (100)
Stated or Implied Objective:				
- Achieve Public Interest	1 (17)	0 (0)	4 (17)	N (0)
- Satisfy Private Interests	1 (17)	0 (0)	6 (25)	N (0)

Table 9.3. (Continued): The Profile of the Submissions in Response to the Ministerial Council Resolution, May 23, 1980

	Respondents	
Response (Agreed with NCSC Release 401 or Proposed) (Policy Issues)	Preparers of Financial Statements	Professional Bodies Firms and Individuals
Other Features:		
- AARF as main or only Standard-setter	4 (36)	4 (80)
- Scope of Standards (applicability of standards to large or small companies)	0 (0)	0 (0)
- Decision by Simple Majority	2 (18)	0 (0)
- Flexibility in Standard-Setting to cope with changing conditions	2 (18)	0 (0)
- Benefits should exceed the of Establishing a Board	1 (9)	0 (0)
- Less Dependence on NCSC	3 (27)	2 (40)
Number of Submissions	11 (100)	5 (100)

Table 9.3. (Continued): The Profile of the Submissions in Response to the Ministerial Council Resolution, May 23, 1980

	Respondents			N.C.S.C.
	Academics	Others	Total	Recommendations (Release 405)
Other Features:				
- AARF as main or only Standard-setter	1 (17)	2 (100)	11 (46)	Y (100)
- Scope of Standards applicability of standards to large or small companies)	1 (17)	0 (0)	1 (4)	N (0)
- Decision by Simple Majority	1 (17)	0 (0)	3 (13)	N (0)
- Flexibility in Standard-Setting to cope with changing conditions	0 (0)	1 (50)	3 (13)	N (0)
- Benefits should exceed the of Establishing a Board	0 (0)	1 (50)	2 (8)	N (0)
- Less Dependence on NCSC	2 (33)	1 (50)	8 (33)	Y (100)[1]
Number of Submissions	6 (100)	2 (100)	24 (100)[2]	

1. N.C.S.C.'s power to nominate one member was removed. Later in the N.C.S.C. and N.S.W. C.A.C. joint recommendations, the Commission's power to endorse or reject standards was also removed and handed over to the Ministerial Council.
2. Includes two submissions not reported in N.C.S.C. Release 405 but were received before the Ministerial Councils meeting discussing these issues.

There were certain important aspects which the N.C.S.C. felt were absent in the respondents' submissions and the Commission itself made no attempt to rectify that in its recommendations. The most important aspect that was missing was the determination of benefits that the recommended legislatively approved standards could provide in a securities market to the users of accounting information. This the Commission noted in the following manner:

> Respondents advocated legislative support for the profession's accounting standards in generalized terms. Few identified specific benefits which would accrue to the users, or to the public generally, from the statutory prescription or recognition of such standards. None described perceived or actual shortcomings or inefficient or inequitable market practices which such prescription would correct. None recognized any impairment of the capital formation process through the activities of those who exploit uncertainties in the present standards for measuring earnings (N.C.S.C. Release 405, para 34).

The Commission itself looked at certain means of providing benefits to the users of accounting information (N.C.S.C. Release 405, para 32) without specifying what benefits would those means lead to. The overall assumption of the Commission and the respondents was that the approved accounting standard through enhanced compliance would some how lead to a better informed market irrespective of the fact that disclosure in financial statements are normally outdated for the market. The Commission also mentioned that there would be additional costs for the review of standards and that the companies would have to bear extra expenses to comply with the mandatory standards (paras 33 and 59). No attempt was made to determine whether the benefits of having a Board would exceed costs.

The Commission's recommendations of <u>Release 405</u> were put forward to the Ministerial Council in its meeting of Nov 26, 1982. In that meeting the Council, in principle, resolved that an A.S.R.B. should be established (<u>N.C.S.C. Release 405</u>, 1981, para 1).

Kelly (<u>Australian Financial Review</u>, December 7, 1982, p. 5) writing about the N.C.S.C. recommendations reported that there was dissatisfaction amongst the accounting bodies about certain aspects of the recommendations. One such aspect was the enlargement of the functions of the Board from being a reviewer of professional accounting standards to a reviewer of standards of any source including the professional ones and also be capable of sponsoring its own standards. In that respect Mr. M. Sharpe, President of the I.C.A.A., emphasized that "An A.S.R.B. should be what it claims to be - a review board to ensure that accountants are doing their job correctly". He said that others who were interested in setting standards could participate through the A.A.R.F. standard-setting mechanism. To do otherwise, he added, would lead to duplication of efforts and extra cost. He reminded those who criticized the profession of being tardy in setting standards that the accounting bodies were contributing enormously, in terms of cost and effort, in the standard-setting process. He also accused them of being unaware of the complexities involved in setting acceptable standards. It was reported that Sharpe lobbied hard to the N.C.S.C. Chairman against the expanded function of the Board. He also disliked the idea of the Board setting priorities for the A.A.R.F. (<u>Australian Financial Review</u>, December 7, 1982, p. 5; and <u>Business Review Weekly</u>, December 11, 1982, p. 58).

Frank Walker expressed dissatisfaction at the mode of compliance recommended by the N.C.S.C.:

I am not happy with the suggestion that individual auditors should be allowed to approve exemptions. The pressures on auditors are already considerable and I suspect that such a discretion could only mean widespread departure from the uniform standard (cited by Thomas, 1982, p. 59).

He suggested that the auditor should convince a panel of his peers on the tribunal (Frank Walker used the term board and tribunal synonymously during the early stages). This would achieve public oversight. He also suggested better protection for the principal accounting officer and summary prosecution by the N.C.S.C. of directors who deliberately breached the standards and the expulsion of offending accountants from professional bodies (Business Review Weekly, December 11, 1982, p. 59).

Meanwhile the controversies persisted. The N.C.S.C. started its campaign to sell its recommendations to various sectors of the community. It emphasized the concept of recognized standards, community endorsement of private standards prepared by the accounting profession and others, setting of priorities by the Board, N.C.S.C.'s power to endorse or reject approved standards, membership of the Board and the remuneration of the members (Business Review Weekly, December 18, 1982, p. 59). The Chairman of the N.C.S.C. took a tough line against flexibility in accounting standards. In a seminar in Sydney, he stressed that flexible standards were worse than no standards. He conceded that departures were necessary, but insisted that such departures should be limited to circumstances where adherence to a standard would not lead to a "true and fair view" and such departures should be fully disclosed. He was however not averse to the setting of standards for particular industries. As for the reason behind expanding the sources of proposed standards, he explained that the profession could not be given the sole authority to reorganize society via the standard-setting process (Business Review Weekly, January 15, 1983, pp. 53-54).

On the other hand the President of the I.C.A.A. pressed ahead with the objections of the profession and stressed that the Board should be a review board to review only those standards which were proposed by the A.A.R.F. (Business Review Weekly, December 18, 1982, p. 59 and p. 61). In addition, Thomas (Business Review Weekly, December 18, 1982, p. 62) pointed out that there had been no review of reporting requirements by company size. He was also critical of the low remuneration of board members.

The Business Review Weekly conducted interviews of nine business leaders including that of the Sydney Stock Exchange, Institute of Chartered Secretaries, Institute of Actuaries of Australia, Association of Superannuation Funds, the Institute of Directors, the Life Insurance Federation and Institute of Internal Auditors. Out of those interviewed six indicated that their organizations were interested in proposing standards to the A.S.R.B., while only one, the Institute of Directors, expressed the intention of working through the A.A.R.F. The remaining two showed little interest in the area of accounting standards (Business Review Weekly, December 18, 1982, p. 61).

There were others who publicly expressed support for or opposed various aspects of the N.C.S.C. recommendations. The Executive General Manager of the B.H.P. objected to the N.C.S.C. veto power of rejecting standards. He was critical of the meagre time and cost estimates made by the Commission for the Board. He suggested that the profession be given a year to establish its own A.S.R.B. and if it could not do so the Government should proceed with its plans for a board. He also suggested that only the chairman of the Board should be appointed by the Government. He supported the idea of public exposure and public hearing of proposed standards by the A.S.R.B. He suggested that standards should be adopted by a simple majority of the Board members, an aspect which was overlooked by the N.C.S.C. (Business Review Weekly, January 15, 1983, p. 53).

In the meeting of November 26, 1982, of the Ministerial Council it was resolved that the N.S.W. C.A.C. prepare a report for consideration by the Ministers at their next meeting (Business Review Weekly, December 18, 1982, p. 59). The N.C.S.C. seemed not to be put out by this resolution, as one N.C.S.C. officer said

> The Attorney-General (N.S.W.) has had an interest for a long time in having an A.S.R.B. [Emphasis added] (Business Review Weekly, December 18, 1982, p. 59).

The Council's intention to reconsider the matter and a further study of the situation by the N.S.W. C.A.C. was seen by the accounting profession as a further opportunity to lobby (Prosser, 1983a, p. 18). In this respect Prosser, the Executive Director of the I.C.A.A., writing in the Chartered Accountant in Australia, saw an opportunity to explain the profession's view point regarding the A.S.R.B. First, he denied what media reports indicated as confrontation between the professional bodies and the N.C.S.C. and/or the Ministerial Council. He assured that the debate was healthy and constructive, but accepted that there were differences. He then clarified the profession's views, foremost amongst which was legislative backing for standards prepared by the accounting bodies in conjunction with other parties. This he claimed would be in the public interest and has always been the profession's rationale for an A.S.R.B. (Prosser, 1983a).

As for legislative backing, he explained that it would enhance compliance and improve the quality of reporting. The additional review step, being secondary in importance to legislative support, he explained could be achieved by external representation in the existing A.A.R.F. structure. However, he added, that the decision for having a government sponsored board did not unduly concern the profession so long as it incorporated essentially those features that the profession demanded (pp. 18-19).

To remove fears that the profession was tardy in its efforts or was not working in the public interest, he argued that the accounting bodies were contributing considerably in terms of cost and time towards standard-setting. Plus, there was sufficient scope for involvement by outside parties. He said that the profession had never claimed or attempted to exercise exclusive control over the development of accounting standards. He concluded that the use of profession's resources and expertise, in appropriate blending with other parties would produce a final A.S.R.B. solution. This, he claimed, would be efficient and economic (Prosser, 1983a, p. 18-19).

Writing in the <u>Australian Stock Exchange Journal</u> in February, 1983 Prosser (1983b) communicated the profession's opposition to A.S.R.B.'s formal recognition of alternative sources of accounting standards as proposed by the N.C.S.C. He explained that it had no precedent in any other country. It would duplicate resources and invite inconsistency in style, format and terminology. It would also lessen co-ordination with other standards and associated audit and other professional statements and priorities (p. 95). R. Walker (1987), studying the files of the Commonwealth Attorney-General's Department, also noted strong lobbying by the accounting bodies against the Board's proposed powers to review standards of other sources and its power to set priorities (p. 272).

On March 21, 1983, the N.S.W. C.A.C. in conjunction with the N.C.S.C. submitted its report on the establishment of the A.S.R.B. to the Ministerial Council. This report did not change the N.C.S.C.'s recommendation regarding the power of the Board to review standards from various sources. It replaced the provision for veto of approved standards of the Board by the N.C.S.C. with a veto provision to be exercised by the Ministerial Council. That is the standards once approved could be rejected only by the Council, under exceptional circumstances, within a period of sixty days of its approval by the Board (N.C.S.C. and N.S.W. C.A.C., A.S.R.B. Report to the Ministerial Council, March 1983, pp. 1-2, and p. 15).

The Report recommended that in addition to the directors statement in the accounts in respect of compliance with the standards the company auditors should provide a similar statement supporting or qualifying the directors' statement. It stated that in case of qualifications auditors should inform the Board by forwarding a copy of their reports to the Board (p. 3). Therefore, as opposed to the previous N.C.S.C. recommendation where it permitted departures with the approval of the auditor, this report placed heavy onus on both the directors and auditors (p. 8). This addition, the report explained, was necessary to act as a deterrence for those auditors who might readily agree to departures from accounting standards (p. 16). This seemed to be in correspondence with the N.S.W. Attorney-General's insistence, mentioned earlier, for more stringent measures for compliance with approved standards.

The powers of the Board remained similar to those recommended earlier by the Commission (p. 3-4). The only item the report added was the mode of voting required to approve the standards. It stated that a majority of five out of the seven members would be needed to approve a proposed standard (pp. 3-4). It also laid down the criteria for approving standards more clearly than the N.C.S.C. Release 405. Those criteria basically required the Board to consider whether the proposed standards were logically formulated; consistent with other approved standards; capable of providing relevant information for the directors and the community when applied; practicable for implementation; and their economic consequences when implemented (p. 4).

The constitution of the Board was changed indicating that the Ministerial Council would appoint only the chairman directly. Amongst the members one member would be appointed from a panel of names submitted by the A.S.A., another from a panel of names submitted by the I.C.A.A. and the rest from panels of names supplied by the N.C.S.C. and other interested bodies. The persons appointed would be selected in their own right and not as delegates of those organizations advancing their names. They would expect to represent a cross-section of interests and at least one would represent the interest of users of accounting reports. All selected persons were expected to possess technical competence in accounting. They would all be part-time members with a term of three years. The members selected from the panels provided by the N.C.S.C. and other bodies would, in the first instance, have a term of two years (pp. 4-5 and pp. 24-25).

One important recommendation was to provide for a research director indicating that the Board could be expected to conduct its own investigations independently (pp. 5-6). The Board's power as regards priorities was further strengthened. It was enhanced from the Board recommending priorities to the accounting bodies to empowering the Board to set priorities and convey them to those bodies (p. 9). This, the report stated was necessary because the Board would need to maintain consistency amongst its approved standards according to the above mentioned criteria of approval and also to provide for matters which militate against informed decision making. In this respect there was also a suggestion of a conceptual framework as one of the priorities (pp. 20-21). The cost estimate for annual expenditure was considerably enhanced from the earlier N.C.S.C. Release 405 estimate of $35,000 to $195,000 (p. 6).

It was mentioned in that report, that before it was prepared the I.C.A.A. and the A.S.A. wrote to the N.C.S.C. and made representations to some ministers regarding its views about the A.S.R.B. The arguments were similar to the ones described by Prosser in February 1983 (see above).[139] It reiterated the profession's desire for a profession sponsored board, but was ready to accept a government sponsored board if legislative recognition for its standards were forthcoming. It was still opposed to the formal recognition of other sources of standards. The Society suggested that if other bodies were interested in setting standards those standards should be proposed to the Board through the A.A.R.F. (pp. 9-11).

The Ministerial Council, in its meeting of March 25, 1983, accepted in principle the recommendations of the joint report of the N.C.S.C. and the N.S.W. C.A.C. Again, their resolution was short of a final decision to establish a board. As mentioned above there were still some differences between the Report's recommendations and the views of the profession, for which the Ministerial Council may have hesitated to take a definite decision. This was evident from the reported intention of the N.S.W. and

---

139   The two bodies wrote to the N.C.S.C. and made representations to the
       Ministers around the same time as Prosser's public comments.

Queensland Attorneys-General to have further talks with the accounting profession and others (not specified) to sort out the details of the draft decision (Business Review Weekly, April 2, 1983, p. 67 and April 9, 1983, p. 81). The discussions between the profession and the Ministers were reported by the I.C.A.A. Executive Director, who also reported the continuing pressures by the profession for the review of only A.A.R.F. standards and the participation of others through the A.A.R.F. (The Chartered Accountant in Australia, April, 1983, p. 5). Apart from that, there were some media reports of split between the N.C.S.C. and the N.S.W. C.A.C. regarding the more stringent compliance requirements and the removal of N.C.S.C. veto powers that the Report recommended (Australian Financial Review, March 25, 1983, p. 11).

Amidst prevailing criticism from the profession of the recommended board, the Ministerial Council decided to go ahead with its establishment, although a firm decision was still needed. The Commonwealth Attorney-General was entrusted with the task of preparing draft legislation to be considered by the Ministers (Business Review Weekly, April 2, 1983, p. 67).

On July 14, 1983, the Ministerial Council finally decided to establish the A.S.R.B. The Council endorsed January 1, 1984 as the date of commencement for the A.S.R.B., in time for the 1984-85 financial year. It was approved that the Board would consist of one part-time chairman, six part-time members and one staff director (N.C.S.C. Annual Report 1983-84, p. 58). The only significant change seems to have been the change in the role of the director from "research" to "staff", meaning that it would be an administrative position rather than "administrative and research" as envisaged in the N.C.S.C. and N.S.W. C.A.C. joint report. This was in congruous to the accounting bodies demands that the Board should not have independent research capability (R. Walker, 1987, p. 272).

The Federal Attorney-General expected to introduce the federal legislation within a few weeks amending the Companies Act to accommodate the provisions for approved accounting standards of the A.S.R.B. (Business Review Weekly, September 10, 1983). A bill for such amendments was finally introduced into the Federal Parliament on October 5, 1983 (Australian Financial Review, October 6, 1983, p. 1). The bill contained various aspects of the company law. As for the A.S.R.B. the only controversy reported, regarding the Board, during the passage of the Bill was that the opposition demanded that the Board be accountable to the Parliament through annual reports and that the approved accounting standards be in the form of regulations so that the Parliament had the power to disallow them, if necessary (Australian Financial Review, November 2, 1983, p. 12). This seems to have been an unachievable requirement because the Board was not a Commonwealth body responsible only to the Commonwealth Government, but was a body under the Co-operative Scheme and responsible to the Ministerial Council composed of Ministers of all the participating States and the Commonwealth. The Bill was passed without further obstacles and changes, making way for the establishment of the Board from January 1, 1984.

In this respect Masel explained that one of the major principles behind the establishment of the A.S.R.B. was that if statutory recognition was to be given to the standards, the standard-setting process should be overt with emphasis on due process and procedural fairness. He added that in a democratic society, the enforcement of professional accounting standards against non-members of the profession can only be carried out with adequate safeguards. He argued, that it was the very nature of a democratic society that the element of coercion, as distinct from consent, required legislative intervention. If accounting bodies were to have rule-making power with rules having penal sanctions, a policy instrument which legitimated such a power should be devised. In this case, he said, the policy instrument was the A.S.R.B. which had the responsibility of reviewing standards set by the accounting bodies and others, subject to disallowance by the Ministerial Council. Thus, he explained, that the interposition of the A.S.R.B. between account setters, the rule-makers and preparers, acted to create a balance between the need to harness technical skills which are essential in the formulation of accounting standards, on the one hand, and the theories of accountability and responsibility which are the hallmark of any democratic society, on the other (Masel, 1983, p. 544 and p. 547).

Meanwhile, another controversy erupted which could have long term effects on the scope of approved accounting standards. The N.C.S.C. Green Paper recommending changes to the disclosure requirements contained in Schedule 7 of the Companies Act was released in June, 1983. This rekindled the earlier debate on whether the concept of "true and fair view" should be defined and used for determining disclosure requirements including the accounting standards or the term "true and fair view" be replaced by a phrase such as "fairly presented in accordance with accepted Australian accounting standards.[140] Media reports indicated that the profession was more inclined towards adopting the latter policy (Australian Financial Review, July 28, 1983, p. 7). This was in line with the profession's earlier suggestions that compliance with generally accepted accounting standards would lead to true and fair

---

140   This debate was further fueled by N.C.S.C.'s consultative document on "true and fair view" issued in October 1984.

reporting (Also see Australian Financial Review, October 14, 1983, p. 79). The same policy, as earlier mentioned, had been adopted by the N.S.W. C.A.C. and recommended by the N.C.S.C. for the establishment of an A.S.R.B. It is also obvious that if the latter policy was adopted, standards would have superseded all other forms of company disclosure regulations and Schedule 7 may have had to be incorporated into the standards. The assimilation of that schedule by the accounting standards was also stressed by the President of the I.C.A.A. (Australian Financial Review, October 14, 1983, p. 79).

At this stage some other critics of the A.S.R.B. emerged. Analyzing the establishment of the A.S.R.B. Peirson and Ramsay (1983) wrote that the A.S.R.B.'s review of professional accounting standards and standards from other sources would make the structure of regulation of financial reporting more diffuse than it already was. Commenting on the various forms of accounting regulation already present in Australia, they explained, that the creation of another form would lead to substantial increase in the cost of regulation. They referred to the amalgamation of the Seventh Schedule into the accounting standards, proposed by the accounting bodies, which could lead to a more co-coordinated and consistent approach to establishing financial reporting requirements at a lower cost (pp. 298-8).

Empowering the Board:

The amended Companies Act 1981, as amended by the Companies and Securities Legislation (Miscellaneous Amendments) Act 1983, did not mention the functions of the Board other than that it could approve standards (See Section 266, Companies Act 1981). At that stage the functions of the Board were those that were laid down in the N.C.S.C. and N.S.W. C.A.C. joint recommendations as approved by the Ministerial Council.

Seemingly for this non-statutory nature of the Board's functions, even before the Board was established, there were criticisms about its functions. Mr. Tony Greenwood, a Commissioner of the N.C.S.C., criticized the amendments for not giving the Board the statutory power of setting priorities for the A.A.R.F. He stated:

> The denial of the Board of any real authority to review project development may not only risk it being subservient to the perceptions of the accounting profession, but we may have denied ourselves of an opportunity to provide a focus for timely and authoritative response to emerging accounting issues.
>
> The failure to accord a priorities approval role to the Board may drastically change its functional role as originally envisaged by the N.C.S.C., from one of conductor of accounting orchestra to that of critic of the concert pieces (Australian Financial Review, November 24, 1983, p. 4).

Mr. Greenwood in his stern message communicated the intention of the Commission that stringent measures would be taken, both with regards to setting standards and enforcement of standards. He warned that the consequences for non-compliance would be severe for both the auditors and the company directors. He warned the profession that the Board would consider adopting international standards or sponsor its own standards if no appropriate standards were forthcoming from the profession. He also pointed out the inconsistencies between existing professional accounting standards (Australian Financial Review, November 24, 1983, p. 4).

The Board commenced operations on January 1, 1984 with the appointment of its first set of members. All members had accounting backgrounds. Although the Ministerial Council may have leaned too far towards accountants, Mr. Greenwood clarified the situation as follows:

> While many are suspicious of legal input, the Board will have quasi-legislative function and it is therefore essential that members be capable of viewing Board decisions in a structured legal way ... This capacity is all the more important because the Board will not have access to permanent legal counsel (Business Review Weekly, January, 21, 1984).

He was reported as urging a "good dose" of legal skill on the Board (Business Review Weekly, January, 21, 1984). In fact the accounting profession had already been warned by the former Federal Minister for Business and Consumer Affairs regarding the intervention of predominantly lawyer-operated N.C.S.C. and the Ministerial Council (Australian Financial Review, February 10, 1982, p. 16).

Meanwhile the accounting profession welcomed the creation of the Board and the appointment of its members (Business Review Weekly, January, 21, 1984). According to R. Walker (1987, p. 272) the accounting profession had more success in the appointment of the members of the Board, specially its chairman, than in other aspects. As mentioned in Chapter 3, the majority of the members of the first board were or had been actively involved in the profession's standard-setting process, but it could not be guaranteed that they would act only in the interest of the accounting profession.

In view of the various controversies persisting regarding the Board's functions and activities, one of the first moves that the Board made was to resolve those issues. In February 1984 it issued its Release 400 inviting submissions with regards to its criteria for approving standards. <u>Release 400</u> also happened to be the first public exposure document in its "Exposures" series. The criteria which it envisaged for approving proposed standards were based on the Ministerial Council's approved criteria recommended to it earlier by the N.C.S.C. and N.S.W. C.A.C. Those criteria were as follows:

(a)　　Is the proposed standard logically well formulated?

(b)　　Is the proposed standard consistent with approved accounting standards?

(c)　　Would the information generated by application of the proposed Standard be relevant for the stewardship function of Directors; for informed decision making and for satisfying community needs?

(d)　　What is the practicability of implementation of the Standard?

(e)　　What are the economic consequences of implementation of the Standard?

The Release also invited comments with respect to the development of a conceptual framework and the perceived priorities of the private sector in relation to existing professional accounting standards.

A total of 74 submissions were received in response to the Release. There were some agreements and disagreements with the envisaged criteria and there were numerous other suggestions. The types of responses have been listed in Column 1 of Table 9.3. The respondents have been classified into six classes, indicating two additional classes of respondents to those identified in Table 9.3. - one of them being that for users and security analysts.

While the Board was still receiving submissions in response to its Release 400, the debate about the scope of the approved standards and their mode of preparation continued. The profession pressed ahead for the assimilation of the Seventh Schedule into the accounting standards. It felt that with the advent of the statutorily backed approved standards such assimilation had greater justification. They also held the view that it would bring about greater consistency between the disclosure and accounting requirements (Australian Financial Review, May, 10, 1984, p. 26).

There was also confusion about the possible existence of dual standards on the same issue and their effects on the obligations of the auditor. This the N.C.S.C. explained should not be the case, because once a certain form of a standard was approved by the Board the professional bodies would reissue their standards to bring them into line with those of the A.S.R.B. (Australian Financial Review, April 5, 1984, p. 55 and The Australian Accountant, January/February 1985, p. 97).

In the meantime the Chairman of the A.S.R.B. responding to the views of others emphasized the need for a conceptual framework. The framework, he said, would reduce the need for accounting standards for every single detail of company reports. He also felt that accounting standards needed to be approved with a single framework in mind. He mentioned that some quarters were expressing the view that all existing professional accounting standards should be approved until further revisions were available. However, he informed that there was a strong body of opinion against such a move. Therefore the Board had decided not to approve standards as they were. He mentioned that one of the Board's tasks would be to stimulate consensus on a conceptual framework. He also expressed the need for public exposure and public hearings on proposed standards before their approval (Australian Financial Review, May 17, 1984, p. 3).

Responding to the suggestions made and the view's held by the respondents of Release 400 the A.S.R.B. issued its Release 100 and Release 200 in February 1985. The first dealt with the criteria for the evaluation of accounting standards and the latter laid out the procedures for the approval of accounting standards. Both were important documents because they outlined the premise on which the standards could be proposed, reviewed and approved.

Commenting on the Board's reaction to the submissions the Release 100 stated:

> The Board received detailed and thoughtful comments on the suggested criteria for the evaluation of accounting standards, and the role of a "conceptual framework" in that process. After careful analysis of these responses, the Board has reached the conclusion that it would be appropriate to link its statement of evaluative criteria with a statement of assumptions concerning some key accounting concepts (p. 1).

As for the evaluative criteria of Release 400, they were restated in Release 100 with very little amendments. Criteria (a), (b) and (c) of the Release 400 became Criteria 2, 3 and 1 respectively of the Release 100. Criteria (d) and (e) became Criterion 4 of the Release 100 (Release 100, p. 3 and p. 4). The overwhelming acceptance of the envisaged criteria was the main reason behind their adoption with minor changes (Release 100, p. 3; also see Table 9.4.). In addition three other suggestions, made by a large number of respondents, were incorporated in the criteria in Release 100. These were conformity of proposed standards with other commercial and legal requirements (pp. 3-4); consistency with overseas standards (p. 3) and the requirements of different classes of companies (p. 4). The Board also kept the criteria open for further review and refinement by stating that it only reflected the Board's current thinking and the Board could amend or extend those criteria in future (p. 3). This could be in response to a number of submissions asking for flexible criteria (See Table 9.4).

In order to apply those criteria, the Board concluded that it would be necessary for it to adopt certain assumptions concerning the accounting process, and it felt that those assumptions be made explicit (Release 100, p. 5). This decision corresponded with the suggestions of a large number of submissions which had recommended that the Board should, as a priority, prepare a conceptual framework to act as a basis of approving proposed standards. There were 25 such submissions as compared to 11 asking for the approval of some or all existing professional standards as the first priority of the Board (Some asked the latter it to be an interim measure). Fifteen other proposals gave importance to both the preparation of a conceptual framework and approval of existing standards (See Table 9.4.).

There were others who felt that assumptions should be defined instead of a conceptual framework. Some simply indicated that definitions of assumptions were necessary and some went further to mention the areas where definitions were necessary (See Table 9.4.).

Although from Table 9.4. we can see that a large number of respondents felt the need for a conceptual framework or a set of assumptions on the basis of which the Board would approve its standards, almost all of them, including those who opposed the preparation of a conceptual framework, expressed the view that preparing a conceptual framework would be a difficult task. It seems that for such reasons the Board developed only a partial set of assumptions defining only some key accounting concepts with the exclusion of a measurement concept (pp. 4-13).[141] The measurement concept was defined later in A.S.R.B. Release 101 (December, 1985), but it did not provide for a particular measurement method or a set of methods.

With respect to its assumptions the Board had this to say:

> While the Board's main brief is to review accounting standards, the Board notes that it would not be practicable for the joint accounting bodies or other organizations to develop an accounting standard to cover every type of transaction or situation. The clarification of the meaning of some key accounting concepts may provide guidance to some directors and auditors when they consider what accounting treatment may be appropriate in a situation for which no approved accounting standards exist. ...
>
> The statements of "assumptions" reflect preliminary views and should be helpful both in focusing the Board's attention on relevant issues, and in assisting those interested in making submissions on proposed standards to address issues of particular concern to the Board (A.S.R.B. Release 100, p. 5).

Apart from responses in respect of the conceptual framework and assumptions criteria, there were some suggestions from the respondents regarding the approval procedures (See Table 9.4.). The largest number of responses were for the public exposure of proposed standards followed by suggestions that the A.S.R.B. support or accept the A.A.R.F. as the standard setter. These two suggestions and some others were incorporated in full or partially in A.S.R.B.'s Release 200, Procedures for the Approval

---

141   R. Walker (1987) called it a mini 'conceptual framework' because it dealt too briefly with accounting attributes of assets and liabilities.

of Accounting Standards, issued along with Release 100. According to Table 9.4. the demand for public exposure of proposed standards mainly emanated from the preparers of accounting statements. Responding to the submissions the Release 200 provided considerable scope for public exposure and debate before a proposed standard could be approved (pp. 3-5). Suggestions for accepting the A.A.R.F. as the main or sole source of accounting standards mainly came from the practitioners (Table 9.4.). Although the possibility of other sources of proposed standards was not eliminated, the Release explicitly stated that the Foundation would normally be the source of proposed standards and the Board would not approve standards of other sources before allowing the Foundation to comment on them (p. 3). The Board also accepted two other suggestions - that of sponsoring its own standards and fixing a time frame for implementing approved standards (p. 2 and pp. 7-8). Another suggestion, that of the Board having the capability of changing standards, was not incorporated into its Release 200, but was eventually included as one of A.S.R.B.'s functions (See Chapter 4 and A.S.R.B. Annual Report 1984-85, p. 3). Surprisingly this proposal mainly came from the accounting practitioners, which was contrary to the view of the professional accounting bodies that in case of partial or total non-acceptance of a proposed standard the Board should return the standard in full to the A.A.R.F. for further consideration (See above). Apart from those changes made on the basis of the submissions and clarifying some procedural matters the Board, at that stage, did not make any significant changes to its terms of operation as approved earlier by the Ministerial Council on March 25, 1983.

Several other issues regarding procedural matters emerged during the Board's first few years of operation. Those issues had not been foreseen by those who initiated and were subsequently involved in the creation of the Board. Some of the issues were controversial and led to certain changes. R. Walker (1987) discussed those changes. Foremost amongst those were, the drafting and copyright of standards which created serious conflicts between the newly formed Board and the accounting profession and led to delays in reviewing existing professional standards (p. 278-80). Since those issues mainly brought about procedural changes and did not affect the organizational or functional aspects of the Board, they fall outside the scope of the discussion of this chapter and Chapter 10. A discussion in that respect is contained in Chapter 11.

Table 9.4.: The Profile of the Submissions in Response to A.S.R.B. Release 400
(Based on Ministerial Council Resolution March 21, 1983 which was in turn based on a N.C.S.C.-N.S.W. C.A.C. Submission)

Suggestions in Response to or Agreement with A.S.R.B. Release 400 (Policy Issues)	Preparers of Financial Statements	Professional Bodies Firms and Individuals	Respondents Academics	Government Bodies	Users and Securities Analysts	Others	Total	Incorporated into A.S.R.B Release 100 Release 200
1	2	3	4	5	6	7	8	
Envisaged Criteria for Approving Proposed Standards:								
(1) Logical Formulation	22 (69)	11 (58)	6 (75)	5 (71)	3 (60)	2 (50)	49 (65)	Y (100) Release 100
(2) Consistency with Approved Standards	23 (72)	11 (58)	5 (63)	5 (71)	3 (60)	1 (25)	48 (64)	Y (100) Release 200
(3) Relevance with Directors' and User needs	24 (75)	10 (53)	3 (38)	5 (71)	4 (80)	2 (50)	48 (64)	Y (100)

Table 9.4. (Continued): The Profile of the Submissions in Response to A.S.R.B. Release 400

Suggestions in Response to or Agreement with A.S.R.B. Release 400 (Policy Issues)	Respondents						Total	Incorporated into A.S.R.B Release 100 Release 200
	Preparers of Financial Statements	Professional Bodies Firms and Individuals	Academics	Government Bodies	Users and Securities Analysts	Others		
1	2	3	4	5	6	7	8	
(4) Practicable for Implementation	23 (72)	8 (42)	5 (63)	5 (71)	3 (60)	2 (50)	46 (61)	Y (100)
(5) Economic Consequences	22 (63)	12 (67)	5 (63)	2 (29)	2 (40)	2 (50)	45 (60)	Y (100) (Continued)

Notes: 1. Figures without parentheses represent actual number of submissions.
2. Figures within parentheses are submissions as a percentage of the total number of submissions for that group. These percentages have been used in the statistical calculations of Chapter 10.
3. In the case of N.C.S.C. recommendations based on those submissions a "Y" represents that the particular response was recommended to the Ministerial Council and an "N" indicates that the response was not recommended to the Council. Since we do not know whether the N.C.S.C. commissioners voted on each issue before such recommendation and as it is not possible to exactly weigh each recommendation, a "Y" has been assigned an arbitrary weight of 100% and an "N" a weight of 0%.

Table 9.4. (Continued): The Profile of the Submissions in Response to A.S.R.B. Release 400

Suggestions in Response to or Agreement with A.S.R.B. Release 400 (Policy Issues)	Preparers of Financial Statements	Professional Bodies Firms and Individuals	Academics	Government Bodies	Users and Securities Analysts	Others	Total	Incorporated into A.S.R.B Release 100 Release 200
1	2	3	4	5	6	7	8	
Criteria Proposed by the Respondents:								
(1) Relevance to Managers' needs	3 (9)	0 (0)	0 (0)	0 (0)	0 (0)	0 (0)	3 (4)	N (0)
(2) Conformity to other Commercial & Legal Requirements	4 (13)	1 (5)	0 (0)	2 (29)	0 (0)	1 (25)	9 (12)	Y (100)
(3) Consistency with International Accounting Standards & Standards of other countries	8 (25)	4 (21)	0 (0)	1(14)	1 (20)	1 (25)	15 (20)	Y (100)

Table 9.4. (Continued): The Profile of the Submissions in Response to A.S.R.B. Release 400

Suggestions in Response to or Agreement with A.S.R.B. Release 400 (Policy Issues)	Preparers of Financial Statements	Professional Bodies Firms and Individuals	Respondents Academics	Government Bodies	Users and Securities Analysts	Others	Total	Incorporated into A.S.R.B Release 100 Release 200
1	2	3	4	5	6	7	8	
(4) Use Historic Costs	0 (0)	0 (0)	2 (25)	0 (0)	0 (0)	0 (0)	2 (3)	N (0)
(5) Criteria should be Flexible (a) Yes	4 (13)	1 (5)	0 (0)	0 (0)	0 (0)	1 (25)	6 (8)	Y (100)
(b) No	0 (0)	0 (0)	1 (13)	0 (0)	0 (0)	0 (0)	1 (1)	N (0)
Prepare a Conceptual Framework as a Priority	8 (25)	3 (16)	6 (75)	3	3	2	25 (33)	Y (100)
Approve some or all the existing Australian Accounting Standards as a Priority	7 (22)	4 (21)	0 (0)	0 (0)	0 (0)	0 (0)	11 (15)	N (0)
Both Preparation of a Conceptual Framework and Approval of Existing Standards as Priorities	7 (22)	5 (26)	1 (13)	1 (14)	0 (0)	1 (25)	15 (20)	N (0)
A.A.R.F. should prepare Conceptual Framework	0 (0)	1 (5)	0 (0)	0 (0)	0 (0)	0 (0)	1 (1)	N (0)

Table 9.4. (Continued): The Profile of the Submissions in Response to A.S.R.B. Release 400

Suggestions in Response to or Agreement with A.S.R.B. Release 400 (Policy Issues)	Preparers of Financial Statements	Respondents					Total	Incorporated into A.S.R.B Release 100 Release 200
		Professional Bodies Firms and Individuals	Academics	Government Bodies	Users and Securities Analysts	Others		
1	2	3	4	5	6	7	8	
Assumptions:								
(1) Assumptions should be defined by the Board	3 (9)	3 (16)	1 (13)	0 (0)	1 (20)	0 (0)	8 (11)	Y (100)
(2) Assumptions which need Definition:								
(a) Purpose of Financial Statements	5 (16)	1 (5)	1 (13)	1(14)	2 (40)	0 (0)	10 (13)	Y (100)
(b) Entity	3 (9)	1 (5)	0 (0)	0 (0)	0 (0)	0 (0)	4 (5)	N (0)
(c) Assets	3 (9)	4 (21)	0 (0)	0 (0)	0 (0)	0 (0)	7 (9)	Y (100)
(d) Liabilities	3 (9)	3 (16)	0 (0)	0 (0)	0 (0)	0 (0)	6 (8)	Y (100)
(e) Equity	3 (9)	2 (11)	0 (0)	1(14)	0 (0)	0 (0)	6 (8)	Y (100)

Table 9.4. (Continued): The Profile of the Submissions in Response to A.S.R.B. Release 400

(f) Measurement Criteria								
(i) Single	1 (3)	0 (0)	1 (13)	0 (0)	0 (0)	0 (0)	2 (3)	N (0)
(ii) Multiple	2 (6)	1 (5)	1 (13)	0 (0)	1 (20)	0 (0)	5 (7)	N (0)
(g) Other Terms	1 (3)	0 (0)	0 (0)	0 (0)	0 (0)	0 (0)	1 (1)	N (0)
Approval Procedure:								
(1) Support or Accept A.A.R.F. as Standard-Setter	2 (6)	5 (26)	1 (13)	0 (0)	0 (0)	1 (25)	9 (12)	Y (100)
(2) Public Exposure of Proposed Standards	6 (19)	3 (16)	0 (0)	0 (0)	1 (20)	2 (50)	12 (16)	Y (100)
(3) Sponsor the Development of Standards	1 (3)	0 (0)	0 (0)	0 (0)	1 (20)	0 (0)	2 (3)	Y (100)
(4) Capability to Change Proposed Standards	2 (6)	4 (21)	0 (0)	0 (0)	0 (0)	0 (0)	6 (8)	N (0)
(5) Provide Reasons for Changing Proposed Standards	0 (0)	1 (5)	0 (0)	0 (0)	0 (0)	0 (0)	1 (1)	N (0)
(6) Convert Schedule 7 into Standards	1 (3)	0 (0)	0 (0)	0 (0)	0 (0)	1 (25)	2 (3)	N (0)
(7) Fix Time Frame for Implementation	0 (0)	2 (11)	1 (13)	0 (0)	0 (0)	0 (0)	3 (4)	Y (100)

Table 9.4. (Continued): The Profile of the Submissions in Response to A.S.R.B. Release 400

Suggestions in Response to or Agreement with A.S.R.B. Release 400 (Policy Issues)	Preparers of Financial Statements	Professional Bodies Firms and Individuals	Respondents Academics	Government Bodies	Users and Securities Analysts	Others	Total	Incorporated into A.S.R.B Release 100 Release 200
1	2	3	4	5	6	7	8	
Others Suggestions:								
(1) Different Reporting Requirements for Large and Small Companies	3 (9)	4 (21)	0 (0)	0 (0)	2 (40)	0 (0)	9 (12)	N (0)
(2) Industry Specific Standards	4 (13)	1 (6)	0 (0)	1 (14)	0 (0)	0 (0)	6 (8)	Y (100)
(3) Set Standards for Entities like Partnerships, Sole Ownerships, Non-business Organizations and Public Sector Organizations	3 (9)	3 (16)	0 (0)	2 (29)	0 (0)	0 (0)	8 (11)	N (0)

Table 9.4. (Continued): The Profile of the Submissions in Response to A.S.R.B. Release 400

Suggestions in Response to or Agreement with A.S.R.B. Release 400 (Policy Issues)	Preparers of Financial Statements	Professional Bodies Firms and Individuals	Respondents Academics	Government Bodies	Users and Securities Analysts	Others	Total	Incorporated into A.S.R.B Release 100 Release 200
1	2	3	4	5	6	7	8	
(4) Fund the A.A.R.F.	0 (0)	0 (0)	0 (0)	0 (0)	0 (0)	1 (25)	1 (1)	N (0)
(5) Monitor Compliance	0 (0)	1 (5)	0 (0)	0 (0)	0 (0)	0 (0)	1 (1)	N (0)
(6) Do not Over Regulate	2 (6)	2 (11)	0 (0)	0 (0)	0 (0)	0 (0)	4 (5)	N (0)
(7) Apolitical Board	0 (0)	0 (0)	1 (13)	0 (0)	0 (0)	0 (0)	1 (1)	N (0)
Totals	32 (100)	19 (100)	8 (100)	7 (100)	5 (100)	4 (100)	75 (100)	

Chapter 10

THE CREATION OF THE A.S.R.B. - AN ANALYSIS

Introduction:

We now examine the facts presented in Chapter 9 regarding the process of the creation of the A.S.R.B. We have already suggested in Chapter 5 that the creation of regulatory bodies and their functions, such as that of the Board, falls in the arena of public policy processes. A similar view of policy making has been taken by Heclo (1972). He explained that:

> Policy does not seem to be a self-defining phenomenon; it is an analytic category, the contents of which are identified by analyst rather than by the policy-maker or pieces of legislation or administration. ... A policy may usefully be considered as a course of action or inaction rather than specific decisions or actions, and such a course has to be perceived and identified by the analyst in question (p. 85).

In respect of the study of public policy Weller (1980) stated that:

> Precisely how that task is done will depend on the scholar; there are many valid approaches. In the field of public policy, what you see depends on where you look (p. 499).

For the purposes of this thesis the model has already been described in Chapter 5. That model incorporated various elements of the policy-making process, amongst which the behaviour of interest groups was one of the elements. The evidence laid down in Chapter 9 indicate that the policy-making process creating the A.S.R.B. was a multi-party process. Here we analyze closely the behaviour of interest groups which were involved in the creation of the Board from the time it was conceived up to the time its first set of functions were publicly stated.

This chapter attempts to explain their participation. The second section of this chapter identifies the stimulants which brought the A.S.R.B. issue into the political agenda. The third and fourth sections respectively deal with the behaviour of the demanders and suppliers of the A.S.R.B. In the fifth section the evidence relating to the creation of the Board is further analyzed to determine the nature of alignment between respondents' demands and the Ministerial Council's decisions. In the final section inferences are drawn regarding the behaviour of the participants.

Entrance of the A.S.R.B. issue into the Political Arena:

Cobb and Elder's model in Figure 5.4. indicates that an issue is created and exists prior to entering the agenda of the politicians and the regulatory process. We have noted in Chapter 5 that for the issue to attain significance and to qualify to enter the regulatory process it should be perceived by the participants in the process as a crisis. The two groups that are expected to expand the issue into crisis proportions are the politicians and the news media.

Our review in Chapters 8 and 9 indicates that the idea for mandatory standards and a government sponsored body to prepare such standards originated in 1967 (Ryan, 1967). Although this was followed by the revelations of widespread non-compliance with accounting standards by the N.S.W. C.A.C., the issue remained insignificant till it came to the attention of the N.S.W. Attorney-General, Mr. F. Walker, in 1977. Already aware of certain instances of involvement of accountants and accounting techniques in corporate frauds and having a low opinion about white-collar professionals, he immediately set upon a campaign of converting the issue into an emotional one. As noted in Chapter 9 he used terms like "anarchy" and "white collar crimes" to stir public sentiment. He also approached his counterparts in other States and the Commonwealth Governments. Not surprisingly, he used the public/community interest rhetoric in suggesting government intervention in standard-setting (F. Walker, 1981a and 1981b). His suggestions were well timed because they followed a period of corporate failures. A number of such failures were alleged to have occurred due to wrong or fraudulent use of accounting methods.

He further pushed the accounting standards issue into the political domain by providing threats of imminent sanctions (F. Walker, 1981a and 1981b). The formation of the Accounting Standards Review Committee of N.S.W. also created an atmosphere of insecurity for the accounting profession. His suggestion for a review board did not provide any convincing argument or evidence as to how corporate crimes and frauds could be solved by reviewing accounting standards. Nevertheless, he provided sufficient impetus to stimulate a debate on the necessity of an accounting standards review board.

The pattern of reporting adopted by the news media clearly followed Watts (1977) explanation that the media entertains the layman. Although the news media closely monitored the developments in the area of accounting standards and the creation of the Board, it never provided an in-depth analysis of the "pros and cons" of a review board.

The following news headlines illustrate the nature of reporting of the creation of the Board and other related issues in the media:

Reform becomes white collar anarchy (Australian Financial Review, August 4, 1977, p. 2)

PROFESSION DELIVERS AN UPPER-CUT (Business Review Weekly, October 9, 1982)

N.C.S.C. PULLS OUT A RABBIT (Business Review Weekly, December 11, 1982 p. 58)

Quixotic plan to maintain standards - BHP financial heavy Bill Hunter has scored some hits and some misses with the N.C.S.C. (Business Review Weekly, January 15, 1983, p. 53).

ACCOUNTANTS CONTROL BROADSIDE (Australian Financial Review, October 5, 1982).

The use of terms such as "anarchy", "delivers an upper-cut", "pulls out a rabbit", "hits and misses" and "broadside" are certainly the kind of language that would attract the attention of the layman to the particular news item.

Some instances of reckless reporting were also detected. For example, under the heading "Moore slams 'appalling' accounting standards" (Australian Financial Review, February 10, 1982, p. 1) it was reported that Mr. Moore, the then Commonwealth Minister for Business and Consumer Affairs, was considering the idea of Government regulation of standard-setting. To this the accounting profession reacted rejecting the 'reported' claims made by the Minister (Australian Financial Review, February 12, 1982). The correct report of the Minister's remarks, which came out ten days latter in the Business Review Weekly (February 20, 1982, p. 47), was that the Minister, a non-Labour politician, was in fact warning the profession that if the Labour party won the 1982 Victorian elections there would be a greater possibility of Government intervention into accounting standard-setting.

From this discussion we can infer that the politicians were responsible for creating an atmosphere of crisis which helped the A.S.R.B. issue to enter the political agenda. On the other hand the news media helped in activating a prolonged public debate about the Board.

Demanders:

This section has four sub-sections. Each sub-section separately analyses the involvement of bureaucrats, accounting bodies and accountants, companies, and others in the process of the creation of the Board and the establishment of its functions.

Bureaucrats:

As already mentioned the origins of the Board lie in the actions of the bureaucrats. As per the established facts, the history of A.S.R.B. starts from 1967 when the then N.S.W. Registrar of Companies, Mr. Ryan, introduced the idea of a statutory commission for the preparation of accounting principles (Ryan, 1967, p. 106). The need for such a commission arose from the prevailing controversy over the "true and fair view" provision of the then Companies Act. As a company law administrator, he found the issue quite perplexing and wrote:

> At the lodgment stage my officers are concerned only to see that the accounts comply with the Ninth Schedule. Obviously it is impracticable for them to form any judgment as to their truth and fairness, which at that stage must be matters for the directors and auditors alone. On the happening of some subsequent event which raises doubts as to the validity of the accounts, I would not for one moment contemplate a prosecution based on so slippery a concept as truth and fairness (Ryan, 1967, p. 107).

Ryan (1967 and 1974) sufficiently elaborated his discomfort with the "true and fair" concept as the basis of company financial disclosure. Subsequently, disenchanted with the low level of compliance with professional accounting standards by companies and their auditors he informed the then N.S.W. Attorney-General, Mr. Frank Walker, about his perceived problem. As we saw earlier, this led to the Attorney-General's call for the creation of a review board. Such a board, having review functions like that of the South African Accounting Practices Board, had been contemplated earlier by Ryan (1974, p. 5). In this case the interest of the N.S.W. Registrar was to facilitate his function of verifying company accounts and take action against directors under the "true and fair view" provisions of the Companies Act. This is in accordance with the notion that bureaucrats can initiate policy issues in their own interest (See Chapter 5).

Various State and Commonwealth committees[142] and bureaucracies[143] were also critical of the accounting standards and/or the company disclosure provisions of the companies statutes. They made various recommendations amongst which some suggested the creation of a national review board or a national statutory commission capable of establishing legislatively backed accounting standards.

The bureaucrats played an active role in the formation of the Board. The May 23, 1980, Ministerial Council resolution accepting the need for an A.S.R.B. was based on N.C.S.C. recommendations which in turn were in conformity with the idea of a standards review board conceived by the N.S.W. Registrar of Companies.

There is evidence that the bureaucrats responsible for the regulation of companies tried to impose their influence over the accounting profession by placing themselves in a supervisory role in the preparation of accounting standards. For example, the N.C.S.C. endeavoured not only to become a permanent participant in the standards review process through acquiring a membership position, but it also tried to secure a key position in the process through acquiring the power to endorse or reject the Board's reviewed standards. The provision for endorsement of standards by the N.C.S.C. was the Commission's own suggestion, and it could empower the Commission to dictate the terms of the review

---

142   Recommendations of committees such as the Eggleston Committee, the Rae Committee and the N.S.W. Accounting Standards Committee have already been dealt with in earlier chapters.

143   The Interstate Corporate Affairs Commission also established an Accounts Sub-committee for greater uniformity in company disclosure requirements between states.

process in its own interest. In this respect, the Commission did admit that the endorsement power was necessary for the purpose of facilitating its primary responsibility, company law administration. Looking from Professor R. Walker's (1987) "capture" notion we may say that it would be possible for the Commission to "capture" the standard-setting process with a view to facilitate the execution of its bureaucratic functions.

The N.S.W. C.A.C. and later the N.C.S.C. also wanted to reduce the role of the accounting profession by keeping the provision that the Board could suggest priorities, approve standards prepared by others in addition to the accounting bodies and sponsor the preparation of standards. Their aim being to strip the accounting profession of its "sole authority" to reorganize society via the standard-setting process (Business Review Weekly, January, 15, 1983, pp. 53-54).

The joint report of the N.S.W. C.A.C. and the N.C.S.C. also recommended responsibilities for auditors with respect to the qualification of accounts and provided for the appointment of a research director to allow the Board to conduct its own investigations independently. It was also suggested that the Board be empowered to set priorities for setting standards by the accounting bodies, thus providing it a role of directing the preparation of standards.

Meanwhile, the officers of the N.C.S.C. took a hard line against flexible standards and warned the auditors and directors of severe consequences for non-compliance. Such a stand to have clear "black and white" rules were directed towards reducing the diversity in accounting procedures. This would reduce the likelihood of the Commission being blamed for future company failures under the provisions of "true and fair" reporting.

The above observations support the arguments placed in Chapter 5. The idea of an A.S.R.B. was initiated by the bureaucrats involved in the task of administering company law. Their main aim was to facilitate their own task and reduce the risk of being blamed under future crises. In doing so, they tried to take over the authority to set and/or approve accounting standards which for a long time was regarded as the responsibility of the accounting profession (See Chapter 6 and 7). Although they failed to secure any of those functions, they did manage to put themselves in the important and conspicuous role of standards enforcer. From that position they could monitor and influence the activities of the Board and, perhaps, that of the accounting profession.

We have also seen that the bureaucrats were better placed in introducing their views into the proposed structure and functions of the A.S.R.B. during its creation process. The N.C.S.C. and the N.S.W. C.A.C. were authorized on different occasions to make recommendations regarding the creation of the Board. At times they made recommendations which were their own creation and had very little or no outside support.

Accounting Profession:

In Chapter 5 we saw that through the imposition of accounting standards the accounting profession could achieve certain benefits. The accounting standards were seen as a device for increasing the profession's revenue (See Figure 3.2.). It was also shown that the demand by the profession for a government sponsored standard-setting body was derived from the demand for mandatory standards. Such a body, under the de facto control of the profession could provide government backing for the profession's standards at little or no extra cost to the profession. It would also ensure that the standards approved by the government body were not contrary to the interests of the members of the profession. From what R. Walker (1987, p. 281) added, we can also infer that the profession's standard-setters would certainly have liked to see this multi-million dollar standard-setting industry in the profession's control.[144]

Furthermore in Chapter 7 we saw that like any other profession the accounting profession (both accountants as preparers of financial statements and auditors as verifiers) was dependent on a special body of knowledge and skills known as accounting. It saw the accounting expertise as an essential skill for the maintenance of a professional identity and development of the standards as the development of that expertise. Accounting standards were an outcome of the process of professional development adopted within the profession and were regarded as an important means of ensuring the adequacy of the skills of the members and the image of the profession. Consequently, the active participation of the accounting bodies in the creation of the A.S.R.B. and keeping the standard-setting process within its control was in the profession's own interest.

Professional accounting standards, over the years, received attention from outside the profession and was eventually recognized as a means of company financial disclosure regulation. In Chapter 8 we noted that accounting standards prepared by the accounting bodies were capable of standardizing the practice of only the members of those bodies. Those bodies could not enforce

---

144   From Appendix D we can see that the accounting bodies already spend well over a million dollars on standard-setting each year and <u>A.S.R.B. Annual Report 1986-87</u>, p. 22, shows that the A.S.R.B. spent $ 212,103 in the year 1986-87 alone.

their standards on company directors. Although there may have been calls for a statutory body for setting standards in the early years of standard-setting, the initiative taken by company regulators for establishing an A.S.R.B. was mainly based on the need for enforceable standards. By this time the accounting bodies had already received wide recognition as standard-setters and the bureaucrats responsible for company regulation felt that only an additional step of "due process", that is review of standards, was needed for community acceptance and statutory recognition of the profession's standards.

We have seen in Chapters 6 and 7 that the criticism of the profession and its standards led to the gearing-up of the standard-setting activities by the accounting bodies. The creation of a separate foundation, the A.A.R.F., was also a part of the concerted effort of the A.S.A. and the I.C.A.A. to develop accounting standards. The threat that the profession constantly feared, was that of government intervention in standard-setting. We have already seen that such threats had been communicated by government bureaucrats, such as Ryan, in the late sixties. Such threats subsided with the increase in the standard-setting activities of the profession in early and mid 1970s, but resumed in the late seventies with the added support of the politicians in government. This time the profession had more to fear, specially because the N.S.W. Attorney-General, Mr. F. Walker, who took the lead in the campaign for government intervention, belonged to the Labour Party. As we shall see in the next section that the Labour Party policies are normally directed towards greater government intervention in economic activities and do not receive much support from white collar professionals.

In 1969 in an accounting convention the accounting profession and its affiliates resolved that the profession should develop accounting standards (Mathews, 1969; also see Table 8.1.). After F. Walker voiced his concern for accounting principles and suggested a government sponsored A.S.R.B., the accounting bodies took the view that legislative support for the standards prepared by the profession was necessary, but not government intervention in the preparation of standards.

The ease with which the Ministerial Council on May 23, 1980, resolved to consider a government sponsored review board can be attributed to the fact that the accounting bodies were once again very slow in countering the criticisms of the profession and its standards. This was pointed out by McKeon (1977a) and can also be noted from the fact that it was as late as 1979 when the accounting bodies, through the Professional Standards Review Committee of the I.C.A.A. made its first authoritative attack on the critics and their criticisms. It recommended statutory and stock exchange support for compliance with the profession's standards, but was strongly opposed to any government intervention in the preparation and enforcement of standards. It argued in favour of the existing mode of compliance adopted by the accounting bodies, that is allowing disclosed non-compliance.

Interestingly, the accounting bodies never seemed to have strongly challenged the results of the N.S.W. C.A.C.'s surveys on compliance and the validity of the tests. Such compliance surveys were the basis for the drive for an A.S.R.B. and mandatory standards. The only criticism from within the profession, in this respect, came from Balmford (1977). He did not support the idea of total compliance and emphasized that there cannot always be "black and white" solutions to accounting problems.

After it was too late to reject the idea of an A.S.R.B. because the Ministerial Council had already formed the opinion that such a review board was needed, the accounting bodies started lobbying for a board compatible with its needs.[145] The accounting bodies accepted the idea of having a board with the power to review only those standards that were prepared and proposed by the A.A.R.F. They wanted a board that would have a majority representation from the profession and would be the means for obtaining legislative backing for the profession's standards.

At first the N.C.S.C., delegated with the task of studying the need for a board, seemed to have responded to the accounting bodies' lobbying. In its first set of recommendations (N.C.S.C. Release 401, 1981) it proposed that the Board would be capable of reviewing standards proposed only by those bodies and approving priorities suggested by them. Subsequently the proposed functions of the Board were enlarged to include the capacity to review standards proposed by other sources and to sponsor standards (N.C.S.C. Release 405, 1982). The accounting bodies reacted strongly demanding that the Board should only be a review board. They preferred a profession sponsored review board, but were ready to accept a board which provided legislative support to the professional accounting standards. They also suggested that interested parties should propose standards to the Board through the profession's A.A.R.F.

The joint recommendations of the N.S.W. C.A.C. and the N.C.S.C. ignored the demands of the profession and made more suggestions having adverse consequences for the profession. Those suggestions included stringent requirements for the auditors with respect to compliance, the appointment of a research director and

---

145   This is the point from where R. Walker (1987) started his "capture" explanation for the creation of the Board.

the Board setting priorities to direct the profession's standard-setting activities.

The lack of response towards the profession's demands did not reduce the spirit of the accounting bodies and they kept on lobbying, this time to the Ministers. The Ministerial Council, during its final deliberations for establishing the A.S.R.B., did in fact respond to at least one of the demands of the profession, by reducing the functions of the research director from "research and administration" to only "administration". Later, the Council while appointing the Chairman of the Board perhaps also accepted the view of the accounting bodies that academic knowledge was not an appropriate selection criterion, and it appointed a non-academic as the Board's first Chairman (R. Walker, 1987, p. 272).

The establishment of the Board went ahead much to the dissatisfaction of the accounting bodies, but the scope for changes in its functions remained. Since the Board was not created as a statutory body and the Companies Act only indicated its review capacity, its functions were put under further public scrutiny through the A.S.R.B. Release 400. The profession started a campaign for the acceptance of its standards, at least as an interim measure. At that stage the Board accepted that the A.A.R.F. would be its main source of proposed standards and that the A.S.R.B. should seek comments from the A.A.R.F. on standards proposed by others.

Although we can see that the accounting bodies did not succeed in getting all their demands accepted, it is quite evident that they were a major force in determining the final outcome. As R. Walker (1987) illustrated, they kept on influencing the A.S.R.B.'s activities well after the Board was established. Our observations clearly demonstrate the keen interest of the accounting profession in the setting of accounting standards and it is evident that the accounting bodies were ready to go to extra-ordinary lengths to retain control of the accounting standard-setting mechanism.

The concept of legislative backing for accounting standards also inherently introduced certain legal concepts and eventually the threat of the participation of the legal profession in the setting of accounting standards. As already mentioned, the principle behind the establishment of the A.S.R.B. was that of statutory recognition of standards. Therefore, if statutory recognition was to be given to accounting standards, the standard-setting process would have to emphasize on the legal concept of due process and procedural fairness (also see Masel, 1983, p. 544 and p. 547). R. Walker (1987, p. 278 and p. 281) also reported that the A.S.R.B. had to take up the task of converting the approved standards from its existing language to a language more compatible with legal requirements. This certainly could introduce the use of legal expertise in the drafting of standards. This was also pointed out by one of the N.C.S.C. Commissioners, Mr. Greenwood, who emphasized that the Board had quasi-legislative functions and therefore the Board's members should have the capacity to view decisions in a structured legal way (See Chapter 9). This was a matter of concern for the accounting profession as it had not contemplated such an influence from another profession. In this respect R. Walker (1987, p. 281) observed the dissatisfaction and opposition of the accounting profession.

The idea of having a review board separate from the accounting bodies and within the bureaucratic and government domain can be seen as an intrusion into what was traditionally the domain of the accounting profession - an area where the profession already had a substantial investment. Although accounting standards had gained prominence as a form of company regulation, their importance to the profession had not diminished. Rather, due to excessive attention their importance to the profession had increased. Therefore, the accounting profession, like any other profession, was unlikely to remain silent to any intervention that was made or proposed by any sector - bureaucratic, legal, political or even academic. Its behaviour during the creation of the Board was aimed at maintaining its control over the standard-setting process which it already enjoyed. We have already noted earlier (Chapter 4) that the creation of the Board did not create a new regulatory environment and provided only a modified version of an existing form of regulation. Consequently, it is not appropriate to explain the behaviour of the profession in terms of "capture" of a new regulatory instrument as shown by R. Walker (1987).

Although the accounting profession retained control over the preparation of the accounting standards, its acceptance of the Board within the regulatory framework of the Co-operative Scheme made it to relinquish its sole authority to approve and enforce standards.

Companies:

Although companies and company directors were the main target of the new regulatory measures, they did not actively participate in the early stages when the notion of mandatory standards was being formed. According to the discussion in Chapter 5, this inaction may be due to the fact that at that stage the companies did not perceive any direct economic consequences because of the vagueness and uncertainty involved in the nature of proposed mandatory standards. Not knowing the consequences, they chose not to incur lobbying costs in the belief that their individual representations could be of little effectiveness.

Once the A.S.R.B. started taking shape and they realized its impact within the growing trend towards regulation of companies in Australia they entered the debate. According to the evidence in Chapter 9, A.I.D.A. was one of the first to strongly express concern from the view point of companies. The Association expressed its views in November, 1981, only a few days before the Ministerial Council was to deal with the A.S.R.B. issue for a second time. From their comments it was evident that the Association, a representative organization of the 50 largest companies in Australia, was not very much aware of the public debate that had been going on since 1977 to have an A.S.R.B.

The Association was critical of the lack of due process in the formation of the Board. Following that criticism the Ministerial Council in its next meeting asked the N.C.S.C. to seek public submissions on the issue. Being an association of companies, not surprisingly, the A.I.D.A. was strongly opposed to the idea of further bureaucratic incursions into the management of the private sector and it favoured the setting of standards in the private sector.

Industrial associations, companies and individual directors, managers and company accountants responded to both N.C.S.C. Release 401 and A.S.R.B. Release 400. In fact, they formed the largest respondent group on both occasions (See Tables 9.3. and 9.4. - this group is classified as preparers of financial statements). Although at times the business community expressed their opposition to government interference in standard-setting, the response to N.C.S.C. Release 401 indicated that they accepted the need for statutory backed mandatory standards as proposed by the N.C.S.C. - that is with room for disclosed departures. They were in favour of an independent review board free from the influence of the government and the profession with the scope of participation for all interest groups. They favoured board members with accounting skills and the board to have only review capacity. Most of those suggestions were incorporated into the organization and functions of the Board.

The response of the preparers of financial statements and/or the business community was also instrumental in forming the criteria for reviewing standards and the procedures of review. According to Table 9.4., in all the policy measures that were accepted by the A.S.R.B. the number of preparers supporting those measures was higher than that of other groups.

Amongst the preparers there were other industrial and professional associations (See Chapter 9), some of whom expressed the support for industry based standards or were interested in preparing their own standards for submission to the A.S.R.B. This may have contributed in providing the A.S.R.B. with the function of reviewing standards from sources other than the accounting profession.

It is interesting to note that although concerned groups within the business sector eventually realized that the companies and their directors were the subject of additional regulation under the concept of legislatively backed standards, there was no concerted effort from that sector to oppose that concept. One explanation that can be forwarded is that the benefits and costs of future approved standards to the companies are difficult to estimate and all standards may not have equal consequences for all companies within the various industries. As a result the companies and industries groups may remain dormant to the general idea of mandatory standards and act only towards specific standards that affect them. Again, the business sector may have been forced to accept the formation of the Board due to the immense criticism they faced because of the company failures and the general trend towards company regulation. In this respect we may predict that, they may serve as a threat for the Board and its mandatory form of standards once the general trend is against greater regulation of companies.

Others:

Amongst others who participated in the deliberations leading to the creation of the A.S.R.B. were the academics, security analysts and the press.

The participation of the academics in the formation of ideas with respect to the organization and functions of the Board, although less than expected, was very persuasive in certain instances. Professor Chambers, in 1969, was one of the first to introduce the idea of government backing for the profession's standards. Later in 1978 as the Chairman of the Accounting Standards Review Committee of N.S.W. he endorsed the idea of a review board with national jurisdiction. That Committee recognized the role of the accounting bodies in preparing standards within the purview of a statutory definition of "true and fair view". Consequently, the idea of endorsement of accounting standards through the scrutiny of a review board and the government backing for standards, introduced through the efforts of Chambers, laid down the foundation for the A.S.R.B.

Only one other academic in A.S.R.B.'s gestation period, Taylor (1977), seems to have expressed support for government backed accounting standards. Later, in response to N.C.S.C. Release 401 and A.S.R.B. Release 400 academics responded in small numbers mostly arguing in favour or against the issues tabled in those releases. Interestingly, the academics who, before the inception of the notion of mandatory accounting standards, played the role of opinion leaders in determining the best principle and practice, seemed to be content with the creation of a process of standard-setting based on the concept of "due process", procedural fairness and compromise - a concept more commonly used by the legal profession and the politicians. Perhaps the trend in the accounting policy literature was the reason for that attitude of the academics. Having contributed substantially towards the technical aspects of accounting, the academics started looking towards the area of acceptance of accounting techniques in the public policy process. For example Moonitz (1974), Wells (1978) and Winsen (1980, p. 250) cautioned the profession that the key to the success of standards lay in involvement of key players outside the profession, such as the company regulators, the companies themselves and financial analysts. As a result, the acceptance by the academics of the principle of review by a body representing all interest groups was inevitable.

The belated and weak participation of the securities analysts and institutional investors can be explained. As noted in Chapter 8, they are interested in greater disclosure by companies because it provides them with costless information. They also act in favour of laws that encourage greater disclosure. In this respect, the upgrading of professional accounting standards to statutorily backed standards may be of no consequence to them. This upgrading of the status of standards only ensures the enforcement of standards and does not ensure any improvement in the quality and quantity of information. Therefore, the establishment of a board capable of enhancing the status of standards may not be of high priority in the security analyst's and institutional investor's agenda.

We also observed that the investors were absent from the A.S.R.B. debate. The reason for this could be that they themselves are difficult to identify or in case of small investors they might have felt that the cost of lobbying would exceed the benefits derived from it. As discussed in Chapter 5 the benefits and costs of a review board to the investors are diffused and a strong response could not be expected from them. Another reason for their silence could be that they may have taken seriously the public interest rhetoric of others such as the politicians, bureaucrats and the accounting profession. In other words they may have felt that something was being done for them.

The press was mainly instrumental in disseminating the views of the various parties involved in the A.S.R.B. debate. There is no apparent reason as to why the press should participate in the debate for serving any of its own needs, except of course serve its interests as a medium of public communication. We have already seen some evidence of the press serving its own purpose through reporting the news in an entertaining fashion, at times manipulating it to the extent of providing a wrong interpretation of the facts. The press at times criticized the profession as regards standard-setting and were instrumental in warning the profession to keep its house in order or face government intervention.

Suppliers (The Politicians):

In Chapter 5 it was illustrated that in this thesis we are concerned with issues regarding public regulation of private activities, because standards with statutory backing can only be provided by the legislative institutions of government. In other words the politicians, who shape the policies of government when they are in power, are the ones who can supply standards which have the coercive powers of the legislature.

We have also discussed in Chapter 5 why politicians supply policies. They sell policies for votes from the electorate and support from interest groups in order to gain or maintain office. All policies have supporters and opposers. The politician, under the given environmental conditions, will promote that policy measure which is expected to provide a support greater in strength than the opposition (See Equation 5.1.). Figure 5.4. (Cobb and Elder's Agenda-Building Model) illustrated that a policy issue to qualify for implementation should coincide with the needs of a political party. If it does so it should then appear in the party's agenda for a systematic entrance into the political process (See also Hawker et al, 1979, pp. 22-23).

Australian democracy is basically a two party system. Webb (1968) and Miller and Jinks (1971, Chapter 3) classified it as such. Although more than two parties exist in practice, they felt that, on ideological grounds, they could be grouped as Labour and Non-Labour. From the evidence available, this simple classification is sufficient to explain the behaviour of politicians in the creation of the A.S.R.B. (Also see Table 10.1. for the groupings of the parties for the purpose of this thesis).

Ideologically, the political parties seem to differ, but at times their goals overlap. Again there are a large number of stated ideologies of each party which also seem to vary over time (Miller and Jinks, 1971, Chapter 3). For the purpose of this thesis, the ideological classification is kept simple. No elaborate discussion on the stated ideologies of the political parties is conducted in this analysis.

Table 10.1.: Political Parties in Governments of Australia (1960-85)

Year	Governments			
	Commonwealth	N.S.W.	Victoria	Queensland
1960	N.L.	A.L.P.	N.L.	N.L.
1961	N.L.	A.L.P.	N.L.	N.L.
1962	N.L.	A.L.P.	N.L.	N.L.
1963	N.L.	A.L.P.	N.L.	N.L.
1964	N.L.	A.L.P.	N.L.	N.L.
1965	N.L.	N.L.	N.L.	N.L.
1966	N.L.	N.L.	N.L.	N.L.
1967	N.L.	N.L.	N.L.	N.L.
1968	N.L.	N.L.	N.L.	N.L.
1969	N.L.	N.L.	N.L.	N.L.
1970	N.L.	N.L.	N.L.	N.L.
1971	N.L.	N.L.	N.L.	N.L.
1972	N.L.	N.L.	N.L.	N.L.
1973	A.L.P.	N.L.	N.L.	N.L.
1974	A.L.P.	N.L.	N.L.	N.L.
1975	A.L.P.	A.L.P.	N.L.	N.L.
1976	N.L.	A.L.P.	N.L.	N.L.
1977	N.L.	A.L.P.	N.L.	N.L.
1978	N.L.	A.L.P.	N.L.	N.L.
1979	N.L.	A.L.P.	N.L.	N.L.
1980	N.L.	A.L.P.	N.L.	N.L.
1981	N.L.	A.L.P.	N.L.	N.L.
1982	N.L.	A.L.P.	A.L.P.	N.L.
1983	A.L.P.	A.L.P.	A.L.P.	N.L.
1984	A.L.P.	A.L.P.	A.L.P.	N.L.
1985	A.L.P.	A.L.P.	A.L.P.	N.L.

A.L.P.   = Austalian Labor Party.
N.L.   = Non-Labor parties, which include the Liberal Party, National
               Party, National Country Party, Country Liberal Party and Country
               Party individually or as a coalition.

Table 10.1. (Continued): Political Parties in Governments of Australia (1960-85)

Year	Governments			Number of Labour Governments
	South Australia	Western Australia	Tasmania	
1960	N.L.	A.L.P.	A.L.P.	3
1961	N.L.	A.L.P.	A.L.P.	3
1962	N.L.	A.L.P.	A.L.P.	3
1963	N.L.	N.L.	A.L.P.	2
1964	N.L.	N.L.	A.L.P.	2
1965	A.L.P.	N.L.	A.L.P.	2
1966	A.L.P.	N.L.	A.L.P.	2
1967	A.L.P.	N.L.	A.L.P.	2
1968	N.L.	N.L.	A.L.P.	1
1969	N.L.	N.L.	N.L.	1
1970	A.L.P.	N.L.	N.L.	1
1971	A.L.P.	A.L.P.	N.L.	2
1972	A.L.P.	A.L.P.	A.L.P.	3
1973	A.L.P.	A.L.P.	A.L.P.	4
1974	A.L.P.	N.L.	A.L.P.	3
1975	A.L.P.	N.L.	A.L.P.	4
1976	A.L.P.	N.L.	A.L.P.	3
1977	A.L.P.	N.L.	A.L.P.	3
1978	A.L.P.	N.L.	A.L.P.	3
1979	N.L.	N.L.	A.L.P.	2
1980	N.L.	N.L.	A.L.P.	2
1981	N.L.	N.L.	A.L.P.	2
1982	N.L.	N.L.	N.L.	2
1983	A.L.P.	A.L.P.	N.L.	5
1984	A.L.P.	A.L.P.	N.L.	5
1985	A.L.P.	A.L.P.	N.L.	5

Sources: Miller and Jinks (1971) p. 46 and Year Books Australia 1960-85.

Through a review of the ideologies of the two groups of parties, it has been found that Labour, dominant amongst which is the Australian Labour Party (A.L.P.), is a "left wing" party and that it favours more government intervention in economic activities than the Non-Labour parties. Amongst its stated objectives, protectionism and a concern for the rights of "the small man" are prominent. It is noteworthy that since World War I the A.L.P. has been the party advocating the greatest net increase in the activities of government, and the biggest spending programmes. On the other hand the Liberal Party, at times in coalition with the Country Party or National Party, is the most dominant amongst the Non-Labour Parties. Its agenda is normally that of an anti-socialist party and its policies are that of low taxation and economic freedom (Miller and Jinks, 1971, Chapter 3). Webb (1968) added that the Labour Party remained formally pledged to increase Commonwealth powers (p. 341).

The two parties can be broadly grouped in terms of social class. Webb (1968) stated that "the Liberal and Labour parties in Australia correspond roughly to the division between the bourgeoisie and the proletariat" (p. 336). Miller and Jinks (1971, p. 68) described A.L.P. as a trade union party with its power base in the lower income groups. Webb (1968) quoted surveys confirming that Labour normally received more support from the "blue collar" workers, whereas the "white collar" workers, such as professionals (white collar) and large businesses supported the Non-Labour parties (p. 337).

Table 10.1. provides information about political parties that held the offices of the Commonwealth and State Governments from 1960 to 1985. 1960 has been taken as the starting point because that was the time from which serious steps towards uniform Companies Acts were first taken in Australia. 1985 is, of course, the last year for this thesis - the year the first set of functions were approved for the A.S.R.B. by the Ministerial Council. The Table shows that the A.L.P. could not gain office of the Commonwealth Government for a long time (23 years to be precise). When the uniform Companies Acts were being enacted the Commonwealth Government and three of the six State Governments were non-Labour governments. Although, as mentioned in Chapter 6, some concern was voiced for the need for a single set of companies law for the whole of Australia, it seems that the Governments were satisfied with uniformity and not unanimity in the laws. This perhaps can be attributed to the presence of a non-Labour government in the centre and a majority of the Governments in Australia being non-Labour.

Despite the constitutional weaknesses of the Commonwealth, when the A.L.P. came back into the office of the Commonwealth Government in late 1972,[146] it tried to enact a Commonwealth Companies and Securities Act and a national companies commission (See Chapter 8). Apart from the benefits of a single companies and securities act and the Labour Party's preference for "big government"[147] there were other reasons for the bold move by the Whitlam Government. One reason was that the decisions of the High Court started favouring the possibility of enacting Commonwealth companies and securities statutes (See

---

146   Table 10.1. shows 1973 because A.L.P. came into office at the end of
       1972. During a major part of 1972 the Liberal-Country Coalition was in
       office. Similar step has been taken to report other years when there was
       a change over from one party to the other. In the Table, any party which
       held more than six months of office in a year, the year has been assigned
       to that party.

147   Also see Bailey (1976) where he illustrated the expansion in Government
       policies and institutions brought about by the Whitlam Government.

CCH, 1986, p. 7). The other could be the growing number of A.L.P. Governments in the Commonwealth and the States. The A.L.P. secured offices in four out of seven State and Commonwealth governments by 1975, after being in the minority for a long period of time (See Table 10.1.).

The situation did not last long enough. The A.L.P. lost its office in the centre in 1975, and with it went the hopes for a Commonwealth companies and securities act. The Labour Party also lost offices in the States. Between 1979 and 1982 it held offices in only two out of the seven governments of Australia. Again, around the time when the A.L.P. was trying to enact a national act, the non-Labour Governments of N.S.W., Victoria and Queensland devised the Interstate Corporate Affairs Commission. This showed a desire for a loose arrangement between the states by the non-Labour governments as opposed to the need for national laws promoted by the Labour Party.[148]

The need for uniformity in laws could not be overlooked by the predominantly non-Labour Governments of the Commonwealth and the States, and in 1978 the Cooperative Scheme for Companies and Securities was born. This scheme provided for the Commonwealth to enact companies and securities statutes with room for the States to withdraw from the Scheme if they desired. Likewise the administration of the company laws would be conducted through the state authorities rather than the National Companies and Securities Commission directly. The Commonwealth Government was also not empowered to generate policies. Rather a committee of all the Ministers of the Commonwealth and States, dealing with company regulation, was

---

148   Labour still prefers national company law and administration (For example see Business Review Weekly, April 9, 1983, p. 82).

created to form the Ministerial Council and entrusted with the role of policy-making. The Council was authorized to decide on policy measures on the basis of a simple majority. In this manner, although provisions for national statutes and administration were made, the liberal policy of the non-Labour parties of loose Commonwealth authority over the States prevailed.

The inter-play of political ideologies of political parties is also evident in the case of the formation of the A.S.R.B. Since the Board and its functions were supplied by the Ministerial Council - a committee composed of politicians, it is inherent that the A.S.R.B., as a policy outcome, was considerably affected by the ideological desires of those politicians. By promoting their party's policies and ideologies those politicians could maintain or enhance their status within the party and also within the government, if the party remained in office. Accordingly, we can surmise that those politicians through their actions could promote their self-interest.

Politicians showed concern for regulating accountants and company accounting as a part of their move to regulate companies. Two states, South Australia and N.S.W., both of which had Labour governments in 1977, showed serious interests in accounting regulation through registration and standard-setting, respectively (Australian Financial Review, August 3, 1977).[149] Since South Australia was trying to regulate accountants through registration, we will not discuss its move here.

---

149   Registration of accountants was what the two accounting bodies were campaigning for, for the last twenty years (Australian Financial Review, August 3, 1977). This was favourable for the accounting bodies because it would bring the supply of accountants under control, possibly restricting it to the advantage of the members of those bodies.

The Attorney-General of the N.S.W. (Labour) Government, Mr. F. Walker, as seen earlier, was one of the first politicians who strongly proposed government intervention into accounting standard-setting and sought the possibility of creating an accounting tribunal to review accounting standards. Although this expression of intent to regulate seemed to be in response to growing concern towards (1) company failures, (2) the accounting bodies' failure to provide acceptable standards and (3) the accounting bodies' capacity to enforce their standards (Australian Financial Review, August 4, 1977, p. 2 and August 5, 1977 p. 2; and Balmford, 1977, p. 555), there may also have been political motivations behind Mr. F. Walker's arguments. We have seen that white collar professionals are mainly non-Labour supporters. Any moves to regulate such professionals can only make the A.L.P. more unpopular in a section of the constituency which is not a traditional Labour base. On the other hand moves to bring a "wealthy" profession under the control of the Government may improve the image of that party within its traditional base, the "small man" and the blue collar trade unions. In turn it could enhance the standing, within the party, of that party-politician who is promoting a policy which benefits the party.

The fact that the accounting profession, as a white collar profession, was a target of Government regulation was expressed by F. Walker himself:

> Accountants must recognize that the relationship between the professions and the community is changing rapidly. The accounting profession, like the legal profession, the medical profession and professions generally, has been and will remain under increasing scrutiny and re-assessment. ...

> The spectacle of wealthy professionals being prosecuted for frauds against Medibank, major defalcations by lawyers and the failure of large and apparently sound financial corporations does nothing to bolster respect for professionals (F. Walker, 1981a, 235).

Seemingly in search for scapegoats, the Attorney-General drew a connection between those responsible for corporate failures and accounting standards.

> When I became Attorney-General for New South Wales in 1976, I found the Corporate Affairs Commission labouring under great difficulties trying to bring to book those responsible for the failure of major corporations.
>
> I was shocked to discover important prosecutions failing through lack of certainty as to what were proper accounting standards (Walker, 1981a, 235).

Thomas (1982, p. 59) also noted that F. Walker's enthusiasm for a review board stemmed from his efforts to prosecute white-collar criminals, mostly charged with financial mis-statements in the course of raising new capital.

Circumstances around 1977 and 1978 seemed to favour the prospects for greater government regulation of accounting as a profession, particularly in the area of standards. The reports of the N.S.W. C.A.C. indicating poor compliance with professional accounting standards and the recommendations of the N.S.W. Accounting Standards Committee's recommendations for a board, as shown in the previous chapter, together with media reports of "white-collar anarchy" involving accounting methods (See Australian Financial Review, August 4, 1977, p. 2), provided fuel for Mr. F. Walker's suggestions for an accounting standards review board.

Similar conditions existed for all professions, generally, under the Labour regimes. The <u>Business Review Weekly</u> reported in 1984:

> The problem is that tax-avoidance schemes and increasingly publicized cases of occasional malpractice have robbed the professionals of much public prestige, particularly when set against their former ivory-tower image. This has strengthened ACTU demands that professional fees come under the ambit of the Arbitration Commission, and their businesses subject to Trade Practices Act. ...

> The Hawke (Labour) Government hopes the professions will at least agree to having their fee or income-setting procedures considered by arbitration (<u>Business Review Weekly</u>, May 5, 1984, p. 24).

Although F. Walker may be the first amongst the politicians to take up the matter of intervention into standard-setting seriously, the issue of standard-setting by a statutory commission was brought up in the Companies and Securities Bill of 1974 (This Bill was also introduced by a Labour Government). The Eggleston and Rae Committees also felt the need for some kind of reform in the area of company financial disclosure.

At this stage one question logically arises - why did it take almost thirteen years (from the time government intervention was first suggested by Mr. Ryan in 1967, till May 23, 1980) for the Governments of Australia to decide that a body capable of providing statutorily backed standards should be considered?

The answer seems to lie in the nature of parties that constituted the Governments in that thirteen year period. Table 10.1. provides a list of the two broad classes of parties, Labour and non-Labour which governed the States and the Commonwealth Governments of Australia from 1960 to 1985. In all years except 1973 and 1975 the A.L.P. was in power less often than the non-Labour parties. This does indicate that A.L.P. policies of greater control, on a nation-wide basis, of companies and professions may not have received support from the non-Labour Governments. The decades of 1960's and 1970's saw the non-Labour dominated Governments try three times to adopt nationally uniform company statutes and administration. The first was the Uniform Companies Acts of early 1960's. The second was the formation of the I.C.A.C. in 1974. The final attempt was made through the Co-operative Scheme for Companies and Securities of 1978. These steps were taken in view of the substantial publicity the corporate failures of 1960's and 1970's had received. All these steps of national or inter-state regulation had a blend of non-Labour policy. They preserved the autonomy of the States as against Labour's policy of a single national system of regulation (For example see Business Review Weekly, April 9, 1983, p. 82).

Apart from a lack of support from non-Labour Governments, the idea of government intervention into standard-setting certainly received no support from the accounting bodies. This may partly explain why the accounting bodies did not participate in the N.S.W. Accounting Standards Review Committee in 1979. There were other instances also where the accounting profession opposed the regulation of the profession (For example, see Business Review Weekly, May 16, 1981, p. 46).

Although a non-Labour dominated Ministerial Council did act on the basis of N.C.S.C. recommendations, its resolution of May 23, 1980, simply asked the Commission to further consider the establishment of the Board. The rift between the members of the Ministerial Council was on party lines. On the one hand we have seen that, Mr. F. Walker, the N.S.W. Attorney-General, was an ardent supporter of the need for a review board and government participation in accounting standard-setting; on the other hand Mr. John Moore, the Federal Minister for Business and Consumer Affairs - a non-Labour Minister, favoured the concept of self-regulation and opposed the creation of a regulatory A.S.R.B. (Business Review Weekly, May 16, 1981, p. 46 and November 28, 1981, p. 46). The Victorian Attorney-General Haddon Storey, also a non-Labour Minister, seemed to be undecided about the establishment of the A.S.R.B. (See Business Review Weekly, November 28, 1981, p. 46).

Due to continuing opposition by the accounting profession and his colleagues within the Ministerial Council, Mr. F. Walker showed signs of moderating his views and started accepting that accountants were making satisfactory progress on self-regulation. At this stage he proposed a compromise solution embodying it in the term "co-regulation" - that is self-regulation under minimal government supervision and participation (Business Review Weekly, May 16, 1981, p. 46 and May 23, 1981, p. 50). While offering his compromise solution he warned the profession that if they were reluctant to accept it he might have to favour more regulation (F. Walker, 1981b).

This solution also seemed acceptable to the profession (Business Review Weekly, May 16, 1981, p. 46 and May 23, 1981, p. 50). By now the profession had accepted through the recommendations of the Savage Committee that the accounting bodies lacked the powers to enforce their standards on companies - therefore there was a need for legislative support for its standards.

In 1981, the Campbell Committee also endorsed the need for an A.S.R.B. to review standards prepared by the accounting bodies. Meanwhile, the debate for the A.S.R.B. progressed with strong opposition from the A.I.D.A.

On the political scene the A.L.P. after dipping into a low position of two out of the seven Governments between 1979 and 1982, made a dramatic come-back. It gained office in Victoria on 8 April 1982, in South Australia in October 1982 and that of the Commonwealth on 11 March, 1983. By 1983 it was in power in five out of seven Parliaments. It seemed that by early 1982 the non-Labour parties could feel that their time to maintain dominance in Australian politics was over for the time being. This meant that there would be fewer non-Labour members in the Ministerial Council than those of the Labour party. That situation prompted Mr. Moore, the Federal Minister for Business and Consumer Affairs, to warn the accounting profession that they had only one year to achieve improved accounting standards. He was still in favour of self-regulation and he informed the accounting profession that if Labour won the Victorian elections then there would be a finely balanced Ministerial Council and he would be left with the casting vote. Such an increase in Labour's participation in the Ministerial Council, he warned, would increase the chances of a national companies act and the regulation of the profession. To add to this situation he pointed out that the lawyer dominated Ministerial Council and the N.C.S.C. may also contribute to the shift towards government intervention. He asked the accountants to put their house in order and take a united stand in the A.S.R.B. issue (Australian Financial Review, February 10, 1982, p. 16).

From the later part of 1982 the Ministerial Council's composition started tipping towards Labour. With the win in the

Victorian and South Australian elections in April, 1982 and October, 1982, respectively, the Ministerial Council was balanced between the States. The Commonwealth Government was yet to become Labour, but this was to follow soon. In 1983, with wins in the Commonwealth and Western Australian elections, the strength of Labour members in the Ministerial Council rose to a majority of five out of seven members (See Table 10.1.). This composition certainly improved the possibility of A.S.R.B.'s creation.

In the light of this changing composition we find that there was some change in the attitude of the Council towards the establishment of the Board. After a long delay of two and a half years since it first decided to consider the need for a board, the Council on November 26, 1982, decided in principle to establish a board. In this meeting Labour was one short of a majority and the Council was still not firm in its decision. Mr. F. Walker, in line with his earlier policies, at this stage demanded stricter public oversight of auditors granting exemptions for non-compliance by directors and suggested more punitive measures against the directors and auditors who breached the standards (Business Review Weekly, December 11, 1982, p. 59). Meanwhile, the Ministerial Council asked the N.S.W. C.A.C. to review and report on the A.S.R.B. issue. As we know the N.S.W. C.A.C. was where the idea of a review board was conceived and that the C.A.C. was also under F. Walker's jurisdiction.

When the composition of the Ministerial Council changed from three to five Labour members, the issue of the A.S.R.B. gained importance on the Council's agenda and the Board started taking shape. The joint report of the N.S.W. C.A.C. and the N.C.S.C. was accepted in principle on March 25, 1983. Some ministers were assigned to meet the interest groups for final consultations and less than four months later, on July 14, 1983, the decision to establish the Board was taken - to start operations from January 1, 1984. Meanwhile, the Commonwealth Attorney-General was entrusted the task of drafting an amendments bill to amend the Companies Act to accommodate the A.S.R.B. and its approved standards. The bill was introduced into the Commonwealth Parliament on October 5, 1982, and because of a Labour majority in that Parliament it was passed with very little opposition.

Even before the Board started operating the Labour Party started to claim the credit for the establishment of the A.S.R.B. and its sister body the Companies and Securities Law Reform Committee. Paul Landa, who replaced F. Walker as N.S.W. Attorney-General, claimed that the decision to establish those bodies was evidence of the co-operative approach to national law reform since Labour's various victories at the polls (Business Review Weekly, April 2, 1983, p. 67).

Such effectiveness of political parties in making policies was explained by Hawker, et al (1979) as follows:

> The capacity of political parties to be effective in policy-making and implementation processes depends on two factors. First they must formulate their own views of what the policies of a government should be; second, they must be able to ensure that their views about desirable policy are accepted as authoritative and final and are later implemented. To do the latter, they must be able to win office and control the machinery of government; there is little that party in opposition can do to influence policy through parliament (p. 31).

This suggests that the creation of the Board was not only the outcome of demand for such a board, but also due to the gaining of office of a political party to a majority of the States and Commonwealth Governments of Australia. That party, being the

Labour Party, found the Board to be compatible to its ideologies and created it as soon as it acquired the power to do so.

Some Further Analysis of the Approach used in the Creation of the Board:

By now it is quite evident that the Board was created through a process which covered a fairly long time span of sixteen years.[150] In the previous chapter we tried to re-enact the creation of the Board from the information that was publicly available.

Within this observable process of creation, two major sets of decisions were taken by the Ministerial Council. The first concerned the formation of the Board and the second was with regard to the establishment of its functions. As seen in the third section and in Chapter 9, both those decisions were based on demands placed by various interest groups, from time to time. In addition to those demands, before any of those decisions were taken, submissions were formally invited. In the first case the Ministerial Council asked the N.C.S.C. to seek submissions from the members of the public regarding the formation of the Board. The N.C.S.C. sought submissions and accordingly recommended to the Council in respect of the need for a board and the form and composition of such a board. In the second case the A.S.R.B. sought submissions regarding its own functions and, on that basis made recommendations to the Ministerial Council.

We have noted in the previous two sections that the members of the Ministerial Council responded to the demands of more than one group of demanders, keeping in view their own

---

150   From 1967 when Ryan first proposed a statutory commission to January 1, 1984, when the Board was finally operationalized.

interests. Tables 9.3. and 9.4. also show that a number of interest groups responded to the invitation for submissions made by the N.C.S.C. and the A.S.R.B., and that the N.C.S.C. and the A.S.R.B. seem to have made recommendations to the Council in most cases according to the strength of those responses. As most of such recommendations were incorporated into the form of the organization and functions of the Board by the Council, we need to investigate whether the regulators responded to the submissions of all the constituents in general or only to the demands of a particular interest group. Since the two previous sections provide indications of regulators responding to various constituents, it may be construed that their actions in these two cases were in response to the demands of the constituents generally. To confirm this we analyze the data of Tables 9.3. and 9.4. below.

The Nature of Tests:

First, we test whether the various responding groups responded in a similar manner, in other words whether they belonged to the same population. If this test is favourable, we have to ascertain whether the regulators' decisions were aligned to the total of all group responses. If the correlation between total responses and the regulators' acceptance is significant, we can conclude on the basis of the two tests, that the groups responded in a similar manner and the regulators had acted on the demands of an homogeneous population.

If the first of the above two tests fails, that is if we find that the respondent groups did not respond in a similar manner, instead of going into the second test we have to ascertain whether the regulators decisions were more aligned to any particular group response or were they more aligned to the total response.

Brown (1981) had used Alternating Least-square Scaling (ALSCAL), a Multi-dimensional Scaling (MDS) algorithm, and Discriminant Analysis (DA) to identify (1) whether there were systematic groupings or relationships of input preferences of the F.A.S.B. respondents, (2) the distinctness of groups and (3) F.A.S.B. alignment with respondent groups. More recently, Coombes and Stokes (1985) used the Quade Test to determine whether the accounting profession released standards which were consistent with the views of a majority of respondents and whether the respondent groups were equally aligned on each policy issue.

Unlike Brown's (1981) case, where specific policy issues could be identified from the predetermined F.A.S.B. project exposure drafts, the respondents in both of our cases responded variedly on a number of issues in addition to those that were identified by the N.C.S.C. and the A.S.R.B. In other words the respondents themselves proposed policy measures in addition to those proposed by the regulators. Other respondents could have responded to such issues if they were also informed about them. Therefore, it is not possible to scale such non-responses as "no response" or as any other form of response as it could have been scaled under Brown's scaling method. Again, as a number of policy issues with such responses were eventually accepted by the regulators, it is not possible to exclude those issues from the analysis. Consequently, ALSCAL and DA are not suitable tests for our analysis.

Again Coombes and Stokes' (1985) method of testing cannot be adopted. They considered "no responses" to identified policy issues as positive responses. In our case the "no responses" for issues that were identified by the respondents themselves cannot be considered as positive responses because all the respondents were not equally aware of those issues and some respondents could have voted against such issues if they were aware of them. Again, as a number of such issues were incorporated in the final decision of the regulators, those issues cannot be overlooked in our analysis.

The Quade Test adopted by Coombes and Stokes' (1985) is also not suitable for our analysis. The Friedman Test has been used here, which is similar to Quade Test but more powerful for five or more treatment groups (Conover, 1980, p. 299). In Table 9.4. there are six respondent/treatment groups. The Quade Test, apart from comparing the ranks of treatment groups, also compares the ranks between issues, assuming that the issues can be ranked according to some criterion (Conover, 1980. p. 206). In our case comparisons between all issues is not possible due to the varying nature of issues. Some issues are organizational, whereas others are functional or procedural. The Friedman Test does not test for rankings between issues (Conover, 1980, p. 299). Therefore, the Friedman Test has been used to identify only whether the groups had similar preferences.

In the case of unfavourable Friedman Test results,[151] Spearman Correlation has been used to identify the nature of alignment between group responses and regulator's preferences and also between total responses and the regulator's preferences. Spearman Correlation Coefficients provide the level of correlation between two variables. It is suitable for our analysis because it has a direct relationship with Friedman Test statistic. According to Conover (1985) the Friedman statistic can be derived from a distribution of Spearman statistics (pp. 305-7).

---

151   Unfavourable Friedman Test results mean that the respondents groups do not have similar preferences.

Results:

Results of the Friedman Test and Spearman Correlation have been furnished in Tables 10.2. and 10.3. respectively. The statistics in both the tables have been calculated using the percentage responses shown in parenthesis in Tables 9.3. and 9.4. The use of percentages is necessary because we are interested in ranking the proportion of respondents of each group preferring an issue rather than the actual number of responses. The percentage of the total response of each group has been taken as an indicator of the proportion of the respondents who preferred a certain policy measure.

The Friedman Test statistics have been calculated twice for Table 9.3. data and twice for Table 9.4. data. For both those tables the Friedman Test statistics is first calculated for responses to all the policy issues (See items 1(a) and 2(a) of Table 10.2.). Then statistics are calculated for only those policy issues that were accepted by the regulators (See items 1(b) and 2(b) of Table 10.2.). The second set of statistics was, of course, to determine whether the group preferences were similar for accepted policy issues in case the preferences were found to be dissimilar for all issues.

The chi-square statistics in Table 10.2. indicate that significant differences at the .10 level of significance or better do not occur for cases 1(a) and 2(b). This suggests that the mean rank of the preferences of respondent groups are not significantly different from each other. From that we can infer that the responses from the different groups, in these two cases, can be considered as being that of one homogeneous group.

For items 1(b) and 2(a) the chi-square statistics indicate that significant differences do occur at the .10 level of significance or better. This signifies that there is a high probability that a difference, at least as large as the ones observed between the mean ranks of the preferences of the various groups, would occur if we accepted that there is no difference between the preferences of the said groups. Therefore, for these two cases, we cannot assert that there is no difference in the respondent group preferences. In other words, the regulators do not seem to have acted on the basis of the preferences of a homogeneous population.

Since from the first test we find that for cases 1(a) and 2(b) the regulators responded to the responses of a homogeneous population we can proceed to the second test. In the second test we identify whether the regulators' decisions were correlated to the total responses of the population. This is done in Table 10.3. To do that, Spearman Correlation Coefficients have been computed to assess the association between all variables. The data are again those of Table 9.3. and 9.4.

Spearman Correlation is a form of non-parametric rank correlation. In Tables 9.3. and 9.4. we determined the proportion of respondents responding for each issue within each group. Here we assume that the higher the proportion of responses for an issue, within the group, the higher was the support of the group for that issue. For the purposes of Spearman Correlation calculation all such responses within a group have been ranked. Correlation coefficients have been calculated on the basis of the rankings to identify whether rankings between groups are similar or not. In other words, we try to identify those groups that responded similarly and those that did not.

Table 10.2.: Friedman Test Results

Data		PR	Mean Rank of Variables PF	AC	GV	US	OT	Cases	Chi-sq.	D.F.	Significance
1(a)	All Responses of Table 9.3.	2.75	2.38	2.52	-	-	2.36	28	1.6607	3	.6457
1(b)	Responses to issues in Table 9.3 which were recommended in N.C.S.C. Release 405	2.80	2.40	1.70	-	-	3.10	10	6.6000	3	.0858
2(a)	All Responses of Table 9.4.	4.39	3.95	3.30	3.11	3.20	3.05	38	16.1466	5	.0064
2(b)	Responses to issues in Table 9.4 which were adopted in A.S.R.B. Release 100 & 200	4.53	3.58	3.16	3.34	3.39	3.00	19	7.9398	5	.1596

Notes: PR = Preparers of Financial Statements; PF = Accounting Bodies, Firms and Individuals; AC = Academics; GV = Government Bodies; US = Users of Financial Statements and Securities Analysts; OT = Others

For any data the Spearman Correlation Coefficient lies between -1 and +1, taking the value +1 when there is a perfect positive correlation, -1 when there is a perfect negative correlation and zero for two unrelated rankings (Leach, 1979, pp. 191-192). For Spearman Correlation we can conduct both a one-tailed test and a two-tailed test at various levels of significance. Here we adopt a one-tail test because we are interested in identifying significantly high positive correlations between the ranks of responses of the groups.

The SPSS-X statistical package has been used to compute the correlation coefficients. In SPSS-X, coefficients with one-tailed observed significance levels less than or equal to 0.01 are designated with a single asterisk; those with one-tailed significance levels less than or equal to 0.001, with two asterisks. For the purpose of this analysis any coefficient with one asterisk is considered as an indicator of significant correlation between two respondent groups responses and that with two asterisks as an indicator of highly significant correlation.

For the data of item 1(a) of Table 10.2. (that is for all issues of Table 9.3.) we find from Table 10.3.A. that there is a highly significant correlation between the total of all responses for the issues and the N.C.S.C. recommendations for those issues. We can also observe that, except for the academics, there is a highly significant correlation between each of the individual group responses and the N.C.S.C. decisions. Adding this observation to the Friedman Test results we can infer that the N.C.S.C. in recommending a review board to the Ministerial Council acted on the basis of the total response of all interested groups or at least to the response of most of the interested parties.

Table 10.3. Spearman Correlation Coefficients

Table 10.3.A. Correlation Coefficients Taking into Account All Policy Issues of Table 9.3.

	PR	PF	AC	OT	TT
PF	.5208*				
AC	.1933	.3686			
OT	.3924	.2802	.0395		
TT	.8830**	.7529**	.5096*	.4969*	
NCSC	.7384**	.5732**	.2159	.6541**	.7792**

Notes:

PR	=	Preparers of Financial Statements
PF	=	Accounting Bodies, Firms and Individuals
AC	=	Academics
GV	=	Government Bodies
US	=	Users of Financial Statements and Securities Analysts
OT	=	Others
TT	=	Total of all Responses
RB	=	Acceptance by the A.S.R.B.
NCSC	=	Acceptance by the N.C.S.C.
*	=	Significance less or equal to .01
**	=	Significance less or equal to .001
".'	=	Coefficient cannot be computed.

Table 10.3. Spearman Correlation Coefficients (Continued)

Table 10.3.B. Correlation Coefficients Taking into Account only those issues of Table 9.3. that were Accepted in N.C.S.C. Release 405

	PR	PF	AC	OT	TT
PF	.1887				
AC	.1033	.0130			
OT	-.1871	.3530	.0966		
TT	.6076	.7803*	.3955	.3113	
NCSC	.	.	.	.	.

Notes:
PR	=	Preparers of Financial Statements
PF	=	Accounting Bodies, Firms and Individuals
AC	=	Academics
GV	=	Government Bodies
US	=	Users of Financial Statements and Securities Analysts
OT	=	Others

TT	=	Total of all Responses
RB	=	Acceptance by the A.S.R.B.
NCSC	=	Acceptance by the N.C.S.C.
*	=	Significance less or equal to .01
**	=	Significance less or equal to .001
"."	=	Coefficient cannot be computed.

Table 10.3. Spearman Correlation Coefficients (Continued)

Table 10.3.C. Correlation Coefficients Taking into Account All Issues of Table 9.4.

	PR	PF	AC	GV	US	OT	TT
PF	.6933**						
AC	.3219	.3385					
GV	.7570**	.5383**	.4960**				
US	.6465**	.5129**	.5813**	.5878**			
OT	.6254**	.4776*	.4345*	.5967***	.5386**		
TT	.9371**	.8239***	.4397*	.7377***	.6862**	.6430**	
RB	.5871**	.4296*	.2911	.5092**	.5092**	.4758*.	6152**

Notes:

PR	=	Preparers of Financial Statements
PF	=	Accounting Bodies, Firms and Individuals
AC	=	Academics
GV	=	Government Bodies
US	=	Users of Financial Statements and Securities Analysts
OT	=	Others
TT	=	Total of all Responses
RB	=	Acceptance by the A.S.R.B.
NCSC	=	Acceptance by the N.C.S.C.
*	=	Significance less or equal to .01
**	=	Significance less or equal to .001
".".	=	Coefficient cannot be computed.

Table 10.3. Spearman Correlation Coefficients (Continued)

Table 10.3.D. Correlation Coefficients Taking into Account only those Issues of Table 9.4. that were Incorporated into A.S.R.B. Releases 100 and 200

	PR	PF	AC	GV	US	OT	TT
PF	.6220*						
AC	.5671*	.6528*					
GV	.8436**	.4987	.6584*				
US	.8070**	.5550*	.7697**	.7319**			
OT	.7715**	.6135*	.5728*	.6076*	.6450*		
TT	.8996**	.7796**	.7227**	.7969**	.8232**	.8056**	
RB	.	.	.	.	.	.	.

Notes:

PR	=	Preparers of Financial Statements
PF	=	Accounting Bodies, Firms and Individuals
AC	=	Academics
GV	=	Government Bodies
US	=	Users of Financial Statements and Securities Analysts
OT	=	Others
TT	=	Total of all Responses
RB	=	Acceptance by the A.S.R.B.
NCSC	=	Acceptance by the N.C.S.C.
*	=	Significance less or equal to .01
**	=	Significance less or equal to .001
"."	=	Coefficient cannot be computed.

An interesting observation is that, despite a favourable Friedman Test result for differences between group responses, except for a significant correlation between the profession and the preparers, there is no significant correlation between any other groups. In this respect we should note that the Friedman Test chi-square statistic is an indicator for the difference between the ranks of the data for all variables, whereas Spearman Correlation coefficients identify the correlation between ranks of the data for only two variables. Therefore, even if the correlation between certain pairs of variables is not significant the overall population as a whole may be homogeneous.

Another observation is, that the correlation coefficient between total of all responses and the N.C.S.C. is higher than that between individual groups and the N.C.S.C. Again, it can also be noted that the correlation coefficient between the accounting profession and the N.C.S.C. is not as high as that between the N.C.S.C. and the preparers, and the N.C.S.C. and others (See Table 10.3.A.). These observations indicate that perhaps the N.C.S.C. responded on the basis of all responses, as inferred earlier, and did respond to the demands of other parties in addition to those of the accounting profession.

In the case of the data for item 2(b) of Table 10.2. the correlation coefficients in Table 10.3.D. indicate that, except for the pair government bodies and the profession, the responses of all groups were either significantly or highly significantly correlated. This contributes to the Friedman Test result that the population was homogeneous. In this case, however, we cannot calculate the correlation coefficient for the total of all responses and the A.S.R.B. recommendations to the Ministerial Council because the data is for only those issues that were recommended by the Board. In this table the coefficients indicate that there is a highly significant correlation between the total of all responses and all individual group responses. From Table 10.3.C. we find that there is a highly significant correlation between the total of all responses and the decisions of the A.S.R.B. on all issues. From these observations we can infer that the A.S.R.B. responded to not only the total responses of a homogeneous group, its decisions for accepting the issues were related to the responses of all individual groups.

For items 1(b) and 2(a) of Table 10.2., since the Friedman Test casts doubts about the homogeneity of the population, before we check whether the total of all group responses were correlated to the regulator's decisions, we proceed to identify the nature of alignment between groups' responses and regulator's preferences.

For issues that were accepted by the Commission, Table 10.3.B. confirms the Friedman Test result (item 1(b) of Table 10.2.) that the respondent groups did not have similar preferences. None of the coefficients for between group association of responses is significant. The correlation coefficients for between the groups and the N.C.S.C. responses cannot be computed for this case because only issues with a "yes" response by the Commission have been used for calculations here. However, the correlation between the profession's response and the total of all responses is significant. As the correlation between the total of all responses and the N.C.S.C. decisions is high in Table 10.3.A., it might be construed that, for the issues accepted by the N.C.S.C., the profession was an effective demander. A firm conclusion in this respect is not possible because from Table 10.3.A. we observed that for all issues the preparers and other respondents were also effective groups and may have been instrumental in the N.C.S.C.'s non-acceptance of certain issues. Therefore, we cannot infer that the N.C.S.C. responded to the profession's demand alone.

Table 10.3.C. figures indicate that the correlation coefficients between most groups are significant at the .001 level and some at the .01 level. The only case of insignificant correlation is between the academics and the preparers, and the academics and the accounting profession. Although the Friedman Test failed to confirm that all the groups had similar preferences, we find here that <u>most</u> respondent groups did have similarities in preferences.[152] As for the similarity between the A.S.R.B.'s adoption of policy measures and the groups' responses, the correlation coefficients between the Board's preferences and that of all but one of the groups, the academics, are significant at a significance level of .01 or less; and are significant at .001 or less for three of the groups. Again the correlation coefficient between the total response and the Board's actions is not only highly significant but also higher than that for the individual groups. Consequently, we can infer that despite the heterogeneous nature of the population we find a strong alignment between the responses of most groups and the A.S.R.B.'s decisions.

Our observations indicate that the N.C.S.C., in recommending to the Ministerial Council that the A.S.R.B. be created, adopted policy measures that were aimed at satisfying the responses of most of the groups and the total responses of all groups. We also observed that the A.S.R.B. seems to have recommended to the Ministerial Council and later adopted the policy measures that satisfied a majority of the groups and, in particular, the total responses of all groups.

---

152   The significance of the chi-square statistics in this case in the Friedman Test was less than .01. Therefore at that level of acceptance we cannot reject the hypothesis that the groups' responses were similar.

Having analyzed the responses to the N.C.S.C. Release 401 and A.S.R.B. Release 400, we may conclude that the regulators responded to the responses of a majority of the respondents and respondent groups in deciding the organizational and functional issues of the Board. Even if there are doubts regarding the homogeneity of the population, there is no sound evidence that the regulators responded to the demands of a particular group of respondents.

Inferences:

Certain important inferences can be drawn from our discussion in this chapter. The A.S.R.B. and mandatory accounting issue existed before it turned into a political debate. The politicians turned the underlying problems, on which the idea for an A.S.R.B. was based, into a crisis. It was further fueled by the news media, and the A.S.R.B. issue eventually entered the political arena. There were several effective participants or participating groups/bodies which acted as demanders of policy measures in the formation of the Board. The bureaucrats, the accounting profession and the companies were the main participants on the demand side. In addition, other parties also took keen interest and participated actively whenever need arose. The suppliers of the Board and the associated policy measures, were the politicians who made-up the Ministerial Council.

All parties did not participate with the same degree of intensity and the intensity of their participation seemed to vary over the various stages of the process. The extent of participation, in terms of a single submission or of continuous lobbying, were linked to the perceived effect on the concerned party's activities through an A.S.R.B. While most participants were found to participate sporadically, some, like the N.C.S.C., the N.S.W.

C.A.C. and the professional accounting bodies, participated actively through out the process and, as shown by R. Walker (1987), even after the Board's functions were set-up. This seems to be in accordance with the mechanics of Equation 5.2. where it is expected that a demand will be placed by a party only if it sees that the expected benefits of a preferred outcome, or the expected loss avoided by not having the outcome, is greater than the cost of effective participation in the regulatory process. Therefore, we can note that the parties participated whenever they were informed of an imminent decision of the regulators adopting a particular form of the A.S.R.B. that would affect them. In some cases they also preempted the need for a review board (at the initial stages) or certain aspects of the Board that would satisfy their own interests.

The A.S.R.B. debate may have originated from the bureaucrats' and politicians' quest for enforceable accounting regulations, but it gained intensity as it turned into a struggle for control over the accounting standard-setting process. It appears to have been a contest between the company law administrators, mainly bureaucrats and lawyers, on the one hand and the accounting profession on the other (Also see Table 10.3.D. and note the low correlation between the government bodies' responses and the profession's responses in respect of the functional aspects that were adopted by the A.S.R.B.). Others, like the A.I.D.A., the company directors and the insurance associations, entered the debate, from time to time, to protect their own/members' interests.

The decisions of the policy-maker (the Ministerial Council) over the entire process did reflect the demands of the participating parties. The nature and content of its decisions at particular stages of the process also varied according to the nature and content of the demands of the parties participating during those stages. We can note from the prior discussion that on several occasions a decision once favourable to one party was amended to accommodate the demands of others who participated effectively at a later stage. The Council, as revealed in the previous section, did in fact respond to the demands of a majority of the effectively participating interest groups and interested individuals in forming the organization and functions of the Board. In terms of the model for this thesis (See Chapter 5) it can be inferred that the Ministerial Council as a policy-making body and a supplier of regulatory policies, being composed of politicians, tried to maximize the support for its actions at each step by supplying policy schemes which corresponded to the demands of a wide cross-section of its effectively participating constituents in the electorate (See Equation 5.1.).

Finally, the most noticeable aspect of the behaviour of the participants in the A.S.R.B. debate was that, although the arguments for and against an A.S.R.B. were mostly cloaked in public interest rhetoric, they were usually aimed at satisfying private/self-interests of the demanders and the suppliers. Significant cases were that of the bureaucrats lobbying with an intention to alleviate the problems of rule enforcement; the accounting profession acted to strengthen its position as a profession and as a standard-setter; the companies joined the debate to secure themselves from over regulation; and the regulators accepted the notion of the Board and supplied it to achieve their own political ambitions. This is consistent with the premise of this thesis - "individuals in government and society supplied and demanded regulation, respectively, primarily to fulfil their self-interest in a rational manner" (See Chapter 5).

Chapter 11

SUMMARY AND CONCLUSIONS

Summary:

The subject of this study was the creation of the A.S.R.B. and the establishment of its functions. The interest in that subject was instigated mainly due to the lack of research on it and by the methodology adopted by R. Walker (1987). R. Walker (1987) used the "capture" argument to explain that the accounting profession, being the regulated party, influenced the regulatory process preceding the creation of the Board and in the two years after the creation of the Board, in order to have a board which would be in its control.

A review of the Board's organization and functions, around the same time as that of R. Walker's study (See Chapter 2 and 3), led to the observation that the Board was dependent on several interest groups and that there was scope for those groups to influence the activities of the Board. Based on the findings regarding the significance of roles acquired by the interested parties in the A.S.R.B. mechanism it was hypothesized, that in order to achieve an influential role in the functioning of the A.S.R.B. all identifiable interest groups participated actively in the Board's establishment. Parties with a significant capacity to influence were the politicians, the bureaucrats, the accounting profession and the companies. Others such as the academics and the stock exchanges had a lesser capacity to influence.

A point to note here is that to make those observations the A.S.R.B.'s organizational and functional aspects have been reviewed within the broader domain of the Cooperative Scheme for

Companies and Securities. This was necessary because the Board, before its merger with the Ac.S.B., was completely under the Cooperative Scheme and had to function in harmony with the other organs of that Scheme.[153] Rather than being an exclusive review of the A.S.R.B. per se, the review was conducted by taking into account all major aspects of the regulatory process - the preparation, review, statutory backing and enforcement of standards.

The above observations and the hypothesis motivated the enquiry into the Board's process of creation. The investigation commenced with the evaluation of the competing theories of regulation with applications in accounting (Chapter 4). The prescriptive theories, for and against, accounting regulation were found to have minimal use in describing the creation of a regulatory body such as the A.S.R.B. Consequently, these theories were set aside. Amongst the descriptive theories, the Public Choice version of explaining economic regulation was found to have the greatest capacity to explain the determination of regulatory policies in a pluralistic regulatory environment. Therefore, it was chosen as the preferred framework for explaining why the regulators created the Board in its current form.

Based on the Public Choice framework and supported by other descriptive theories of regulation a model was developed (Chapter 5). The model illustrated that regulatory policies were initiated by perceived crises. Crises stimulated the demand[154] for

---

153   It still has to do the same, but now its functions extend beyond that of the Cooperative Scheme.

154   Demand for policy measures may have existed before those crises, but only in a dormant form.

such policies. The regulators responded by supplying the policies. Both the demanders and suppliers were motivated by self-interest. The resulting policy was the equilibrium outcome of the demand and supply functions. Such policies represented a state, at a point in time, in a dynamic regulatory process and were subject to change with changing demand and supply patterns. A reasonably long time interval was recommended to identify all the major participants in the regulatory process. It was suggested that to understand the role of the participants in the policy outcome it was important to understand their behaviour in the process preceding the outcome.

After establishing the model, the history of accounting regulatory policies up to 1970 was briefly reviewed (Chapter 6). This review provided an insight into the forms of accounting regulatory policies and accounting/financial disclosure regulations that preceded the accounting standards. It showed how the accounting standards gained prominence as a form of company disclosure regulation. The notion that the regulatory process is dynamic and that the regulatory policies are the equilibrium points within the process was substantiated by this review.

The role of the accounting bodies in setting accounting standards was further analyzed (Chapter 7). This was essential in the light of the focus by R. Walker (1987) on the participation of those bodies in the formation of the Board and because they were found to be the main source of accounting standards. That analysis revealed that professional accounting pronouncements, later to be known as standards, evolved as a means of guiding and developing the skills of accountants and auditors, in particular, and the image of the profession, in general. Having received considerable attention and criticism in the past, specially in the sixties and the seventies, the accounting profession responded by issuing an increasing number of accounting standards with increasing authority. On the one hand accounting standards have become one of the significant means by which the accounting profession can, at least, be seen to be keeping its "house in order;" and on the other hand it is being seen as a means of company financial disclosure regulation.

The professional accounting standards and the profession as a whole, though often criticized, have received the recognition of the other sources of accounting regulation - the courts, the legislators, the stock exchanges and the A.I.M. That recognition has been mainly in the area of providing measurement requirements. The evidence and arguments also suggest that, by around late 1970's and early 1980's, professional accounting standards and the accounting bodies were firmly entrenched as a form of company financial disclosure regulation and rule-makers, respectively.

The decades of 1960s and 1970s saw an increasing trend towards company regulation in Australia. That led to the formation of the Co-operative Scheme for Companies and Securities. In the later part of that period there was growing concern regarding the weaknesses of the profession based accounting standard-setting mechanism accompanied by demands for government involvement in it (Chapter 8).

The co-operative scheme provided a single national regulatory system which seemed to provide improved grounds for government involvement in the professional standard-setting system. Despite the presence of various anomalies, non-compliance with professional standards and the profession's lack of power to enforce standards received greater attention - specially in the later half of the seventies.

Meanwhile, the company regulators recognized the legislature's lack of capacity to define a "true and fair" view or specific accounting standards. In that light, the scheme which seemed to receive more attention, for the removal of anomalies in accounting standards, was a government-profession based co-regulatory scheme.

The notion of a co-regulatory scheme materialized into a review board, the A.S.R.B., with the power to approve accounting standards having legislative backing. The process of the creation of the Board and the installation of its functions was studied in detail in Chapter 9. That covered an interval from the time the idea of the Board was conceived up to the time its functions were publicly stated in 1985.

Three stages were noted in the creation of the A.S.R.B. The first dealt with the debate prior to the Ministerial Council for Companies and Securities resolution dated May 23, 1980, in which the Council formed the opinion that the A.S.R.B. was needed. The second stage was that of the formation of the Board with some tentative functions. The specific functions and criteria for approving proposed standards were finalized in the third stage.

The evidence laid down in Chapter 9 was closely analyzed in Chapter 10. Certain important inferences were drawn from this analysis. It was inferred that the A.S.R.B. and the mandatory accounting issue originated and existed before it entered the political debate. The politicians turned the underlying problems, on which the idea for an A.S.R.B. was based, into a crisis. It was further fueled by the news media, and the A.S.R.B. issue eventually entered the political arena.

There were several effective participants or participating groups/bodies which acted as demanders of policy measures in the formation of the Board. The bureaucrats, the accounting profession and the companies were the main participants on the demand side. In addition, other parties also took keen interest and participated actively whenever need arose. The suppliers of the Board and the associated policy measures were the politicians who made-up the Ministerial Council.

All parties did not participate with the same degree of intensity and the intensity of their participation seemed to vary over the various stages of the process. The extent of their participation was linked to how they perceived the effect of a review board on their activities. The parties participated whenever they were informed of an imminent decision of the regulators adopting a particular form of A.S.R.B. that would affect them. In certain cases they also preempted the need for a review board (at the initial stages) or certain aspects of the Board that would satisfy their own needs.

The decisions of the policy-maker (the Ministerial Council), over the entire process, did reflect the demands of the participating parties. The nature and content of its decisions at particular stages of the process also varied according to the nature and content of the demands of the parties participating during those stages. On several occasions a decision once favourable to one party was amended to accommodate the demands of others. The Council did in fact respond to the demands of a majority of the effectively participating interest groups and interested individuals in forming the organization and functions of the Board. It can be inferred that the Ministerial Council as a policy-making body and a supplier of regulatory policies, being composed of politicians, tried to maximize the support for its actions at each step by supplying policy schemes which corresponded to the demands of a wide cross-section of its effectively participating constituents in the electorate.

Finally, the most noticeable aspect of the behaviour of the participants in the A.S.R.B. debate was that, although the arguments for and against an A.S.R.B. were mostly cloaked in public interest rhetoric, they were usually aimed at satisfying private/self-interests of the demanders and the suppliers. Significant cases were that of the bureaucrats lobbying with an intention to alleviate the problems of rule enforcement; the accounting profession acted to strengthen its position as a profession and as a standard-setter; the companies joined the debate to secure themselves from over-regulation; and the regulators accepted the notion of the Board and supplied it to achieve their own political ambitions. This is consistent with the premise of this thesis that the suppliers and demanders of regulation act rationally on the basis of self-interest.

Conclusions:

As has been noted, the major impetus for the creation of the Board and the introduction of the notion of approved accounting standards was the non-compliance by companies and their auditors with professional accounting standards. The underlying notion was that compliance (say C) is a function of acceptability of standards (say A) by major interest groups and statutory backing of approved standards (say S). In short:

$$C = f(A, S)$$

The participatory mode adopted for enhancing acceptability made the Board dependent on interest groups. It is quite evident from the discussion here that the Board was not under the complete control of any particular interest group. Rather it relied on several parties for its efficient functioning. That reliance had provided the interest groups the scope to influence the Board's activities. It was certainly not an independent regulatory body as envisaged by those who devised it. It seems that the term "independent" was a misnomer for the purposes of describing the organisation and activities of the Board.

Through the establishment of the Board the powerful influencing interests institutionalized their roles in the standard-setting process. They did that by participating effectively in the process through which the A.S.R.B. was created. In order to acquire their roles they acted on the basis of self-interest.

The Board, as described here, served the purpose of balancing the interests of all interested parties namely, the politicians as law-makers; the bureaucrats as law-enforcers; the accounting profession as standard-setters and law-abiders; and the companies also as law-abiders. It seemed to be a "political" power sharing formula ensuring that the Board did not come under the de facto control of any of those parties. This sort of mechanism may be unacceptable to those who perceive politics from a derogatory sense, but it seems essential for a task of the kind the A.S.R.B. was entrusted with. The competing interests will always exist. The A.S.R.B., to survive in an environment where politically effective groups decided the fate of public bodies, would have to bring about a balance amongst the different interests it served.

Gerboth (1973), Moonitz (1974) and Wells (1978) also pointed out the importance of political and constituent involvement and support for the survival of standard-setting agencies and their established standards. This is consistent with the concept of "due process" enshrined in the legislative and judicial procedures of government in Australia and other Western democracies (Chisholm and Nettheim, 1978, pp. 69-70). Since approved accounting standards are a form of delegated legislation, the delegation of authority to set standards to the law-enforcers, technical experts, the regulated and others is in conformity with the notion of delegated legislation. It provided a mechanism of producing technical rules, for which the legislature had neither the time nor the expertise, without foregoing democratic safeguards necessary for preparing such rules - "public exposure" and "due process" of issues, subject to Parliamentary supervision (Also see Chisholm and Nettheim, 1978, pp. 17-18; Gifford and Gifford, 1983, pp. 44-47; and Masel, 1983).

The users of accounting information as the purported beneficiaries of the policy measure encompassing the Board and the legislatively backed standards were numerous, but with no direct participation in the Board's activities. This did not mean that their interests were at risk. The politicians on the Ministerial Council were responsible for the activities of the Board. Under the notion of responsible government and as elected office-bearers, it was in their interest to monitor and direct the activities of the Board in a manner so that it at least looked as if it was serving its beneficiaries. In the event of the Board's failure to provide its intended services it would be in the best interest of the Council to terminate its life. The example of the C.A.S.B. in the U.S.A. has already been cited earlier. Therefore it was in the interest of those who were involved in the activities of the Board to act in a manner that they did not overlook the interests of the beneficiaries.

The active participation of the accounting profession in the determination of the organization and functions of the Board was related to its position as the standard-setter before the creation of the Board. The professional accounting bodies were involved in setting standards well before those standards received recognition as a form of company regulation. Their purpose was the development of the skills of its members and the enhancement of the image of the profession. The incursions of the bureaucrats and politicians in the domain of standard-setting was seen as a threat to one of its essential and established activities. Therefore, the actions of the professional bodies were quite rational. Nevertheless, they only succeeded in maintaining their control over the standard-preparation process and in securing a position to influence the review process, that also in a manner that it was not against the interests of other major parties.

We have seen accounting regulation and regulatory bodies as elements of the changing regulatory policies adopted by the regulators - the government. The various forms of regulatory policies that are noticeable from this research are no regulation, self-regulation by the accounting profession or the stock exchange or industry groups such as the A.I.M., regulation through statutes and the courts and finally the form of co-regulation as in the case of the A.S.R.B. We have noted that the changes that occur are initiated by certain forms of crises that reveal the deficiencies in the existing regulatory policies. The response of the government in respect of supplying regulations itself or allowing some other body to do so, depends on the intensity and the nature/direction of the demand for regulations. Depending on that, the government chooses either to directly get involved or delegate its responsibilities of law-making to some other body to which the demanders have directed their attention. As the environmental conditions change the pattern of demand shifts. Meanwhile, the composition of the government in terms of politicians and political parties in power and their ideologies may also change. This brings about changed regulatory conditions leading to changes in the regulatory policies of the government. Alterations made in the regulatory policies may alter old forms of regulation or introduce new forms with new sources of regulation.

Corollary - R. Walker (1987) Re-explained:

The weaknesses of R. Walker's (1987) model and methodology have been explained in Chapter 4. Here we attempt to provide an alternate explanation for the changes in the Board's operations that he was so critical about.

Our review of the creation of the A.S.R.B. in Chapter 9 covered the major aspects of the establishment of the Board and its functions. It stopped short of a detail account of the events discussed by R. Walker (1987). The changes discussed by R. Walker were mainly that of procedures rather than that of organization and functions. Nonetheless, they should not be overlooked because they may have long run implications for the standard-setting process.

From R. Walker's (1987) discussion it is apparent that the accounting profession tried to consolidate its position under the changed conditions of accounting standard-setting and it also tried to protect itself from further government and bureaucratic incursions in that area. Such moves of the profession do not appear to diminish the importance of other interest groups in the standard-setting process and, as is shown later, the A.S.R.B. setup was also in accord with the earlier demands of other parties.

The standards' copyright dispute (R. Walker, 1987, pp. 274-275) indicated that the accounting bodies did not want to part with the ownership of the standards after they were approved by the A.S.R.B. This move, as R. Walker claimed, was in the interest of the accounting bodies and their members. The reasons for this are quite simple. Those bodies have invested a great deal of money and effort in the accounting standard-setting process. As seen in Chapter 7, the per capita expenditure of the members on standards have risen continuously. After the creation of the A.S.R.B. the expenditure of the accounting bodies on standard-setting stands at around five to six times of that spent on the A.S.R.B. by the government. Apart from the issue of expenditures, there is the aspect of the scope of the standards. After the professional standards were approved by the A.S.R.B. they became company financial regulations, but they also remained as professional accounting standards for the purpose of non-corporate sector accounting and auditing. Therefore, standards which may be applicable to the companies under the company law, from the perspective of the accounting profession, are also applicable to other entities. The wider importance of the standards to the members of the profession and the extent of expenditure incurred by the professional bodies gave those bodies ample reason for trying to retain the ownership of the standards and their commercial exploitation.[155]

Other procedural changes, such as the adoption of the fast-track method of reviewing standards, do indicate that the professional bodies were trying to consolidate their role as preparer of standards. However, those changes did not represent the views of the profession alone. They also reflected the suggestions that were made earlier by others. Although neither the N.C.S.C. nor

---

155   The A.S.R.B. Annual Report 1986-87, p. 20, stated that under an agreement reached between the Ministerial Council and the accounting bodies, the copyright of the standards will be transferred to the Crown and the Crown will in turn grant a license to those bodies for the commercial exploitation of the standards.

the A.S.R.B. called for submissions on the question of whether the A.A.R.F. of the professional bodies should be the sole source of standards for the A.S.R.B., there were parties from all the classes of respondents to N.C.S.C. Release 401 and A.S.R.B. Release 400 who proposed that the A.A.R.F. should be the main or only source of proposed accounting standards (Tables 9.3. and 9.4.). We have also seen that the A.I.D.A., a powerful business sector association, also expressed preference for the profession's standard-setting mechanism. Therefore, to provide greater procedural powers, in terms of preparation of standards, to the A.A.R.F. satisfied the demands of a wide range of interest groups, in addition to that of the profession.

R. Walker (1987, p. 282) distinguished the members of the Board as mainly the members of the accounting bodies, implying that the Board was not independent of those bodies. We have already discussed in Chapters 2 and 3 that such affiliations do not necessarily mean that those members of the Board would work in the interest of the accounting bodies.

The controversy surrounding the redrafting of standards (R. Walker, 1987, pp. 278-279) implies that the professional bodies were trying to protect themselves from further bureaucratic and legal incursions into its established pattern of standard-setting and the manner in which its standards could be interpreted. The more purposive style of drafting standards, to reduce ambiguity in the standards with a view to making them legally enforceable, had implications for the accounting practitioners and the companies. According to Parker et al (1987, p. 239), the legal style of drafting made the meaning of the standards more precise, hence requiring compliance with greater precision. That would make compliance with the standards by the members of the professional bodies more difficult in certain situations. For example, there might be situations where precise standards may not be appropriate for disclosing a "true and fair view." This may lead to the dilemma of whether the accountant should follow the sprit of true and fair reporting or the requirements of the standards.

On the demand side it is evident that the accounting bodies were the most vocal beneficiaries of the procedural changes that were criticized by R. Walker (1987), but that does not explain why the Ministerial Council accepted such demands.

By simply looking at the resources allocated for the operations of the Board we can deduce that the Ministerial Council never allowed the Board to be a major regulatory organization. Mr. Bottrill, the first chairman of the A.S.R.B., was critical of the "shoe-string" budget of the Board (Business Review Weekly, December 8, 1984) and identified it as one of the major causes of the Board's lack of aggressiveness (Business Review Weekly, November 21, 1986). He was concerned about funding to the extent that he suggested self-financing of the Board through a levy on filings by companies.

It was mentioned in Chapter 3 that poor financing and dependence on others for funds, specially in its early years, can force a regulatory body to adopt a restrictive view of its powers and that view could continue to shape its consciousness. From our observations we find that the Board was in a similar position. The lack of funding ensured the dependence of the Board on the interest groups for expertise and resources. Since the Ministerial Council with the recommendation of the N.C.S.C. was responsible for funding the Board, it is not appropriate to blame the accounting bodies alone for the lack of aggressiveness of the Board.

R. Walker (1987) explained that the Council, due to continuous changes in its membership, no longer saw the A.S.R.B. as a vote winning exercise, for which it accepted the demands of the accounting bodies. An alternate explanation for the Ministerial Council's acceptance of the demands favourable to the accounting profession is that, by establishing a review board contrary to the demands of the profession, the politicians or the political parties represented in the Council had presumably lost support from the accounting profession. Since the demands for procedural modifications later placed by the accounting bodies also had support from others, with hardly any vocal opposition, the Council approved the changes to win back some of its lost support. Therefore, the politicians in the Council used accounting policy-making once more as a vote winning exercise.

Apart from such alternate explanations to R. Walker's (1987) arguments, Parker et al (1987, p. 237) argued that all standards prior to the formation of the Board or after its formation did not originate from the accounting bodies. According to them there were several sources of origin for the standards. They noted that the standard on foreign currency translation, which was proposed by the N.C.S.C., was such a standard and that the A.S.R.B. had created a precedence by approving it. This, they claimed, was contrary to Walker's "capture" notion (Parker et al, 1987, p. 243) because it illustrated how the N.C.S.C. without any direct participation in the activities of the Board could influence it from outside. We have also noted earlier that the corporate sector would take increased interest in the processing of approved accounting standards due to their mandatory nature. The recent changes have not done anything to alter that situation.

Implications:

Since this research is descriptive it is not possible nor is it intended to make recommendations. However the observations made here and the conclusions drawn from them have their implications. Besides that, this research introduces a powerful model (parts of which have been tested before by others[156]) and demonstrates its effectiveness in explaining several aspects of a regulatory process, in general, and the accounting regulatory process, in particular.

The broader concept of "regulatory process" rather than "regulatory organization" provided a better illustration of the A.S.R.B. and its environment. The checks and balances installed in the mechanics of the approved accounting standards framework, although not yet fully tested, can discourage excessive dominance of a single party at the expense of other parties. For example, if the Board's standard-setting and review functions were captured by the accounting profession, as R. Walker (1987) explained, it could not go without the notice of others (R. Walker (1987) himself is a good example of the criticism of alleged dominance of an interest group). We have noticed, that in the past when the accounting profession showed less inclination towards developing certain standards, such as the foreign currency translation standard, the intervention of bodies such as the N.C.S.C. prompted the profession to develop standards in those areas.

The perception that regulatory processes are dynamic implies that the form and even the existence of the A.S.R.B. and its standards can change. Any attempt to reduce the efficiency of the Board can lead to a situation where the deficiencies will be

---

156   See Chapters 4 and 5.

revealed. This may lead to further government intervention and to a situation where the interest group responsible for creating obstacles to efficiency may have its share of involvement in the regulatory process reduced.

The scope for participation of several interest groups through the review process could be used by the accounting profession to its own advantage. The profession by encouraging and involving the other major groups to participate in the approval of standards can reduced its risk of being singled out and blamed for future corporate collapses.

The description of the creation of the Board using the model described in this thesis sheds light into the "black box" of the political activity that normally precedes the formulation of a regulatory policy. Although a completely new form of regulation did not evolve through the creation of the Board, there was sufficient activity preceding the change in the form of regulation of accounting. It provided ample evidence to illustrate the model. Once vaguely described as "political/social choice/socio-economic/evolutionary/revolutionary", the use of the model provided an insight into the mechanics of the regulatory process. It helped us understand why regulatory policies take the shape as they do and why and how various participants in the process behave.

The research has illustrated that the model is capable of describing the origin and creation of regulatory policies. Likewise, it can also explain or predict the change or termination of policies. The explanation that the A.S.R.B. was created in a certain manner through the actions of politically effective participants leads us to predict that any change in the participant composition or participants' needs may lead to further change in the regulatory policies. Similarly, we may argue that when the major participants in the regulatory process find that it is in their own interest that the Board be dissolved the life of the Board will be terminated. Such a situation, as already mentioned, may occur if a single party tries to achieve dominance at the expense of others. This may be further strengthened by a general trend towards the deregulation of the economy.

The adoption of the notion of demand and supply in a continuous regulatory process made it necessary to use a long time span for the purpose of this research. That approach facilitated the identification of a number of interest groups involved in the accounting regulatory process on both the demand and the supply sides, as opposed to only one on the demand side as shown by R. Walker (1987). The identification of interest groups and an understanding of their behaviour in the creation of the A.S.R.B. can help predict the nature of involvement of those groups in accounting standard-setting in the future. This also implies that the standards set by an organization such as the Board are not the outcome of an independent process. Rather the standards are the product of a process of demand and supply where that organization is the supplier and the interest groups are the demanders of standards.

The use of a broader perspective than that of R. Walker (1987) provides a more elaborate and neutral explanation of the creation of the Board and its current form. It shows the manner and the extent to which the participating interests can involve themselves in the Boards activities. Since the participants in the regulatory process act on the basis of self-interest, it is implied that they will participate in the Board's activities to safeguard their own interests.

Finally, this research unveils the facts behind the often unexplained "pristine" legislative purpose of the politicians. The reason for which the actions of politicians is not investigated may be the public interest rhetoric in which they are normally cloaked. With the help of the model of this thesis it has been shown in detail how the politicians as the suppliers of the Board, behaved during the creation of the Board and why they established the Board. It was certainly far from a convincing effort to reduce the information asymmetry in the capital markets. Rather the politicians tried to satisfy all the major parties in the regulatory process, with a view to achieving their own political ambitions. From that perspective, it is expected that the Board will face changes whenever dissatisfaction with its activities is voiced by the major participants of the accounting standard-setting process and that such changes satisfy the needs of the politicians.

Postscript:

The A.S.R.B. was reorganised in 1988-89. The Accounting Standards Board (Ac.S.B.) of the A.A.R.F. was merged with the A.S.R.B. The latter was then expanded in size to accommodate two more members, one each from the I.C.A.A. and the A.S.A. That increased the representation of each of the accounting bodies from one to two members. The A.A.R.F., still funded by the professional bodies, prepared accounting standards for approval by the A.S.R.B. and not by the professional bodies. The Foundation continued with its other duties, such as preparing auditing and public sector accounting standards, for the profession. The Government continued funding the A.S.R.B. at the previous level (Business Review Weekly, July 8, 1988, p. 105 and Business Review Weekly, July 22, 1988, p. 99). The merged body retained the name "Accounting Standards Review Board."

This change in the mechanics of accounting standard-setting eliminated the stage of professional approval previously conducted by the Ac.S.B. According to its chairman, Mr. Stan Droder, the new arrangement as transitional and expected a further merger of the Board with the Public Sector Accounting Standards Board[157] (Business Review Weekly, July 22, 1988, p. 99 and Australian Financial Review, September 23, 1988, p. 22).

Since the expanded Board would eventually have expanded functions of setting private (corporate and non-corporate) and public sector standards, it was expected that the State and Commonwealth Parliaments would enact laws to enforce its public sector standards (Business Review Weekly, July 22, 1988, p. 99). The enforcement of private corporate sector standards would remain as the responsibility of the N.C.S.C. and the C.A.C.s and the non-corporate sector enforcement would continue to be the responsibility of the accounting profession. All other provisions for the review of standards under the Companies Act and within the Cooperative Scheme remained unchanged (Australian Financial Review, September 23, 1988, p. 22).

Contrary to the "capture" notion, the reorganised A.S.R.B. could be perceived differently. The accounting bodies seem to have given up more than they received in return. For a nominal increase in their membership they have handed over the supervisory role of preparation of standards to the review board in

---

157   The merger with the Public Sector Accounting Standards Board will be considered by the Ministerial Council in December, 1988 (Australian Financial Review, September 23, 1988.

which they did not hold a confirmed majority[158] and which was under the control of the Ministerial Council. Some vocal opponents to the merger have already criticized the change as a handing over of the standard-setting role by the profession to the Government (Australian Financial Review, September 29, 1988, p. 31). This observation of the critics seems to be true in the light of the earlier proposals by the accounting bodies for a profession sponsored review board or an expanded Ac.S.B. with outside participation in it (See Chapter 9). The reorganisation was opposite to the board conceived by the accounting profession, that is instead of others participating in a profession sponsored board the profession could be seen as participating in a government sponsored board. Moreover, the profession committed to spend far more on accounting standard-setting than its representation on the reconstituted Board. It also reduced its role in the setting of standards by disbanding its Ac.S.B. and thereby surrendering its power of veto over accounting standards before they are submitted for approval.

The only way to understand the impact of the current changes is by re-enacting the process through which the change was brought about. We should recall from the conclusions and implications of this research, discussed earlier, that for any change affecting the operations of the Board there should be sufficient support from parties on both the supply and the demand sides of the regulatory process. The major participants acting for and reacting to the need for the change are expected to act on the basis of self-interest. Others who do not perceive any major impact from the change will provide tacit approval by not opposing the change. From that perspective and using the available information

---

158   They may hold a majority from time to time by seeking support from others on the Board.

we can provide an explanation in terms of the model adopted in this research.

On the demand side the accounting profession had advocated standard-setting by the profession or profession's dominance in standard-setting as early as the late 1960s (See Chapter 8 and Mathews, 1969, p. 632) and had, on many occasions, made various moves to oppose government involvement in accounting standard-setting (Chapters 8 and 9). We have also seen that accounting standard-setting is in the interest of the profession (Chapter 7). Therefore, the Board with enhanced representation of the profession in it, is more likely to be the idea of the profession.

We have already observed that the Board was set-up in a manner that was not to the complete liking of the accounting profession and that they later acquired procedural changes to consolidate their position in the preparation of accounting standards. Despite those moves and some increase in the pace of standard-setting by the A.S.R.B. the profession remained critical of the review and approval process. The accounting bodies criticized the redrafting of professional standards and the additional time and money spent on re-exposure of all standards by the Board after the A.A.R.F. had done it once (Business Review Weekly, June 20, 1986, p. 138). Apart from the differences arising between approved standards and professional standards due to drafting style, the professional bodies expressed their criticism regarding amendments made to their standards by the Board which brought about changes, such as differential applications. Since the accounting profession regarded accounting standards as being applicable to a much wider area than just the corporate sector, a separate set of standards different from theirs and applicable only to the corporate sector was not to the liking of the accounting bodies, specially when the A.A.R.F. was expected to redraft professional standards to meet the requirements of the approved standards (Peirson, 1988, p. 4). This duality of purpose seemed to create problems for the standard-preparers - the A.A.R.F. The profession had earlier predicted that the creation of a second set of accounting standards by the A.S.R.B. would make accounting regulations more dispersed increasing the cost of financial reporting (Peirson and Ramsay, 1983, p. 299) .

It has been mentioned in the Corollary that procedural aspects of reviewing and approving standards may have serious implications. It is quite evident here that aspects such as re-drafting and amending standards by the Board became a contentious issue and also an excuse for the accounting bodies to demand an amalgamation of the A.S.R.B. with the A.A.R.F.

A year after the A.S.R.B. was created the accounting profession started expressing its views for amalgamating the Board with its A.A.R.F. In view of the initial procedural problems faced by the Board, both the I.C.A.A. and the A.S.A. started arguing for the merger. David Boymal, a former member of the Ac.S.B., expressed similar views in 1986 (Boymal, 1986, p. 36). At that time the problems perceived by the profession had not affected financial reporting and a feeling of crisis had not developed. Hence, the issues were mainly dealt by introducing procedural changes.

With the introduction of the fast-track system of review, agreement on copyrights and the understanding reached on drafting standards the procedural problems seemed to have been solved. The solution was only temporary. As the A.S.R.B. treaded into more contentious areas, such as foreign exchange disclosure, the problem of duality became more vivid. It not only seemed to

create difficulties in standard-setting, but also appeared to lead
towards different accounting practices for the corporate and public
sectors. This situation created a sense of confusion amongst the
preparers of financial statements (Australian Business, July 22,
1987, p. 25). Problems of application and hence of enforcement
were showing up and the N.C.S.C. and the accounting bodies were
clearly perplexed with the prevailing level of non-compliance with
standards (For example see Australian Financial Review: January
14, 1987, p. 16; March 5, 1987, p. 14; April 7, 1987, p. 24; April
21, 1987, p. 56; June 5, 1987, p. 23,; and Australian Business July
22, 1987, p. 25). Meanwhile, the equity accounting guidelines of
the N.C.S.C. led to further complaints from the business and
professional quarters about the variety of requirements established
for similar issues by the different standard-setting and regulatory
bodies (The Australian, September 22, 1987, p. 16). In the light
of the ensuing debate about standards, the I.C.A.A. and the A.S.A.
emphasized the merger of the A.A.R.F. and the A.S.R.B. to
produce uniform standards. They visualized an eight member
board, four appointed by the Government and four (two each) by
the two accounting bodies (Business Review Weekly, April 16,
1987, p. 111 and Business Review Weekly, and May 8, 1987, p.
150). There was feeble opposition to that proposal, that also from
the A.S.R.B. itself, only claiming that the merger was premature
(Business Review Weekly, April 24, 1987, p. 126).

The N.C.S.C., which was one of the proponents of the
fast-track method of reviewing standards, having realized the more
recent problems confronted by the standard-setters and the
companies, started looking towards some form of amalgamation of
the A.S.R.B. and the profession's Ac.S.B. and P.S.A.S.B.
(Australian Business, February 3, 1988, p. 87 and Australian
Business, February 10, 1988, p. 96). Although no submissions
were called from the public, it is understood that shortly after the

N.C.S.C.'s consideration of an amalgamation the accounting bodies placed a detailed submission emphasizing the merger. The submission explained how the three standard-setting bodies, the A.S.R.B., the Ac.S.B. and the P.S.A.S.B., worked on similar issues but with different outcomes. It pointed out that such a method of accounting standard-setting would lead to inconsistent reporting requirements for companies, public sector organizations and other non-corporate sector entities. It explained that apart from such inconsistencies, the work of standard-setting was being duplicated by the A.S.R.B. and the accounting profession, with the wasteful use of limited resources. To reduce the inconsistencies between standards, the wastage of resources and the time taken to set standards, the profession's submission suggested a single national standard-setting body. That body, the submission contemplated, would absorb the resources and expertise of the A.A.R.F. and the A.S.R.B. and be controlled by the Government and the accounting bodies. Since the standards of that body would be applicable to both the private (corporate and non-corporate) sector and the public sector bodies, the body's functional boundary would extend beyond that of the Cooperative Scheme. Accordingly, the submission proposed that the Parliaments of the States and the Commonwealth would have to pass legislations to adopt the standards of that body for application in the public sector. To facilitate the new changes, the accounting bodies expressed their readiness to dismantle or reconstruct the existing Ac.S.B. and P.S.A.S.B.; orient its other activities towards the standards of the proposed body; discontinue the practice of approval and issuance of standards by the two accounting bodies; and make the resources of the A.A.R.F. available for use by that national body. In short, the profession was ready to relinquish its supervisory role over the preparation of accounting standards (Proposal for the Formation of a National Standard-Setting Body - an unpublished submission by the I.C.A.A. and the A.S.A., March 15, 1988). At that stage it did not disclose the extent of participation it would demand in the new body in return for the price it was ready to pay. Perhaps, as mentioned earlier, the profession was still contemplating a fifty percent representation in the reconstituted board.

Meanwhile the controversy regarding the applicability of standards entered into 1988 (For example see Business Review Weekly, February 12, 1988, pp. 107-108 and Australian Financial Review, February 15, 1988, p. 45). The arrangements for the proposed merger also went on without much public debate or any demand for public exposure about the change. This indicates that there was no effective opposition to the change. In fact it was later reported in the media that the proposed merger had the support of the business sector (Australian Financial Review, September 29, 1988, p. 31) and, of course, the N.C.S.C. which was responsible for recommending it to the Ministerial Council.

The Ministerial Council approved the merger, in principle, in July, 1988 (Business Review Weekly, July 8, 1988, p. 105 and Business Review Weekly, July 22, 1988, p. 99). The profession expressed its satisfaction with the "compromise", indicating that although it could not achieve all its demands, it at least acquired an increased representation on the expanded Board (Business Review Weekly, July 8, 1988, p. 105). There was some belated opposition from within the profession, with the perception that the merger would mean a complete transfer of standard-setting from the profession to the Government (Australian Financial Review, September 29, 1988, p. 31), but it seemed to be of no consequence.

An early decision to implement the merger was expected from the Ministerial Council, but it came about sooner than expected. It was earlier expected that the Council would approve the merger in its December 1, 1988 meeting (<u>Australian Financial Review</u>, September 6, 1988, p. 22), but the Council announced its approval on September 22, 1988 (<u>Australian Financial Review</u>, September 23, 1988, p. 22). The Council's decision was immediately hailed by the accounting profession and the business sector. The accounting bodies also publicly claimed credit for engineering the merger (<u>Business Review Weekly</u>, September 30, 1988, p. 120). According to its earlier commitment it dismantled the Ac.S.B. (<u>Business Review Weekly</u>, October 7, 1988, p. 179).

On the supply side of the merger, it once again seems that the politicians in the Ministerial Council have used accounting policy making to their own advantage. On the one side they satisfied the demands of the major interest groups. For example, they satisfied the demands of the profession backed by the business sector for greater privatization of accounting rule-setting. The merger also provided, in form, some assurance to the bureaucrats within the N.C.S.C. that accounting standards will be less diversified and produced faster and more efficiently, thus removing obstacles to enforcement.

On the other hand the Ministerial Council formally kept the Board under its control by retaining the power to appoint all members without allowing the professional nominees to have a majority. It also retained the power to veto the standards and, more importantly, the authority to decide upon any policy issue pertaining to the Board. Therefore, the change portrays that, in form, the Board was still a public body independent of private interests.

The politicians could also receive public support for their merger decision because it suited the prevailing popular demand for privatization and rationalization. The increase in the representation of the accounting bodies may satisfy those who opposed the concept of government involvement in standard-setting and enforcement of standards (Business Review Weekly, September 20, 1985, p. 151). To them the change may indicate lesser government involvement in standard-setting.

As for rationalisation, the merger, as announced by the Chairman of the Ministerial Council, was necessary to rationalise the standard-setting process. The A.S.R.B., from its outset, was a victim of spending cuts by the Commonwealth Government (Business Review Weekly, December 8, 1988 and Business Review Weekly, September 21, 1986, p. 149). The dilemma was that the Government had accepted the need for a review board but could not provide sufficient funds for it to function effectively on its own (Business Review Weekly, September 21, 1986, p. 149, The Chartered Accountant in Australia, July, 1986, p. 26 and The Chartered Accountant in Australia, November, 1986, p. 32). The merger brought the Board closer to the profession's mechanism of preparing standards, removing or reducing the need for the Board to conduct its own investigation on standards. Such a reduction in the Board's functions may have convinced the Ministerial Council that the merger would enhance the effectiveness of the Board without increasing its level of spending. Thereby the merger would, as the Council expected, on the one side provide an image of streamlining the standard-setting process and on the other side contribute towards its programme of rationalization of government activities (Australian Financial Review, September 23, 1988, p. 22).

Finally, the concept of a single national accounting standard-setting body may have also appealed to the Commonwealth Labour Government because of it was a move towards a national companies and securities legislation and an

Australian Securities Commission (<u>Australian Business</u>, February 3, 1988, p. 87). A Commonwealth legislation in this respect was favoured by the business sector and was supported by the recent rulings of the High Court of Australia and the April 1987 findings of the Senate Standing Committee on Constitutional and Legal Affairs (Ford, 1988, p. 11). A Commonwealth scheme was also preferred by the bureaucrats as opposed to the more dispersed Co-operative Scheme for Companies and Securities, because it would enhance and strengthen their role as company law administrators (<u>Australian Accountant</u>, September, 1988, p. 55). It also conformed to the Labour Party's policy of a stronger Federal Government (See Chapter 10).

To sum-up, it can once more be asserted that the change in the accounting policy framework through the merger of the A.S.R.B. and the Ac.S.B. was brought about to satisfy the major interests involved in accounting policy making. The policy was amended in a manner that the Board would serve the interests of the major interest groups, namely the accounting profession, the business sector, the bureaucrats and the politicians - possibly better than it served under the previous form. Also observable was, that the implementation of this change was considerably faster and smoother than the creation of the Board. The reason for that, as already identified, was that it satisfied all interested parties, both on the supply and the demand sides.

Appendix 1

Events and Crises Having Direct or Indirect Impact
on Australian Company Financial Disclosure Regulations

Year	Events and Crises
Mid 1850s	William Clay's campaign for "Limited Liability: paid-up capital: perfect publicity" in U.K. (Gibson 1971, p. 6).
1850's, 70's & 80's	Mining and real estate boom in Australia. (Daly, 1982, p. 173).
1880's	Speculation in real estate in Victoria (Gibson 1971, p. 39).
1890-92	Bankruptcies and company insolvencies in Victoria. Severe criticism of the parliamentarians by the public and the media regarding their involvement in the scandals and disasters and ignoring what was happening (Gibson 1971, p. 39).
1894	Liberal-protectionist Party sweeps into victory with promises of reform at the elections. Sir Isaac Isaacs, who entered politics with the objective of amending companies law, becomes Attorney-General of Victoria (Gibson 1971, pp. 39-41).
1900-7	The Victorian and English Companies Acts drift apart in terms of disclosure requirement (Gibson 1971, p. 48).

1910   Parliamentary Select Committee appointed in Victoria to review the Victorian Companies Act in the light of the amendments to English laws (Gibson 1971, pp. 48-49).

1920   Victorian Companies Act requires balance sheet and profit and loss account (Gibson 1971, p. 51).

1928   I.C.A.A. founded through the gradual merger of various accounting bodies and finally the receipt of the royal charter (Graham, 1978, p. 140).

1929   Biannual meeting of stock exchanges resolves to require audited balance sheets to be put before the annual general meeting (Gibson, 1971, p. 78).

1931-33   Continuing mining and land speculation and other business considerations result in a strong demand for stricter and uniform disclosure requirements in W.A., N.S.W. and Queensland (Gibson, 1971, p. 57).

1935   Concern regarding share options in the stock exchanges (Gibson, 1971, p. 79).

1936   Sir A. Fitzgerald, during the Australasian Congress on Accounting, suggested a joint standing committee of major accounting bodies to report upon the question of accounting terminology (Zeff, 1973, p. 29).

1937   Following a motion by Sir A. Fitzgerald the General Council of the Commonwealth Institute of Accountants (C.I.A.) decides that the Institute will issue opinions on general principles regarding professional practice of universal application. A committee appointed to look into the Institute's developmental matters later recommended the creation of committees on accounting principles and terminology (Zeff, 1973, p. 29).

1944   The General Council of the I.C.A.A. considers issuing formal guidance to members (Zeff, 1973, p. 2).

1945   The old guard within the General Council of the I.C.A.A. resist any pronouncement by the Institute and, if there has to be any pronouncement, they want the I.C.A.E.W. ones. Contrary to this attitude affirmative response was received from other quarters within the Institute (Zeff, 1973, pp. 2-3).

1947-48   Concern about non-compliance with the I.C.A.A. 1946 recommendation (Zeff, 1973, p. 4).

1949   Second Australian Congress of Accounting held. All areas of accountancy profession reviewed. Promulgation of authoritative standards of accounting and auditing, among other things, seen as a necessary condition of professional status. General acceptance expected from wide dissemination and discussion of proposed standards, self imposed discipline of accountants in following them and from voluntary acceptance. Compulsion, regimentation and legislative sanction were to follow general acceptance. Need for an organizational machinery for standard setting realized. Unanimous agreement that accounting provides historical record of stewardship based on historical cost. Therefore, it provides historical truth. Need for integration voiced (Birkett and Walker, 1971, pp. 98-101).

1950s   Confusion and public criticism of accounts and accountants. Profession accepts the responsibility to educate the public (Birkett and Walker, 1971, p. 104).

1950   C.I.A. undertakes to form a Joint Committee of Accountancy Bodies in Australia to which four bodies other than the I.C.A.A. join (Zeff, 1973, p. 32).

1950-54   Considerable demand for guidance on accounting principles from I.C.A.A. members and the demand for an institutional set-up for developing accounting principles from certain State councils and influential members (Zeff, 1973, p. 6 and Graham, 1978, p. 56).

1951-53   The General Council of the C.I.A., later the A.S.A. seeks ways of conducting accounting research and publicizing the results (Zeff, 1973, p.33).

1952   A.S.A. founded (Zeff, 1973, pp. 32-33).

1952-60   A.S.A. emerges as the largest accounting body through the merger of various institutes (Birkett and Walker, 1971, p. 101).

1955	The stock exchanges express concern over lack of data and urge a half yearly report for all listed companies (Gibson, 1971, p. 280).
1957	Survey by some South Australian I.C.A.A. members indicates many are critical of the failure of companies to comply with I.C.A.A. recommendations.
1957-58	Demand by various quarters of the I.C.A.A., for example the South Australian State Council and Sir A. Fitzgerald, for revising the 1946-48 recommendations (Zeff, 1973, p. 7).
1958	I.C.A.A. General Council resolves to revise the 1946-48 recommendations (Zeff, 1973, p. 7).
1959	Debate on whether Australia professional bodies should issue own principles or adopt those issued in U.K. (Zeff, 1973, p. 9).
1960	Credit Squeeze and financial crises (Dean, 1985).
1961	Sydney Guarantee collapses after attracting new subscriptions of over $1 million. Investors lose $8 million. Latec and Australian Motor Industry (AMI) also collapse along with other companies. A total of $30 million lost (Birkett and Walker, 1971, pp. 106-107).
1962	Reid Murray Group collapses 42 days after attracting debenture sales (Birkett and Walker, 1971, p. 107).

1962-63	The A.R.C. of the A.S.A. reassesses its programme of activity and reaffirms the view that it should conduct applied research to provide guidance on accounting principles (Zeff, 1973, p. 35 and p. 37).
1963	Six more companies collapse (Birkett and Walker, 1971, pp. 107-108).
1963	Directors, company accountants and auditors blamed by the financial press for fraud and misinformation. Academics, stock exchange officials and the press criticize accounting methods used. Profession responds by indicating that it is the doing of only one percent of the accountants (Birkett and Walker, 1971, pp. 108-109).
1963	Financial journalists critical of the profession for not recognizing its shortcomings (Birkett and Walker, 1971, p. 110).
1963-67	Inspectors Reports tabled (Dean, 1985). Reid Murray inspector highlights the need for "true and fair" disclosure to the debenture holder in addition to that to the share holders (Gibson 1971, p. 12). Accountants and auditors and their accounting principles and auditing practices are criticized (Birkett and Walker, 1971, p. 112).
1963	Criticism of the Institute and the profession generally in the Victorian Parliament for the absence of professional self regulation and threats for government legislation to register accountants (Birkett and Walker, 1971, p. 112).

1963   Committee on the Whole Future of the Accountancy
               Profession considers the suggestion by E.W.Savage
               for a standing committee on accounting principles
               (Zeff, 1973, p. 11).

1964   Company collapses continue. Neon Signs (A'asia)
               Ltd. declared insolvent, despite claims of profit by
               its directors (Birkett and Walker, 1971, p. 112).

1964   Majority of the participants in the I.C.A.A.
               conference believe that historical cost accounting is
               deficient (Birkett and Walker, 1971, p. 114).

1964   The I.C.A.A. General Council entrusts the task of
               proposing recommendations to a standing committee
               after realizing that the *ad hoc* approach with varying
               modus operandi was inadequate. Accounting
               Principles and Auditing Practice Committee
               appointed (Zeff, 1973, p. 11).

1964   The A.S.A. appoints a special committee to study the
               accounting implications of government inspectors'
               reports on company failures (Zeff, 1973, p.37).

1964-65   Interim reports of listed companies criticized in the
               financial press as misleading (Gibson, 1971, pp.
               282-82).

1965   H.G. Palmer (Consolidated) Ltd. placed in
               receivership. N.S.W. Registrar of Companies starts
               investigation on the company. N.S.W.
               Attorney-General shows concern and promises action
               if it is found that the financial position of the

company had been misrepresented at any time (Birkett and Walker, 1971, p. 116).

1965 Australian Shareholders Association created (Dean, 1985).

1965 I.C.A.A. hires public relations consultants to improve its image (Birkett and Walker, 1971, p. 114).

1965 I.C.A.A.'s Third Australian Congress held. Unease at recent company failures and inspectors' criticisms. Problems of consolidated statements and uncertainty of auditors duties and responsibilities discussed (Birkett and Walker, 1971, p. 115).

1965 H.G. Palmer (Consolidated) Ltd. put into receivership. Excessive valuations of assets, insufficient write-offs and falsification of prospectuses detected (Birkett and Walker, 1971, p. 116).

1965 Latec's inspector proposes statutory requirements for the disclosure of adequate information and explanation of accounts. He also suggests a requirement for a directors' statement as to the "true and fair view" (Birkett and Walker, 1971, pp. 116-117).

1965 Joint statement by the presidents of the I.C.A.A. and the A.S.A., at the creation of the A.R.F., that the major issue confronting the accountancy profession is the means by which accountancy principles are to be determined (Birkett and Walker, 1971, p. 118).

1966   The Accounting and Audit Research Committee of the A.R.F. recognizes the poor publicity received by the profession due to company failures and asserts that the profession must seek to improve the standing of the profession. Methods suggested by the Committee and its parent bodies, the A.S.A and the I.C.A.A. included higher educational qualifications for entry into the profession, such as university graduation, standards for accounting and auditing, disciplinary measures for the members, one national accountancy body with statutory backing (Birkett and Walker, 1971, p. 119).

1966   A.S.A. asks members to procure professional indemnity insurance (Birkett and Walker, 1971, p. 121).

1966   Neon Signs, Reid Murray and Second United Permanent Building Society inspectors criticize unresolved technical problems in accounting (Birkett and Walker, 1971, p. 121).

1966   Victorian Chamber of Manufacturers pointed out the overall decline of ethical standards in accounting (Birkett and Walker, 1971, p. 122).

1967   Victorian State President of the A.S.A. recognizes the connection between company failures and a few accountants, but overlooks the findings of inspectors that application of accounting principles produced misleading data (Birkett and Walker, 1971, p. 122).

1967   I.C.A.A. criticizes critics of the profession of being
                ill-qualified and ill-informed (Birkett and Walker,
                1971, p. 123).

1967   Mr. Ryan, N.S.W. Registrar of Companies critical of
                the "true and fair" criteria of reporting (Birkett and
                Walker, 1971, p. 124). He suggests that a statutory
                body be constituted under the Companies Act and
                authorized to make regulations as to the form and
                contents of accounts and as to the accounting
                principles to be applied in their preparation; such a
                body to be constituted of representatives of the legal,
                accountancy and secretarial professions and
                representatives of government, and that the
                regulations made by such a body should be subject
                to disallowance by Parliament in the same manner as
                other regulations made under the authority of an Act
                of Parliament (Ryan, 1967, p. 106).

1967   Investors of Stanhill, which collapsed in 1966, lose
                $48 million. Inspector's report indicates that
                investors were misinformed due to misleading profit
                figures (Birkett and Walker, 1971, p. 124).

1967   Auditing profession points out difficulties of
                preparing mid-year reports (Gibson, 1971, p. 283).

1967   Company Law Advisory Committee (Eggleston
                Committee) Established to review company law
                (Dean, 1985).

1968   Criticism of the professional practices in Australia in
                the Fifth Conference of Asian and Pacific

Accountants, but rejection of the idea of statutory development of accounting practices (Birkett and Walker, 1971, p. 125).

1968   A.R.F. research shows many respondents are critical of contemporary accounting practices (Birkett and Walker, 1971, p. 127).

1968   First interim report of the Eggleston Committee dealt with disclosure of information in accounts and reports of directors; powers duties and responsibilities of auditors; and a proposal for a Companies Commission (Dean, 1985). It also raised the issue of an Australian Companies Commission which, among other duties, would include the altering of statutory requirements for company accounts, group accounts and directors' report (Gibson, 1971, p. 302).

1969   Further company collapses (Birkett and Walker, 1971, pp. 129-30).

1969   Auditors of H.G. Palmer jailed. Chartered accountants guilty of professional negligence in the Pacific Acceptance Ltd. case (Birkett and Walker, 1971, p. 130).

1969   Second interim report of the Eggleston Committee dealt with nominee shareholdings and takeovers (Dean, 1985).

1969	Third interim report of the Eggleston Committee dealt with investigations under the Companies Act (Dean, 1985).
1969	Directors resist publication of profit trends as required by the stock exchanges in mid-year reports (Gibson, 1971, p. 283).
1969	Companies which failed as a result of the Speculative Mining Boom, which started in 1967, and were subject to criticism: Poseidon, Tasminex, Queensland Mines/Kathleen Investments and Antimony Nickel (Dean, 1985).
1970	A.S.A. and I.C.A.A. seek strengthening of minimum disclosure requirements of the Companies Act (Birkett and Walker, 1971, p. 134).
1970	Fourth interim report of the Eggleston Committee dealt with misuse of confidential information; dealing in options; disclosure by directors (Dean, 1985).
1970	Fifth interim report of the Eggleston Committee on the control of fund raising, share capital and debentures - prospectuses (Dean, 1985).
1970	Following criticisms of short selling and after "sharp" practices the Senate Select Committee on Securities and Exchange (Rae Committee) was appointed (Dean, 1985).

1971   First version of K1 opposed by influential quarters, like the Institute of Directors in Australia (Zeff, 1973, p. 23).

1971   Sixth interim report of the Eggleston Committee on share hawking (Dean, 1985).

1971   Money Market squeeze: Mineral Securities insolvency and JBL collapse (Dean, 1985).

1972   Seventh interim report of the Eggleston Committee on registration of charges (Dean, 1985).

1972   N.S.W. C.A.C. raises the possibility of approaching the Supreme Court in respect of conflicts between directors and auditors as to the appropriate accounting principles to apply in the preparation of accounts (Morley, 1979, p. 35).

1974   Mr. Ryan, now Commissioner of N.S.W. C.A.C., seemed in favour of a board with statutory support and wide community representation, capable of endorsing accounting standards (Ryan, 1974, p. 16).

1974   The Rae Committee tables report and recommends national legislation and regulation of companies and securities industry similar to the SEC in USA. It also drew attention to shortcomings in accounting standards and disclosure (Dean, 1985).

1974   Accounting profession fears possibility of legislative action in the event of failure to define standards and recognizes the need for reducing the wide range of acceptable alternatives in accounting (Editorial, The Chartered Accountant in Australia, 1974).

1974   Mainline failure. Cambridge Credit placed in receivership (Dean, 1985).

1975   Company law administrators in Victoria and ACT publicly expressed reservations in respect of Tax Effect Accounting (Dean, 1985).

1977   Mr. Frank Walker, Attorney-General N.S.W., approached by deputations of company directors and some accountants seeking to stop the introduction of C.C.A. He was critical of the fact that the accounting profession was entrusted with the power to make such a major economic decision without reference to the government and without input from the consumers of accounting services. He also proposed an Accounting Standards Tribunal (Peirson and Ramsay, 1983, p. 296).

1978   Mr. Frank Walker, Attorney-General N.S.W., links "white collar crime" with the lack of acceptable accounting standards and expresses the need for an Accounting Standards Review Committee (Kirby, 1980, pp. 517-18).

1980   The Savage Committee findings reveal the following areas of criticism about the profession:
              (1)   Adherence to an accounting standard found to be inappropriate to the particular case,
              (2)   Failure to observe an accounting standard,
              (3)   Deficiencies in an existing standard, and

(4)   Apparent lack of an appropriate standard (Vincent, 1981, p. 237).

1981   N.C.S.C. recommends to the Ministerial Council that an A.S.R.B. should be established (Peirson and Ramsay, 1983, p. 297).

1981   Australian Financial System, Final Report of the Committee of Enquiry (Campbell Committee Report) recommends:

(1)   I.C.A.A. and A.S.A. should continue to be responsible for the design and development of accounting standards.

(2)   An A.S.R.B. should be established with the responsibility of deciding on the adoption of accounting standards, having regard to the needs of the users; the N.C.S.C., the professional accounting bodies and other interested parties should be represented on the Board.

(3)   Accounting standards recommended by such a board should be given legislative support (Campbell Committee Report, 1981, p. 372).

Also recommended:

(1)   stock exchange listing requirements should include provision for quarterly reporting.

(2)   The requirements of such reports should be less onerous than for annual reports (Campbell Committee Report, 1981, p. 375).

1981   The N.S.W. Attorney-General, Mr. Frank Walker, indicates that the most appropriate form of regulation of the accounting profession may ultimately be a blend of self-regulation, community participation and government supervision - that is co-regulation (Walker, 1981, p. 24).

1982

The Ministerial Council accepts, in principle, the concept of an A.S.R.B. independent of the N.C.S.C. (Peirson and Ramsay, 1983, p. 297).

Feb. 1983

Accounting Profession supports N.C.S.C.'s proposal for the provision of legislative recognition of accounting standards through the A.S.R.B., but opposes the idea of recognition of proposed standards of sources other than the Profession. It stresses the contribution of other parties through the A.A.R.F. to ensure consistency with other standards and avoid duplication of cost and expertise (Prosser, 1983, p. 95).

Mar. 1983

N.S.W. C.A.C. and the N.C.S.C. jointly re-propose the form of the A.S.R.B.:
(1)   It shall have seven members.
(2)   Ministerial Council to select one member each from the A.S.A. and the I.C.A.A. and four members from panels of names submitted by the N.C.S.C. and other interested parties.
(3)   At least one member to represent the users.
(4)   The chairman and two other members to have technical competence (Peirson and Ramsay, 1983, p. 297).

Appendix 2

Supply of Accounting Regulations - Case Law
(Decisions and dicta of courts)

Year	Institutional Set-up and Requirements
1824	Baldwin v Lawrence 2 Sim and St 18: Unless the articles expressly provides it, no member as such has the right to inspect books of account (Ford, 1982, p. 404).
1828	N.S.W., Victoria, Queensland and Tasmania adopt English laws to date (Gibson, 1971, p. 24).
1829	Western Australia adopts English laws to date (Gibson, 1971, p. 24).
1836	South Australia adopts English laws to date (Gibson, 1971, p. 24).
1864	*Macdougall v. Jersey Imperial Hotel Co. Limited*: Dividends to be made out of clear profits and not from capital stock - the "capital maintenance" rule (French, 1977, p. 307).
1864-82	More cases confirming the "capital maintenance rule", but the meaning of capital was never clearly defined (French, 1977, p. 308).
1869-82	In a number of cases on capital maintenance it was established that if asset valuation was done fraudulently for the calculation and payment of dividends then the court could order the refund of

the dividends. No rule for asset valuation established (French, 1977, pp. 310-11.).

1877   Re *Ebbw Vale Steel, Iron and Coal Company*: The idea of making out a balance sheet to determine profit as surplus after recognizing liabilities to creditors and company members suggested (Gibson, 1971, p. 31).

1879   *Dent v. London Tramways Company*: If stipulated in the articles, depreciation is to be charged as an expense for profit calculation (French, 1977, p. 311).

1879   *Davison v. Gillies*: Depreciation is to be charged as expense for profit calculation, even if it is not mentioned to do so in the articles, provided it is necessary in the light of the commercial circumstances of the business (French, 1977, p. 311).

1885   *Moller v Spence* 4 SC 46 (South Africa): Director has the right to inspect books of account (Ford, 1982, p. 403).

1887   *Leeds Estate Building and Investment Society Ltd. v. Shephard*: The law is content to grant full recognition to accounting methods and procedures determined by the accounting profession (Dixon, 1979, p. 207). Care should be exercised by the directors while presenting annual reports. Reliance on the managers is not sufficient (Dixon, 1979, pp. 217-218). Auditor not to confine himself merely to the task of ascertaining the arithmetical accuracy of the balance sheet, but to see that it was a true and accurate representation of the companies affairs (Chambers, 1973, p. 26).

1889   *City of Glasgow Bank v. Mackinnon*: In order to ascertain profits earned and divisible at any time, the balance sheet must contain a fair statement of the liabilities of the company, including the paid up capital, and on the other hand, a fair or more properly bona fide valuation of assets - the balance, if in favour of the company, being profits (French, 1977, p. 309).

1889   *Lee v Neuchatel Asphalt Company*: A quarrying company allowed to omit charging depreciation on its mineral lease in calculating profits available for dividend. Principle that depreciation need not be charged on depreciable assets established. This was against the established practice of the profession (Morris, 1986, pp. 71-72).

1890   *Phillips v Melbourne and Castlemaine Soap and Candle Co.*: Followed the principle in *Lee v Neuchatel Asphalt Company* (Morris, 1986, p. 76).

1890   *Burn v London and South Wales Coal Co* 7 TLR 118: Unless the articles expressly provide it no member as such has the right to inspect books of account (Ford, 1982, p. 404).

1892   *Lubbock v. British Bank of South America*:
              There could be no objection to the distribution of
              surplus realized on fixed capital (fixed assets)
              (French, 1977, p. 324).

1894   *Verner v General and Commercial Investment
              Trust Company*: Extended *Lee v Neuchatel
              Asphalt Company* ruling (Morris, 1986, p. 78).
              Accounts must show the truth and not be misleading
              or fraudulent (Chambers, 1973, p. 26).

1895   *Re London and General Bank* Ltd.: A full and fair
              balance sheet must convey a truthful statement as to
              the companies position (Chambers, 1973, p. 26).

1896   *Kingston Cotton Mill Case*: Auditors can rely
              on a certificate from the appropriate company officer
              as evidence to substantiate the balance sheet figures
              for inventories (Gibson 1971, p. 147). Auditor is a
              "watch dog" not a "blood hound" (Mannix and
              Mannix 1982, p. 43 and 44).

1906   *Newton v. Birmingham Small Arms Co.*: The
              purpose of the balance sheet is to show that the
              financial position of the company is at least as good
              as stated and not to show that it is not or may be
              better (Ryan, 1967, p. 99).

1911   *Young v. Brownlee*: Follows the *dicta* in Newton
              v. Birmingham Small Arms Co. (Ryan, 1967, pp.
              99-100).

1918   *Ammonia Soda Company Limited v.Chamberlain*: Dividend can be paid out of circulating capital as long as there is a profit (French, 1977, p. 326).

1925   *Re City Equitable Fire Insurance Co. Ltd.*: Directors should be satisfied as to the value of the assets of the company before presenting their annual report and balance sheet. Reliance on the chairman is not sufficient (Dixon, 1979, p. 218).

1926   *Lothian Chemical Co. Ltd. v Rogers*: Where the ordinary principles of accounting are not invaded by the statute they must be allowed to prevail (Ryan, 1974, p. 14).

1931   *The Royal Mail Case*: Pointed out the uninformative nature of acceptable financial statements. Identified the need for a clear statement of current operating profits and the isolation of other extraordinary items. (Gibson 1971, p. 103) The accounting profession and the companies started showing an inclination towards "fullest practicable disclosure" (Edwards 1976, p. 302-303).

1939   *McKesson and Robbins Case*: The auditor to verify stock to his/her own satisfaction. No legal influence in Australia, but it did catch the attention of the Australian accounting profession (Gibson 1971, p. 150).

1940   *Dickson v FCT* 62 CLR 687 at 708, 711-2 and 726-7: There is a possibility that the market value of a company's shares may not reflect the current value of its fixed assets (Dixon, 1979, p. 207).

1949   *Re Press Caps Ltd* 1 All ER 1013: Historical cost method under fire. Balance sheet can effect valuations in takeovers. It fails to give an indication of the value of the company and its assets, at the time of accounts, it fails to present to shareholders or the public, information upon which they could act or benefit from (Mannix and Mannix, 1982, p. 33 and 34 and Chambers, 1973, pp. 133-34).

1953   *FCT v James Flood Pty. Ltd.* 5AITR 579: Although courts will refer to generally acceptable accounting principles, the High Court made it clear that it is the court which makes the final decision on the issues in dispute.

1960   *Westburn Sugar Refineries Limited v. Commissioner of Inland Revenue* (A Scottish case): Dividend <u>cannot</u> be paid out of capital surplus resulting from an appreciation in value of unrealized fixed assets (French, 1977, pp. 324-25).

1961   *Dimbula Valley (Ceylon) Tea Co. Limited v. Laurie* (An English Case): Dividend <u>can</u> be paid out of capital surplus resulting from an appreciation in value of unrealized fixed assets (French, 1977, p. 325 and Baxt, 1970).

1961   *Ostime v Duple Motor Bodies Ltd*: Accounting method should be chosen to suit the circumstances of a particular business. The method chosen must be applied consistently and should not be changed without proper reason (Mannix and Mannix, 1982, p. 32).

1961   *Downey v Prior* ALR 310: Director has the right to inspect books of account (Ford, 1982, p. 403).

1963   *Re Funerals of Distinction Pty Ltd.* NSWR 614: Ex-director does not have the right to inspect books of account (Ford, 1982, p. 403).

1967   *Re Grierson Oldham and Adams Ltd* 1 All ER 192: Historical cost method under fire. Balance sheet can effect valuations in takeovers. It fails to give an indication of the value of the company and its assets, at the time of accounts, it fails to present to shareholders or the public, information upon which they could act or benefit from (Mannix and Mannix, 1982, p. 33). Critical of the fact that figures in the balance sheet are not being put forward as the current value of the assets in question (Afterman and Baxt, 1979, p. 409).

1971-2 *Odeon Associated Theatres Ltd. v. Jones*: Courts to adopt established commercial accountancy practice provided it is not contrary to any statute and the courts will decide upon the best established practice. (Ryan, 1974, pp. 14-15).

1973   *Haw Par Bros (Pte) Ltd v Dato Aw Kow* 2 MLJ 169: Director's agent cannot authorize inspection of books of account after director ceases to be a director (Ford, 1982, p. 403).

Appendix 3

Supply of Accounting Regulations - Accounting Requirements Prescribed by the Legislature

Year	Institutional Set-up and Requirements
1856-62	All Colonies in Australia except South Australia adopt English companies legislation (Morris, 1984, p. 56).
1863	Queensland Companies Act: Presentation of directors' report, balance sheet and profit and loss account optional. Accounting and auditing requirements to be determined by individual companies and laid down in the articles of the respective companies (Gibson, 1979, p. 24).
1864	Victoria Companies Statute and South Australia Companies Act: Presentation of directors' report, balance sheet and profit and loss account optional. Accounting and auditing requirements to be determined by individual companies and laid down in the articles of the respective companies (Gibson, 1979, p. 24).
1874	N.S.W. Companies Act: Presentation of directors' report, balance sheet and profit and loss account optional. Accounting and auditing requirements to be determined by individual companies and laid down in the articles of the respective companies (Gibson, 1979, p. 24).

1893   Western Australia Companies Act: Presentation of
               directors' report, balance sheet and profit and loss
               account   optional.   Accounting   and   auditing
               requirements to be determined by individual
               companies and laid down in the articles of the
               respective companies (Gibson, 1979, p. 24).

1896   Victorian Companies Act based on the U.K. Davey
               Committee Inquiry into Company Law in 1895 -
               balance sheet and audit required. Concept of
               proprietary company introduced to allow limited
               liability without disclosure, with limitations on share
               transactions (Gibson, 1971, p. 41).

1920   Tasmania Companies Act: Presentation of directors'
               report, balance sheet and profit and loss account
               optional. Accounting and auditing requirements to be
               determined by individual companies and laid down
               in the articles of the respective companies (Gibson,
               1979, p. 24).

1920-43   Companies Acts' disclosure requirements (including
               the proprietary company requirements) in other states
               brought in line with the Victorian Act of 1896
               (Gibson, 1971, p. 57). Statutory recognition of the
               balance sheet as an important document for financial
               reporting (Gibson, 1971, p. 65).

1931/6   Catch up legislation in Queensland, South Australia
               and New South Wales - based largely on 1928/9
               English developments including English Companies
               Act 1929. Required directors' report, balance sheet

classifying fixed and floating assets and profit and loss account (Miller, 1978, p. 95).

1936   N.S.W. Legislation requires disclosure of investment in subsidiaries (Whittred, 1986, p. 107).

1938   Victorian Companies Act: Demands more adequate profit and loss details and group consolidated statements or separate statements for each company in a group (Miller, 1978, p. 95 and Whittred, 1986, p. 107).

1943   Western Australian Companies Act: Requires Profit and loss details and balance sheet. Holding companies to submit consolidated statements or statements of all subsidiaries (Gibson, 1979, p. 26).

1955   Victorian Companies Act: "true and fair" disclosure requirement introduced (N.C.S.C. Release 405, 1982).

1956   Tasmania Companies Act : Requires Profit and loss details and balance sheet. Holding companies to submit consolidated statements or statements of all subsidiaries (Gibson, 1979, p. 26).

1958/9   Acts in Victoria and Tasmania to extend and upgrade disclosure (Miller, 1978, p. 95).

1961/3   Uniform legislation in all states: Requires Profit and loss details and balance sheet. Holding companies to submit consolidated statements or statements of all subsidiaries (Gibson, 1979, p. 26 and Miller, 1978, p. 95).

1961   Power of Companies Registrar enhanced by adding investigative powers to the existing power of simply receiving and filing certain documents and providing public access to them (Morley, 1979, p. 35).

1963/4   The Companies (Public Borrowings) Act passed to protect the public in respect of borrowing and guarantor corporations - required greater disclosure to trustee for debenture holders and the public including half-yearly balance sheet and profit and loss account (Miller, 1978, p. 95).

1965   Section 74 added to the Companies (Public Borrowings) Act requiring the following from the borrowing companies (Dean, 1985):
             (i)   specification of duties and responsibilities of the trustees.
             (ii)   provision of quarterly reports to the trustees.
             (iii) provision of mid-year and annual audited reports.
             (iv)   increased amount of disclosure.

1969   Corporate Finance and Accounting Division established in the office of the N.S.W. Registrar of Companies and entrusted with the task of administering and developing the protection afforded by the disclosure provisions of the Companies Act (Morley, 1979, p. 35).

1970   N.S.W. Securities Industry Act passed providing for
            a Commissioner for Corporate Affairs and the
            establishment of a C.A.C. (Morley, 1979, p. 35).

1971   National Accounts Sub-Committee set up for
            consultation on accounting matters between States
            (Morley, 1979, p. 35).

1971/3   Extensive revision of State Companies Acts on the
            advice of Eggleston Committee and amendments to
            the Acts in respect of current assets valuation (Dean,
            1985).

1972   Corporate Affairs Advisory Committee set up to
            facilitate regular consultation with those affected by
            the legislation and its administration (Morley, 1979,
            p. 35).

1974   Analysis check by N.S.W. C.A.C. to determine, for
            example, whether a company may have difficulty in
            meeting its liabilities or whether the accounts are
            misleading by reason of an overstatement of the
            book value of assets. Under this programme Marra
            Developments profit figure was challenged by the
            N.S.W. C.A.C. for including preacquisition profits of
            a subsidiary as a group profit. This was in spite of
            the auditors opinion that the accounts were true and
            fair (Morley, 1979, p. 35).

1974   Interstate Corporate Affairs Commission (I.C.A.C.)
            created between N.S.W., Victoria and Queensland
            (Dean, 1985), to bring about greater uniformity in
            the relevant legislation and its administration, and to

eliminate multiple registration and lodgment in member states. Also the National Accounts Sub-committee replaced by an I.C.A.C. Accounts Sub-committee (Morley, 1979, p. 35).

1974   National Companies and Securities Industry Bill introduced by Labour Government (Dean, 1985).

1975   Standards check (checking compliance with accounting standards) added to the disclosure and analysis checks (Morley, 1979, p. 35).

1975   Securities Industries Acts passed - N.S.W., Victoria, Queensland, W.A. (Dean, 1985).

1975   W.A. joins I.C.A.C. (Dean, 1985).

1976   N.S.W. C.A.C. adopts policy that non-compliance with professional accounting standards was prima facie evidence that the accounts may not show a true and fair view (Morley, 1979, p. 36).

1976   Cooperative Scheme announced by the Joint Standing Committee of Attorneys General (Dean, 1985).

1978   The Co-operative Scheme for Companies and Securities established (Campbell Committee Report, 1981, p. 364).

1979   The N.C.S.C. Act passed (Dean, 1985).

1980   The N.C.S.C. established (Dean, 1985).

1981   Commonwealth Companies Act for adoption by all
               states under the Co-operative Scheme. Accounts
               provisions relegated to Regulation and Principal
               Accounting Officer provision deleted (Dean, 1985).

1983   Amendments made to the Companies Act 1981 for
               the statutory recognition of accounting standards
               approved by the A.S.R.B. (Companies and Securities
               (Interpretation and Miscellaneous Provisions) Code
               1983).

1984   A.S.R.B. created (Companies and Securities
               (Interpretation and Miscellaneous Provisions) Code
               1983).

1984-Jun '87
               Eleven accounting standards approved (A.S.R.B.
               Annual Report 1986-87).

Appendix 4

Supply of Accounting Regulations - Stock Exchange Requirements for Financial Disclosure

Year	Institutional Set-up and Requirements
1904	Companies seeking to list on the Sydney Stock Exchange agree to supply to the exchange their balance sheet and material information like dividends, alteration of capital, etc. (Morris, 1984, p.62).
1912	Requirement of audit by professional accountants in active practice introduced. Profit and loss statement encouraged (Morris, 1984, p.62).
1922	Recommendation for separation of tangible and intangible assets on company balance sheets (Morris, 1984, pp.62-63).
1923	Requirements enhanced to include directors report on the state and conditions of the company dividends proposed and intended appropriation to reserve fund (Morris, 1984, p.63).
1925	Sydney and Melbourne Stock Exchanges require profit and loss account to accompany balance sheet. Requirement for the supply of the balance sheet and profit and loss accounts of subsidiary companies (Morris, 1984, p.63 and Gibson, 1971, p. 75).
1925	Requirement in Victoria and Tasmania to disclose balance sheet of the holding company (Gibson, 1979,

p. 27). Victoria requires provisions for appointment of auditors (Gibson, 1971, p. 75).

1927   Sydney and Melbourne Stock Exchanges modify requirements to permit parent company to submit consolidated balance sheets and profit and loss accounts (Morris, 1984, p. 63).

1927   Melbourne exchange requires separation of tangible and intangible assets in the balance sheet. Recommends the publication of associate company accounts (Gibson, 1971, pp. 78-79).

1929   Qualified audit reports to be disclosed to shareholders and filed with the stock exchange (Morris, 1984, p. 63).

1930   Melbourne Stock Exchange requires audited balance sheet to be presented in an annual general meeting (Gibson, 1971, pp. 78-79).

1931   Sydney requires separate subsidiary accounts or aggregation of subsidiary accounts (Whittred, 1986, p. 107).

1936   Exchanges require disclosure of stock options as footnote to the balance sheet. Also require disclosure of directors' remuneration (Gibson, 1971, p. 79).

1937   A.A.S.E. formed (Gibson, 1971, p. 74).

1939   A.A.S.E. resolution for half yearly reports for new listing (Gibson, 1971, p. 81). Companies with new issues required by the stock exchanges to provide a general report after the first six months of operations (Gibson 1971, p. 280).

1941   Sydney and Melbourne Stock Exchanges separate subsidiary accounts or consolidated accounts (Whittred, 1986, p. 107).

1946   Companies applying to list in Sydney and Melbourne Stock Exchanges required to enter into a "form of agreement" to abide by the Stock Exchanges' Official List Requirements. This "form of agreement was amended in 1954 to include a dragnet clause aimed at making future amendments to the listing requirements retrospective (Gibson, 1971, p. 81 and Whittred, 1986, p. 106).

1949   Sydney Stock Exchange listing requirement for balance sheet and profit and loss accounts after every fifteen months and for a directors report on dividend payment. The exchange recommends that the companies follow the preparation practice set by leading banking and industrial companies (Sub-section E 31-33 of the Sydney Stock Exchange Official List Requirements 1949).

1952   New listing requirements for Sydney Stock Exchange, but financial disclosure requirements remain unchanged (Sydney Stock Exchange Official List Requirements 1952).

1954   Listing requirements issued under the imprimatur of the A.A.S.E.. Required amongst other things: (1) consolidated accounts and (2) income tax provisions. (Dean, 1985; and Gibson, 1971, p. 81)

1955	Mid year sales figures of current and previous years and any other information affecting the companies earning capacity to be disclosed in the half-year directors' report (Gibson 1971, p. 281).

1964	Stock exchanges require the disclosure of the relationship between the company and its corporate group, if any (Gibson 1971, p. 281).

1964　　　　Exchanges require information from borrowing companies. For example:

(1) Give the exchanges any reports required by the Public Borrowings Acts.

(2) Explaining the reason where a provision for taxation differs by more than 15% from the prima facie amount payable on the declared profit.

(3) Identification of subsidiaries which have incurred a loss and the amount of loss (Gibson, 1971, p. 85).

1965	A.A.S.E. requires a descriptive or quantitative statement of trend of sales and profitability in the mid-year reports (Gibson 1971, p. 284).

1967	A.A.S.E. recommends inclusion of a statement of relationship between the current years profitability and sales with that of the previous year. Mid year report to be filed within three months of the end of the first six months of the year (Gibson 1971, p. 283).

1968	A.A.S.E. requires a quantitative statement of trend of sales and profitability in the mid-year reports (Gibson 1971, p. 284).
1974	A.A.S.E. listing requirements, require mid year profit statements, and annual audited reports according to the Companies Act (Sub-sections 3B and C of the listing requirements). Also requires disclosure of loans to directors (Dean, 1985).
1974	A.A.S.E. recommends that published accounts are to be prepared in conformity with the Recommendations and Statements of Accountancy Practice issued by the I.C.A.A. and the A.S.A. Non-compliance should be disclosed by the directors with proper explanations. Turnover to be disclosed (Dean, 1985; and Balmford, 1974, pp. 6-7).
1979	Complete revision of A.A.S.E. requirements: If during a takeover it is announced that assets have a value in excess of book value, then it is required to (a) have an independent valuers opinion on the revalued amounts, or (b) provide a statement by two directors on the value of the assets, and also to disclose the tax effect of the revaluation (Dean, 1985).
1980	Securities Industries Act passed by the Commonwealth Parliament providing for the establishment and control of stock exchanges by the Ministerial Council for Companies and Securities or other Government agencies delegated to do so, like the N.C.S.C. Sub-section 42(1) of this Act made

. compliance with the A.A.S.E. listing rules mandatory (Securities Industries Act 1980).

1980   A.A.S.E. relax provisions in respect of debentures trust deeds re guaranteeing subsidiaries (Dean, 1985).

1985 (August 1)

A.A.S.E. requires half yearly consolidated profit and loss and dividend statements; audited consolidated reports according to the Companies Act with additional information like turnover, contingent liabilities etc.; and funds statements (A.A.S.E. Listing Requirements 1985).

Appendix 5

Supply of Accounting Regulations - Professional Accounting Bodies Institutional Set-up and Requirements

Year	Institutional Set-up and Requirements
1938	The Commonwealth Institute of Accountants (C.I.A.) appoints a Committee on Accounting Principles (C.A.P.) and a Committee on Accounting Terminology (C.A.T.) (Zeff, 1973, p. 29)
1940	The C.I.A. General Council publishes a statement on cash discounts (Zeff, 1973, pp. 29-30).
1944	First technical committee formed by the I.C.A.A. (Graham, 1978, p. 56).
1946	Recommendations based on I.C.A.E.W. recommendations of 1942-44, on the following aspects issued by the I.C.A.A.:

- Form of balance sheet and profit and loss accounts.
- Treatment of taxation in accounts.
- Inclusion in accounts of proposed profit appropriations.
- Reserves and provisions.
- Disclosing the financial position and results of subsidiary companies in the accounts of holding companies.
- Depreciation of fixed assets.

Emphasis placed on specification of items in

Emphasis placed on specification of items in statements, classification of items and the standardization of terms. Therefore they dealt mainly with the form of the statements (Zeff, 1973, pp. 3-4 and Graham, 1978, p. 56).

1946-7   C.A.P. of C.I.A. reviews the I.C.A.E.W. and I.C.A.A. pronouncements and prepares various draft pronouncements, none of which is approved by the C.I.A. General Council (Zeff, 1973, pp. 31-32).

1948   I.C.A.A. issues its seventh recommendation, that on valuation of stock-in-trade (Zeff, 1973, p. 4).

1948   I.C.A.A. sets up a Research Co-ordination Committee for the purpose of guiding and assisting the work of the Research Society in the various states (Zeff, 1973, p. 5).

1948   C.A.P. and C.A.T. of C.I.A. replaced by an Accounting Research Committee (A.R.C.) to coordinate the activities of the State Research Committees (Zeff, 1973, p. 32).

1953   A.S.A. publishes interim research report on "Accounting Terminology" (Birkett and Walker, 1971, p. 102).

1954   A.S.A. appoints full-time research officer (Birkett and Walker, 1971, p. 102). [1955 as per Zeff, 1973, p. 32].

1956 A.S.A. begins producing "Statements on Accounting Practice" and "Technical Bulletin" in line with the "practice notes" of The Society of Incorporated Accountants of U.K. Its purpose is to bring about uniformity and consistency in accounting practice and develop generally accepted accounting standards (Zeff, 1973, p. 33 and Birkett and Walker, 1971, p. 102).

1956 The Research Co-ordination Committee dissolved by the I.C.A.A. and the Australian Chartered Accountants Research and Service Foundation (A.C.A.R.S.F.) created (Zeff, 1973, p. 6 and Graham, 1978, p. 57).

1956-65 A.S.A. issued nine "Statements on Accounting Practice" but none of these were submitted to the General Council for approval (Zeff, 1973, p. 35 and Birkett and Walker, 1971, p. 117).

1957-63 Seven technical bulletins published by the A.C.A.R.S.F. (Graham, 1978, p. 57).

1963-4 I.C.A.A. approves three recommendations, one each on the presentation of balance sheet and profit and loss account, the treatment of stock-in-trade and work-in-progress, and accountants' reports for prospectuses. The first two replaced four of those issued in 1946-48 (Zeff, 1973, p. 9).

1964 Committee on Accounting Principles and Audit Practice (C.A.P.A.P.) formed by the I.C.A.A. (Graham, 1978, p. 57).

| 1964 | Idea of a joint Accounting Research Foundation (A.R.F.) of the A.S.A. and the I.C.A.A. discussed by the two bodies (Graham, 1978, p. 61). |

| 1964 | I.C.A.A. issues "Recommendations on Accounting Principles" based on I.C.A.E.W. recommendations of 1958-60 (Birkett and Walker, 1971, p. 110). |

| 1964 | A.S.A. sets up committee to study the findings of company investigators (Birkett and Walker, 1971, p. 118). |

| 1965 | I.C.A.A. publishes "Statement on Accounting Principles and Recommendations on Accounting Practice" (Graham, 1978, p. 58). |

| 1965 | A.R.F. approved by the two accountancy bodies and the terms of the joint undertaking published in their professional journals (Zeff, 1973, p. 43). |

| 1965-8 | A.S.A. publishes four Technical Bulletins (Zeff, 1973, pp. 35-36). |

| 1966 | A.R.C. of the A.S.A. renamed Research and Technical Committee to promote applied research as opposed to basic research (Zeff, 1973, p. 35). |

| 1966 | A.S.A. publishes "Accounting Principles and Practices Discussed in Reports on Company Failures" (Birkett and Walker, 1971, p. 118). Professional deficiencies recognized (Dean, 1985): |

a.   The formulation, promulgation and regular review of accounting principles.

b.   Adherence to accounting principles by members.

c.   Audit of accounts.

d.   Relationship between management and accountant.

e.   Adequacy of the form and content of published financial statements.

1966   A.R.F. incorporated (Graham, 1978, p. 61).

1966   The General Council of the I.C.A.A. appointed a Development and Planning Committee to make a comprehensive review of the Institute's committee structure and mode of operation (Zeff, 1973, p. 12).

1967   A.S.A. issues its first General Council approved authoritative pronouncement (Zeff, 1973, p. 38).

1967   C.A.P.A.P. disbanded after an unproductive life (Graham, 1978, p. 58).

1967   A Research and a Technical Committee formed by the I.C.A.A., which produced two exposure drafts, one each in accounting and auditing (Graham, 1978, p. 58).

1967-8   I.C.A.A. issues pronouncements on auditors qualifications and group accounts (Graham, 1978, p. 58).

1968   A.R.F. conducts survey to discover what is wrong
             with financial statements. Profession does not
             respond to the results (Birkett and Walker, 1971, p.
             127).

1968   Discussion for merger of A.S.A. and I.C.A.A. starts
             (Birkett and Walker, 1971, p. 127).

1968-71   A.S.A. Research and Technical Committee issues a
             number of exposure drafts none of which take the
             shape of authoritative pronouncements (Zeff, 1973,
             pp. 39-40).

1969   The Research and Technical Committees of the
             I.C.A.A. replaced by the Accounting Principles
             Committee (A.P.C.) of the I.C.A.A. (Zeff, 1973, p.
             16 and Graham, 1978, p. 58).

1969   A.R.F. reconstituted in the light of its poor
             performance and to meet the needs of both the
             I.C.A.A. and the A.S.A. (Graham, 1978, p. 62).

1969   A.S.A. and I.C.A.A. integration move fails. A.S.A.
             members accept, but I.C.A.A. members reject the
             merger proposal (Zeff, 1973, p. 20 and Birkett and
             Walker, 1971, p. 127).

1969-70   Five draft statements issued by the A.P.C. of the
             I.C.A.A. and approved by the General Council of the
             I.C.A.A. (Graham, 1978, p. 58).

1970   A.R.F. publishes "A Statement of Australian
             Accounting Principles" (Zeff, 1973, p. 46).

1970	A.C.A.R.S.F. liquidated (Graham, 1978, p. 57).
1970-3	Four standards jointly issued/endorsed by the A.S.A. and the I.C.A.A. (Balmford, 1974, p. 5).
1971	The title of I.C.A.A. pronouncements changed from "Statements of Accounting Principles and Recommendations on Accounting Practice" to "Statements on Accounting Practice". This is similar to the change from "recommendations" to "Statements of Standard Accounting Practice" made by the I.C.A.E.W. in 1969 (Zeff, 1973, pp. 19-20).
1971	Statement K1. Conformity by members with Accounting Standards published by the I.C.A.A. introducing the idea of compulsory standards rather than optional recommendations or principles (Dean, 1985).
1971	A.S.A. Research and Technical Committee renamed as Accounting Principles Committee (A.P.C.) (Zeff, 1973, p. 40).
1972	I.C.A.A. revises K 1 and issues a modified and softened version. I.C.A.A. clarifies that the pronouncement was educational and not disciplinary in nature. It was made clear that the obligation of the members was to report significant departures from I.C.A.A. accounting standards in the company accounts and directors' reports (Zeff, 1973, p. 23).
1972	I.C.A.A. forms the Audit Practice Committee and relieves the A.S.C. of its auditing responsibilities (Zeff, 1973, p. 22).

1972 I.C.A.A.'s A.P.C.'s name changed to Accounting Standards Committee (A.S.C.) (Graham, 1978, p. 59).

1972 A.S.A. formally accepts two I.C.A.A. statements as "general guidelines" (Zeff, 1973, p. 40).

1972 The Australian Accounting Standards Committee (A.A.S.C.), a joint A.S.A./I.C.A.A. body under the A.R.F. created. DS series of accounting standards commenced (Dean, 1985).

1972 Statement K1 revised to allow non-compliance, provided it is disclosed. The financial effects of those departures should also be estimated and disclosed. Any non-disclosure of estimates should be explained (Gibson, 1979, p. 31).

1972 A.R.F. publishes a comprehensive examination of accounting practices and financial disclosure of Australian companies called "Australian Financial Reporting" (Zeff, 1973, p. 46).

1972 A.R.F. publishes the "Objectives and Concepts of Financial Statements" based on a study of users informational needs and their implications for the valuation of assets and determination of profits (Zeff, 1973, p. 47).

1973 A.S.A. publishes "Forging Accounting Principles in Australia" prepared by Zeff and advocating the merger of A.S.A. and I.C.A.A. (Balmford, 1977, p. 547).

1973   A.S.A. publishes Statement 300 the equivalent of statement K1 of the I.C.A.A. (Balmford, 1974, p. 5).

1974   A.S.C. of the I.C.A.A. merged into the A.A.S.C. (Graham, 1978, p. 59).

1974   Joint Standing Committee of the A.S.A. and the I.C.A.A. formed (Balmford, 1974, p. 6).

1974-6   C.C.A. provisional standard prepared and issued (Graham, 1978, p. 59).

1974-83   Nine accounting standards produced jointly by the A.S.A. and the I.C.A.A. (Peirson and Ramsay, 1983, p. 289).

1976   Statements K1 and 300 reissued jointly by the A.S.A. and the I.C.A.A. (Balmford, 1977, p. 547).

1976   Accounting Standards Review Committee set up by the A.S.A. and the I.C.A.A. to review problem areas like standard on company income tax (Balmford, 1977, p. 548).

1976   N.S.W. C.A.C. survey reveals significant non-compliance by companies with professional accounting standards (Morley, 1979).

1978   Accounting Standards Review Committee (Chambers Committee) appointed by the N.S.W. Government, which reported in November (Dean, 1985).

1978   Amended provisional C.C.A. standard issued (Miller, 1978, p. 100).

1979   I.C.A.A. and A.S.A. codify statements, re-titled as Australian Accounting Standards (A.A.S.) (Dean, 1985).

1980   Proposals for A.S.A./I.C.A.A. integration (Dean, 1985).

1982   Integration proposals rejected (Dean, 1985).

REFERENCES

Abdel-khalik, A.R., R.B. Thompson and R.E. Taylor, "The Impact of Reporting Leases off the Balance Sheet on Bond Risk Premiums: Two Exploratory Studies", Economic Consequences of Financial Accounting Standards - Selected Papers, F.A.S.B., July 1978.

Abrams, B.A. and Russell F. Settle, "The Economic Theory of Regulation and Public Financing of Presidential Elections", Journal of Political Economy, 1978.

Accounting Standards Committee (U.K.), Setting Accounting Standards: A Consultative Document, 1978.

Accounting Standards Review Board, Criteria for the Evaluation of Accounting Standards, A.S.R.B. Release 100, February, 1985.

_____, Evaluation of Accounting Standards, A.S.R.B. Release 101, December, 1985.

_____, Procedures for the Approval of Accounting Standards, A.S.R.B. Release 200, February, 1985.

_____, Statutory Requirements for Approved Accounting Standards, A.S.R.B. Release 201, June 1985.

_____, A.S.R.B. Annual Report for the Period 1 January to 30 June 1984.

_____, A.S.R.B. Annual Report 1984-85, A.S.R.B. Release 301, November, 1985.

_____, A.S.R.B. Annual Report 1985-86, A.S.R.B. Release 302, October, 1986.

_____, Public Comment Invited on Accounting Standards Criteria, A.S.R.B. Release 400, February, 1984.

_____, Media Release 86/9, December 1, 1986.

Afterman, A. and R. Baxt, Cases and Materials on Corporations and Associations, Butterworths, Sydney, 1979.

American Accounting Association, Statement of Accounting Theory and Theory Acceptance, 1977.

American Institute of Certified Public Accountants, Establishing Financial Accounting Standards (Report of the Study on the Establishment of Accounting Principles), March 1972.

_____ (A.I.C.P.A.), A.I.C.P.A. Professional Standards, Vol. b, as at June 1, 1984.

Aranya, N., "The Influence of Pressure Groups on Financial Statements in Britain", Abacus, June, 1974.

Ashton, R.K., U.K. Financial Accounting Standards: A Descriptive and Analytical Approach, Woodhead - Faulkner Limited, Cambridge, 1983.

_____, "The Royal Mail Case: A Legal Analysis", Abacus, March 1986.

Arrow, K., Social Choice and Individual Values, John Wiley and Sons, N.Y., 1963.

"Auditor's Report - Approved Accounting Standards", The The Australian, "Single body urged to set company report standards", September 22, 1987.

The Australian Accountant, "New Accountancy Research Structure Announced" April, 1974.

_____, "Australian Accounting Profession Joint Submission, 31 March, 1982", June, 1982.

_____, March, 1984.

_____, "A.A.R.F. Submission of Accounting Standards to the Accounting Standards Review Board", January/February, 1985.

_____, "Corporate Regulation", September, 1988.

Australian Accounting Profession, "Submission on The Corporations and Securities Industry Bill 1974", The Chartered Accountant in Australia, May, 1975.

_____, Submission of the Australian Accountancy Profession to the N.C.S.C. Commenting on the N.C.S.C.'s Media Release 21/1981 of 29 November 1981 Recommending the Establishment of an A.S.R.B., 31 March 1982.

_____, Joint Submission to the N.C.S.C. regarding Company Acts and Codes Accounts and Group Accounts of Companies, 16, August 1982.

_____, Proposal for the Formation of a National Standard-Setting Body, March 15, 1988.

Australian Associated Stock Exchanges, Official Listing Requirements, 1974.

_____, The Role and Functions of the Australian Stock Exchanges, A submission to the Trade Practices Commission, November, 1981.

_____, Official Listing Requirements, 1 August, 1985.

Australian Business, "New standards cause confusion, even experts disagree on applications", July 22, 1987 p. 25.

_____, "A.S.R.B. Changes", February 3, 1988.

_____, "Not so fast setting standards", February 10, 1988.

_____, "A merger not made in haven", November 9, 1988.

Australian Financial Review, "Accountants Called to Account", August 3, 1977.

_____, "Reform becomes white collar anarchy", August 4, 1977.

"Standards review board proposed", November 11, 1981.

_____, "Accounting standards move criticised", November 16, 1981.

_____, "Moore slams 'appalling' accounting standards", February 10, 1982.

_____, "'Appalling accountancy' claim rejected by profession", February 12, 1982.

_____, "Accountants set to battle N.C.S.C.", April 14, 1982.

_____, "Accountants oppose Govt hand in proposed standards review", May 17, 1982.

_____, "Accountants hit back against Govt controls", October 5, 1982.

_____, "Accounting watchdog's fate in balance", November 17, 1982.

_____, "Account rendered to the profession", November 24, 1982.

_____, "Accounting standards face a shake-up", November 29, 1982.

_____, "Accountants' balancing act on review board", November 30, 1982.

_____, "Giving an account of themselves", November 30, 1982.

_____, "N.C.S.C. casts a wider net for accounting standards review", December 7, 1982.

_____, "Division on standards plan for accounting", March 25, 1983.

_____, "Paper on financial reporting confusing, says firm", July 28, 1983.

_____, "Sweeping Changes to Company Law", October 6, 1983.

_____, "Institute president criticises N.C.S.C. disclosure proposals", October 14, 1983.

_____, "'Tighten reform' - Opposition", November 2, 1983.

_____, "A.S.R.B. functions threatened by N.C.S.C. official's proposal", November 24, 1983.

_____, "N.C.S.C. outlines accountants' obligations", April 5, 1984.

_____, "Slim chance of new form being adopted by N.C.S.C.", May 10, 1984.

_____, "A.S.R.B. Looks at Company Reports", May 17, 1984.

_____, "A Correction for Creative Accountants", May 15, 1985.

_____, "N.C.S.C. and accountants agree on method to enshrine professional standards in law", December 10, 1985.

_____, "Top companies ignore goodwill treatment standard", January 14, 1987.

_____, "Dissension still rules on a forex accounts standard", March 5, 1987.

_____, "A.S.R.B. adds sweetener to proposed forex standard", April 7, 1987.

_____, "N.C.S.C. to administer first public rebuke over adherence to standards", April 21, 1987.

_____, "N.C.S.C. plans accounting crackdown", May 15, 1987.

_____, "N.C.S.C., profession clash over equity accounting", June 5, 1987.

_____, "Merger likely of accounting boards", September 6, 1988.

_____, "Go-ahead for merger of accounting boards", September 23, 1988.

_____, "Government 'should not set accounting standards'", September 29, 1988.

Australian Financial System, Final Report of the Committee of Inquiry, Australian Government Publishing Services, Canberra, September 1981.

Australian Industries Development Association (A.I.D.A.), "Accounting Standards Review - the N.C.S.C. Scheme", A.I.D.A. Bulletin, May, 1982.

Australian Institute of Management N.S.W. Limited (A.I.M.), Annual Report Award Handbook and Report of the Adjudicators, 1965.

_____, 1983.

_____, 1984.

_____, 1985.

_____, 1986.

_____, 1987.

Australian Society of Accountants, "Letter to the Executive Director, N.C.S.C.", (Unpublished), June 9, 1980.

_____, The Institute of Chartered Accountants in Australia, "Letter to the Chairman, N.C.S.C.", (Unpublished), August 4, 1980.

_____, "The Role of the A.S.R.B. in the Standard-Setting Process", Accounting Communique', Number 6, 1988.

Bailey, P.H., "The Political Factor in Administrative Change", Australian Journal of Public Administration, March, 1976.

Balmford, J.D., "Accounting Standards", The Chartered Accountant in Australia, June, 1974.

_____, "Accounting Standards - Developments and Prospects Since 1972", The Australian Accountant, October, 1977.

Barber, W.J., A History of Economic Thought, Penguin Books, England, 1967.

Basu, S. and Milburn, J.A. (Editors), Research to Support Standard Setting In Financial Accounting: A Canadian Perspective, Clarkson Gordon Foundation, Toronto, Ontario, 1981.

Baxt, R., "True and Fair Accounts - A Legal Anachronism", The Australian Law Journal, November 30, 1970.

Baxt, R. (Ed.), "The Campbell Report - a blueprint for the future or destined for the scrap heap?", The Chartered Accountant in Australia, March, 1982.

Baxter, W.T., and S. Davidson, Studies in Accounting, I.C.A.E.W., 1977.

Beaver, W.A., Financial Reporting: An Accounting Revolution, Prentice-Hall, Englewood Cliffs, N.J., 1981.

Becker, G., 'Comment', The Journal of Law and Economics, 1976.

Belkaoui, A., Accounting Theory, Harcourt Brace Jovanovich, San Diego, 1985.

Bell, P. W., "Accounting as a Discipline for Study and Practice: What Content? ... In Whose Interest", <u>Accounting Association of Australia and New Zealand Conference Papers</u>, Canberra, August 29, 1988.

Benson, H., "The Professions and the Community", <u>The Australian Accountant</u>, May, 1981.

Benston, G.J., "Required Disclosure and the Stock Market: An Evaluation of the Securities Exchange Act of 1934", <u>The American Economic Review</u>, March 1973.

_____, <u>Corporate Financial Disclosure in the U.K. and the U.S.A.</u>, Saxon House, England, 1976.

_____ and M.A. Krasney, "The Economic Consequences of Financial Accounting Statements", <u>Economic Consequences of Financial Accounting Standards - Selected Papers</u>, F.A.S.B., July 1978.

Bernstein, M.H., <u>Regulating Business by Independent Commission</u>, Princeton University Press, Princeton, N.J., 1955.

Birkett, W.P., " Regulation through the profession: the Case in Accounting", in Tomasic (Ed.), op cit, 1984.

Birkett, W.P. and R.G.Walker, "Response of Australian Accounting Profession to Company Failures in the 1960s", <u>Abacus</u>, December, 1971.

_____, "Accounting a Source of Market Imperfection", <u>Journal of Business Finance and Accounting</u>, Summer 1974.

Bishop, J., "A Challenging Year", <u>The Chartered Accountant in Australia</u>, December, 1978.

Botrill, G.W., "The Role and Function of Accounting Standards Review Board", <u>Recent Developments in Corporate Reporting Requirements</u>, I.C.A.A. Seminar, July 5, 1984.

Boymal, D., "Accounting Standards - The Profession's Spectator Sport", The Chartered Accountant in Australia, February, 1986.

Briloff, A.J., <u>Unaccountable Accounting</u>, Harper and Row, 1972.

Bromwich, M., <u>The Economics of Accounting Standard Setting</u>, Prentice-Hall International, London, 1985.

Brown, P.R., "A Descriptive Analysis of Select Input Bases of the Financial Accounting Standards Board" <u>Journal of Accounting Research</u>, Spring 1981.

Bryant, M.J. and D.B.Thornton, "Public Choice of Corporate Accounting Standards", in Mattessich (1984).

Buckley, J., "F.A.S.B. and Impact Analysis", <u>Management Accounting</u>, April, 1976.

_____, and P.O'Sullivan, "Regulation and the Accounting Profession: What are the Issues?", in Buckley and Weston (Eds.), 1980.

_____, and J.F. Weston, Regulation and the Accounting Profession, Lifetime Learning Publications, Belmont, California, 1980.

_____, "Policy Models in Accounting: A Critical Commentary", Accounting, Organizations and Society, 1980.

Business Review Weekly, "Why the industry is seeking self-regulation", May 16, 1981.

_____, "Regulation Compromise", May 23, 1981.

_____, June 27, 1981, p. 30.

_____, "Regulation: the big test for accounting", June 13, 1981.

_____, November 28, 1981, p. 46.

_____, "Accounting bodies restive over uncertainty", November 28, 1981.

_____, "Inquiry findings", November 28, 1981.

_____, "How inaction could spell disaster for accountants", February 20, 1982.

_____, "Accountancy Hotline", October 9, 1982.

_____, "Accountancy Hotline", December 4, 1982.

_____, "Accountancy Hotline", December 11, 1982.

_____, "Quixotic plan to maintain standards", January 15, 1983.

_____, "Masel takes tough line on flexibility", January 15, 1983.

_____, "Accountancy Hotline", April 2, 1983.

_____, "Accountancy Hotline", July 9, 1983.

_____, "Accountancy Hotline", September 10, 1983.

_____, "Accountancy Hotline", October 22, 1983.

_____, "Accountancy Hotline", November 26, 1983.

_____, "Accountancy Hotline", January 21, 1984.

_____, "Review Board Members Roll up their Sleeves", January 21, 1984.

_____, "Ministerial Council opts for rigid reporting standard", September 15, 1984.

_____, "Accountancy Hotline - Review Board on $200,000 Shoestring", December 8, 1984.

_____, "Accountancy Hotline - Morgan Calls for Less Regulation", September 20, 1985.

_____, "Standards block cleared at last", September 27, 1985.

_____, "Accountancy Hotline - Big Shake-up Changes A.S.R.B. Balance", December 13, 1985.

_____, "Accountancy Hotline - Standards Delay Irks A.S.A. Chief", June 20, 1986.

_____, "Standards are worth the cost", November 21, 1986.

_____, "Accountancy Hotline - Flushing out the Issues", December 5, 1986.

_____, "Accountancy Hotline - Standards first merger later", April 24, 1987.

_____, "Accountancy Hotline - Merger urged for uniform standards", April 16, 1987.

_____, "Accountancy Hotline - Society disappointed with A.S.R.B.", May 8, 1987.

_____, "Accountancy Hotline - Timing Defended", May 13, 1988.

_____, "Accountancy Hotline - Single standards", July 8, 1988.

_____, "Accountancy Hotline - Boards Find Unity of Purpose", July 22, 1988.

_____, "Accountancy Hotline - Standard hailed", September 30, 1988.

_____, "Accountancy Hotline - Old guard says goodbye", October 7, 1988.

Carey, J.L., The Rise of Accounting Profession - From Technician to Professional 1896-1936, A.I.C.P.A., Inc., N.Y., 1969.

_____, The Rise of Accounting Profession - To Responsibility and Authority 1937 - 1969, A.I.C.P.A., Inc., N.Y., 1970.

Carrington, A.S., "A Critical Look at the Accounting Profession," The Chartered Accountant in Australia, June, 1973.

CCH Australia Limited, Guidebook to Australian Company Law, Sydney, 1986.

Chambers, R.J., Accounting Evaluation and Economic Behavior, Prentice-Hall, Englewood Cliffs, N.J., 1966.

_____, Securities and Obscurities, Gower Press Australia, Sydney, 1973.

_____, "Accounting Principles and Practices - Negotiated or Dictated?" in G.J. Previts (Editor), 1977

_____, T.Sri Ramanathan and H.H. Rappaport, Company Accounting Standards. Report of the Accounting Standards Review Committee, N.S.W. Government Printer, 1978.

_____, The Design of Accounting Standards, University of Sydney Accounting Research Centre Monograph No. 1, August, 1980.

The Chartered Accountant in Australia, "Truth, Fairness and the Financial Press", August, 1971.

_____, "Press Release: Submission on The Corporations and Securities Industries Bill 1974", May, 1975.

_____, "Accounting Standards Review Committee", March, 1978.

_____, "Criticism, Independence and Discipline - The Report of the Professional Standards Review Committee", April, 1979.

_____, "The Campbell Report - a blueprint for the future or destined for the scrap heap?", March, 1982.

_____, Talking Point", May, 1982.

_____, Submission to the N.C.S.C. on the proposed Accounting Standards Review Board", June, 1982.

_____, "Submission on the 7th Schedule", November, 1982.

_____, "Accounting Standards Review Board", February, 1983.

_____, "Current issues and communications with members", April, 1983.

_____, 1983 Companies Bill and the A.S.R.B. November, 1983.

_____, May 1984, p 25.

_____, "A.S.R.B. under pressure", July, 1986.

_____, "A.S.R.B. misses the mark", November, 1986.

Chatov, R., Corporate Financial Reporting, The Free Press, N.Y., 1975.

Chishlom, R. and G. Netheim, Understanding Law, Butterworths, Sydney, 1978.

Chow, C.W., "The Demand for External Auditing: Size, Debt and Ownership Influences", The Accounting Review, April 1982.

_____, "Empirical Studies of the Economic Impacts of Accounting Regulations: Findings, Problems and Prospects", Journal of Accounting Literature, 1983, Volume 2, pp. 73-107.

Christenson, C., "The Methodology of Positive Accounting", The Accounting Review, January, 1983.

Chua, W.F., and F.L.Clarke, "Disclosure Regulation: An Alternative Explanation", (Unpublished) Sydney University Research Seminar, 1984.

Cobb, R.W. and C.D. Elder, Participation in American Politics: The Dynamics of Agenda Building, Boston: Allyn and Bacon, Boston, 1972.

Cohen, S. and J. Young (Ed.), Manufacture of News: Social problems, deviance and the mass media, London, Constable, 1973.

Collins, D.W., M.S.Rozeff and D.S.Dhaliwal, "The Economic Determinants of Market Reaction to Proposed Changes in Oil and Gas Industry", Journal of Accounting and Economics, 1981.

Collins, D.W., M.S.Rozeff and D.S.Dhaliwal, "The Economic Determinants of Market Reaction to Proposed Mandatory Accounting Changes in the Oil and Gas Industry", Journal of Accounting and Economics, 1981.

Conover, W.J., Practical Nonparametric Statistics, John Wiley & Sons, Inc., New York, 1980.

Conybeare, J.A.C., "Politics and Regulations the Public Choice Approach", Public Administration, 1982.

Cooke, J.C., "Company Reporting: A Regulator's View", The Australian Accountant, September, 1981.

Coombe, B, "Accounting Standards", The Australian Accountant, September, 1983.

Coombes, R.J. and D.J.Stokes, "Standard Setters' Responsiveness to Submissions on Exposure Drafts: Australian Evidence", Australian Journal of Management, 1985.

Cooper, K. and G.D.Keim, "The Economic Rational for the Nature and Extent of Corporate Financial Disclosure Regulation: A Critical Assessment", Journal of Accounting and Public Policy, Vol 2, No 3, 1983.

Craig, R., "Government Involvement in the Setting of Accounting Standards - Some views for and against", The Australian Accountant, May, 1985.

Cranston, R.F., "Regulation and Deregulation: General Issues", The University of New South Wales Law Journal, 1982.

Craswell, A.T., Qualified Audit Reports, Unpublished Doctoral Thesis, The University of Sydney, December, 1983.

_____, Audit Qualifications in Australia 1950 to 1979, Garland Publishing, Inc., N.Y. and London, 1986.

Currie, C. P. Robinson and R. Walker, Political Activity and the Regulation of Accounting: Gaps in the Literature", AAANZ Conference, Auckland, New Zealand, 1987.

Curnow, G.R., Quangos - The Australian Experience, Hale and Iremonger, Sydney, 1983.

Curran, B. "Developing a Statement of Accounting Standards", The Australian Accountant, September 1983.

Daly, M.T., Sydney Boom Sydney Bust, George Allen & Unwin, Sydney, 1982.

Davis, S. W. and K. Menon, "The Formation and Termination of the Cost Accounting Standards Board: Legislative Intervention in Accounting Standard-Setting", Journal of Accounting and Public Policy, 1987.

Dean, G.W., (Unpublished) Lecture Notes for the Course Development in Accounting Thought, 1985.

Demski, J., "The General Impossibility of Normative Accounting Standards", The Accounting Review, October, 1973.

Dhaliwal, D.S., "The Impact of Disclosure Regulations on the Cost of Capital", Economic Consequences of Financial Accounting Standards - Selected Papers, F.A.S.B., July 1978.

Dixon "The Disclosure of Corporate Financial Standing - Can the Companies Act Protect the Community from Corporate Insolvency" Australian Business Law Review, 1979.

Dopuch N. and D. Simunic, "The Nature of Competition in the Auditing Profession: A Descriptive and Normative View", in Buckley and Weston (Eds.), 1980.

_____, and S. Sunder, "F.A.S.B.'s Statement on Objectives and Elements of Financial Accounting: A Review", The Accounting Review, 1980.

Downs, A., "An Economic Theory of Political Action in a Democracy", Journal of Political Economy, 1957a.

_____, An Economic Theory of Democracy, Harper & Row, N.Y., 1957b.

Durie, J., "Accounting watchdog's fate in balance", Australian Financial Review, November 17, 1982.

_____, and K.Kelly, "Accounting Standards a Shake-up", Australian Financial Review, November 29, 1982.

Dyckman, T.R. and D. Morse, Efficient Capital Markets and Accounting: A Critical Analysis, Prentice-Hall, Englewood Cliffs, N.J., 1986.

Editorial, "The Shape of a Profession", The Chartered Accountant in Australia, December, 1970.

"Editorial: New Role for Accountancy Research Foundation", The Chartered Accountant in Australia, April, 1974.

Edwards, J.R., "The Accounting Profession and Disclosure in Published Reports, 1925-1935", Accounting and Business Research, Autumn, 1976.

_____, Company Legislation and Changing Patterns of Disclosure in British Company Accounts 1900-1940, I.C.A.E.W., 1981.

Edwards, S.A., The Principal Accounting Officer's Duty to Conform to the Accounting Profession's Accounting Standards, Unpublished Master of Business Administration Dissertation, University of Sydney, February, 1979.

Evans, E.J., Prospectuses and Annual Reports: An Historical Look at Rule Development, New England Accounting Research Study Number 3, Accounting Systems Research Centre, University of New England, Armidale, N.S.W., 1974.

F.A.S.B., Economic Consequences of Financial Accounting Standards - Selected Papers, 1978.

Faggotter, C.R., "Accounting Standards: Preparation and Use", The Australian Accountant, April, 1978.

Fainsod, M.,"Some Reflections on the Nature of the Regulatory Process", in Public Policy, C.J.Friedrich and Edward S. Mason, eds., Cambridge, Mass.: Harvard University Press, 1940.

Fainsod, M. and L.Gordon, Government and the American Economy, W.W. Norton and Co., Inc., N.Y., 1941 and 1948.?

Fama, E.F., "Efficient Capital Markets: A Review of Theory and Empirical Work", Journal of Finance, May 1970.

_____, "Agency Problems and the Theory of the Firm", Journal of Political Economy, April, 1980.

Fels, A., "The Political Economy of Regulation", The University of New South Wales Law Journal, 1982.

Feller, B., "Accounting Standards - Objectives, Problems, Achievements", The Australian Accountant, August, 1974.

Fesler, J.W., "Independent Regulatory Establishments", Elements of Public Administration, Prentice-Hall-Inc., F.M. Marx (Ed.), N.Y., 1946.

The Financial Accounting Foundation, Report of the Structure Committee (Palmer Committee Report), April 1977.

Financial Reporting and Accounting Standards, University of Glasgow Press, 1978.

Ford, H.A.J., Principles of Company Law, Butterworths, Sydney, 1982.

_____, W.E. Paterson, H.H. Ednie, F.J.O. Ryan and R. Watzlaff, Guide to the National Companies and Securities Scheme, Butterworths, Sydney, 1984.

_____, Guide to the National Companies and Securities Scheme, Butterworths, Sydney, 1988.

Foster, G., Financial Statement Analysis, Prentice-Hall, Englewood Cliffs, N.J., 1978.

_____, "Externalities and Financial Reporting", The Journal of Finance, May, 1980.

_____, Financial Statement Analysis, Prentice-Hall, Englewood Cliffs, N.J., 1986.

_____, Companies and Securities Law, Butterworths, Sydney, 1988.

French, E.A., "The Evolution of Dividend Law of England", in Baxter and Davidson (1977).

Gallagher, "Accounting Standards - A Positive Approach, The Case for Voluntary, Not Mandated Accounting Standards", A.A.A.N.Z. Conference, August, 1986.

Gavens, J. and G. Carnegie, "Company Attitudes to the Accounting Standards Setting Process: An Empirical Survey", AAANZ Conference 1987, Auckland, New Zealand.

Gerboth, D.L., "Research, Intuition, and Politics in Accounting Inquiry", The Accounting Review, July, 1973.

Gibson, R.W., Disclosure by Australian Companies, Melbourne University Press, 1971.

_____, "Development of Corporate Accounting in Australia", Accounting Historians Journal, Fall 1979.

Gifford, D. and K. Gifford, Our Legal System, The Law Book Company, Sydney, 1983.

Gonedes, N. and N. Dopuch, "Capital Market Equilibrium, Information Production, and Selecting Accounting Techniques: Theoretical Framework and Review of Empirical Work", Journal of Accounting Research, 1974, Supplement to Volume 12.

Graham, K.M., M.O.Jager, and R.B. Taylor, Company Accounting Procedures, Butterworths, Sydney, 1984.

Griffin, P.A., "Management's Preferences for F.A.S.B. Statement No. 52: Predictive Ability Results", Abacus, December 1983.

Haring, J.R., "Accounting Rules and Accounting Establishment" Journal of Business, 1979.

Harison, W.T., "Accounting Changes in Principles and Estimates: How Different are They?", Economic Consequences of Financial Accounting Standards - Selected Papers, F.A.S.B., July 1978.

Harrowell, J.R., "Accounting Standards", The Chartered Accountant in Australia, July, 1973.

Hawker, G., R.F.I. Smith, and P. Weller, Politics and Policy in Australia, University of Queensland Press, Queensland, 1979.

Heclo, H., "Review Article: Policy Analysis", British Journal of Political Science, 1972.

Hein, L.W., The British Companies Acts and the Practice of Accountancy 1844-1962, Arno Press, N.J., 1978.

Henderson, S., and G.Peirson, Introduction to Accounting Theory, Longman Cheshire, Melbourne, 1977.

Henderson, S., "The Impact of Financial Accounting Standards on Auditing", The Australian Accountant, April, 1985.

Hepworth, J.A., "The Story of the Development of Accounting Standards in Australia", The Chartered Accountant in Australia, 1972.

Hines, R., "Economic Consequences of Accounting Standards: A good reason for a representative A.S.R.B.", The Chartered Accountant in Australia, July, 1983.

Hirshleifer, J., 'Comment', The Journal of Law and Economics, 1976.

Holthausen, R., and R.Leftwich, "The Economic Consequences Accounting Choice: Implications of Costly Contracting and Monitoring", Journal of Accounting and Economics, August 1983.

Hood, C., "Keeping the Centre Small: Explanations of Agency Type", Political Studies, 1978.

Horngren, C.T., "The Marketing of Accounting Standards", Journal of Accountancy, October, 1973.

Houghton, K.A., "True and Fair View: An Empirical Study of Connotative Meaning", Accounting Organizations and Society, 1987.

Huck, S.W., W.H. Cormier and W.G. Bounds, Reading Statistics and Research, Harper and Row Publishers, N.Y. 1974.

Hughes, C.A. (Ed.), Readings in Australian Government, University of Queensland Press, Queensland, 1968.

Hunter, B., "Accountants' Responsibility for Corporate Failures", The Chartered Accountant in Australia, July, 1980.

Hussien, M.E. and J.E.Ketz, "Ruling Elites of the F.A.S.B.: A Study of the Big Eight", Journal of Accounting, Auditing and Finance, Summer, 1980.

Hussien, M.E., "The Innovative Process in Financial Accounting Standard Setting", Accounting Organization and Society, 1981.

Hutcheson, Australian Financial Review, September 1, 1977, p. 2.

Institute of Chartered Accountants of England and Wales, Accounting Standards 1981, 1981.

Irish, R.A., Auditing, Sydney Law Book Co., 1972.

Jarrell, G.A., "Pro-Producer Regulation and Accounting for Assets", Journal of Accounting and Economics, 1979.

Jensen, M.C., and W.H.Meckling, "Theory of the Firm: Managerial Behavior, Agency Costs and Ownership Structure", Journal of Financial Economics, 3 1976.

_____, "Reflections on the State of Accounting Research and the Regulation of Accounting", Stanford Lectures in Accounting, May 21, 1976.

Johnson, S.B. and W.F.Messier, "The Nature of Accounting Standard Setting: An Alternative Explanation", Journal of Accounting and Auditing, Spring 1982.

Johnston, T.R. and M.O. Jager, The Law and Practice of Company Accounting in Australia, Butterworths, Sydney, 1963.

Keane, S. M., The Efficient Market Hypothesis, The Institute of Chartered Accountants of Scotland, 1980.

Kelly, K., Australian Financial Review, May 21, 1981, p. 14.

Kelley, L., "Corporate Lobbying and Changes in Financing or Operating Activities in Reaction to F.A.S. No. 8", The Journal of Accounting and Public Policy, Winter 1982.

_____, "Corporate Management Lobbying on F.A.S. No. 8: Some Further Evidence", Journal of Accounting Research, Autumn 1985.

Kent, P.L., "Changes to the Directors' Statement and the Genesis of the Accounting Standards Review Board", Recent Developments in Corporate Reporting Requirements, I.C.A.A. Seminar, July 5, 1984.

King, R.K., The Stock Exchange, George Allen and Unwin Ltd., 1947.

Kirby, M.D., "Reform of Professions", The Australian Accountant, September, 1980.

Kripke, "Commentary", Issues in Financial Regulation, F.R. Edwards (Ed.), 1979.

Kuhn, T.S., The Structure of Scientific Revolutions, 2nd Ed., University of Chicago Press, 1970.

Lapin, L.L., Statistics for Modern Business Decisions, Harcourt Brace Jovanovich, Inc., N.Y., 1978.

Lee T.A. and R.H. Parker, The Evolution of Corporate Financial Reporting, Thomas Nelson and Sons Ltd., 1979.

Leftwich, R., "Market Failure Fallacies and Accounting Information", Journal of Accounting and Economics, 1980.

_____, "Accounting Information in Private Markets: Evidence from Private Lending Agreements", The Accounting Review, January, 1983.

Lev, B. and J.A. Ohlson, "Market-Based Empirical Research in Accounting: A Review, Interpretation, and Extension", Journal of Accounting Research, Supplement, 1982.

Lev, B., "Toward a Theory of Equitable and Efficient Accounting Policy", The Accounting Review, January, 1988.

Makin, J.H., "Measuring the Impact of Floating and F.A.S.B. Statement No. 8 on Cost of Capital for Multinationals", Economic Consequences of Financial Accounting Standards - Selected Papers, F.A.S.B., July 1978.

Mannix, E.F., and J.E.Mannix, Professional Negligence, Butterworths, Sydney, 1982.

Masel, L., "The Future of Accounting and Auditing Standards", The Australian Accountant, September, 1983.

_____, "Financial Reports: Guiding Investors Through the Maze", Australian Financial Review, July 27, 1987.

_____, "How Regulatory Systems Allocate Responsibility", Australian Financial Review, July 28, 1987.

_____, "Testing the Methodology of Reporting", Australian Financial Review, July 29, 1987.

Mathews, R., "Uniformity in Accounting Principles - a commentary", The Chartered Accountant in Australia, January, 1969.

Mattessich, Modern Accounting Research: History, Survey, and Guide, The
       Canadian Certified General Accountants' Research Foundation, 1984.
May, R.G. and G.L.Sundem, "Research for Accounting Policy: An Overview",
       The Accounting Review, October, 1976.
Mayer, H. (Ed.), Australia's Political Pattern, Cheshire, Melbourne, 1973.
McKeon, A., "Communication in Annual Reports", The Australian Accountant,
       August, 1976.
McManamy, "Should Accounting Standards Carry Legal Force?", The
       Accountants Journal, July, 1984.
Merino, B.D. (Editor), The Impact of Regulation on Accounting Theory, Charles
       Waldo History Seminar, April 20, New York University, 1978.
_____, and M.D.Neimark, "Disclosure Regulation and Public Policy - A
       Sociohistorical Reappraisal", Journal of Accounting and Public Policy,
       1982.
_____, B.S. Koch and K.L. MacRitchie, "Historical Analysis - A Diagnostic
       Tool for "Events" Studies: The Impact of Securities Act of 1933", The
       Accounting Review, October, 1987.
Meyer, P.E., "The APB,s Independence and Its Implications for the F.A.S.B.",
       Journal of Accounting Research, Spring 1974.
Miles, J., "Accounting Standards - in Retrospect and Prospect", The Australian
       Accountant, March, 1986.
Miller, M., "The Impact of Government Regulation on Financial Accounting:
       The Australian Experience", in Merino [1978].
Miller, J.D.B. and B. Jinks, Australian Government and Politics, Gerald
       Duckworth and Co. Ltd. London, 1971.
Mitnick, B.M., The Political Economy of Regulation, Columbia University
       Press, N.Y., 1980.
Moonitz, Maurice, Obtaining Agreement on Standards in the Accounting
       Profession, Studies in Accounting Research No. 8, A.A.A., 1974.
Morgan, T.D., Economic Regulation of Business, West Publishing Co., St. Paul,
       Minnesota, 1976.
Morley, B.A., "Administering the Law on Company Accounts: Current Policy
       and Trends", The Chartered Accountant in Australia, December, 1979.
Morris, R.D., "Corporate Disclosure in a Substantially Unregulated
       Environment", Abacus, 1984.
_____, The Relationship Between Agency and Signalling Theories, With Some
       accounting Applications, University of N.S.W., Accounting Department
       Working Paper, 1986a.

_____, "Lee v. Neuchatel Asphalt Company (1889) and Depreciation Accounting: Two Empirical Studies", Accounting and Business Research, Winter 1986b.

Mueller, D.C., "Public Choice: A Survey", Journal of Economic Literature, June 1976.

Murray, B.L. and B.T. Shaw, Final Report of an Investigation into the Affairs of Reid Murray Holding Ltd., Victorian Government Printer, Melbourne, 1966.

National Companies and Securities Commission, Second Annual Report and Financial Statements 1 July 1980 to 30 June 1981.

_____, Third Annual Report and Financial Statements 1 July 1981 to 30 June 1982.

_____, Fourth Annual Report and Financial Statements 1 July 1982 to 30 June 1983.

_____, Fifth Annual Report and Financial Statements 1 July 1983 to 30 June 1984.

_____, Release 401, 26, November, 1981.

_____, Release 405, 3, December, 1981.

_____, Release 600,

_____, Release 625,

_____, Release 650,

_____ (N.C.S.C.) and the New South Wales Corporate Affairs Commission (N.S.W. C.A.C.) Accounting Standards Review Board Report to the Ministerial Council, March 1983.

_____, Financial Reporting Requirements of the Companies Act and Codes, (The green paper), National Companies and Securities Commission, Canberra, December, 1983.

Newman, D.P., "An Investigation of the Distribution of Power in the A.P.B. and F.A.S.B.", Journal of Accounting Research, Spring 1981a.

_____, "The S.E.C.'s Influence on the Accounting Standards: The Power of Veto", Journal of Accounting Research, Supplement 1981b.

Olson, M., The Logic of Collective Action, Harvard University Press, Cambridge, Mass., 1965.

Parker, R.H., "Australia's First Accountancy Body - The Adelaide Society of Accountants" The Chartered Accountant in Australia, December, 1961.

_____, "Why are Australian Accounting Standards Different?", Australian Society of Accountants: Research Lecture, June 10, 1982.

_____, Accounting Standards and the Law: An Australian Experiment, Accounting Research Centre, University of Sydney, Working Paper No. 18, October, 1986.

_____, C.G. Peirson and A.L. Ramsay, "Australian Accounting Standards and the Law", Company and Securities Law Journal", November, 1987.

Parker, R.S., "Structure and Functions of Government", Public Administration in Australia, R.N. Spann (Ed.), Government Printer, Sydney, 1965.

Paterson, W.E. and H.H. Ednie, Aspects of the Corporations and Securities Industry Bill, 1974, Butterworths, Sydney, 1975.

Peers, M., The Financial Review, November 14, 1985, p 22.

Peirson, G. and A.L.Ramsay, "A Review of Regulation of Financial Reporting in Australia", Company and Securities Law Journal, November, 1983.

_____, "Regulation of the Accounting Profession in Australia", Company and Securities Law Journal, February, 1984.

Peltzman, S., "Toward a More General Theory of Regulation", The Journal of Law and Economics, August, 1976.

Phillips, S.M., and J.R.Zecher, The SEC and the Public Interest, The MIT Press, Cambridge, Massachusetts, 1981.

"Policing the Accountants", The Australian Financial Review, October, 7, 1982.

Posner, R.A., "Theories of Economic Regulation", Bell Journal of Economics and Management Science, Autumn, 1974.

Prakash, P., and A.Rappaport, "Information Inductance and its Significance for Accounting", Accounting Organization and Society, 1977.

Previts, G.J., 1976 Accounting Research Convocation: Emerging Issues, University of Alabama, 1977.

_____, The Development of S.E.C. Accounting, Addison-Wesley Publishing Co., 1981.

_____, and B.D. Merino, A History of Accounting in America, A Ronald Press Publication - John Wiley and Sons, N.Y., 1979.

Priddice, J.A., "A practitioner's View", Recent Developments in Corporate Reporting Requirements, July 5, 1984.

Prosser, V., "Proposed Accounting Standards Review Board", Australian Stock Exchange Journal, February, 1983.

Puro, M., "Audit Firm Lobbying Before the Financial Accounting Standards Board: An Empirical Study", Journal of Accounting Research, Autumn, 1984.

Ramsay, A., "Disclosure of departures from an accounting standard", The Chartered Accountant in Australia, February, 1982.

Rappaport, A., "Economic Impact of Accounting Standards - Implications for the F.A.S.B.", Journal of Accounting, May, 1977.

Reiter, P., Profits, Dividends and the Law, Ronald Press Company, N.Y., 1926.

Report from the Senate Select Committee On Securities and Exchange, The Government Printer of Australia, Canberra, 1974. (Rae Committee Report)

Richardson, A.J., "Accounting Knowledge and Professional Privilege", Accounting Organizations and Society, 1988.

Riley, R.B., "Directors and Accounting Principles - Quo Vadis", The Chartered Accountant in Australia, June, 1973.

Rockness, H.O. and L.A.Nikolai, "An Assessment of APB Voting Patterns", Journal of Accounting Research, Spring 1977.

Ross, S.A., 'Disclosure Regulations in Financial Markets: Implications of Modern Finance Theory and Signaling Theory", Issues in Financial Regulation, F.R. Edwards, McGraw Hill, 1979.

Rowe, G.C., "Economic Theories of the nature of regulatory activity", in Tomasic, R. (Ed.) 1984.

Ryan, F.J.O., "A True and Fair View", Abacus, December, 1967.

Ryan, F.J.O., "A True and Fair View Revisited", The Australian Accountant, February, 1974.

Samuelson, P.A., "The Pure Theory of Public Expenditure", Review of Economics and Statistics, 1954.

Savage, E.W., "President's New Year Message", The Chartered Accountant in Australia, January, 1970.

Schaffer, B. "On Politics of Policy", Australian Journal of Politics and History, 1977.

Scott, M.R., "Information, Economics and Accounting Regulation", Accounting Association of Australia and New Zealand Conference, August, 1978.

Solomons, D., "The Politicization of Accounting", The Journal of Accountancy, November, 1978.

Solomons, D., Making Accounting Policy - The quest for Credibility in Financial Reporting, Oxford University Press, N.Y., 1986.

Spann, R.N., Government Administration in Australia, George Allen and Urwin, 1979.

Stacey, N.A.H., English Accountancy 1800-1954, Arno Press, 1980.

Stamp, E., Accounting Auditing Standards Present and Future, From an International Viewpoint, the Australian Society of Accountants and the University of Sydney Endowed Lecture, 17, September, 1979.

Standish, P.E., The Rationale for Accounting Standard Setting, April 1982.

Sterling, R.R, Theory of Measurement of Enterprise Income, Kansas University Press, Lawrence, Kansas, 1970.

Stigler, G.J., "The Theory of Economic Regulation", The Bell Journal of Economics and Management Science, Spring, 1971.

Strickland, A.D., Government Regulation of Business, Houghton Mifflin Co., Boston, 1980.

Studdy, J.B., "Self Regulation or Government Regulation - Management's View", The Chartered Accountant in Australia, July, 1979.

Sunder, S. and Haribhakti, S., "Economic Interest and Accounting Standards" in Mattessich, 1984.

Sutton, T.G., "Lobbying of Accounting Standard Setting Bodies in the U.K. and the U.S.A.: A Downsian Analysis", Accounting, Organization and Society, Vol. 9, 1984.

Swieringa, R.J., "Consequences of Financial Accounting Standards", Accounting Forum, May, 1977.

Sydney Stock Exchange, Official List Requirements, 1949.

_____, Official List Requirements, 1952.

Taylor, D.W., "Financial Accounting Objectives and Standards Setting, Part 2", The Chartered Accountant in Australia, October, 1977.

The Report of the Commissioner for Corporate Affairs (N.S.W.) for the Year ended 31st December, 1971.

The Report of the Corporate Affairs Commission (N.S.W.) for the Year ended 31st December, 1972.

_____, 1973.

_____, 1974.

_____, 1975.

_____, 1976.

_____, 1977.

_____, 1978.

_____, 1979.

_____, 1980.

_____, 1981.

_____, 1982.

_____, 1983.

_____, 1984.

_____, 1985.

_____, 1986.

_____, 1987.

"The Report of the Professional Standards Review Committee", The Chartered Accountant in Australia, April, 1979.

The Report of the Registrar of Companies for the year ended 31st December, 1970.

Thomas, T., "Standards Shake-up Looms as a Top Issue", Business Review Weekly, December 11, 1982.

_____, "Standards Issue is Far from Settled", Business Review Weekly, December 18, 1982.

_____, "Draft Agreement on Review Board Released", Business Review Weekly, April 9, 1983.

Tomasic, R., Business Regulation in Australia, C.C.H. Australia Ltd., Sydney, 1984.

_____, "Business Regulation and the Administrative State", in Tomasic, R., op cit, 1984.

U.S. Congress, Committee of Interstate and Foreign Commerce, Report of the Advisory Committee on Corporate Disclosure to the SEC, November 3, 1977.

Vincent, G., "Co-Regulation: The Background", The Australian Accountant, May, 1981.

_____, "Do We Need and Accounting Standards Review Board?", The Australian Accountant, January/February, 1982.

_____, "Where is Corporate Accounting at?", 7th Schedule (Green Paper) Compendium, October, 1983.

Walker, F. 1979, in Kent [1984], pp. 17-18.

_____, "An Address by the N.S.W. Attorney-General Frank Walker to the Young Accountants", Seminar, Victor Harbour, South Australia, March 1, 1980.

_____, "Regulation of the Accounting Profession", The Australian Accountant, May, 1981a.

_____, "Address to the Institute's N.S.W. Branch Members", The Chartered Accountant in Australia, October 1981b.

Walker, R.G., "The Hatry Affair", Abacus, June 1977.

_____, (lecture in) Recent Developments in Corporate Reporting Requirements, I.C.A.A., July 5, 1984.

_____, "The A.S.R.B.: Policy Formation, Political Activity and 'Research'", A.A.A.N.Z. Annual Conference, 1985.

_____, Australia's A.S.R.B. - A Case Study of Political Activity and Regulatory "Capture", Working Paper, University of New South Wales, 15 December, 1986.

_____, "Australia's A.S.R.B. - A Case Study of Political Activity and Regulatory "Capture"", Accounting and Business Research, Summer 1987.

Waterhouse, J.H., "A Descriptive Analysis of Selected Aspects of the Canadian Accounting Standard Setting Process", in Basu and Milburn (Eds.), 1981.

Watts, R.L., "Corporate Financial Statements, A Product of the Market and Political Processes", Australian Journal of Management, April, 1977.

_____, and Zimmerman, J.L., "Towards a Positive Theory of the Determination of Accounting Standards", The Accounting Review, January, 1978.

_____, "Accounting Theories: The Market for Excuses", The Accounting Review, 1979.

_____, Positive Accounting Theory, 1986.

Webb, L.C., "The Australian Party System", in Hughes (1968).

Weller, P., "The Study of Public Policy", Australian Journal of Public Administration, September/December, 1980.

Wells, M.C., "A Revolution in Accounting Thought?", The Accounting Review, July 1976.

_____, "Is it Futile to Impose Accounting Standards", A.S.A. Lecture, The University of Melbourne, October 26, 1978.

Weston, J.F., "Regulation and the Accounting Profession: An Evaluation of Issues", in Buckley and Weston (Eds.), 1980.

Wettenhall, R.L., "Classification of Agencies", Public Policy and Administration in Australia: A Reader, R.N. Spann and G.R. Curnow (Ed.), John Wiley and Sons Australia Pty. Ltd., Sydney, 1975.

_____ and Bayne, P., "Administrative aspects of regulation", in Tomasic, R., op cit, 1984.

_____, "Statutory Authorities", Australian Government Administration - Report of Royal Commission, Appendix I.K, Vol. 1, Commonwealth Government Printer, 1977.

Whittred, G., "Australian Accounting standards - Some Anomalies", The Australian Accountant, September, 1978.

_____, "The Evolution of Consolidated Financial Reporting in Australia", Abacus, September 1986.

Willmott, H., "Organizing the Profession: A Theoretical and Historical Examination of the Development of the Major Accounting Bodies in the U.K.", Accounting Organization and Society, 1986.

Wilson, J.Q. "The Politics of Regulation", In James W. McKie, ed., <u>Social Responsibility and the Business Predicament</u>, pp. 135-68, Washington, D.C.: Brokings Institution, 1974.

_____, "The Politics of Regulation", In J.Q. Wilson, ed., The Politics of Regulation, pp. 357-394, Basic Books, New York, 1980.

Winn D.N., "The Potential Effect of Alternate Accounting Measures on Public Policy and Resource Allocation", <u>Economic Consequences of Financial Accounting Standards - Selected Papers</u>, F.A.S.B., July 1978.

Winsen, J.K., "Regulation of Financial Reporting", <u>Australian Business Law Review</u>, August, 1980.

Wise, T., and V. Wise, "A.S.R.B. under pressure", The Chartered Accountant in Australia, July, 1986.

_____, "A.S.R.B. misses the mark", The Chartered Accountant in Australia, November, 1986.

Wolnizer, P.W., <u>Auditing as Independent Authentication</u>, Unpublished Doctoral Thesis, The University of Sydney, November, 1985.

Wyatt, A.R., "The Economic Impact of Financial Accounting Standards", <u>Journal of Accounting</u>, October, 1977.

Zeff, S.A., "Chronology of Significant Developments in the Establishment of Accounting Principles in the United States 1926-1972", <u>Journal of Accounting Research</u>, Spring 1972.

_____, <u>Forging Accounting Principles in Australia</u>, A.S.A. Bulletin No. 14, March 1973.

_____, "Chronology of Significant Developments in the Establishment of Accounting Principles in the United States 1926-1978," in T.A. Lee and R.H. Parker (1979).

_____, "The Rise of "Economic Consequences"," <u>The Journal of Accounting</u>, December, 1978.

_____, "Towards a Fundamental Rethinking of the Role of the "Intermediate" Course in the Accounting Curriculum", (Unpublished), <u>Plenary Session 3, A.A.A.N.Z. Conference 1986</u>.

For Product Safety Concerns and Information please contact our EU representative GPSR@taylorandfrancis.com
Taylor & Francis Verlag GmbH, Kaufingerstraße 24, 80331 München, Germany